Unexplained Wealth Orders and the UK's Anti-Corruption Regime

Unexplained Wealth Orders and the UK's Anti-Corruption Regime

ÁINE CLANCY
Lecturer, Department of Law, University of Liverpool, UK

OXFORD
UNIVERSITY PRESS

OXFORD
UNIVERSITY PRESS

Great Clarendon Street, Oxford, OX2 6DP,
United Kingdom

Oxford University Press is a department of the University of Oxford.
It furthers the University's objective of excellence in research, scholarship,
and education by publishing worldwide. Oxford is a registered trade mark of
Oxford University Press in the UK and in certain other countries.

Published in the United States of America by Oxford University Press
198 Madison Avenue, New York, NY 10016, United States of America.

British Library Cataloguing in Publication Data
Data available

Library of Congress Control Number: 2025935198

ISBN 9780198907282

DOI: 10.1093/9780198907312.001.0001

Printed and bound by
CPI Group (UK) Ltd., Croydon, CR0 4YY

The manufacturer's authorised representative in the EU for product safety is
Oxford University Press España S.A. of Parque Empresarial San Fernando de Henares,
Avenida de Castilla, 2 – 28830 Madrid (www.oup.es/en or product.safety@oup.com).
OUP España S.A. also acts as importer into Spain of products made by the manufacturer.

MIX
Paper | Supporting
responsible forestry
FSC® C013604

Acknowledgements

I am grateful to Profs Peter Alldridge and Miriam Goldby at Queen Mary University of London for agreeing to supervise the thesis on which this monograph is based, and for providing careful and generous feedback, direction, and suggestions throughout the process. I struck lucky in having them as supervisors: working with them was a total delight. Thanks are also due to Prof Jackie Harvey and Dr Andromachi Georgosouli for their examination of and feedback on the thesis.

Since completing the PhD, I have encountered time and again academics who have contributed generously to how I think and write about the issues addressed in this monograph. These include (without limitation) Liz Campbell, Micheál O'Floinn, Colin King, David Ormerod KC, Radha Ivory, Arie Frieberg, and Gregory Dale. Heartfelt thanks to you all. I am grateful too to the anonymous reviewers who provided feedback on the proposal to Oxford University Press leading to this work, and to the editorial team at OUP for all of their help. Thanks to Hans Peter Bauer and Gemma Aiolfi of the Basel Institute on Governance and the senior officers at the National Crime Agency for providing valuable insights in the course of interviews undertaken in researching this volume. Thank you to my erstwhile colleagues at the School of Law at the University of Sheffield and my current colleagues at the School of Law and Social Justice at the University of Liverpool for providing sounding boards, pep talks, and distractions over innumerable coffees and pints throughout the writing of this work.

I am very grateful to my parents, Julianne and Maurice, for a lifetime supply of support and encouragement.

Finally, my deepest love and gratitude to Pádraig McAuliffe for everything. This work is dedicated to him and Ned.

Contents

Detailed Contents

Illustrations

Figures

Tables

Abbreviations

A1P1	Article 1 of the First Protocol to the ECHR
ACN	Anti-Corruption Network
AEIA	Automatic Exchange of Information Agreements
AFO	Account Forfeiture Order
AFrO	Account Freezing Order
AML	Anti-Money Laundering
AML Regulations	Anti-Money Laundering, Terrorist Financing and Transfer of Funds (Information on the Payer) Regulations 2017 (SI No 692 of 2017).
ARIS	Asset Recovery Incentivisation Scheme
BCBS	Basel Committee on Banking Supervision
BVI	British Virgin Islands
CAA	Civil Aviation Authority
CD	Crown Dependency
CJA 1987	Criminal Justice Act 1987
CPS	Crown Prosecution Service
CRO	Civil Recovery Order
DAML	Defence Against Money Laundering
DfID	Department for International Development
DISP	Dispute Resolution: Complaints Sourcebook
DPP	Director of Public Prosecutions
ECCTA	Economic Crime and Corporate Transparency Act 2023
ECHR	European Convention on Human Rights
ECJ	European Court of Justice
ECTEA	Economic Crime (Transparency and Enforcement) Act 2022
ECtHR	European Court of Human Rights
EDD	Enhanced Due Diligence
EEA	European Economic Area
FATF	Financial Action Task Force
FCA	Financial Conduct Authority
FCDO	Foreign, Commonwealth & Development Office
FCPA	Foreign Corrupt Practices Act (US)
FDI	Foreign Direct Investment
FOI	Freedom of Information
FT	*Financial Times*
HMRC	His Majesty's Revenue Commissioners
IMF	International Monetary Fund
KYC	Know Your Customer
LSE	London Stock Exchange
NCA	National Crime Agency

NGO	Non-Governmental Organisation
OECD	Organisation for Economic Co-operation and Development
OT	Overseas Territory
PEP	Politically Exposed Person
POCA	Proceeds of Crime Act 2002
PRA	Prudential Regulation Authority
PSC	Person of Significant Control
RICO	Racketeer Influenced and Corrupt Organizations Act
ROE	Register of Overseas Entities
SAMLA	Sanctions and Anti-Money Laundering Act 2018
SAR	Suspicious Activity Reporting
SFBC	Swiss Federal Banking Commission
SFO	Serious Fraud Office
SLAPP	Strategic Lawsuit Against Public Participation
SRA	Solicitors Regulation Authority
StAR	Stolen Assets Recovery Initiative
UBO	Ultimate Beneficial Owner
UN	United Nations
UNCAC	United Nations Convention Against Corruption
UNODC	United Nations Office on Drugs and Crime
UWO	Unexplained Wealth Order
WBES	World Bank Enterprise Survey

Introduction

1. Introduction

The powers available to criminal enforcement authorities to investigate and seize the UK-based proceeds of overseas grand corruption are piecemeal in nature and collectively under-researched. There is much available academic commentary and empirical work which considers the cultural, political, and economic reasons for official corruption globally, its impact on the populaces of the states in which it is endemic, and individual international and domestic structures designed to combat its occurrence. In considering how the UK uses its laws to address the proceeds of overseas political corruption being laundered within its territory, this book is the first that examines the broader anti-corruption enforcement architecture of a 'destination' country for the proceeds of grand corruption. This volume assesses the efficacy, the pitfalls, and the advantages of the options available to destination countries to deter laundering of corruptly acquired 'dirty money' in their states, and to recover and, where appropriate, to return misappropriated assets to states of origin. In this way, this book aims to inform current anti-corruption policy and future reform both in the UK and in other states harbouring dirty money.

2. The United Kingdom and Grand Corruption

The Russian invasion of Ukraine has reignited the discussion on the London property and financial markets' statuses as top destinations for the spoils of forms of grand corruption including kleptocracy. Although the UK does not have an obvious widespread problem with large amounts of its *own* public funds being diverted through criminal activity like bribery, graft, and embezzlement, it is widely viewed as a haven state for the proceeds of such proceeds.[1] The enormity of the proceeds of foreign corruption being laundered in the UK has been flagged by, amongst others, crime enforcement authorities,[2] parliamentary

[1] Even so, relatively isolated incidents of serious impropriety in UK public office for personal gain are alleged from time to time. See Chapter 1, n 3, and generally Kevin Morgan and Nadir Kinossian, 'Dismantling Londongrad: The Dark Geography of Dirty Money' (2023) 32 European Planning Studies 169.

[2] See eg National Crime Agency (NCA), *National Strategic Assessment of Serious and Organised Crime 2020–2021*, at 54: '[it is] a realistic possibility that the scale of money laundering impacting on

Unexplained Wealth Orders and the UK's Anti-Corruption Regime. Áine Clancy, Oxford University Press.
 DOI: 10.1093/9780198907312.003.0001

committees,[3] non-governmental organisations (NGOs),[4] and even other governments.[5] It should be emphasized that there is no empirical evidence available to establish definitively the *scale* of the proceeds of grand corruption being laundered, nor is there evidence available to suggest that foreign senior public officials are more or less likely to launder the proceeds of crime in the UK than other individuals. Nevertheless, work undertaken by various civil society groups, amongst others, strongly suggests that there exist huge and inexplicable discrepancies between assets in the UK including real estate in expensive parts of London being held by high-ranking foreign officials, their associates, and their family members (collectively, 'politically exposed persons' or PEPs), and those individuals' known lawful incomes.[6] The anti-corruption laws discussed in this book are targeted primarily at overseas PEPs who use the UK as a 'holding state', a 'haven state', or a 'destination state' in which to invest their illicit assets. Throughout this volume, the countries from which those stolen or misdirected assets originate are referred to variously as 'states of origin', 'countries of origin', or 'victim states'.

3. Unexplained Wealth Orders

The recovery levels of the proceeds of foreign official corruption in the UK are low.[7] Within the past decade, however, a series of legal and policy developments have been introduced with the aims of preventing those proceeds entering the British economy and pursuing those assets that *have* been laundered in the UK. The most widely publicized of these is the unexplained wealth order (UWO) targeted specifically at corrupt PEPs. In theory, the UWO holds enormous potential as an anti-corruption device because it allows law enforcement authorities to investigate and, with ostensibly relative ease, to seize the UK-based proceeds of kleptocracy and to return them to the citizens of the states in which the assets originated. Since they were first introduced in 2018, however, only one set of UWOs has been deployed successfully against a PEP, in a case involving the wife of a former chairman of the International Bank of Azerbaijan.

the UK (including through UK corporate structures or financial institutions) is in the hundreds of billions of pounds annually'.

[3] House of Commons Foreign Affairs Committee, *Moscow's Gold: Russian Corruption in the UK Eighth Report of Session 2017–19* (Stationery Office 21 May 2018).

[4] Transparency International UK and Thomson Reuters, *London Property: A Top Destination for Money Launderers*, 2 December 2016.

[5] See eg Catherine Philip and Chris Smyth, 'US Sounds Alarm over Russian Cash in London' *The Times* (London, 16 January 2022) 1 and 7.

[6] See eg John Heathershaw and others, *The UK's Kleptocracy Problem: How Servicing Post-Soviet Elites Weakens the Rule of Law* (Chatham House 2021).

[7] See eg Chapter 1, nn 134–37 and accompanying text.

A UWO is an investigative tool requiring respondents who hold unexplained wealth to positively establish to law enforcement authorities the licit origin of their assets or face having those assets being made the subject of civil recovery proceedings. UWOs were introduced with the intention of making it easier for enforcement authorities including the National Crime Agency (NCA) to obtain evidence or raise inferences of the standard required to freeze and investigate the suspected proceeds of corruption and crime, with a view ultimately to apply for civil recovery orders in respect of those assets. In considering the policy approaches adopted by the British government in tackling dirty money originating overseas, this book considers whether the introduction of the UWO in the form that is specifically exercisable against PEPs was legitimate, justifiable, or necessary. A PEP is anyone who is, or has been, entrusted with prominent public functions by an international organization or by a state other than the UK, or a European Economic Area (EEA) state; or who is a family member of, is known to be a close associate of, or is 'otherwise connected to' that person.[8] In April 2016, the multitude of PEPs owning property through offshore trusts incorporated in so-called 'secrecy' jurisdictions was thrown into sharp relief through the leaking of a trove of documents detailing the ownership of over 200,000 corporate vehicles and other ownership entities known as the Panama Papers. Twelve national leaders and a total of 143 known PEPs were disclosed as holding interests in offshore companies administered through Mossack Fonseca, the Panamanian law firm and corporate services provider from which the Panama Papers were leaked.[9] The documents' publication seemed to corroborate what NGOs including Transparency International's UK office had long argued: that senior public officials in some countries were misappropriating their states' assets and laundering them abroad. Significant sums of these proceeds were laundered, Transparency International UK argued, through PEP-owned corporate vehicles incorporated offshore acquiring properties in the UK, and in London in particular.[10]

The first draft of legislation providing for a new investigative measure known as the UWO was published in October 2016. That UWOs were introduced reflected 'the fact that it may be difficult for law enforcement agencies to satisfy the evidential standard at the outset of an investigation given that all relevant information may be outside of the jurisdiction'.[11] The orders allow enforcement authorities to require

[8] Proceeds of Crime Act 2002 (POCA), s 362B(7). In this context, a 'person' is defined as including both natural persons and incorporated bodies—see sch 1 of the Interpretation Act 1978. In this book, all references to the POCA are references to the legislative provisions that apply in England and Wales. Some chapters (including those providing for UWOs) also apply to Northern Ireland. Scotland has a different (though substantially similar) regime for UWOs provided for under ss 396A–V of the POCA. References to POCA powers throughout this book refer to the provisions applicable in England and Wales unless otherwise specified. References to High Court throughout this book are references to the High Court of England and Wales unless otherwise specified.

[9] Luke Harding, 'What Are the Panama Papers?' *The Guardian* (London, 6 April 2016) 3.

[10] Transparency International UK and Thomson Reuters (n 4).

[11] *Explanatory Notes to the Criminal Finances Act 2017*, [13].

asset holders to account for how assets were acquired in circumstances where there is no obvious explanation for how those asset holders could have afforded them.[12] Where a respondent fails to respond without reasonable excuse with the information required pursuant to an order within the time frame set out therein, a presumption will arise that the assets specified in the order are 'recoverable property' obtained through 'unlawful conduct' for the purposes of the Proceeds of Crime Act 2002 (POCA).[13] The High Court will take this (rebuttable) presumption into account where enforcement authorities subsequently apply for civil recovery orders against the relevant assets.[14]

As of 31 January 2018, enforcement authorities became entitled to apply to the High Court for UWOs. Less than three weeks after first becoming available, following an *ex parte* application and a High Court hearing in private, the NCA obtained its first UWOs. The then-unnamed respondent, subsequently identified as an Azerbaijani PEP named Zamira Hajiyeva, together with her husband, beneficially owned, inter alia, a house in Kensington in London and a golf club in Berkshire and had allegedly spent £16m in Harrods over a ten-year period. The UWOs made against Mrs Hajiyeva required her to explain the origins of those assets, something that was not immediately apparent to the NCA as the respondent had no obvious sources of income. Mrs Hajiyeva's husband had been the chairman of a state-owned bank in Azerbaijan from 1993 until 2015.[15] In 2015, he was prosecuted and convicted for major fraud and embezzlement offences involving the bank of which he was the chairman.[16] The value of the assets forming the subject matter of the orders was inexplicable given his relatively modest income as a senior public servant. Upon Mrs Hajiyeva's failure to comply with the orders, a rebuttable presumption arose that her assets were 'recoverable property'. There followed a lengthy appeals process against the orders on various grounds during which Mrs Hajiyeva failed to establish the legitimate provenance of those assets.[17] Over six years after the UWOs against her properties were first granted, some of her assets had civil recovery orders issued against them by the High Court.[18] This case illustrates how UWOs can be used to investigate PEP assets of allegedly suspicious origin.[19]

[12] 'Enforcement authorities' in this context are, in England and Wales: the NCA, HM Revenue & Customs (HMRC), the Financial Conduct Authority (FCA), the Director of the Serious Fraud Office (SFO), and the Director of Public Prosecutions (DPP)—s 362A(7) of the POCA. In Northern Ireland, enforcement authorities for the purposes of UWOs are the NCA, HMRC, the FCA, the SFO, and the Director of Public Prosecutions for Northern Ireland. In Scotland, they are the Scottish Ministers and their delegates.

[13] POCA, s 362C(2).

[14] POCA, s 304(1).

[15] *NCA v Hajiyeva* [2018] EWHC 2534 (Admin), [2018] 1 WLR 5887 [17].

[16] *Hajiyeva* (n 15) [18].

[17] The Supreme Court turned down the respondent's application to appeal on 21 December 2020.

[18] The details of which are discussed in further detail in Chapter 7, Section 2.

[19] See *Hajiyeva* (n 15), and on appeal: *NCA v Hajiyeva* [2020] EWCA Civ 108, [2020] All ER (D) 34.

The stated policy underpinning UWOs is to 'make the UK a more hostile place for those seeking to move, hide or use the proceeds of crime or corruption'.[20] Granting enforcement authorities the ability to require respondents to explain the funding of assets held by them is an attractive proposition, particularly when viewed in light of the disastrous impact of corruption on states from which corruptly acquired assets originate.[21] Where properly enforced, UWOs potentially offer a means of depriving corrupt PEPs of the proceeds of crime and restoring those proceeds to the citizenries of those victim states. If widely enforced, they may deter other corrupt PEPs from laundering the proceeds of their corruption in the UK by creating a credible risk that the origins of their assets too will become the subject of unwanted attention from enforcement authorities.[22] However, despite the early promise of UWOs against PEPs, their success to date in achieving either outcome is questionable. Mrs Hajiyeva's case is the only one so far in the UK in which UWOs against PEPs have been upheld by the courts.[23] It is doubtful that the introduction of the measure can therefore be said to have contributed meaningfully to recovering the proceeds of official corruption in the years since it was first made available. It is not known whether the measure's availability has stemmed the flow of corrupt assets into London.[24] Based on a political and media narrative prevailing at the time of writing, one where foreign diplomats, senior domestic politicians, and NGOs all decry the UK's ongoing and reportedly pervasive problem with 'dirty money' representing the proceeds of overseas corruption, it seems unlikely.[25]

The triggers for the examination of UK anti-corruption measures through the lens of PEP-specific UWOs in this book are as follows. UWOs against PEPs were introduced at a particularly politically opportune time for a UK government burdened by public perceptions that it was failing to staunch the flood of illicitly acquired assets cascading through the London property market from abroad. The problem with the measure's introduction in response to this issue is that UWOs against PEPs are useful as an investigative and evidential tool only to the extent that they (i) are actually used in practice and (ii) are backed by the political support and funding necessary to ensure proper and widespread enforcement. This

[20] House of Lords, *Explanatory Notes related to the Criminal Finances Bill* as brought from the House of Commons on 22 February 2017 (HL Bill 104).

[21] See eg Susan Rose-Ackerman, 'The Law and Economics of Bribery and Extortion' (2010) 6 Annual Review of Law and Social Science 217.

[22] Discussed further in Section 4(a) of Chapter 3.

[23] A second set of UWOs sought against PEPs formed the subject matter of *NCA v Baker* [2020] EWHC 822 (Admin). In the High Court, Lang J discharged the orders on the ground that she was not satisfied that the NCA had met all of the statutory tests necessary to sustain the orders, noting the NCA's case was 'flawed by inadequate investigation into some obvious lines of enquiry' (at [217]).

[24] Owing to the clandestine nature of laundering activities, it is not possible to establish any quantitative or other empirical benchmark from which this might be accurately measured in any event.

[25] See eg Nicola Sturgeon, 'Britain's Failure to Tackle Russian Dirty Money has Enabled Putin's Aggression' *The Guardian* (London, 1 February 2022).

is a prevailing theme in the discussion of anti-corruption measures more generally throughout this volume. On a cynical view, the UWO's introduction might be regarded as a form of political window-dressing; something that was only discussed by the executive when there was a critical mass of media and international attention driving that discussion. Introducing UWOs against PEPs allowed the UK government to convey to the public and to the international community the impression that 'something is being done' about the state's use as a laundry for the proceeds of foreign corruption, without having to expend further political capital (by, for example, implementing meaningful and effective company and property ownership identification reforms at the time[26]) or financial capital (thereby allowing for more robust enforcement of existing measures). Similar political impetuses to those prompting the introduction of UWOs have driven or expedited subsequent pieces of legislation and policy introduced with the stated aims of inter alia thwarting the proceeds of grand corruption being routed through or held in the UK.[27]

In early 2022, following over four years of near non-use since their introduction, UWOs against PEPs were *again* being invoked as a political tool, repeatedly cited by lawmakers as a way in which the UK was tackling corruption amid a resurgent outcry in the media about the spoils of kleptocracy being laundered in London following the Russian invasion of Ukraine.[28] The apparent reluctance of enforcement authorities to use UWOs against PEPs in practice and the relative dearth of measures subsequently introduced to counter the ease with which foreign assets can be laundered in the UK do little to assuage this perception. One of the aims of the research in this volume is to highlight circumstances where the introduction of anti-corruption measures risks constituting politically expedient but perhaps ultimately largely empty gestural lawmaking. It is argued that where a new legal innovation transpires to act primarily as a window-dressing exercise to show that 'something is being done' about a particular problem, that mechanism is not wholly legitimate. When evaluating whether the UK's available anti-corruption measures in general and UWOs against PEPs in particular are 'legitimate', 'justifiable', or 'necessary', the

[26] See Chapter 7, Section 4 on criticism of the measures introduced pursuant to the Economic Crime (Transparency and Enforcement) Act 2022, and Oliver Bullough, 'Boris Johnson Claims the UK is Rooting out Dirty Russian Money. That's Ludicrous' *The Guardian* (London, 25 February 2022).

[27] See eg the passing by Parliament of the Economic Crime (Transparency and Enforcement) Act 2022 some eight days after the Russian invasion of Ukraine. The Act introduced, amongst other items, the Register of Overseas Entities (discussed in Chapter 7), some amendments to improve the operation of the UWO regime, and an expedited process to make sanctions regulations.

[28] UWOs and their effectiveness in tacking the UK's kleptocratic proceeds problem were mentioned in seven separate parliamentary debates in the House of Commons and the House of Lords in the six weeks surrounding Russia's invasion of Ukraine in February 2022. These references are exclusive of references to UWOs made in the context of debating the Economic Crime (Transparency and Enforcement) Act, which was passed three weeks after the invasion and which made minor amendments to the laws governing UWOs.

meanings and parameters of those terms, together with the meaning of 'grand corruption itself', first must be understood.

a. Grand Corruption

The definition of 'corruption' is infamously inexact, to the extent that the drafters of the United Nations Convention against Corruption (UNCAC) were unable to formulate a single agreed definition of the word when negotiating the instrument's terms.[29] This is unsurprising. Attempting to exhaustively define corruption by reference to specific crimes ignores the reality that the interpretation of those offences under domestic laws can vary from country to country and are subject to change.[30] With regard to grand corruption, there are however factors common to almost all discussions of the concept. Activities that, when directly or indirectly involving public officials, are widely viewed by commentators and enforcement authorities as forms of 'grand' official corruption include, without limitation, 'bribery, lobbying, extortion, cronyism, nepotism, parochialism, patronage, influence peddling, graft and embezzlement'.[31] Grand corruption occurs where members of the political elite of a country or those with close ties to those members use their power and connections to misappropriate or otherwise illegitimately misdirect the assets of that country for their personal gain.

Transparency International defines grand corruption as 'the abuse of high-level power that benefits the few at the expense of the many'.[32] While broad, this definition captures three key concepts common to all definitions of grand corruption. First, it typically involves an abuse of public trust, either because the corrupt party is a senior public official who is misusing their public position for private gain or because the corrupt party in question wields status of a kind that enables them to use political contacts to profit from their misdeeds. It follows that crimes of grand corruption may be committed both by individuals who hold high public office, and by people who may not have a formal public function but are, for example,

[29] In considering the relative subjectivity of the term 'corruption', Susan Rose-Ackerman has observed that it 'is often used to condemn behavior that violates the speaker's values . . . But if not everyone shares the same values, the term can imply an overbearing insistence on one's own view of what is right and good. This produces much conceptual confusion'. Susan Rose-Ackerman, 'Corruption & Purity' (2018) 147(3) Daedalus 98.

[30] 'A startling example of this is the Supreme Court of the United States' recent majority decision in *Snyder v United States* (603 U.S. 1 (2024)) that the acceptance by public officials of gratuities after the grant of a political favour by them to the giver of those gratuities is incapable of constituting bribery as a matter of US federal law'.

[31] Fen Osler Hamson and Robert I Rotberg, 'Introduction: Measuring Grand Corruption and Inventing New Legal Barriers' in Osler Hamson and Robert I Rotberg, *Grand Corruption: Curbing Kleptocracy Globally* (Routledge 2025) 1, 5.

[32] Transparency International, *Our Priorities: Grand Corruption* <www.transparency.org/en/our-priorities/grand-corruption>.

'wealthy business leaders with a great deal of political influence'.[33] Each case involves an abuse of public office, whether directly or indirectly, meaning that grand corruption is, by definition, a form of official corruption. That those who commit acts of grand corruption misuse public office (generally) to profit at the expense of the public to whom a duty of responsibility and trust is owed sets corruption apart from other types of crime. Whilst other crimes are often characterized in a relatively abstract way as crimes against society, grand corruption is anathema to the 'public good', both in a literal material sense, as it diverts assets to which the state has an entitlement, and in terms of subverting the mutual expectations of loyalty between a state's authorities and its populace.[34]

Second, Transparency International's definition usefully connotes the idea that the scale of the personal financial gain to an individual committing an act of grand corruption is significant. An alternative formulation of grand corruption previously posited by Transparency International sought to define the concept by reference to the financial context of the state suffering the corruption.[35] Although that definition succeeded in distinguishing grand corruption from more mundane forms of petty corruption, in so doing it suggested a perhaps unhelpful fiscal threshold at which grand corruption might be deemed to have occurred. Under that definition, corrupt officials from countries with higher minimum subsistence incomes would have to misappropriate more assets for an act to qualify as 'grand corruption'. Moreover, Transparency International's current definition allows some constructive ambiguity around the scale of 'grandeur' that a corrupt act needs to achieve to constitute grand corruption, allowing for greater flexibility in interpretation. The necessity of a link between a corrupt activity and the abuse of a senior public office, coupled with the requirement that the scale of misappropriation is consequential, might be viewed as a sufficiently precise test to determine whether an act constitutes grand corruption.

Third, and helpfully, Transparency International's definition does not attempt to conflate the terms 'grand corruption' and 'kleptocracy', notwithstanding the

[33] Louise Shelly, 'Post-Soviet Oligarchs and Kleptocrats: Their Rise, Their Survival, and Western Complicity' in Robert I Rotberg and Fen Osler Hampson (eds), *Grand Corruption: Curbing Kleptocracy Globally* (Routledge 2025) 70.

[34] The 'public good' in this context being used in the Razian sense of types of common goods 'which, in a certain community, serve the interests of people generally in a conflict-free, non-exclusive and non-excludable way'. Joseph Raz, *Ethics in the Public Domain* (OUP 1994) 52.

[35] It defined 'grand corruption' as occurring: 'when a public official or other person deprives a particular social group or substantial part of the population of a State of a fundamental right; or causes the State or any of its people a loss greater than 100 times the annual minimum subsistence income of its people; as a result of bribery, embezzlement or other corruption offence'. The UN Office on Drugs and Crime (UNODC) and the Organisation for Economic Co-operation and Development (OECD) each tacitly endorsed this definition. See UNODC, *Grand Corruption Definition with Explanation* (2016) <www.unodc.org/documents/NGO/Grand_Corruption_definition_with_explanation_19_August_2016_002_1.pdf>; and OECD, *Frequently Asked Questions: How to Address Bribery and Corruption Risks in Mineral Supply Chains* (OECD General Secretariat 2021).

tendency to use those expressions synonymously.[36] Conceptually, they are similar, but their interchangeable use is not always apt. The notion of kleptocracy, or 'rule by thieves' is suggestive of political systems subject to endemic corruption. It is narrower in scope than grand corruption. The United States has, for example, defined kleptocracy as follows: 'a government controlled by officials who use political power to appropriate the wealth of their nation. [It c]an include state capture'.[37] Not all large-scale embezzlement by a public official, for example, or acceptance of significant bribes for influencing the award of public contracts will necessarily occur within a kleptocratic state but can still constitute grand corruption.[38] As kleptocracy can be a politically loaded term, its use may allow corrupt official actors who are not within states deemed 'kleptocratic' or within clearly authoritarian regimes to avoid scrutiny from the authorities of allies that are running anti-kleptocracy clampdowns. One US federal commission, in outlining its government's various anti-kleptocracy initiatives, referred specifically to targeting the corrupt activities of 'US adversaries'.[39] In other words, the use of kleptocracy as a descriptor in national policy literature can have a potentially unhelpful diplomatic undertone that is less obviously present where the term 'grand corruption'—which can be used more neutrally to describe the activities of individual actors—is employed. Strictly speaking, therefore, it is appropriate to categorize kleptocracy as a subset of, rather than the same as, grand corruption.

b. Legitimacy

'Legitimacy' is similarly a notoriously slippery concept, and its meaning is to some extent dependent on the context within which it is discussed. Even then, commentators adopt varying understandings of the term.[40] In this work, understanding something as 'legitimate' should be taken by reference to the 'conditions under which it can be rightfully asserted that something has the kind of moral standing that goes with . . . the relationship the state . . . needs to have over those who [it] claims the right to rule'.[41] There is no scholarly consensus on what those conditions

[36] See eg JC Sharman, *The Despot's Guide to Wealth Management: On the Campaign Against Grand Corruption* (Cornell University Press 2017) 2.

[37] The White House, *United States Strategy on Countering Corruption Pursuant to the National Security Strategy Memorandum on Establishing the Fight Against Corruption as a Core United States Security Interest* (December 2021) 6.

[38] It is highly debatable whether Malaysia during the occurrence of the 1MDB scandal could, for example, fairly be characterized as a kleptocracy. The more recent alleged bribery of EU officials by the governments of Qatar and Morocco falls outside of an obviously kleptocratic context.

[39] US Commission on Security and Cooperation in Europe, *Anti-Kleptocracy Initiatives Supported by the Helsinki Commission* (23 January 2020) <www.csce.gov>

[40] On which, see Colin King and Nicholas Lord, *Negotiated Justice and Corporate Crime: The Legitimacy of Civil Recovery Orders and Deferred Prosecution Agreements* (Springer 2018) 24–25.

[41] Silja Voeneky and Gerald Neuman, 'Introduction' in Silja Voeneky and Gerald Neuman (eds), *Human Rights, Democracy and Legitimacy in a World of Disorder* (CUP 2018) 2.

might comprise. Broadly, modern conceptions of legitimacy of laws or state acts distinguish between 'input legitimacy', meaning the validity of the institutions or processes by which a particular law or measure is developed and enacted, and 'output legitimacy', meaning the relevant measure's success in practice and how the measure and its success (or lack thereof) is accepted by its audience.[42] In evaluating the PEP-specific UWO's input legitimacy, I focus on the socio-political and legal narratives informing and motivating the government's decision to introduce it. Output legitimacy is analysed with reference to factors which commentators have identified as especially important conditions for legitimacy in anti-corruption contexts, namely, inclusiveness or non-discrimination, and a relevant measure's effectiveness as a fair and proportionate means of meeting the objectives sought through its introduction.[43] The impact on individual rights through the state's use of anti-corruption measures like the UWO forms a further important component of output legitimacy, and this is also assessed.

c. Necessity

Determining the applicable criteria to establish whether an anti-corruption mechanism can be viewed as 'necessary' is an altogether more straightforward exercise. Legislative claims for the necessity of PEP UWOs, for example, can be summarized broadly as being based in the need to (i) express the UK's intolerance of the proceeds of foreign corruption being laundered in its territory; (ii) ease the evidential burden of enforcement authorities seeking Civil Recovery Orders (CROs); (iii) deter crime by depriving criminals of criminal proceeds; and (iv) return stolen assets to the states in which they originated.[44] In evaluating whether UWOs against PEPs were necessary, this book determines whether there is something novel about the measure which allows it to effectively achieve these objectives in some way that other measures cannot. Several corollaries follow from the question of whether the measure is necessary. First, does it actually work in practice? Second, are measures which pre-existed the PEP-specific UWO or the form of UWO which is designed for use against the assets of those suspected of involvement of serious crime capable of achieving the same legislative objectives? Assuming they are, this may undermine the case for the PEP-specific UWO. Third, is there something distinctive about UWOs against PEPs when compared to alternative routes to achieving the legislative objectives that somehow renders the former more effective or in some

[42] See Friedrich Kratochwil, 'On Legitimacy' (2006) 20 International Relations 302.

[43] Cecily Rose, *International Anti-Corruption Norms: Their Creation and Influence on Domestic Legal Systems* (OUP 2015) 30–39.

[44] These statutory objectives are discussed in detail in Chapter 3.

way superior to those alternatives? If there is, this would move the dial back in favour of concluding that PEP-specific UWOs are necessary.

d. Justifiability

The question of whether a given measure is justifiable is centrally concerned with the interference of the measure with respondents' individual rights, and whether any such interference might be viewed as a disproportionate means of meeting the objectives pursued in its introduction. In examining the justifiability of new anti-corruption mechanisms, it is necessary to interrogate their rights implications both for individuals directly impacted and for wider society. UWOs were introduced at a time when a number of academics expressed ambivalence about the legitimacy of civil recovery from an individual rights perspective.[45] Concerns about civil recovery's character as a 'hybrid' measure have been expressed widely because it utilizes a process bearing certain criminal justice hallmarks and outcomes yet has been statutorily designated as a civil mechanism.[46] Enforcement authorities need only establish their cases against respondents to a civil standard. Furthermore, respondents are not formally entitled, inter alia, to the benefit of 'criminal limb' protections afforded to defendants provided for under Article 6 of the European Convention on Human Rights (ECHR or the 'Convention'), or established as norms of English criminal law.[47] From a human rights perspective, this gives pause to commentators who view civil recovery (and especially publicized civil recovery cases) as impacting punitively upon respondents in circumstances where respondents are denied the more stringent procedural protections typically afforded to criminal defendants. These commentators suggest that increased reliance on civil recovery powers to tackle the UK's 'dirty money' problem are emblematic of a legislative drift towards highly efficient but potentially procedural fairness-deficient forms of crime control.[48]

This concern is all the more acute in the case of UWOs against PEPs. UWOs can be sought by enforcement authorities against (i) foreign PEPs or (ii) individuals reasonably suspected of involvement in serious crime or those connected to them (referred to throughout this volume as 'Serious Crime UWOs'), in each case provided certain conditions are first met.[49] One might expect that if PEPs are the subject of an enforcement authority investigation, those PEPs are suspected of (at

[45] See Chapter 4, Section 4(a).

[46] See eg the comprehensive liberal rights-based analysis of civil recovery employed by Colin King and Jennifer Hendry in *Civil Recovery of Criminal Property* (OUP 2023).

[47] eg the presumption of innocence and the principle that individuals accused of crimes must be proven guilty beyond reasonable doubt.

[48] See the discussion on Herbert Packer's models of criminal justice in Chapter 3.

[49] POCA, s 362B.

least holding the proceeds of) serious crime and are thus connected in some way to someone involved in serious crime. If this is correct, then the form of UWO designed to tackle the proceeds of serious crime should be sufficient.[50] And yet to obtain a UWO against a PEP, it is not necessary for enforcement authorities to show any link with crime, serious or otherwise. Provided the High Court is satisfied on the balance of probabilities that (i) a respondent is a PEP; (ii) who holds the property specified in the UWO application; (iii) the value of which is apparently incommensurate with the PEP's income or which is reasonably suspected of having been obtained through unlawful conduct; and (iv) is valued at more than £50,000, a UWO will be issued.[51] This unprecedentedly lowers the bar to be met by enforcement authorities seeking to use investigative powers against respondents in a civil recovery context. It raises the prospect that enforcement authorities not needing to establish a nexus between a property and criminality before pursuing asset recovery processes will become normalized and applied more broadly under future legislation against members of society. Moreover, it prompts questions on the impact of UWOs on respondents' other individual rights including property, privacy, non-discrimination, and reputation rights, and on the rigour of criteria to be met before the state can interfere with those interests.

This work therefore evaluates the justifiability of PEP-specific UWOs and other anti-corruption measures considering their relative benefits against the negative consequences that can ensue from their introduction. It discusses how anti-corruption measures can impact on both individual rights and on the wider state-citizen relationship and assesses whether, given the rationale underpinning those measures, their efficacy in practice, and the scale of state intrusion that can follow from their introduction, such measures are justified.

4. Anti-Corruption Innovations: Key Points of Contention

The book uses questions on the legitimacy, justifiability, and necessity of UWOs against PEPs as a lens through which to critique the UK's anti-corruption regime more broadly. It specifically advances the discussion around corruption reform in the following ways. It refocuses critical deviance techniques in a contemporary context in its analysis of the socio-political and legal narratives preceding the UWO's introduction and its use against a specified category of individuals.

[50] POCA, s 362B. To obtain a Serious Crime UWO, enforcement authorities must establish (i) that the property the subject of an order application is held by the respondent and is worth more than £50,000; (ii) a reasonable suspicion that the sources of a respondent's lawful income are insufficient to allow them to obtain the relevant assets or that the property was obtained through unlawful conduct; and (iii) that there are reasonable grounds for suspecting that the respondent or someone connected to them is involved in serious crime.

[51] POCA, s 362B.

It builds on the conversation around hybrid measures by highlighting the tenor and impacts of using publicized civil recovery processes against respondents, and by citing UWOs as a good example of why bifurcating rights into distinct 'civil procedural rights' and 'criminal procedural rights' classes is deeply unhelpful when contextualizing appropriate procedural safeguarding for hybrid measures. Historically, little of the literature on both hybrid measures and non-conviction-based forms of asset recovery has drawn on the application of those measures to elites. Analysis of incrementalism in crime control measures is enhanced through the discussion of specific measures being applicable to sub-categories of individuals who are predominantly non-citizens. Finally, in this volume, I seek to reframe anti-corruption policy debate by offering analysis on additional and alternative legislative and policy options for recovering the UK-based proceeds of foreign kleptocracy and for increasing the difficulty with which the proceeds of corruption can be laundered.

In addressing the proceeds of overseas grand corruption, enforcement authorities and lawmakers are required to confront a particularly challenging area of law; namely, dealing with the proceeds of financial crime. In doing this, they are frequently required to grapple with numerous complicating factors, many of which are relatively new considerations in crime control. These include, without limitation: secrecy jurisdictions and ownership structures which by design obstruct the process of investigators; evidence-gathering from multiple jurisdictions, including uncooperative or institutionally incapable jurisdictions; the lack of expert resources implicit in austerity policing policies; diplomatic or political pressures to pursue or abandon particular courses of action; and civil society, public, and media scrutiny. This book acknowledges that the issues are complex, and that no perfect solution exists. Nevertheless, I argue that more robust, ambitious, and holistic approaches to tackling corruption are necessary, and that the experience with UWOs and PEPs serves as both a cautionary tale and a teachable moment in devising future anti-corruption strategy.

Domestic laws specifically aimed at recovering proceeds of grand corruption, amendments to legislation governing transparency around the ownership of properties and companies, and new sanctions provisions are all potentially helpful means of ensuring that corrupt actors cannot enjoy their ill-gotten UK-based gains. Each of these developments shows promise in principle in helping to deter laundering, but critics note that taken individually, they are reasonably easy hurdles for committed launderers to circumvent. More effective but hitherto less-discussed recent measures for recovering corruptly acquired assets and deterring the laundering of those assets include account freezing orders (AFrOs) and the negotiation by law enforcement authorities of settlement agreements with those suspected of holding the proceeds of corruption. There is an obvious legislative appetite to address—or at the very least, to be seen to be addressing—the proceeds of grand corruption being laundered in the UK. Nevertheless, this book argues that there is scope for significantly greater strides to be made at a policy level in tackling the proceeds of overseas graft. A lack of resourcing to allow for proper enforcement including against domestic professional service providers who facilitate laundering, the use of reactive rather than proactive policy approaches, and a failure to adopt more holistic strategies to prevent corruptly acquired assets from entering the UK enable a flood of 'dirty money' to continue to stream through the jurisdiction. The hasty conception and design of some newer measures aimed at thwarting the laundering of the proceeds of assets stolen by foreign political elites means that potential pitfalls in some newer measures' operation are not fully anticipated, or that existing measures are under-explored. Moreover, policy trends suggest a waning interest in the UK towards pursuing solutions in cooperation with other states and a reluctance to engage in more fundamental reforms in dealing with kleptocracy and other forms of corruption.

This book argues that whilst new anti-corruption measures tend to be politically popular, unless they are backed by meaningful financial and political resources, they risk constituting little more than empty rhetoric. In making this argument, it highlights the strengths and weaknesses of the UK's anti-corruption regime. It focuses predominantly on domestic laws and policies targeting the proceeds of grand corruption, but given the transnational nature of the underlying crimes, it will draw upon the experiences of other common law jurisdictions in considering the effectiveness and legitimacy of anti-corruption measures of the present and options for future reform. The introduction of any measure designed to address and deter corrupt assets being laundered in the UK is, in theory, a desirable addition to the state's anti-corruption armoury. However, some aspects of recent innovations—UWOs against PEPs in particular—in the outcomes sought in introducing them, in their operation in practice, and in terms of their wider implications within the anti-corruption paradigm, warrant closer investigation and discussion on their necessity, legitimacy, and justifiability.

5. Methodology

This book uses doctrinal methods primarily, though not exclusively, in undertaking its analysis. It draws on policy papers, parliamentary discussion, domestic legislation and case law, the jurisprudence of the European Court of Human Rights (ECtHR), and international legal instruments. The rights implications of the UK's anti-corruption machinery are evaluated using a liberal human rights framework. Some additional methods conduced to completing this enquiry into the UK's efforts to tackle grand corruption. A literature review covering theoretical conceptions of what constitutes 'crime' and what constitutes 'punishment' was important in framing a discussion on the procedural rights implications of UWOs against PEPs. Works from theorists influential to those discussions, and to discussions on civil recovery as a form of crime control, are referenced throughout the text. Additionally, some empirical methods were employed in addressing specific issues.

a. Media Surveys

The discussion in this book around the socio-political and legal narratives precipitating and influencing the introduction of UWOs against PEPs is premised on a research assumption that, owing to the lack of empirical evidence showing that PEPs are more likely to launder ill-gotten gains in the UK property market than other individuals, UWOs against PEPs may be the product of a moral panic.[52] To evaluate this assumption, I looked at the work of critical deviance theorists whose commentary on interactions between public concern, media coverage of wrongdoing, moral entrepreneurship, and deviance creation informed my decision to undertake media surveys to discern trends between publicized corruption scandals and the introduction of asset recovery powers. One survey looked at the prevalence of news articles containing specific terms including 'proceeds of crime' and 'dirty money' published in the main British non-tabloid format daily newspapers (ie *The Times*, *The Independent*, *The Telegraph*, and *The Guardian*) in the period from 2000 to 2017. Its purpose was to find whether media attention toward stories on these themes was especially prevalent at times preceding or coinciding with the publication of draft legislation aimed at strengthening asset recovery powers. The data were collected by undertaking a search of the Lexis®Library News Search function, which allows users to search all UK national non-tabloid format newspaper publications except for the *Financial Times* (FT). A second survey was used to demonstrate public (or, at least, media) perceptions of links between UWOs and criminality by checking the prevalence in the same media sources up to May 2022 of articles referring to both 'unexplained wealth orders' and the term 'McMafia'. A third media survey was undertaken to track the frequency with which references to 'money laundering' were made using all articles published in the FT referring to instances of foreign official corruption in the year 2016 (the year in which the draft legislation proposing UWOs against PEPs was first published). The FT's reportage on corruption was selected for analysis because (i) of its focus on business and economics reporting; (ii) of the ability to search by reference to date-range on its website; (iii) of a perception that its media bias rating skews relatively centrist;[53] and (iv) the FT is the preferred broadsheet of the UK's financial sector, key stakeholders in the PEP discussion. The media surveys provide insight into the

[52] See Chapter 4, Section 3 for a definition of moral panic.

[53] See <www.allsides.com/news-source/financial-times-media-bias>, a media analysis website which claims to be staffed by individuals from a range of political biases. It is acknowledged that any such rating will always be imperfect because it will be informed by biases of the individuals responsible for compiling such ratings.

frequency and tenor of news reportage in the periods preceding and following the introduction of civil recovery measures generally and UWOs against PEPs specifically. They are therefore helpful in identifying prevailing media narratives at relevant times.

b. Interviews

Early proponents of PEP-specific rules were interviewed to discern the key concerns driving, and rationales underpinning, the decision of the financial sector to develop PEP-specific rules and practices. Two members of the Wolfsberg Group (one of whom participated in the Group's inaugural conferences) were interviewed individually in February 2020. Each interview was of approximately sixty minutes' duration. Additionally, to establish enforcement authorities' perceptions on the efficacy of UWOs against PEPs and to help understand why UWOs were regarded as preferable to pre-existing measures, three senior NCA officers were interviewed together in a single interview of roughly seventy-five minutes' duration in December 2020.[54]

c. Court Attendance

I attended the second day of a two-day High Court hearing for *NCA v Baker* to observe how enforcement authorities' and respondents' counsel interpreted the statutory requirements in one of the two cases to date involving UWOs against PEPs.[55] This informed the discussion on satisfying the application criteria for UWOs set out in Chapter 3.

d. FOI Requests

Finally, in an attempt to ascertain the quantitative efficacy of UWOs against PEPs by reference to the amount of assets actually recovered since the measure's

[54] All interviews received prior ethical clearance from the institution where I was undertaking my doctoral thesis at the time, Queen Mary University of London. Participants were provided with information sheets outlining the uses to which the content of the interviews might be put and a list of questions that would form the basis for discussion in the interviews, with the opportunity to digress or expand on issues as the interviews progressed. All interviews took place via Skype. Consent to digitally record and transcribe the interviews was granted by all interviewees. Each interviewee was sent a copy of the transcript of their interview to allow them to review, clarify, or expand on any of the points made, and to verify the accuracy of what was recorded. Each interviewee duly provided their sign-offs to their respective transcripts.

[55] *NCA v Baker* [2020] EWHC 822 (Admin).

introduction, I submitted a Freedom of Information (FOI) request to the Home Office seeking clarity on discrepancies in historical reports on the value of assets restrained and recovered through UWOs. The only enforcement authority that has applied for UWOs against PEPs to date, the NCA, is not subject to FOI requirements and therefore a request to it was not possible.[56] Information on data held and not held by the Home Office is in itself insightful, because it is an indicator of the degree of executive oversight implicit in the operation of particular measures. An FOI was also submitted to HMRC to determine the number of number of trust data requests received from parties with legitimate interests in determining the beneficiaries of UK and non-UK trusts used directly or indirectly to hold UK properties, and the number of requests granted.[57] This information is useful because it provides insight on the transparency (or ongoing lack thereof) in the operation of trusts holding properties in the UK.[58]

6. Chapter Outline

This book centres the PEP-specific unexplained wealth order in considering the anti-corruption regime in the UK, and, in particular, the use of asset recovery processes to deter corruption. Before embarking on the book's substantive analysis, the first chapter provides the context within which the British anti-corruption machinery operates. It traces the historical, political, and social origins of the country's status as an attractive destination in which to transform stolen wealth into apparently licit investment in real estate and other assets. The difficulties in establishing the scale of wealth of illegal origin both globally and domestically are explained, and the UK's international law obligations in relation to the recovery and repatriation of corruptly acquired assets are described. This chapter explains how factors including a somewhat laissez-faire approach towards scrutinizing the origins of monies invested from abroad coupled with its pronounced under-resourcing of the authorities responsible for investigating complex multi-jurisdictional financial crimes has led to UK becoming a safehouse for illicit wealth.

Discourse around anti-corruption innovation unsurprisingly centres around the individuals holding political and financial decision-making powers and who

[56] Freedom of Information Act 2000, s 23.

[57] Letter from HMRC Information Rights Unit to the author dated 30 April 2024 (HMRC FOI 2024/36578).

[58] Two final general methodological notes are necessary. First, this book was completed at a time when new transparency laws have been enacted but the finer detail of how these laws will be implemented in practice has not yet been published. Where relevant, these developments are noted but are not extensively discussed. The discussion and analysis of law in force in this book is current and up to date as at 1 December 2024. Second, there are internet sources and websites cited throughout this volume for sources unavailable in hard print copy. All website addresses were last accessed on, and are correct as of, 1 December 2024.

therefore have the most opportunity for committing acts of corruption, namely senior public officials. Chapter 2 introduces the reader to the concept of the 'PEP' or 'politically exposed person' by examining its development in money laundering and asset recovery laws at national, European, and international levels. The concept of the 'PEP' as defined under the law is broad: it covers any senior public official from outside the UK or the EEA, their family members, and any of their close associates. PEP-specific rules originated with financial institutions, their regulators, and the Financial Action Task Force (FATF) developing anti-money laundering (AML) laws and rules in response to the reputational fallout for banks from political corruption scandals in the 1990s. The chapter highlights the remarkably limited parliamentary scrutiny afforded by lawmakers to the 'PEP' concept in the EU and the UK prior to passing laws aimed at preventing overseas political elites from laundering stolen assets, and examines the rationales frequently posited in justifying such rules. It argues that the mismatch in the definition of 'PEP' in asset recovery and anti-money laundering settings is unhelpful. It further contends that, in either context, the idea of the 'politically exposed person' is so broadly conceived that it risks diffusing focus from the individuals in whom political and financial influence is concentrated.

Chapter 3 begins by explaining how the proceeds of crime regime works in the UK. It explains the difference between conviction-based confiscation measures and non-conviction-based civil recovery measures and sets out some key criticisms made of civil recovery including its hybrid status. Notwithstanding lowered bars to enforcement, there has been markedly little success in the UK in instituting or sustaining civil recovery proceedings against those suspected of stealing state assets from other countries. Having provided this context, the chapter explores the objectives forwarded by the government in introducing UWOs against PEPs and assesses the extent to which these legislative aims have been met in practice.

Chapter 4 examines the socio-political and legal narratives precipitating the introduction of the PEP-specific UWO through a critical criminological lens. The chapter argues that the process surrounding recent anti-corruption legislation's introduction conformed to tropes typical of moral panics. In making this contention, the chapter draws on the work of critical deviance theorists and uses media surveillance and review of parliamentary debates to assess the public discourse surrounding the introduction of tools designed to help investigate unexplained wealth. Historic correlations between periods of heightened publicity as regards official foreign corruption scandals and the extension of PEP-specific measures internationally are identified. The chapter goes on to examine media coverage preceding and contemporaneous to the introduction of UWOs and recent sanctions provisions to determine whether the reportage surrounding their introduction conforms to processes historically evident in the enactment of panic-induced and typically ineffective laws. Drawing comparisons with the operation of targeted sanctions, the chapter concludes that whilst the introduction of PEP-specific UWOs was well-meaning and potentially helpful, many such measures might be viewed as effective in practice for politically expressive purposes but little else.

Chapter 5 suggests that in the fervour to be seen to be 'doing something' about the dirty money flowing through the UK's real estate and financial markets, lawmakers, enforcement authorities, and other interested parties may be overlooking options already provided for on the statute books or available through the courts using regulatory, private law, and criminal law options. It highlights possibly under-exploited pre-existing measures which may be capable of staunching the flood of corruption proceeds laundered in the UK. It considers options for bolstering deterrence from within the jurisdiction by looking at how domestic legal, financial, corporate, and property service providers can be used as instruments of money laundering. First, it details civil and regulatory routes to dealing with regulated professionals who facilitate kleptocracy. It argues that regulatory and enforcement practice and policy should be revisited and updated to ensure that potential money-laundering enablers are deterred credibly from assisting in corruption. Second, it highlights the domestic under-prosecution of criminal offences over which the UK has clear enforcement and adjudicative jurisdiction. It argues in favour of more aggressive prosecution of financial and legal service providers based in the UK who assist kleptocrats using criminal facilitation laws. Third, it looks at private law options for recovering the proceeds of corruption. It assesses the relative efficacy and utility of (i) 'victim' states instituting civil proceedings through the civil courts in England; and (ii) privately instituted prosecutions. The aim of the chapter is to foreground the multiplicity of legal avenues open to private, public, and regulatory parties in tackling stolen wealth. It argues that to meaningfully address the problem, it is necessary for a multiplicity of private and state actors to exert pressure from several directions to ensure that the conditions necessary to hoard illicit wealth in the UK are as inconvenient and uncomfortable as possible for corrupt elites and their associates.

Chapter 6 addresses several principled and practical implications arising from the use of investigative measures employed to target the proceeds of grand corruption. Some commentators have argued that the individuals against whose assets such measures are imposed are being subjected to state-made claims of criminal guilt without benefiting from a presumption of innocence. These concerns are particularly acute where the use of the relevant measures is widely publicized. Others have expressed concerns about the impact of anti-corruption measures on privacy and property rights. A broader criticism relates to the under-scrutinized development of anti-corruption processes more generally. Where draconian laws are introduced against a specified cohort in a population on an exceptional and limited basis and their operation becomes normalized, similar measures applicable against society more generally might be introduced subsequently with little dissent. The chapter discusses the idea of anti-corruption laws paving the way for incremental expansion of harsher measures capable of employment against the general domestic population.

Since Russia's invasion of Ukraine in early 2022, the UK has introduced new laws aimed, amongst other matters, at improving transparency on the identities of the natural persons who are entitled to the ultimate beneficial ownership of property in the jurisdiction and companies and trusts registered there. Chapter 7 highlights these and other recent anti-corruption legal and policy developments and suggests that they represent a welcome shift in policy approaches to allow for more a proactive and systematic fight against grand corruption. It goes on to consider some potential reforms currently under discussion in the anti-corruption discourse.

The volume concludes with an appeal towards more empirically rigorous evaluations of the scope, the effectiveness, and the broader consequences of potential solutions when considering policy options to deal with the proceeds of kleptocracy. It argues for greater deliberation in formulating anti-corruption policy, with a renewed turn towards consciousness of the civil liberties consequences of untested measures. It joins the chorus of works arguing in recent decades for a reimagining of the civil/criminal dichotomy of procedural rights as enshrined in the jurisprudence of the European Court of Human Rights and the UK's courts to ensure that respondents to anti-corruption measures are afforded due process. Finally, it exhorts the political establishment to back anti-corruption measures with sufficient political will and financial resourcing to ensure proper enforcement. It acknowledges the political impulse to focus resourcing on crimes with visible UK-based victims but argues that to ignore overseas corruption is to ignore the fact of globalization and its enormous impact, good and ill, upon domestic society.

7. Conclusion

A failure to staunch the proceeds of corruption from flooding the domestic financial system negatively impacts both upon 'victim' states and upon the domestic populace. It follows that it is essential for everybody's benefit that the fight against grand corruption is prosecuted more effectively and more legitimately.

1

The UK's Relationship with Overseas Grand Corruption

1. Introduction

The turn of this century coincided with a transformation in public and academic discourses on grand corruption and kleptocracy. Once viewed as a wholly parasitic process predicated on the actions of leaders of 'poorer' states, grand corruption began to be characterized more accurately as akin to a symbiosis whereby wealthy global financial centres profit by serving and facilitating kleptocrats in less developed states who line their pockets at their countries' expense.[1] Moreover, on a social if not a legal level there seems to be a nascent recasting of what exactly official corruption can compromise.[2] The citizenries of wealthier countries are now uncomfortably aware that senior public officials having conflicts between their personal and public interests is not solely the preserve of states in the Global South.[3] Despite this shift in the understanding of grand corruption, however, policy changes engendered by this shift in socio-political consciousness have been slow to emerge in the UK. Since the start of this century, several international political scandals have highlighted the UK's unwitting but negligent complicity in enabling foreign corrupt senior public officials and their cronies to personally enrich themselves through the misuse of public office. It has become apparent that foreign

[1] See eg Alexander Cooley and JC Sharman, 'Transnational Corruption and the Globalised Individual' (2017) 15 Perspectives on Politics 732; Kevin Morgan and Nadir Kinossian 'Dismantling Londongrad: the Dark Geography of Dirty Money' (2023) European Planning Studies 1; Jackie Harvey 'Tracking the International Proceeds of Corruption and the Challenges of National Boundaries and National Agencies: The UK Example' (2020) 40 Public Money & Management 360.

[2] Peter Alldridge observes that '[t]he three main forms of corruption which have never, without more, been criminal in English law are the linked ones of nepotism, asynchronous exchanges, and unreciprocated but corrupt doing of favours'. Peter Alldridge, 'The U.K. Bribery Act: The Caffeinated Younger Sibling of the FCPA' (2012) 73 Ohio State Law Journal 1181, 1184.

[3] Recent matters attracting public ire include House of Lords member Michelle Mone's alleged link to suspected criminal offences committed in the public procurement of personal protective equipment during the Covid pandemic: Emily Dugan and David Conn, 'UK's National Crime Agency says it is "not scared" of PPE Medpro's lawyers' *The Guardian* (London, 15 August 2024); and misgivings about conflicts of interest between Donald Trump's private commercial holdings and those of his family members, and his public duties as President of the United States.

Unexplained Wealth Orders and the UK's Anti-Corruption Regime. Áine Clancy, Oxford University Press.
 DOI: 10.1093/9780198907312.003.0002

illicitly acquired assets have been invested in significant—perhaps even market-distorting—quantities in London's property market and through the UK's domestic and offshore financial centres and institutions, facilitated by a coterie of the UK's professional financial and legal advisers.[4]

This problem was thrust into focus immediately following the Russian invasion of Ukraine in February 2022. Legislation aimed at strengthening both corporate transparency and the ability of criminal law enforcement authorities to pursue the proceeds of overseas corruption was rushed through Parliament in eight days.[5] A raft of economic sanctions took effect shortly thereafter.[6] By this time, London had already answered to the sobriquet of 'Londongrad' for over a decade. This term was used at first in a value-neutral way to refer to the number of wealthy individuals from states in the former USSR buying property in upmarket areas of London. It later took on a pejorative undertone as the sources of some wealthy emigrees' assets began to be questioned.[7] The UK's harbouring of illicitly acquired assets (or, at best, assets acquired in legally questionable circumstances) was not limited to those originating in Russia. Unexplained wealth investigations into UK-based assets originating in Azerbaijan and Kazakhstan,[8] as well as investigations into assets acquired using funds allegedly corruptly acquired in Libya, Pakistan, Chad, Malaysia, Nigeria, and Pakistan, are amongst those instituted by UK law enforcement authorities since 2000.[9] There are indications that the *known* instances of suspected kleptocratic wealth form only the tip of the iceberg. Civil society groups including Transparency International UK have pointed to the tens of thousands of properties in Central London acquired by companies registered in so-called secrecy jurisdictions.[10] At the times of the acquisition of these properties,

[4] John Heathershaw and others, *The UK's Kleptocracy Problem: How Servicing post-Soviet Elites Weakens the Rule of Law* (Chatham House 2021); Transparency International UK and Thomson Reuters, *London Property: A Top Destination for Money Launderers*, 2 December 2016 <https://issuu.com/transparencyuk/docs/final_s041329_v8_hrnc__1_>.

[5] The Economic Crime (Transparency and Enforcement) Act 2022 received Royal Assent on 15 March 2022.

[6] Somewhat belatedly: see Chapter 4, n 85.

[7] According to a search across all newspapers searchable using the Lexis+ UK database, the term started to become widely used by the British media in 2005.

[8] In *NCA v Hajiyeva* [2018] EWHC 2534 (Admin), [2018] 1 WLR 5887, and *NCA v Baker* [2020] EWHC 822 (Admin), [2020] 4 WLUK 113, [2020] Lloyd's Rep FC 240, respectively.

[9] See Áine Clancy, 'A Better Deal: Negotiated Responses to the Proceeds of Grand Corruption' (2022) 33 Criminal Law Forum 149.

[10] The following helpful definition of 'secrecy jurisdiction' was provided by Quentin Reed and Alessandra Fontana in *Corruption and Illicit Financial Flows: The Limits and Possibilities of Current Approaches* (2011, U4 Anti-Corruption Research Centre) 15:

'The central characteristic of a secrecy jurisdiction is that it is a legal jurisdiction that provides secrecy to entities that do not in fact operate within its physical space . . . This secrecy is created through a range of regulations [. . . that] include laws that allow a low degree of transparency in the establishment and accounting by corporate entities, the creation of trusts whose real beneficiaries remain anonymous, zero or low tax rates and minimal exchange of tax information with other tax jurisdictions, banking secrecy, and barriers to exchange of information on criminal matters'.

these companies were not required to disclose details of the individuals holding the ultimate beneficial ownership in their shares.[11]

This chapter examines the UK's contemporary relationship with corrupt foreign politically exposed persons (PEPs) and their use of the jurisdiction as a place to store their wealth. Some of the pull factors leading to this status are outlined in Section 2. The third section sketches the current legal enforcement environment which, it is argued throughout this volume, has contributed to the UK's image as a place where the proceeds of graft can be held with relative impunity. The fourth section assesses the UK's fulfilment of its international law obligations to tackle grand corruption, retrieve its proceeds, and return them to states of origin. This background helps to establish why the UK in general and London in particular are so appealing to kleptocrats as locations in which to invest their ill-gotten gains. The discussion in this chapter forms a foundation for evaluating appropriate responses to overseas corruption, with which the remainder of this book is concerned.

2. The UK's Relationship with Overseas Grand Corruption: A Brief Recent History

In this part, literature published by civil society groups, policy-makers, historians, news media, academics, and anti-corruption commentators is reviewed to identify why overseas elites (corrupt and otherwise) use the UK as a base for their assets. The reasons for which the UK has become such an attractive destination for suspected dirty money are numerous and complex. It is not intended (nor is it possible), to provide an exhaustive list of the reasons for this state of affairs. Nevertheless, some key factors are outlined here. Sub-sections (a) to (e) discuss salient aspects of the UK's recent economic history, its post-colonial constitutional relationships, its social infrastructure, its property and corporate ownership regimes, and its legal and commercial environments respectively.

a. Some Modern Origins of the Problem

London's prominence as a modern global financial centre was achieved in large part owing to economic tectonic shifts in world economics in the last century. Britain's global commercial dominance and the impact of its empire-building is well documented.[12] As the British Empire started disintegrating in the

[11] See Transparency International UK and Thomson Reuters (n 4). Transparency International UK has highlighted the heightened risk of corporate bodies organized in these jurisdictions engaging in money laundering.

[12] Notable recent works include John Darwin, *The Empire Project: The Rise and Fall of the British World-System, 1830–1970* (CUP 1999) and for a more specific focus on the intertwining of British commercial and administrative interests in extending the British Empire in India, see William Dalrymple,

mid-twentieth century, its facilitation of individuals wishing to obscure the origins of their wealth began to develop in earnest. Throughout the 1930s, the availability of cheap credit and the ability of states to rapidly devalue their own currencies creating ungoverned flows of cash across borders was viewed as an important factor in enabling Germany to build its military to an ultimately disastrous extent, leading to the Second World War. By the time the Bretton Woods Conference was convened in 1944, all forty-four allied nations were unanimous on the need to regulate economic relationships between states and to control currency flows to avoid the fiscal conditions leading to the war being replicated.[13] The outcomes of the Conference included the formation of the International Monetary Fund (IMF) and the fixing of the par value of signatories' currencies to the US dollar, the value of which in turn was pegged at US$35 per ounce of gold.[14] Deviations from these currency valuations were possible only with the prior consent of the IMF. The ease of cross-border transactions thus was curbed considerably.[15] Over the following decades, the pound sterling suffered speculative pressure as the British Empire faced independence campaigns in its colonies. The UK's economy suffered as it struggled to find the resources to maintain the pound's parity with the US dollar, to the extent that its government applied for a significant bailout from the IMF in 1956 to allay a financial crisis catalysed in part by the Suez Canal debacle.[16] The City of London's dominance as a world finance centre faltered.

There is some consensus among commentators that this state of economic decline ended with the development of the 'Eurodollar' in the late 1950s. The growth of the Eurodollar market through the 1960s and the realization that it was possible to open bank branches physically located in London yet deemed offshore for regulatory and tax purposes assisted the City of London's great revival.[17] Although the nature and origins of the Eurodollar market are contested,[18] a dominant account is that by the late 1950s, British banks were limited in the amounts of GBP they could lend owing to currency controls imposed following the Suez Crisis. As US banks

The Anarchy: The Relentless Rise of the East India Company (Bloomsbury 2019). On the development of empire through British trading and the ongoing impact of empire on former colonies, see Kojo Koram, *Uncommon Wealth: Britain and the Aftermath of Empire* (John Murray 2022). On the City of London's evolution into a global financial powerhouse, see David Kynaston, *City of London: The History* (Chatto & Windus 2011).

[13] Donald Markwell, *John Maynard Keynes and International Relations: Economic Paths to War and Peace* (OUP 2006).

[14] Given effect in the UK pursuant to the Bretton Woods Agreements Act 1945 (c.19).

[15] Bullough (n 160) 30.

[16] James M Boughton, 'Northwest of Suez: The 1956 Crisis and the IMF' 48(3) IMF Staff Papers (Palgrave Macmillan Journals on behalf of the IMF 2001).

[17] See Elena Blanco and Miguel José Arjona Sánchez, '"Follow-ing the Money" Ten Years On: Transparency and the Fight against Banking Secrecy' in Nicholas Ryder and Lorenzo Pasculli (eds), *Corruption, Integrity and the Law: Global Integrity Challenges* (Routledge 2020) 185, 190–92.

[18] Ronen Palan, Richard Murphy, and Christian Chavagneux, *Tax Havens: How Globalization Really Works* (Cornell University Press 2013) 131–33.

were subject to regulatory interest rate restrictions and capitalization requirements, they were restricted in the value of US dollars *they* could lend.[19] When one City of London bank, Midland Bank, began taking huge US dollar deposits from overseas clients unrelated to any specific trade activity—something prohibited under the Bretton Woods Agreement on the basis that it constituted speculative activity—the Bank of England opted not to intervene, in part because the activity bolstered Britain's dollar reserves.[20] Huge reserves of US dollars began to be deposited in UK banks by Eastern bloc countries mistrustful of US banks. Banks in London started using these dollar deposits to fund international financing transactions. Interest on dollar loans issued by UK banks attracted tax liability, so banks in London (and Switzerland) instead began to use their dollar reserves to issue Eurobonds—bonds denominated in US dollars with high interest rates. Although these bonds often were arranged through London banks, they were formally issued in European countries that did not tax bond issuances, and interest was repaid in jurisdictions that did not tax those payments. Oliver Bullough describes Eurobonds as 'a highly convenient bond paying a good rate of interest, on which no one had to pay tax of any kind, and which could be turned back into cash anywhere. It was the ultimate expression of offshore'.[21] The Bank of England apparently decided that attempting to regulate transactions involving non-resident parties and denominated in foreign currencies fell outside of its bailiwick, even though the transactions were arranged in the City of London. An almost entirely unregulated and untaxed market for dollars in London was born.[22] This non-interventionist approach, coupled with the fact that no other country's banking authorities had jurisdiction to impose regulatory limitations has led some commentators to suggest that 'the British state established the Euromarket'.[23]

The majority of Eurobond-bearers were made up of 'standard tax-dodgers', but as Bullough and others note, the availability of bonds subject to scant regulatory oversight and no tax liability was attractive too to a range of international elites holding wealth of questionable origin.[24] Their number included corrupt politicians from newly democratic countries whose state institutions were somewhat precarious following de-colonization, and a hodgepodge of individuals with unexplained wealth who settled in South America after the Second World War or from

[19] Oliver Bullough, 'The Dark Side of Globalization' (2018) 29 Journal of Democracy 25, 29–30. See also Blanco and Arjona Sánchez (n 17) discussing the active solicitation by Midland Bank of foreign currency deposits, allowing it to service the 'financial activity of non-residents' and transform a London branch into a *de jure* if not de facto overseas branch.

[20] Nicholas Shaxson, *The Finance Curse: How Global Finance is Making Us All Poorer* (Vintage 2019) 54–56.

[21] Bullough (n 19) 42.

[22] Shaxson (n 20) 55–58.

[23] Palan and others (n 18) 132.

[24] Bullough (n 19) 42. And see Palan and others (n 18); and Shaxson (n 20) 56: 'The Euromarkets' . . . lack of controls made them a paradise for tax cheats, scammers and criminals'.

Soviet bloc states.[25] In this way, banks based in the City of London together with their colleagues in Switzerland and New York facilitated the availability of stateless or 'offshore' arrangements allowing individuals to hold funds using high levels of banking secrecy and negligible or no tax liability. The Eurodollar market grew exponentially throughout the 1960s and beyond. The UK government's neoliberal economic (de)regulation policies introduced via the 'Big Bang' in the Thatcher era onwards added further impetus to international investors.[26] Taken in the round, the increasingly laissez-faire approach in the second half of the twentieth century towards regulating the flow of funds from outside and through the country significantly contributed to Britain's transformation from financially listless to an economic powerhouse.

b. Crown Dependencies and Overseas Territories and Tax 'Efficiency'

In tandem with and inspired by the loosening of regulatory oversight in the UK, international banks started engaging in further light-touch regulatory tourism, motivated variously by low or no tax liability, convenient time zones, lower overhead costs, and strict banking secrecy rules.[27] Some of the UK's semi-autonomous overseas territories (hereafter 'Overseas Territories') including Bermuda, the Cayman Islands, and the British Virgin Islands (BVI) began expanding and developing offshore financial sectors, facilitated by a knowledge base of tax, financial, and legal experts in London.[28] Overseas Territories, which were transitioning towards autonomy following the dissolution of the British Empire, were explicitly encouraged by the UK government to develop their financial services sectors as a means of achieving self-sufficiency and financial independence.[29] The physical off-shoring of much of the Euromarkets also addressed concerns within the City of London that this booming and largely unregulated sector could result in reputational contagion for the City if conditions soured. The UK's development of offshore tax havens appealed to international financing houses, who required jurisdictions in which to organize non-resident investment, borrowing, and holding vehicles falling outside the ambit of their national regulators. The legacies of colonialism mean that Overseas Territories, although largely self-governing, maintain

[25] Bullough (n 19) 44–45.

[26] See eg Morgan and Kinossian (n 1) 7–8; Blanco and Aronja Sánchez (n 17).

[27] Palan and others (n 18) 133–49.

[28] Blanco and Aronja Sánchez (n 17) 192–93.

[29] Tony Freyer and Andrew P Morriss, 'Creating Cayman as an Offshore Financial Center: Structure and Strategy Since 1960' (2013) 45 Arizona State Law Journal 1297. The UK has fourteen Overseas Territories, seven of which operate 'sophisticated financial sectors': Dominic Thomas-James, *Offshore Financial Centres and the Law: Suspect Wealth in British Overseas Territories* (Routledge 2022) 48. The relevant seven territories are: BVI, Cayman Islands, Gibraltar, Anguilla, Bermuda, Turks and Caicos Islands, and Montserrat.

constitutional links to the UK, speak English as their official language, have familiar common law legal systems, use the Privy Council as their court of final appeal, and recognize the concept of trusts. These factors allowed international firms and banks to operate in those jurisdictions in reassuringly familiar legal and corporate contexts. Moreover, the Overseas Territories' and the UK's three Crown Dependencies'[30] legislative autonomy has allowed their tax regimes sufficient malleability to enable innovations to be developed in a way specifically aimed at attracting international banks and their clients to establish branches, companies, and trusts within those jurisdictions.[31]

By the end of the twentieth century, a business model had evolved whereby financial institutions based in the City of London actively solicited money from all corners of the world to a relatively light-touch regulatory environment. The City's financial strength coupled with the UK's somewhat constitutionally ambiguous but influential relationship with its Overseas Territories and Crown Dependencies ensured that the Treasury was well positioned to influence money-laundering policy and other forms of international financial policy in a way that served its own interests.[32] To the extent that asset holders wished to maintain privacy, numerous corporate and trust models subject to low tax and high levels of discretion were available offshore. These features of the Crown Dependencies and Overseas Territories subsist today, with many of them consistently named as among the 'most complicit in helping individuals to hide their finances from the rule of law'.[33] Some defending those low or no tax regimes and low levels of financial transparency argue that there is at times a 'disproportionate focus' on these jurisdictions in calling for greater transparency in their corporate ownership registers and query the disproportionality in 'compelling small island territories to take the lead' on improved levels of transparency.[34] Dominic Thomas-James, for example, has called for more nuance in distinguishing between the practices of various Crown Dependencies and Overseas Territories, noting that whilst 'some tax havens are

[30] The Crown Dependencies comprise the Isle of Man, the Bailiwick of Jersey, and the Bailiwick of Guernsey, the latter of which comprises the islands of Guernsey, Alderney, Sark, and Herm.

[31] See Nicholas Shaxson's (n 20, 56–69) discussion of the benefits of the Overseas Territories' willingness to trade in both pounds sterling and US dollars as a means of circumventing Bretton Woods requirements, and the involvement in the Cayman Islands of what an official at the Bank of England described in correspondence in 1967 as 'an expatriate tax council, who overnight persuaded [the Cayman authorities] to enact trust legislation which goes beyond anything yet attempted elsewhere' (at 62).

[32] See Mary Alice Young and Michael Woodiwiss, 'A World Fit For Money Laundering: The Atlantic Alliance's Undermining of Organised Crime Control' (2021) 24 Trends in Organized Crime 70; and Nicholas Shaxson, *Treasure Islands: Tax Havens and the Men Who Stole the World* (The Bodley Head 2011).

[33] See eg the Tax Justice Network *Global Secrecy Index 2022* <https://fsi.taxjustice.net>. The United States is ranked as the most complicit jurisdiction, but the Cayman Islands, Guernsey, Jersey, and the BVI all rank amongst the top twenty.

[34] See Dominic Thomas-James, *Offshore Financial Centres and the Law: Suspect Wealth in British Overseas Territories* (Routledge 2021) 173. He notes, very reasonably, that the US, which has a number of 'secrecy' states including Delaware, Florida, and South Dakota, receives little corresponding attention yet is in a much stronger position to lead by example.

capable of misconduct . . . the phrase in its negative connotation cannot be equally applied to all offshore financial centres'.[35]

The symbiotic growth of the City of London and the UK's Overseas Territories and Crown Dependencies as global financial hubs since the 1950s and 1960s has contributed to the ease with which assets can move across borders. This has created a distinctly favourable culture for individuals abroad wishing to move assets to a stable environment with high levels of protection for private property and minimal scrutiny as to the origins of those assets. Developments on the banking side have been accompanied in more recent decades by strategies designed specifically to enable wealthy foreigners to move themselves and their wealth to the UK with relative ease.

c. Societal Factors

Fundamental to the UK's contemporary status as a playground for the super-rich are the social factors making it such an attractive destination for high and ultra-high-net-worth individuals, regardless of the provenance of their assets.[36] This sub-section highlights four noteworthy influences. First, London has served as a hub for global diasporas for centuries.[37] Wealthy individuals wishing to invest and/or ultimately settle in the UK from almost any country in the world will find compatriots with whom to socialize and build community. Until relatively recently, they could do this with conspicuous ease. Up to its ultimate closure one week before the Russian invasion of Ukraine in 2022, the operation of the UK's Tier 1 visa scheme provided a straightforward process for wealthy individuals from outside the UK or the EEA to apply for and obtain residency visas in the UK. The scheme conferred a visa and, after five years, residency rights on applicants in return for a minimum £2m investment in UK bonds or shares.[38] From 2008 to 2015, over 6,000 Tier 1 investors came to the UK during a 'blind faith' period whereby the Home Office's visa authorities did not examine the sources of funds invested by successful applicants.[39] Whilst the scheme was in operation, the Home Office apparently primarily relied on the anti-money laundering compliance checks of information provided by applicants to financial institutions when setting up their bank accounts in the UK to establish that the sources of funds invested into the scheme were legitimate

[35] Thomas-James (n 34) 47.

[36] See generally Rowland Atkinson, *Alpha City: How London Was Captured by the Super-Rich* (Verso 2020).

[37] John Eade, *Placing London: From Imperial Capital to Global City* (Verso 2000).

[38] The operation of the scheme is described in detail in *R (on the application of Wang) v Secretary of State for the Home Department* [2023] UKSC 21 [8]–[14].

[39] Written Statement by the Home Secretary, Suella Braverman MP, 'The Tier 1 (Investor) Route: Review of Operation between 30 June 2008 and 6 April 2015' 12 January 2023, Statement UIN HCW492.

in origin. It also relied on due diligence provided by wealth managers, financial advisors, and private family offices who benefited from their clients succeeding in the latter's visa applications. These parties were therefore conflicted.[40] It subsequently emerged that individuals suspected of involvement in corruption including the respondent in the *Hajiyeva* case, numerous other PEPs, and at least ten Russian oligarchs who subsequently had sanctions imposed against them by the UK government were among those accepted under the so-called 'Golden Visa' scheme.[41] At the conclusion of a review into the scheme in 2023, the Home Office acknowledged that 'there are inherent difficulties in an investment-based immigration route based on passive wealth, both in terms of security and economic value'.[42] To date, and much to the chagrin of anti-corruption campaigners, the Home Office has refused to publish its detailed review.[43] In publishing some key findings, it noted that those accepted under the scheme had included:

> a small minority of individuals connected to the Tier 1 (Investor) visa route that were potentially at high risk of having obtained wealth through corruption or other illicit financial activity, and/or being engaged in serious and organised crime.[44]

In any event, kleptocrats drawn by the social capital of UK residency are now more likely to face obstacles when seeking to fast-track residence rights than they would have before 2022. The Tier 1 (Investor) visa scheme saga is a good example of a lax approach towards potential inflows of dirty money where the super-rich are involved. The abrupt cessation of the scheme's availability came at a time when public and media interest in plutocratic suspicious wealth was at its peak, providing one of several examples identified throughout this book of politically expedient anti-corruption policy measures having been taken only once a critical mass of public concern is reached.[45]

A second reason that the super-rich are drawn to the UK is that its education system is regarded as excellent. Fourteen of the top 100 universities and over forty of the world's top fee-paying private secondary schools in the world are located in the UK.[46] Wealthy foreign parents who send their children to these prestigious

[40] Susan Hawley, George Havenhand, and Tom Robinson, *Red Carpet for Dirty Money: How the UK's Golden Visa Regime Urgently Needs Further Reform and More Transparency* (Spotlight on Corruption July 2021).

[41] For reporting on the oligarchs, see William Wallis, 'Russian Oligarchs Used "Golden Visa" Scheme to Settle In UK' *Financial Times* (London 12 January 2023). On the PEPs, see Hawley and others (n 40). The relevant case is *NCA v Hajiyeva* [2020] EWCA Civ 108, [2020] All ER (D) 34.

[42] Braverman (n 39).

[43] Peter Geoghegan, 'Home Office Accused of Cover-up over "Golden Visas" for Super-rich Russians' *The Observer* (London, 25 February 2023).

[44] Braverman (n 39).

[45] See Chapter 4, Section 3.

[46] According to the QS World University Rankings 2024, albeit it should be noted that the criteria for determining what the world's 'top' educational institutions are, and the reliability and subjectivity

institutions can benefit from the social and cultural capital implicit in being associated with them.[47] Helpfully for corrupt foreign PEPs sending their children to be educated in the UK, educational institutions are not required by the anti-money laundering regulations to carry out due diligence checks on parties paying tuition fees, nor are they required to establish the sources of funds used.[48] Consequently, payment of school and university fees and donations will not, as a rule, attract the attention of anti-money laundering enforcement authorities.[49] For the same reason, bribes by way of paying the tuition and accommodation fees of bribees' children attending schools and universities in the UK tend to go undetected unless and until they are incidentally discovered as part of a larger corruption investigation.[50]

Third and relatedly, political and charitable donations and involvement are a relatively straightforward means by which ultra-high net worth individuals can quickly assimilate themselves into the higher echelons of British society and benefit from a halo effect of legitimacy.[51] Accounts of Dmitry Firtash, the Ukrainian businessman recently under investigation by US authorities on suspicion of bribery allegedly granting millions of pounds to Cambridge University, and endowments from Muammar Gaddafi's family to the London School of Economics are two notable instances of such (ultimately unsuccessful) reputation laundering.[52] Research including work undertaken by Chatham House has highlighted how donations to

of such rankings are widely contested. See further Lila Jones, 'Best Private High Schools in the World 2024' *CEO World* (April 2024) <https://ceoworld.biz/2024/04/04/worlds-best-international-high-schools-2024/>.

[47] Matthew T Page, *The Cleansing Power of Ivory Towers: How Elite Educational Institutions Legitimize Kleptocrats' Children*, National Endowment for Democracy Global Insights Series, March 2022.

[48] For more on the anti-money laundering obligations of UK higher education institutions and the significant disparity between institutions in adherence to those regulations that they and their employees *do* have obligations under, see Nicholas Ryder and others, 'Higher Education Institutions and the Anti-Money Laundering And Counter-Terrorism Financing Regulations' (2023) 9 Criminal Law Review 560.

[49] reg 8 of the Money Laundering, Terrorist Financing and Transfer of Funds (Information on the Payer) Regulations 2017, SI 2017/692) (the AML Regulations).

[50] See eg Luke Harding and others, 'UK at Centre of Secret $3bn Azerbaijani Money Laundering and Lobbying Scheme' *The Guardian* (London, 4 September 2017).

[51] A prominent example of this involves Evgeny Lebedev, the Russian son of a billionaire former KGB agent. He became the majority shareholder of the London Evening Standard in 2009 and was befriended by, and offered support in his media interests to, the then-mayor of London Boris Johnson. Thirteen years later the now-Lord Lebedev was named as a life peer of the House of Lords, reportedly notwithstanding advice provided from the intelligence services to the Lords Appointment Commission who in turn advised Boris Johnson (the Prime Minister at this point) against proceeding with the offer of a peerage. See Richard Kelly, *Research Briefing: Advice Relating to the Appointment of Lord Lebedev* (House of Commons Library, 29 March 2022). There is no evidence available to suggest that Lord Lebedev was involved in corrupt activity.

[52] See, respectively, Oliver Bullough, 'Gas-Powered Kingmaker: How the UK Welcomed Putin's Man in Ukraine' *The Guardian* (London, 8 March 2022); Alistair MacDonald and Cassell Bryan-Low, 'Institutions Scramble to Determine Libya Entanglement' *The Wall Street Journal* (New York, 7 March 2011).

universities in the UK have almost tripled in the past ten years, with universities and other organisations with charitable status in the UK exempt from any legal requirement to publish the sums donated, the identities of donors, or any conditions attached to endowments.[53] This is occurring in circumstances where the financial position of UK universities is becoming increasingly precarious owing to cuts in public funding and reduced revenue from EU students and research funding post-Brexit, making it all the more expensive for these institutions to be discerning in determining from whom they should be accepting donations. Sending one's children to and/or making donations to educational institutions thus remains one avenue that remains open to foreign elites—whether corrupt or blameless—to cultivate establishment links within the UK.

Fourth, the UK provides ample opportunity for the super-rich to invest discreetly and with relative ease in high-value assets. Its shipping and aircraft registries each have excellent global reputations. It is necessary for aircraft and marine vessel owners to ensure that their assets are maintained to a high standard to obtain and retain registration on those registers.[54] This is useful for ultra-high net worth individuals because in addition to ensuring that high safety and operational standards are adhered to, registration on the British registries helps to maintain the value and optimize the resale value of the relevant vessel or aircraft. Moreover, for aircraft, the Civil Aviation Authority's (CAA) aircraft register does not necessarily record a UK-registered aircraft's beneficial or legal owner against the aircraft's publicly searchable details. The 'registered owner' of an aircraft as it appears on the register is the entity legally entitled to operate the aircraft as advised to the CAA. The entities recorded as registered owners are often charterers-by-demise—operating companies acting as agents on behalf of, rather than an aircraft's actual owner.[55] In this way, it is possible to own a UK-registered aircraft such that the details of the legal and/or ultimate beneficial owners of that high-value asset are not available to the public. In addition to registrable high-value moveable assets, London is home to some of the world's leading auction houses and other dealers of art, antiques, fine jewellery, collectable wine, and other valuable assets. The ownership of none of these asset types is subject to public registration requirements. Art dealers and other dealers in high-value goods are subject to due diligence and reporting obligations under the money-laundering regulations.[56] Nevertheless,

[53] Heathershaw and others (n 4) 35. The Report notes that when regulations were introduced in the United States in 2019 requiring universities to disclose donation details, some US$6.5bn worth of previously unknown donations were published, many originating from autocratic states.

[54] For aviation, see the regulations made pursuant to the Civil Aviation Acts 1982 and 2006. For shipping, see the Merchant Shipping (Registration of Ships) Regulations 1993, SI 1993/3138, as amended.

[55] The Air Navigation Order 2016, SI 2016/765, reg 26(4).

[56] 'High value dealer' means, per reg 14(1) of the Money Laundering, Terrorist Financing and Transfer of Funds (Information on the Payer) Regulations 2017, SI 2017/692, traders in goods involved in transactions of 10,000 euros or more. Some academic scepticism has been expressed as to whether imposing anti-money laundering obligations on art dealers is capable of effectively deterring money

trading in those types of valuable assets is remarkably untransparent and presents opportunities for corrupt kleptocrats to acquire mobile and valuable assets in settings of privacy and confidence.

As should be clear from the foregoing, there are avenues open across society in the UK to overseas elites who wish to acquire valuable assets and access to excellent education, allowing wealth to be absorbed into the economy with ease.

d. Transparency: Corporate Entities and Trusts

The 'light touch' modes of commercial regulation championed under Thatcherism and subsequently by New Labour and its successors have manifested in ways beneficial to the corrupt.[57] A prominent example of this is that details recorded on the register of companies maintained by the UK's registry of limited companies, Companies House, were, until new rules were introduced in 2024, unverified by Companies House or by independent third parties.[58] Before the Economic Crime and Corporate Transparency Act 2023 (the ECCTA) received Royal Assent in October 2023, the UK companies register was, like many corporate registries internationally, regarded as 'archival and passive in nature'.[59] From April 2011 until March 2024 when the roll-out of some changes to the application processes took effect, it was straightforward for anyone anywhere in the world with an internet connection and a credit card to pay £13 to incorporate a company to obtain the perception of legitimacy and good governance seemingly afforded by UK-registered companies, safe in the knowledge that any details submitted would be subject to minimal or no verification processes.[60] With hindsight, this permeability to money launderers and fraud, rather than affording the UK a reputational advantage as a jurisdiction that is open for business, may have had a net negative impact on international perceptions of the trustworthiness of its corporate vehicles. The 2023 Act introduced a raft of measures designed to improve the quality of the data deposited at Companies House including increased powers on the part of the companies registrar to, inter alia, reject documents for inconsistencies, strike off companies registered on a false basis, and require additional information before proceeding with a registration.[61] It is still too early to build an empirically sound picture of

laundering. See Saskia Hufnagel and Colin King, 'Anti-Money Laundering Regulation and the Art Market' (2020) 40 Legal Studies 131.

[57] See n 26.

[58] With the coming into force of ss 1110A and 1110B of the Companies Act 2006.

[59] Emile van der Does de Willebois and others, *The Puppet Masters: How the Corrupt Use Legal Structures to Hide Stolen Assets and What To Do About It* (StAR 2011) 74.

[60] The 'web incorporation service' was introduced under The Registrar of Companies (Fees) (Companies, Overseas Companies and Limited Liability Partnerships) (Amendment) Regulations 2011, SI 2011/309.

[61] ECCTA, ss 79, 70, and 38, respectively.

how rigorous or effective Companies House will be in its review and verification of details submitted in applications for new companies and retrospective review and monitoring of the veracity of documents already submitted to it.[62] At a minimum, however, the heightened verification processes (the roll-out phase of which will continue until at least 2027) represent a shift away from the previous ambient tolerance of dishonesty or negligence within the companies registration infrastructure in the UK.

Companies House maintains a Register of Overseas Entities, on which all legal entities (ie entities having a legal personality and organized under the laws of a country or territory outside of the UK)[63] holding real property in the UK are required to register details of, amongst other things, their 'persons of significant control' or PSCs.[64] Broadly, a company's PSC is any individual who (whether directly or indirectly—through a holding company, for example) holds more than 25 per cent of shares or voting rights in the relevant company, or who has the right to appoint or remove the majority of the company's board of directors.[65] The Register of Overseas Entities is publicly searchable but is subject to the same transparency criticisms that apply to PSC information for UK companies.[66] Trusts, regardless of their jurisdiction of establishment, are of further concern. Express UK and non-UK trusts holding property in the UK are subject to reporting requirements on beneficial ownership. And a register of trusts is maintained by HMRC but again, this is not publicly searchable.[67]

In summary, until recently, it was easy for bad actors seeking to register or update details of companies, their registered offices, their officers, and their PSCs at Companies House using false details with relative impunity. Whilst recent reforms on how companies are registered and their details maintained in the UK are promising, potential challenges to the public accessibility of information concerning the owners of those companies loom on the horizon. These challenges, together with transparency developments around trust and company ownership, are discussed in further detail in Chapter 7.

e. Legal and Commercial Environment

A further pull factor for wealthy elites is the vast and internationalist nature of the UK's legal, financial, and corporate services industries. All countries which

[62] For more information on process and timings, see <changestoukcompanylaw.campaign.gov.uk>.
[63] ECCTA, s 2.
[64] ECCTA, s 4.
[65] Companies Act 2006, s 790C.
[66] See Chapter 7, n 108 and accompanying text.
[67] The Money Laundering, Terrorist Financing and Transfer of Funds (Information on the Payer) Regulations 2017, SI 2017/692, regs 44 and 45. The Trusts Register is discussed in more detail in Chapter 7.

formerly formed part of the British Empire retain either a common law-based legal system or systems comprising a mixture of civil and common law aspects. As of 2024, twenty-seven Commonwealth countries use the Privy Council as their final court of appeal. These factors have facilitated large English law firms in establishing their own offices or relationships with correspondent firms across the globe.[68] Additionally, English law (in addition to New York law) tends to be the dominant law of choice governing contracts in multi-jurisdictional commercial agreements in the Global North as a result of the amount of financing concluded through the City of London and given the reputation, predictability, and extensive body of precedent of the English commercial courts.[69] This means that London hosts an enormous market of lawyers, tax advisers, finance houses, and accountants adept at facilitating multi-jurisdictional parties and deals. Approximately 16 per cent of UK legal services provided in 2021 were to clients based overseas.[70] Kojo Koram has illustrated the exponential growth of the legal and financial services industries in England and Wales in the following terms:

> While the total national population grew by around 9 per cent over the past thirty years, the number of solicitors working in England and Wales has grown by over 300 per cent during the same period. The UK also has more accountants per capita than anywhere else. In 2019, disputes between foreign companies made up 70 per cent of the cases heard in London's Commercial Court.[71]

Commentators observe that corruption is almost always intermediated by professional facilitators.[72] In the UK, there are plenty of specialist experts on hand to blindly, negligently, recklessly, or knowingly assist in moving the proceeds of grand corruption between jurisdictions. Where kleptocratic clients are concerned, commentators have noted the ostensible and actual legitimacy of much of the work that legal and financial facilitators undertake on behalf of those clients, making detection difficult or impossible.[73] The underlying tension for many professional service providers in attempting to serve the twin imperatives of strong commercial performance and assiduous application of the money-laundering rules are each discussed further in Chapter 7.[74]

[68] Three of the world's top ten law firms measured by turnover and headcount are headquartered in London <www.law.com/international-edition/law-firms/>.

[69] Ewan McKendrick, *Contract Law* (14th edn, Bloomsbury 2021) 10.

[70] Office for National Statistics, 2023 Input–output supply and use tables. See <www.ons.gov.uk/economy/nationalaccounts/supplyandusetables/datasets/inputoutputsupplyandusetables>.

[71] Koram (n 12) 44.

[72] Cooley and Sharman (n 1) 733.

[73] See eg Nicholas Lord, Liz Campbell, and Karin Van Wingerde, 'Other People's Dirty Money: Professional Intermediaries, Market Dynamics and the Finances of White-Collar, Corporate and Organized Crimes' (2019) 59 British Journal of Criminology 1217.

[74] This tension is recognized by academics, NGOs, and financial practitioners. See eg Antoinette Verhage, *The Anti Money Laundering Complex and the Compliance Industry* (Routledge 2011) 68; comments of experts from Transparency International UK and Global Witness to the

In addition to access to legal and financial facilitators, strong property rights and the well-established right to protection from reputational damage draw elites to the UK. The right to quiet enjoyment of private property, bolstered by the jurisdiction and jurisprudence of the European Court of Human Rights,[75] means that unlike some of the authoritarian states from whence some kleptocrats come, the likelihood of property appropriation by the state for spurious reasons is non-existent.[76] The right to privacy jurisprudence provides further reassurance. The protection of reputation is a subsidiary right to the right to privacy and is recognized in the UK's courts and the European Court of Human Rights' jurisprudence.[77] The way in which the UK's strict defamation laws have evolved means that this protection can now be used—and misused and weaponized—by international elites intent on reputation control. These laws notoriously have been co-opted by well-resourced oligarchs to attempt to silence journalists, civil society groups, and enforcement authorities who allege corruption against them.[78] This phenomenon, known as 'lawfare', involves the tactical (ab)use of lawsuits (strategic litigation against public participation, or SLAPPs) to exhaust the attention and resources of critics and their publishers as a means of punishing them for their public dissent, and to impose a chilling effect on others considering similar commentary.[79] SLAPPs have been used variously 'with the intention of harassing, intimidating and financially or psychologically exhausting opponents via improper use of the legal system'.[80] The government has acknowledged that SLAPPS benefit individuals who want to suppress or minimize adverse media attention.[81] The ECCTA introduced provisions allowing SLAPPs claims to be struck out before trial where, inter alia, the

Treasury Committee: House of Commons Treasury Committee, *Economic Crime: Eleventh Report of Session 2021–22* HC 145, 22 February 2022, paras 39–40; and various estate agents' comments in Ilaria Zavoli and Colin King, 'The Challenges of Implementing Anti-Money Laundering Regulation: An Empirical Analysis (2021) 84 Modern Law Review 740.

[75] Article 1 of the First Protocol to the European Convention on Human Rights (A1P1) recognizes the right to peaceful enjoyment of property. In the UK, s 6(1) of the Human Rights Act 1998 specifies that it is unlawful for public authorities to 'act in a way that is incompatible' with the Convention.

[76] In the worst-case and statistically unlikely scenario, assets may be made the subject of confiscation or civil recovery orders following a successful POCA investigation against a property holder but only following the scrutiny of the courts on the merits of such claims. In a sanctions context, the difficulties for the state inherent in the move from 'freeze' to 'seize' have been extensively highlighted by anti-corruption experts. See eg Maria Nizzero, *From Freeze to Seize: How the UK Can Break the Deadlock on Asset Recovery* (Royal United Services Institute 10 October 2022).

[77] See the discussion in NA Moreham, 'Privacy, Defamation and ZXC v Bloomberg' (2022) 14 Journal of Media Law 226.

[78] Prominent recent examples of SLAPPs-style litigation include the multiple libel lawsuits instituted against Harper Collins and Catherine Belton for the bestseller *Putin's People* (William Collins 2020) by three prominent oligarchs, and against the FT journalist Tom Burgis for his investigative reportage on the multinational energy company ENRC in *Kleptopia* (William Collins 2020).

[79] See Geoffrey Robertson KC, *Lawfare: How Russians, The Rich and The Government Try to Prevent Free Speech and How to Stop Them* (TLS Books 2023).

[80] Economic Crime and Corporate Transparency Act 2023 Explanatory Notes (ECCTA Explanatory Notes) para 60.

[81] ECCTA Explanatory Notes, paras 60–63.

subject matter of a SLAPPs claim is a matter of public interest, concerns allegations related to economic crime, and 'the claim has, or is intended to have, the effect of restraining the defendant's exercise of the right to freedom of speech'.[82] It is too early to assess whether these measures will meet their legislative objectives.[83] As with reform to the Companies House document verification processes, the tipping point for reform of the law to address 'lawfare' only eventuated after many years of civil society activists and commentators highlighting the adverse implications for the rule of law.[84] Corrupt members of the super-rich class who are interested in protecting or bolstering their public images in more subtle ways also have the option of employing UK-based public relations consultancies specializing in managing and massaging reputations.[85]

Lawfare is only one prominent example of the ways in which the legal system in the UK is susceptible to abuse by corrupt elites. Anti-corruption campaigners continue to highlight lax regulation and oversight in diverse areas open to misuse by wealthy corrupt elites including, without limitation, political donations,[86] the role of the legal profession in facilitating overseas corruption,[87] under-enforcement of sanctions breaches,[88] and ongoing vulnerabilities in transparency of ownership in real estate.[89] As part of any clearing out of the UK's legal and asset-ownership

[82] ECCTA, s 195(1)(a). The progress of a private member's bill, the Strategic Litigation Against Public Litigation Bill, Bill (2023–24) [21], which would have removed the requirement for SLAPPs claims to involve links to alleged economic crimes, proceeded to Committee Stage in the House of Commons in May 2024, but the Bill was not carried over upon the election of a new government in July 2024, notwithstanding its cross-party support.

[83] The Explanatory Notes to the ECCTA note (at para 62) that the relevant provisions 'aim to ensure that misconduct and improper use of the legal system to suppress legitimate reporting on matters of public interest related to combating economic crime will be prevented'.

[84] See eg Douglas W Vick and Linda Macpherson, 'An Opportunity Lost: The United Kingdom's Failed Reform of Defamation Law' (1997) 49 Federal Communications Law Journal 621.

[85] A notable example of one such consultancy is that of which the former Prime Minister Tony Blair is a partner. It has been paid at least US$13m by the Kazakh authorities for its services. See Luke Harding, 'How Tony Blair Advised Former Kazakh Ruler after 2011 Uprising' *The Guardian* (London, 7 January 2022).

[86] See eg Spotlight on Corruption, 'Press Release: Government snubs final chance to take action on foreign political donations' (27 June 2023) <www.spotlightcorruption.org/final-foreign-political-donations>. A notorious example of another London-based reputation management consultancy is the now-defunct London-based Bell Pottinger Private which, in acting for the billionaire Gupta family, collapsed in disgrace after accusations of stoking racial animosity in South Africa to benefit its clients' political allies. And on lobbying and clientelism, see Peter Geoghegan, *Democracy for Sale: Dark Money and Dirty Politics* (Head of Zeus 2020).

[87] Helen Taylor and Daniel Beizsley, 'A Privileged Profession? How the UK's Legal Sector Escapes Effective Supervision for Money Laundering' (Spotlight on Corruption and ACE Global Integrity, October 2022) <www.spotlightcorruption.org/report/a-privileged-profession-how-the-uks-legal-sector-escapes-effective-supervision-for-money-laundering/>.

[88] Helen Taylor, 'All Bark and No Bite? Taking Stock of the UK's Enforcement of Sanctions' (Spotlight on Corruption, 24 July 2024) <www.spotlightcorruption.org/sanctions-all-bark-and-no-bite>.

[89] Matthew Collin and his colleagues note for example that a reporting equivalent of Automatic Exchange of Information Agreements (AEIA) pursuant to which countries share tax details of their inhabitants with each other is not available in the context of property transactions and ownership. Matthew Collin, Florian M Hollenbach, and David D Szakonyi, 'The End of Londongrad? The Impact of Beneficial Ownership Transparency on Offshore Investment in UK Property' (2023) WIDER Working Paper 2023/11. Helsinki: UNU-WIDER.

systems' Augean stables, policy-makers will need to ensure that any regulatory and legal reforms introduced to tackle these issues are adequately resourced and enforced to prevent them from being viewed as mere window-dressing.

3. Anti-Corruption Policy and Enforcement

Before the introduction of legislation enacted in response to increased public concern around the proceeds of grand corruption and particularly kleptocracy from early 2022 onwards,[90] it seemed as though anti-corruption strategy largely had been deprioritized by various iterations of the UK government. Two indications of this will be highlighted briefly here. The first is the demotion of what was formerly the Department for International Development (DfID) as a stand-alone ministerial department into a de facto subsidiary department by merging it with what was previously the Foreign Office to form the Foreign, Commonwealth & Development Office (FCDO).[91] This, coupled with the diminution in the ratio of the UK's Gross National Income contributed to overseas development aid from 0.7 per cent to the 0.5 per cent (introduced as a 'temporary measure' in 2020) has undermined claims the UK has to providing global anti-corruption leadership.[92] That 'temporary measure' appears to have crystallized into a permanent measure for now,[93] notwithstanding the UK's own self-imposed statutory duty to contribute 0.7 per cent.[94] The reduction in funding perhaps reflects a wider political tendency globally to develop policies 'as a reaction or response to specific scandals, or . . . to *prevent* particular forms of behaviour [sic]',[95] while neglecting the positive

[90] Notably, the Economic Crime and Corporate Transparency Act 2022 and the Economic Crime and Corporate Transparency Act 2023.

[91] One former Minister of State at DfID and the Foreign and Commonwealth Office, Sir Alan Duncan, referred to the merger as a 'crime and a catastrophe' which has 'diminished the UK at a critical period of post-Brexit scrutiny' at an event convened by the Institute for Government entitled 'The FCDO: Is the Reunification of Foreign and Development Policy Working?' in London on 19 May 2022. The demotion of DfID was perhaps indicative of a wider crisis in the Conservative government around corruption both domestically and internationally. This is perhaps best illustrated by its own anti-corruption champion and its independent advisor on ministers' ethics each resigning in 2022 in protest at the government's permissive attitudes towards its own members' activities. The latter's replacement was appointed six months later; the former was not replaced in the lifetime of that government.

[92] Sir Alan went on to remark that since the merger, the UK has a 'less effective presence in international institutions where [it] used to dominate and shape the policy and expenditure of many of the UN organisations to which we gave money, and now we won't have enough ministers simply to go to their meetings' (n 91). The UN has a target for countries to contribute a sum equivalent to 0.7 of their gross national income (GNI) on official development assistance to intended to promote the economic development and welfare of developing countries. See Philip Loft and Philip Brien, *The 0.7% Aid Target,* House of Commons Research Briefing no 3714, 30 July 2024. Sir Alan Duncan (n 91) described the decision to reduce official development assistance upon the amalgamation of the Foreign Office and DfID as undertaken by 'sleight of hand'.

[93] But see n 161 and accompanying text below.

[94] International Development (Official Development Assistance Target) Act 2015, s 1.

[95] Paul Heywood, 'Combatting Corruption in the Twenty-First Century: New Approaches' (2018) 147 Daedalus 83, 84.

promotion of integrity overseas or adopting more coherent systems-wide practices to help defeat corruption. The piecemeal 'corruption-busting' policy approach exemplified by the fanfare surrounding the introduction of the PEP-specific UWO is antithetical to the slower and less visible but potentially more consequential forms of development work involved in assisting other states in establishing and promoting effective models of integrity in public office. It ignores recent calls from anti-corruption thinkers to avoid falling into the trap of 'over-individualising' corruption rather than recognizing that corruption is, above all, a systemic issue.[96] Moreover, DfID played an active role in managing and distributing the return of stolen overseas assets. The reorganization of DfID into a sub-department contributed to the departure of many senior civil servants with institutional memory and experience around how best to manage that asset return.[97]

Second, enforcement authorities investigating the alleged proceeds of overseas corruption are significantly under-resourced given the enormity of the crimes involved and the resources at the disposal of those whom those enforcement authorities are pursuing. The scale of the problem was neatly summarized by Dame Margaret Hodge discussing an unsuccessful PEP-related UWO case[98] in the House of Commons in 2023:

> [O]n cost caps, crooks have such deep pockets. We saw that with the unexplained wealth orders. It is outrageous that the people who managed to win the case in the courts—although investigative journalists have subsequently suggested that they lied to the courts, in effect; that the evidence that they gave was not the truth—have claimed £1.5 million in costs from the National Crime Agency (NCA). The NCA's total budget for fighting corruption is £4 million a year. If it loses £1.5 million on one case alone, the idea that it will have any confidence in litigating when it comes across cases of bad actors and malpractice is for the birds. If we do not tackle the cost-capping issue, we will never get on top of the really bad people whom we want to eliminate from our economy.[99]

Beyond low levels of institutional funding and its deep-pocked adversaries, the NCA faces challenges in retaining individual officers with relevant expertise. Its staff are consistently drawn towards better paid investigative and compliance work in the private sector, to the point that the NCA's Command and Control Centre has the equivalent of a full staff turnover every three years on average, with most of its employees going to work for financial institutions; including for their anti-money

[96] See Anne Peters, 'Human Rights and Corruption: Problems and Potential of Individualising a Systemic Problem' (2024) 22 International Journal of Constitutional Law 538.

[97] See Lord Duncan's speech (n 91).

[98] *NCA v Baker* [2020] EWHC 822 (Admin).

[99] HC Deb, Economic Crime and Corporate Transparency Bill, 4 September 2023, vol 737, cols 110–11.

laundering compliance teams.[100] Similar problems have beset the Serious Fraud Office which as of its annual report in 2024 had a staff vacancy rate of over 16 per cent.[101] In response to its 'continuing recruitment challenges', the NCA announced in its 2024 report plans to introduce a 'transformational pay business case' aimed at attracting and retaining high-quality investigators.[102] This is a welcome development, suggesting a turn towards a more meaningful governmental commitment to resourcing anti-corruption investigation and enforcement initiatives.

At an agency level, there is little economic incentive for enforcement authorities to pursue laundering offences linked to suspected foreign corruption.[103] Typically, where enforcement authorities recover the proceeds of domestic crime, a portion of those proceeds are retained and redistributed to the agencies involved in the asset recovery process.[104] For grand corruption proceeds however, the best practice expectation is that proceeds recovered through confiscation or civil recovery actions (less reasonable investigation and enforcement expenses) will be restored to states of origin.[105] This means that proactive unilateral pursuit of the proceeds of overseas grand corruption by an enforcement authority must be premised at least partially on their acting on an altruistic sensibility.[106] Such action is unlikely given enforcement authority under-resourcing to date.[107] To paraphrase an observation made by Jason Sharman, 'English cops are paid with English taxes to solve English problems'.[108] The gravest and most immediate impacts of overseas grand

[100] Oliver Bullough, *Butler to the World* (Profile Books 2022) 203.

[101] This is an improvement from the previous year, where the vacancy rate was over 23 per cent. See SFO, *Annual Report and Accounts 2023–24*, HC 179, 11.

[102] NCA, *Annual Report and Accounts 2023–24*, HC 66, 39.

[103] See observations made by senior members of the NCA that had a specialized Overseas Corruption Unit (funded using the UK's foreign aid budget) not been set up, 'the pattern of incentives means there would have been no prospect of them investigating foreign corruption proceeds'. JC Sharman, *Report to the Cullen Commission: Money Laundering and Foreign Corruption Proceeds in British Columbia: A Comparative International Policy Assessment*, June 2022.

[104] For wholly domestic matters, enforcement authorities are incentivized by the prospect of the award of a portion of the sums recovered through asset recovery processes. This distribution occurs through the Home Office-administered Asset Recovery Incentivisation Scheme (ARIS). A snapshot of the use to which enforcement authorities put ARIS proceeds is set out in Home Office, *Asset Recovery Statistical Bulletin: Financial Years Ending March 2018 to March 2023*, 7 September 2023 <www.gov.uk/government/statistics/asset-recovery-statistical-bulletin-financial-years-ending-2018-to-2023/asset-recovery-statistical-bulletin-financial-years-ending-march-2018-to-march-2023#asset-recovery-incentivisation-scheme-aris>. For a critique of what is essentially a 'policing for profit' model, see Mary Alice Young and Amber Phillips, 'Challenges in Policing Financial Crime' in Barry Rider (ed), *A Research Agenda for Financial Crime* (Edward Elgar 2022) 89.

[105] UNCAC, art 57(3). Note however that pursuant to that provision, unless a 'final judgment in the requesting State Party' has been handed down, States Parties in which the proceeds of corruption are held are required only to give 'priority consideration' to returning assets to states of origin.

[106] See Kevin E Davis, 'What Counts as a Good Settlement?' in Tina Søreide and Abiola Makinwa (eds), *Negotiated Settlements in Bribery Cases: A Principled Approach* (Edward Elgar 2020) 260, 265.

[107] As one senior NCA official put it in an interview with the author on 16 December 2020: 'PEP respondents [to unexplained wealth orders] by definition have almost bottomless money and can get the best QCs'.

[108] JC Sharman, *The Despot's Guide to Wealth Management: On the International Campaign Against Grand Corruption* (Cornell University Press 2017) 8.

corruption will be experienced far from the UK, and its victims hold little political influence. This diminishes the impetus for the UK's enforcement authorities to engage in overseas anti-corruption work, notwithstanding arguments that overseas corruption should be conceptualized as a human rights violation that triggers international state responsibility.[109]

A further disincentive from a crime control perspective to giving priority to tackling the proceeds of grand corruption lies in the idea that a key justification for making broad asset recovery powers available is that seizing the proceeds of crime will prevent further crimes. The argument is that, unless seized, criminals will invest the proceeds of crime into further criminality.[110] It seems, based on the limited case studies available, that foreign PEPs who seek to invest corruptly acquired cash in the UK tend to launder by investing in 'legitimate' assets rather than in further criminal enterprises. Consequently, the same concerns around proceeds of crime being used to finance further criminal enterprise (other than the act of laundering itself) do not apply where the proceeds of grand corruption are concerned.

A final possible explanation for the under-resourcing of proceeds of grand corruption enforcement in the UK may be linked to policy concerns around disincentivizing foreign direct investment (FDI). FDI has a net positive impact on the economy regardless of its origin, and the British economy's reliance on FDI has become heightened post-Brexit.[111] These *obiter* comments from Tugendhat J presiding over a High Court case in which a wealthy Serbian businessman based in London who sought to have English libel proceedings served against a Serbian media publication give a sense of some of the considerations in play:

> [M]embers of this elite class are attracted to London, and many of them own properties in London, and spend as much time in London as the Claimant says that he does. And it is in the public interest that the reputation of such people should not be unlawfully damaged. Their business activities are of importance to the economic well-being of this country.[112]

Tugendhat J's references to foreign elites' importance to the UK's 'economic well-being' and the 'public interest' are interesting, highlighting that there are a number of elements and policy choices at work in 'pulling' money to the UK (or at least not dissuading its arrival). The factors are not idiosyncratic to the UK—many other countries provide high standards of protection for private property, for example.

[109] For an overview of the arguments, see Peters (n 96).

[110] See Peter Alldridge, *Money Laundering Law: Forfeiture, Confiscation, Civil Recovery, Criminal Laundering and Taxation of the Proceeds of Crime* (Routledge 2003) 241–42.

[111] See Valentina Romei, 'New FDI Projects in UK Fall to Near 12-Year Low' *Financial Times* (London, 27 June 2024).

[112] *Ahuja v Polotika Novine I Magazini Doo* [2015] EWHC 3380 (QB), [2016] 1 WLR 1414 [71].

There are other relatively wealthy countries with lax visa requirements,[113] or that provide opportunities to acquire high-value assets on an unregulated basis, or which are used as havens for dirty money because of limited investigation capacity or enforcement resources.[114] Within the UK, the operation all of these factors and others like the recent lack of corporate verification requirements, the lax oversight over the origin of funds in certain sectors, and the City of London's status as a hub for global wealth have ensured collectively that conditions are particularly ripe for the proceeds of overseas grand corruption to be held within the jurisdiction. Given the UK's international law obligations to assist in retrieving and returning the proceeds of corruption, this is problematic. Those obligations will now be outlined.

4. International Law Obligations to Tackle Grand Corruption

International law rules contemplating domestic and foreign senior political officials and their associates using public office for personal gain can be categorized broadly within three distinct but divergent legal frameworks: the anti-corruption, bribery, and money-laundering regimes. The UK has signed up to international legal frameworks imposing obligations in all three areas, and its responsibilities to implement each in the context of tackling grand corruption will now be outlined in turn. The evolution of 'PEP'-specific rules in international law will be considered in more detail in the next chapter.

a. Anti-Corruption Rules

The main international legal instrument addressing the retrieval and return to states of the proceeds of foreign corruption is the United Nations Convention Against Corruption (UNCAC).[115] The UNCAC was adopted by the UN General Assembly in October 2003 and entered into force in December 2005.[116] It is close to universally subscribed.[117] The Convention requires all States Parties to criminalize, amongst other actions, the 'embezzlement, misappropriation or other diversion by a public official for his or her benefit',[118] the offering to or acceptance

[113] As of the time of writing (December 2024), Malta, Cyrus, Hungary, and Italy are among the EU countries which continue to operate Golden Visa-type schemes.
[114] JC Sharman (n 108) details, for example, the recent histories of the US, the UK, Switzerland, and Australia as havens for kleptocratic wealth.
[115] United Nations, UN Convention Against Corruption (2003) Treaty Series, 2349, 41.
[116] UNGA Res 58/4 of 31 October 2003.
[117] As of December 2024, it has 191 States Parties.
[118] UNCAC, art 17.

of bribes by domestic public officials,[119] and the bribery of foreign public officials and officials of public international organizations.[120] The Convention prima facie imposes far-reaching asset recovery obligations on States Parties. Article 51 provides that:

> The return of assets pursuant to this chapter is a fundamental principle of this Convention, and States Parties shall afford one another the widest measure of co-operation and assistance in this regard.

Chapter Five of the Convention requires States Parties to cooperate with each other in identifying, tracing, freezing, and seizing assets representing the proceeds of crimes established in accordance with the Convention.[121] It urges countries to 'consider entering bilateral or multilateral agreements or arrangements to enhance the effectiveness of international cooperation'.[122] In addition to requiring states harbouring the proceeds of corruption to assist in enforcing (criminal) confiscation orders issued by states of origin, the Convention encourages States Parties to consider taking 'such measures as may be necessary to allow confiscation of such property without a criminal conviction'.[123] Notwithstanding that the return of assets is stated to be a 'fundamental principle' of the Convention, however, a number of conditions must be met before States Parties become entitled to the return of assets. Article 57 of the Convention requires holding states to return assets only where a final judgment has been executed in a requesting state (ie the state in which the corruptly acquired assets originated) and a formal request for the return of the assets has been made, though the requirement of a final judgment can be waived by the relevant holding state.[124] In the absence of a formal request accompanied by an appropriate final judgment, States Parties are merely required to 'give priority consideration to returning confiscated property to the requesting State Party, returning such property to its prior legitimate owners or compensating the victims of the crime'.[125] This procedural rigour is unsurprising: there are obvious reasons militating against the return of assets to states beset by kleptocracy

[119] UNCAC, art 15. The UN Convention against Transnational Organized Crime, which came into law a month before the UN Resolution adopting the UNCAC was passed, similarly required its parties to criminalize the giving of and acceptance of bribes by public officials.

[120] UNCAC, art 16.

[121] UNCAC, art 55.

[122] UNCAC, art 59. Those offences include, without limitation, bribery of, and solicitation and/or acceptance of bribes by national public officials (art 15); bribery of foreign public officials and officials of international organizations (art 16); embezzlement, misappropriation or other diversion of property by a public official (art 17); and money laundering (art 23).

[123] UNCAC, art 54(1)(c).

[124] UNCAC, art 57(3)(a) and (b). For discussion, see Anton Moiseienko, 'The Ownership of Confiscated Proceeds of Corruption Under the UN Convention Against Corruption' (2018) 67 International & Comparative Law Quarterly 669.

[125] UNCAC, art 57(3)(c).

problems. Chief among them is the risk that returning assets to an endemically corrupt administration may result in the assets once again 'disappearing'.[126] That said, a number of supervised returns models (where the primary supervising parties are non-governmental organizations (NGOs) or civil society groups or foundations established specifically for that purpose at the instigation of the relevant holding state) have been implemented successfully in recent decades.[127] Where holding states insist on the Article 57 requirements being met before returning assets, it may create impediments for states of origin which are, for example, in transitional post-conflict periods or which lack institutional capacity for other reasons and consequently are unable to produce a final judgment as a basis for an asset return request.[128] The converse, of course, may also be true: states with questionable rule of law records could conceivably rely on final judgments of dubious legitimacy in seeking the return of assets.[129]

As of the end of 2023,[130] the Stolen Assets Recovery Initiative's (StAR) database of asset recovery cases with an international dimension reported that the UK had returned assets to overseas jurisdictions in twenty-six out of the seventy-eight cases in which it was involved.[131] The earliest of these recorded returns was in 2007, the most recent was in 2021, and over half a billion dollars' worth of assets has been returned during that period (almost US$0.2bn of which involved the return to Nigeria of assets misappropriated by its former president, Sani Abacha).[132] Of those returns, nine cases are recorded as involving assets returned following a request from a country of origin following a criminal conviction, with the legal basis

[126] See eg Pablo J Davis, 'To Return the Funds at All: Global Anticorruption, Forfeiture, and Legal Frameworks for Asset Return' (2016) 47 University of Memphis Law Review 291, 322–24, in which he cites a cautionary example of the prompt disappearance of funds returned to Bayelsa State, Nigeria.

[127] Davis (n 126) and Michael J Biondi, 'Building Trust(s): Rethinking Asset Return in Kleptocracy Forfeitures' (2023) 72 Duke Law Journal 1079.

[128] A lack of institutional capacity was central, for example, to Haiti's difficulties in finalizing appropriate mutual legal assistance (MLA) requests in seeking return of assets misappropriated by its former president, Jean-Claude 'Baby Doc' Duvalier, from Switzerland. See further Chapter 5, n 127 and accompanying text.

[129] This line of argument was unsuccessfully invoked by the respondent's lawyers in *Hajiyeva* (n 41) [64]–[85], where they suggested that the respondent's husband's conviction for embezzlement offences in Azerbaijan should have no probative value given the 'very detailed evidence of the deficiencies in [Azerbaijan's] criminal justice system' (at [79]). Although this hearing was not concerned with a return for assets request, the issues are relevant as it is possible that Azerbaijan may seek repatriation of the respondent's assets in future based on the UK's obligations under the UNCAC.

[130] Which, at the time of writing (December 2024) was the most recent time the StAR database had been updated.

[131] A partnership between the World Bank Group and the United Nations Office on Drugs and Crime, StAR supports international efforts to end safe havens for corrupt funds by conducting research, issuing best practice guidelines, maintaining anti-corruption databases, and assisting states pursuing corruption and asset recovery proceedings. Of the matters reported in the StAR database in which the UK's involvement is noted, forty-nine cases involved overseas corruptly acquired assets being held in the UK. The remainder are recorded as having UK involvement either because UK companies or individuals were involved in bribery of overseas countries, the UK was a transit country for overseas assets, or assets were ordered to be frozen in various countries based on rulings made in UK courts.

[132] It is possible that more recent returns have not yet been recorded in StAR's database.

for each of those returns being cited as the UK's UNCAC obligations. Notably, many of the cases involving the UK cite its three Crown Dependencies as locations to which corruptly acquired assets were tracked.

The database provides a useful broad snapshot of the range the countries of origin for 'dirty money' the subject of asset recovery investigations in the UK.[133] It should however be emphasized that the database is incomplete at any given time.[134] It appears to be updated on an ad hoc basis, no state is under any obligation to record asset recoveries thereunder, there are inconsistencies in how various factors are recorded, and the quality and amount of information on each case vary.[135] With those caveats in place, two comments are necessary. The first is that, notwithstanding the provisional nature of the data recorded, there is a marked dissonance between the scale of the 'dirty money' feared by NGOs and enforcement authorities to be laundered in the UK on the one hand, and the number of successful asset recoveries on the other.[136] One of three conclusions may be drawn. Either retrieval of corruptly acquired assets is vastly under-enforced, the problem has been overstated, or, most likely, this dissonance reflects the difficulties inherent in identifying, investigating, and pursuing the proceeds of corruption across borders. Second, whilst the spirit in which the UNCAC was passed imputes an obligation on its States Parties to investigate credible claims of dirty money in their jurisdictions, there is no justiciable legal obligation to pursue investigations. At best, States Parties to the Convention may come under diplomatic pressure to deter and tackle the harbouring and/or laundering of stolen assets in their jurisdictions. The success of initiatives to retrieve and return the proceeds of overseas corruption is therefore contingent on their being politically prioritized in jurisdictions that serve as holding states like the UK. It is noteworthy from the information available on the StAR database that where the proceeds of overseas grand corruption are seized in the UK, this tends not to be a result of its enforcement authorities acting unilaterally to institute investigations into those assets.[137]

[133] Those countries include, without limitation, Nigeria, Brazil, Uganda, Chad, Moldova, Costa Rica, Egypt, and Kuwait.

[134] There are cases in which UK enforcement authorities have reported asset returns to countries of origins which are not included on StAR's list. See eg the case of Malik Riaz Hussain discussed in Clancy (n 9) 149.

[135] This is attributable in part to the fact that the information recording process is not systematized. Those recording key facts appear to include variously StAR researchers and representatives acting on behalf of both states of origin for the assets and destination states. The training of the inputters and the legal systems with which they are familiar impact upon how data are recorded. The development of a style guide and data input oversight—perhaps by a StAR representative—would allow for a more reliable record.

[136] See NCA, *National Strategic Assessment of Serious and Organised Crime 2020–2021*, 54: '[it is] a realistic possibility that the scale of money laundering impacting on the UK (including through UK corporate structures or financial institutions) is in the hundreds of billions of pounds annually'.

[137] By contrast, assets held in the UK are frequently recovered and returned to their originating countries because of investigations undertaken by the United States, most notably recently in the context of the One Malaysia Berhad Development scandal.

b. Bribery Laws

A wave of high-profile corruption scandals in the 1990s[138] added momentum to the US push to pass the Organisation for Economic Co-Operation and Development's (OECD) Anti-Bribery Convention which prohibited, inter alia, the active bribery of any 'foreign public official'.[139] The UK, together with forty-seven other countries collectively representing almost 90 per cent of the world's total foreign direct investment outflows, has ratified the Anti-Bribery Convention. It is explicitly modelled on the US's Foreign Corrupt Practices Act (FCPA),[140] and prohibits the making of bribes *to* foreign public officials but, like the UNCAC, not the *acceptance* of such bribes *by* foreign public officials. The rationale for this was that acceptance of bribes would already be unlawful under domestic laws and an approach of 'collective unilateralism' to tackle bribery from the supply-side would therefore be a sufficient and effective means of addressing the problem.[141] The OECD's decision not to criminalize the acceptance of bribes reflects the FCPA's 'local laws' provisions,[142] which confirm that it is a defence to a charge of bribery if hospitality, gifts, or payments in dispute are permissible under the local written laws of the recipient.[143] Although recommendations for the reform of bribery laws had long been under discussion,[144] it was not until after the UK ratified the Anti-Bribery Convention that it introduced into its criminal laws an offence of bribery of an overseas public official.[145] Together with general offences relating to bribing and being bribed,[146] that offence has extraterritorial application where it is committed by someone with a 'close connection' with the UK.[147] The UK's extraterritorial

[138] See Chapter 3, Section 3.

[139] art 1.4(a), OECD Convention on Combating Bribery of Foreign Officials in Business Transactions (entered into force on 15 February 1999).

[140] 15 USC §§ 78dd-1ff. For discussion, see Elizabeth Spahn, 'Implementing Global Anti-Bribery Norms: From the Foreign Corrupt Practices Act to the OECD Anti-Bribery Convention to the UN Convention against Corruption' (2013) 23 Indiana International & Comparative Law Review 1, 11. US businesses protesting that the FCPA was, for them, anti-competitive ensured that when amendments were made to the FCPA in 1988, a provision was included expressly requiring the US President to pursue negotiations with the OECD to pass what would eventually become the Paris Convention. See Peter Alldridge, 'The U.K. Bribery Act: The Caffeinated Younger Sibling of the FCPA' (2012) 73 Ohio State Law Journal 1181, 1187.

[141] See Mark Pieth, 'Introduction' in Mark Pieth, Lucinda Low, and Peter Cullen (eds), *The OECD Convention on Bribery: A Commentary* (2nd edn, CUP 2014) 30.

[142] 15 USC §§ 78dd-1(c)(1), 78DD-2(c)(1), and 78dd-3(c)(1) (1998).

[143] It also 'rebuts the charge that [the instruments are a form of] moral imperialism imposing its naïve values on hapless sovereigns abroad': Spahn (n 140) 9. Elsewhere, Spahn cites laws on the statute books in Japan and Hong Kong as examples of 'local law' provisions: Elizabeth Spahn, 'Local Law Provisions under the OECD Anti-Bribery Convention' (2012) 39 Syracuse Journal of International Law & Commerce 249.

[144] See Alldridge (n 140).

[145] First under ss 108–10 of the Anti-Terrorism, Crime and Security Act 2001 and subsequently under s 10 of the Bribery Act 2010.

[146] Bribery Act 2010, ss 1 and 2.

[147] Bribery Act 2010, s 12. Those with a close connection include, inter alios, British citizens, any body incorporated under the laws of any part of the UK, and any individual ordinarily resident in the UK.

enforcement jurisdiction was further expanded by a new offence enforceable against companies of failure to prevent bribery, which allows for prosecution of bribery by companies and partnerships organized under UK laws, regardless of where that bribery occurs. It further allows for the prosecution of bribery offences committed by non-UK companies or partnerships where they carry on any part of their business in the UK.[148]

The UK has been subject to close monitoring of its implementation and enforcement of the Anti-Bribery Convention. The OECD requires ratifying parties to submit to its Working Group on Bribery's peer monitoring and evaluation system, whereby a panel of experts drawn from other signatories of the Convention periodically review each other signatory's progress in meeting its obligations thereunder.[149] In its most recent evaluation report on the UK, the OECD Working Group confirmed that it was broadly satisfied that the UK had satisfied its obligations under the Convention.[150] However, it expressed concerns, inter alia, that the independence of UK enforcement authorities in taking investigation and prosecution decisions was compromised by the existence of Shawcross exercises. The Shawcross process involves the Attorney General exercising their discretion, having consulted with government ministers on the public interest implications of a particular course of action, to advise enforcement authorities on whether to proceed with an investigation or prosecution. The Working Group also expressed concerns on the secretive nature of the use of the Shawcross exercise.[151] The OECD's reasonable concern is that the use of the Shawcross process prevents the UK from adhering to Article 5 of the Convention, which provides:

> Investigation and prosecution of the bribery of a foreign public official shall be subject to the applicable rules and principles of each Party. They shall not be influenced by considerations of national economic interest, the potential effect upon relations with another State or the identity of the natural or legal persons involved.[152]

A further weakness identified by the OECD's Working Group was the under-implementation or enforcement of and, in some cases, the non-ratification by the UK's Overseas Territories (OTs) and Crown Dependencies (CDs) of the

[148] Bribery Act 2010, s 7.

[149] OECD, *OECD Anti-Bribery Convention and the Country Monitoring Process* (OECD Publishing 2024).

[150] OECD, *Implementing the OECD Anti-Bribery Convention Phase 4 Follow-Up Report Addendum: United Kingdom: 2019 Two-Year Follow-Up Updated 2021* (OECD Publishing 2021).

[151] OECD Directorate for Financial and Enterprise Affairs and OECD Working Group on Bribery in International Business Transactions, *Phase 4 Evaluation of the United Kingdom's Additional Written Follow-up Report* (OECD Publishing July 2023) 4.

[152] OECD Convention on Combating Bribery of Foreign Public Officials in International Business Transactions (entered into force on 15 February 1999) art 5.

Convention. It was argued in response that those jurisdictions are autonomously governed, and the UK is therefore unable to direct them to implement policy and law reform.[153] This abdication of responsibility on the UK's part has been met with scepticism in some quarters.[154]

c. The AML Regime

The third regime explicitly contemplating the risks of senior public officials transferring corruptly acquired assets abroad is the anti-money laundering framework. The development of the anti-money laundering (AML) regime and its PEP-specific rules will be discussed in the next chapter, and the potential enforcement of AML offences against kleptocrats is considered in Chapter 5. The Financial Action Task Force (FATF) is a hugely influential ad hoc inter-governmental body that serves as the global AML policy watchdog. In formulating financial crime policy, the UK government has tended to refer explicitly to FATF monitoring processes and Recommendations in introducing new measures or reforms.[155] FATF's oversight process of its participant states operates in much the same way as the OECD's mutual evaluation process. FATF deemed the UK as of the date of its most recent evaluation in 2022 to be largely or fully compliant with all but one of the FATF's Recommendations. Nevertheless, FATF drew attention to its ongoing concerns that the NCA, which serves as the UK's central Financial Intelligence Unit responsible for receiving and analysing disclosures of financial information under the AML Regulations, was insufficiently resourced 'to conduct operational and strategic analysis needed given the size of the UK economy and financial sector'.[156]

Notwithstanding areas of weakness and the generally low levels of prosecution of overseas bribery offences, the OECD and FATF have each deemed the UK largely compliant with their obligations as parties and member jurisdictions to the Anti-Bribery Convention and the FATF Recommendations respectively despite low rates of prosecution of bribery and high-end anti-money laundering offences.[157] Similar observations might be made of the UK's performance of its

[153] OECD, *Group Phase 4 Evaluation* (n 151).

[154] The justification provided to date has been that imposing requirements on OTs and CDs is contrary to established constitutional relationships—but such constitutional relationships have not precluded the UK 'repeatedly legislat[ing] in respect of overseas territories—for example, on issues relating to corruption, abolishing the death penalty, pirate radio, and the decriminalisation of homosexuality'—Joanne Cherry MP, HC Deb 25 October 2016, vol 616, col 215. The UK government's decision in 2009 to suspend the ministerial government of Turks and Caicos is a more conspicuous and relatively recent use of its influence.

[155] See eg the multiple references to FATF's assessments of the UK in the policy background set out in the Explanatory Notes to the Economic Crime and Corporate Transparency Act 2023, paras 39–47.

[156] *Anti-Money Laundering and Counter-Terrorism Financing Measures: United Kingdom Follow-up Report and Technical Compliance Re-Rating* (FATF 2022) 3.

[157] See Chapter 4, n 42 and accompanying text.

UNCAC obligations. It has fulfilled all of its obligations under the Convention, but the UK's actual realization of the asset recovery aims contemplated by the UNCAC are limited. This is instructive for anti-corruption lobbyists. Once the UK has agreed to adhere to international standards, even where those standards may not yet necessarily have achieved international normative force, it tends to make a strong good-faith effort to implement those standards. It is the rate and success of investigation and enforcement (and the political support and resourcing in furtherance of these norms) which are notable weak points.

5. Conclusion

The reasons for the UK's status as a magnet for dirty money are numerous, complex, and, in some instances, have developed in part as a result of decades or even centuries of policy decisions aimed at cultivating wealth. Here, through negligence or by design, insufficient checks and balances have been built into the systems implementing those policies. This has allowed the UK to evolve into a state that at times seems to have displayed an attitude of constructive ambivalence in trying to tread a line between deterring dirty money from flooding into the jurisdiction and encouraging FDI. However, there exists some preliminary evidence suggesting that the UK's highly publicized anti-corruption policies introduced in recent years may be finally bearing some fruit. First, since the introduction of a requirement that companies incorporated in overseas jurisdictions are required to disclose the names of the natural persons who hold the ultimate beneficial ownership interests in the relevant entities to the UK's Land Registry,[158] the number of properties being acquired by companies incorporated in tax havens has fallen significantly.[159] Second, the UK appears to be haemorrhaging high-net-worth individuals more generally. The jurisdiction saw an estimated net outflow of 9,500 millionaires in 2024.[160] The chief drivers of this exodus likely include the economic impact of Brexit and the scrapping of the UK's non-dom tax regime, which allowed individuals resident but not permanently settled in the UK to avoid tax on foreign earnings. Although respondents to the survey that generated these data are unlikely to

[158] Economic Crime and Transparency Act 2022, s 12.

[159] Collin and others (n 89).

[160] These data are based on research undertaken by Henley & Partners, a company that describes itself as 'the global leader in residence and leadership by investment': Henley & Partners, *The Henley Private Wealth Migration Report 2024* <www.henleyglobal.com/publications/henley-private-wealth-migration-report-2024/top-10-country-inflows>. Henley has been criticized as being instrumental in the development of so-called 'Golden Visa' schemes, the UK iteration of which is discussed earlier in this chapter. The source methodology is based on the individuals in question residing for at least six months in their new countries of residence. See Oliver Bullough, *Moneyland: Why Thieves & Crooks Now Rule the World & How to Take it Back* (Profile Books 2018). Somewhat ironically, this makes information published by the company a useful source of global data recording the migration trends of the super-rich.

acknowledge it publicly, one wonders whether a nascent environment of heightened scrutiny of wealth and growing public intolerance of dirty money might play a part in the departure of some. An increasing dearth of the UK-resident super-rich makes it more likely that those interested in profligate expenditure of unexplained wealth might become more visible and thus more detectable in future.

On a political level, the Labour Party in its manifesto for government indicated that it was 'committed to restoring development spending at the level of 0.7 per cent of gross national income' but only 'when fiscal circumstances allow'.[161] The manifesto paid relatively cursory attention to overseas corruption, only making a passing reference to working with the UK's 'allies and international financial centres to tackle corruption and money laundering, including in Britain, Crown Dependencies, and in British Overseas Territories'.[162] In the wash-up of legislation following the 2024 election, the new Labour government declined to carry over work commenced on the Strategic Litigation against Public Participation (SLAPPs) Bill, a private member's bill introduced by a Labour MP which had enjoyed cross-party support and had reached Committee Stage in the House of Commons. The SLAPPs Bill had proposed amongst other matters to increase defendant protection for costs against SLAPPs, and to expand the range of cases to which SLAPPs protections apply.[163] Immediately reinstating the 0.7 per cent contribution and saving the SLAPPs Bill would have been two relatively straightforward ways for the new government to signal a meaningful commitment to tackling elite corruption and to championing overseas development. The relative sparsity of overseas anti-corruption policy published to date is reason to worry that the government may view (or may view the public as viewing) Britain's status as haven for the proceeds of overseas corruption as a relatively unimportant issue. The public concern or even panic around the UK's harbouring of dirty money that reached its peak in the aftermath of the invasion of Ukraine has ebbed, and with it the political impetus for action and reform in tackling overseas elites' ill-gotten gains.

The Labour manifesto has made encouraging noises around reforming domestic standards and increasing levels of integrity in public office. This development is redolent of Sharman's observations on parochialism in crime control policy.[164] The risk is that some or all of the momentum engendered by the public outrage on 'Londongrad' which helped to expedite the introduction of transparency-focused anti-corruption reforms will stall, allowing for the re-introduction of a mood of policy complacence towards dirty money. One of the key issues examined in the

[161] David Lawder, 'UK Plans to Boost Development Aid When Fiscal Circumstances Allow, Minister Says' *Reuters* (London, 24 July 2024).

[162] Labour Party, *Change: The Labour Party Manifesto 2024* <labour.org.uk/change>.

[163] These protections were introduced in the Economic Crime and Corporate Transparency Act 2023 but are limited to claims where defendants purport to exercise their right to freedom of speech in allegations related to economic crime.

[164] See n 108 and accompanying text above.

next chapter and in Chapter 4 is how that public concern can be harnessed—in ways resulting in both positive and negative policy outcomes—by moral entrepreneurs interested in capitalizing on it by introducing new policy. The challenge for anti-corruption lobbyists and campaigners is to ensure that this momentum continues to be channelled into effective and systemic reform.

2
Targeting the Politically Connected

1. Introduction

In the UK, each new anti-corruption measure introduced in law tends to follow fast on the heels of either scandals highlighting the abuse of high political office for personal financial gain or international crises of some kind. The resulting laws specifically aimed at addressing crimes of official corruption committed by overseas senior public officials and their associates fall into two main legal categories: the anti-money laundering rules and the proceeds of crime laws. Each of these legislative regimes includes provisions specifically targeting the individuals that the law recognizes as central to the commission of acts of grand corruption: politically exposed persons (PEPs). This chapter introduces the reader to the concept of the 'PEP' and questions the legitimacy and effectiveness of its use in domestic and international anti-corruption laws. It explains how those rules originated. The rationales frequently posited in justifying PEP-specific rules are examined and the socio-political and legal narratives preceding their introduction are assessed through a critical criminological lens. A discussion of the legitimacy of the PEP concept and its origins is important because anti-corruption rules are often directed at ensuring that PEPs cannot benefit from official corruption.[1] It concludes that whilst, in principle, bespoke tools to facilitate the recovery of stolen assets are to be welcomed, attempts to focus high levels of scrutiny on enormous cohorts of PEPs are not necessarily the most constructive or pragmatic means of tackling the proceeds of grand corruption.

2. The Origin of 'Politically Exposed Persons'

Despite its ubiquity, there is no single understanding of the expression 'politically exposed person' within the AML and asset recovery paradigms in which it is used. The first recorded use of the term 'politically exposed person' that this writer

[1] For example, the European Union's anti-money laundering directives and the UK's money-laundering regulations require financial institutions to undertake enhanced due diligence processes against customers who are PEPs and the Proceeds of Crimes Act 2002 provides for lower tests to be met by enforcement authorities seeking UWOs against PEPs.

Unexplained Wealth Orders and the UK's Anti-Corruption Regime. Áine Clancy, Oxford University Press.
 DOI: 10.1093/9780198907312.003.0003

was able to identify was made by the Bank for International Settlements' Basel Committee on Banking Supervision (BCBS) in 2000,[2] when it observed that:

> Business relationships with individuals holding important public positions and with persons or companies clearly related to them may expose a bank to significant reputational and/or legal risks. Such politically exposed persons (PEPs) are individuals who are or have been entrusted with prominent public functions.[3]

In its original definition, BCBS suggested that PEPs are (i) natural persons; (ii) who are or who have been entrusted with prominent public functions. Depending on the context in which the term is used, however, PEP can have different meanings. Under the Proceeds of Crime Act 2002 (POCA), the legislation providing for unexplained wealth orders, the definition of a PEP is expanded to include within its ambit (i) any person holding or who has held a prominent public office; (ii) the family members and close associates of such individuals; and (iii) any person who is 'otherwise connected with' such individuals.[4] For these purposes, persons 'otherwise connected with' the holder of a prominent public office can include companies (ie non-natural persons).[5]

It is not entirely clear what is meant by *politically* exposed persons. BCBS says that PEPs include: 'heads of state or of government, senior politicians, senior government, judicial or military officials, senior executives of publicly owned corporations and important political party officials'.[6] Not all of those roles involve overtly 'political' functions.[7] Furthermore, it is not clear *to what* politically exposed persons are purportedly exposed. It might be exposure to, without limitation: political

[2] This result is based on a Google Scholar search made on 1 October 2024 for the date range between 1990 and 2003. False positives were removed. Similar searches were made on the library catalogue of the University of Liverpool. No earlier references were found as a result of those searches. The BCBS comprises a joint group of central banks and bank supervisors from twenty-eight jurisdictions.

[3] BCBS, *Customer Due Diligence for Banks*, Basel Committee Publications No 85, October 2001, para 41 <www.bis.org/publ/bcbs85.pdf>.

[4] POCA, s 362B(7).

[5] s 1122 of the Corporation Tax Act 2010 applies in determining whether a person is 'connected'. The definition of 'person' as provided for under sch 1 of the Interpretation Act 1976 includes 'a body of persons corporate or unincorporated'. Unlike the provisions of the POCA, under the EU's anti-money laundering directives and the UK's AML regulations, only people who are (i) natural persons; and (ii) themselves 'entrusted with prominent public functions' (and not their family members or connected persons) are PEPs.

[6] See n 3.

[7] The *Oxford English Dictionary* defines 'political' as '[o]f, belonging to, or concerned with the form, organization, and administration of a state ...' Political, adj' (OED Online, <www.oed.com/view/Entry/146887>). In a UWO case from 2018 involving a woman who spent £16.1m of unexplained wealth in Harrods in London, for example, the respondent Zamira Hajiyeva's husband was found to be a PEP in his capacity as chairman of a bank in which the Azerbaijani State had a controlling shareholding: see *National Crime Agency v Hajiyeva* [2018] EWHC 2534 (Admin), [2018] 1 WLR 5887. Mr Hajiyev may not have been undertaking a role inherently 'political' in nature, but as a member 'of the administrative, management or supervisory bodies of [a] State-owned enterprise', he is a PEP for the purposes of s 362B(8) of the POCA.

influence generally; foreign or domestic corrupting influences; opportunity to misappropriate public funds; opportunities to accept bribes in decision-making on how to use public funds or in awarding public contracts or licences; or all, or none, of the above.[8] The term as now defined under the POCA captures, amongst other individuals, all past and present non-UK or European Economic Area (EEA) parliamentarians or other legislative body members; senior judges; senior military personnel; diplomats; senior members of political parties; members of the administrative, management, or supervisory bodies of state-owned enterprises; *and* each of their respective family members and close associates.[9] This is an enormous cohort of individuals, the size of which is increasing exponentially.

An earlier consultation draft of the BCBS's 2000 publication used the word 'potentate' instead of 'politically exposed person'.[10] This term is one that is favoured by some members of the Wolfsberg Group (Wolfsberg)[11] in anti-corruption rules, 'because people associate [the word potentate] with people in very high office, and it also reflects on a political system that does not follow a system of general checks and balances'.[12] Leaving aside the questionable implication that corruption will not occur in a reasonably well-functioning political system, the main thrust of this argument is that by expanding the meaning of 'PEP' beyond the most senior members of a state's ruling class (ie theoretically those with easiest access to that state's coffers), attention is diverted away from the individuals best placed to commit offences of grand corruption.[13] Alternative formulations of the expression might have the problems of being less pleasingly alliterative and, more pertinently, more directly aspersive. A 'graft-susceptible person', for example, might be a more accurate but less delicate descriptor than 'politically exposed person'.

[8] Some standard-setting bodies have referred to *financial sectors and banks* being exposed to risks presented by PEP customers but have not elucidated exactly to what the PEPs themselves are exposed. See eg the Wolfsberg Anti-Money Laundering Principles for Private Banking (2012) <www.wolfsberg-principles.com/sites/default/files/wb/pdfs/wolfsberg-standards/10.%20Wolfsberg-Private-Banking-Prinicples-May-2012.pdf> and para 75 of the FATF *Report on Money-Laundering Typologies 2003–2004* (FATF Secretariat 2004).

[9] POCA, s 362B(7). This definition encompasses the PEPs of a total of 162 countries.

[10] BCBS, *Consultative Document: Customer Due Diligence for Banks*, January 2001, paras 33–34 <www.bis.org/publ/bcbs77.pdf>.

[11] A group comprised of facilitators from Transparency International, the Basel Institute on Governance, and primarily of representatives from banks comprising 85 per cent of the world's private banking business. The Wolfsberg Group and its activities are discussed in more detail in subsection (b).

[12] Author interview on 6 February 2020 with Hans-Peter Bauer, now of the Basel Institute on Governance, who has attended meetings of the Wolfsberg Group since its inception, first acting on behalf of UBS and subsequently as an Institute facilitator. See also Wolfsberg's submission to FATF preceding the 2012 publication of FATF's 40+9 Recommendations, noting 'that the notions of the seniority of the politician, the type of account being requested and who controls the purse strings are [the] essential criteria to be taken into consideration' when determining whether a financial institution's client should be designated as 'high risk'. Wolfsberg Group Comment Letter on FATF Consultation Paper—06/01/2011, 5 <www.wolfsberg-principles.com/sites/default/files/wb/pdfs/comment-letters/22.%20Wolfsberg_Group_Comment_Letter_on_FATF_Consultation_Paper_Jan-6th-2011_unsigned.pdf>.

[13] See the discussion on the definition of 'grand corruption' in the Introduction to this volume.

'Potentate' is similarly a value-laden (and, perhaps, racially loaded) term. The slightly nonsensical construction of 'PEP' is, at least, inoffensive. Nevertheless, it is not ideal that the expression was used, inter alios, by the Financial Action Task Force (FATF) in its Recommendations and by the European Union (EU) and HM Treasury in drafting laws without consideration of what it means to be 'politically exposed', yet the term 'politically exposed person' is now an accepted part of the AML and asset recovery lexicon. This unquestioning acceptance is, perhaps, symptomatic of a wider lack of legislative rigour around the treatment of PEPs in law and policy.

a. The Evolution of PEP-Specific Rules

There is nothing new in activities involving foreign senior public officials being the subject of specific doctrines and laws.[14] The development of enhanced regulatory standards involving PEPs in domestic laws followed the discovery of over US$600m stolen from the Philippines by its president Ferdinand Marcos and his associates in Swiss bank accounts.[15] This scandal led the Swiss Federal Banking Commission (SFBC) to adopt a practice recommendation in 1987 requiring that decisions within banks to establish business relationships with high-ranking government officials should only be taken at the highest management levels.[16] Bankers found to have approved the deposit of assets of corrupt origin would face personal disqualification.[17] The effectiveness of the requirements was subsequently shown to be limited but not without teeth. Following an investigation by the Commission in 2000 into money misappropriated by former Nigerian dictator Sani Abacha, at least US$660m of which was found to be held in seventeen Swiss banks, several bankers were ordered to resign from their positions.[18] Aside from the Swiss activism in the 1980s, however, no further developments in other states' domestic laws on PEPs in an anti-money laundering context were to follow for many years.[19]

[14] See eg the immunities enjoyed by heads of state and other senior officials, or the US Foreign Corrupt Practices Act, enacted in 1977, which prohibits the bribery of foreign public officials: 15 USC §§ 78dd-1–78qq.

[15] JC Sharman, *The Despot's Guide to Wealth Management: On the International Campaign Against Grand Corruption* (Cornell University Press 2017) 91–94.

[16] Following a merger and reorganization in 2007 of banking and markets supervisors in Switzerland, the SFBC's functions were assumed by the Swiss Financial Market Supervisory Authority.

[17] Eva HG Hüpkes, 'Keeping Dirty Money and Terrorist Funds Away: The Proposed Money Laundering Regulation of the Swiss Federal Banking Commission' (2002) 10 Journal of Financial Regulation and Compliance 317, 319.

[18] SFBC, *'Abacha Funds at Swiss Banks': Report of the Swiss Federal Banking Commission* (Swiss Federal Banking Commission, 30 August 2000).

[19] Hüpkes (n 17).

b. The Global Banking Sector Recognizes the 'PEP Problem'

In November 1999, instances of grand corruption orchestrated by PEPs in Pakistan, Mexico, Nigeria, Indonesia, Venezuela, and Gabon using the services of just one bank—Citibank—were all highlighted in a report published by the US Senate Permanent Subcommittee on Investigations.[20] The report exposed how private banks facilitated PEP corruption, and its publication precipitated the convening of the Wolfsberg Group in 2000 in Chateau Wolfsberg, then UBS Bank's training centre in Switzerland. As convened, Wolfsberg comprised a group of international banks, each with private banking arms, and the gathering was facilitated by Transparency International and Professor Mark Pieth who at the time chaired the Organisation for Economic Co-operation and Development's (OECD) Working Group on Bribery.[21] Wolfsberg was founded in part out of banks' frustration at the slow progress of regulators and FATF in acting to produce a globally harmonized set of customer due diligence principles.[22] Wolfsberg developed a voluntary set of anti-money laundering guidelines for the financial sector which came to be known as the Wolfsberg Principles. The first published version of the text provided that:

> Individuals who have or have had positions of public trust such as government officials, senior executives of government corporations, politicians, important political party officials etc. and their families and close associates require heightened scrutiny.[23]

This reference to PEPs' families and their close associates constitutes the first time of which the author is aware that a concept very close to the current scope of the broad contemporary understanding of the 'PEP' was proposed on a supranational basis.[24]

In convening, Wolfsberg's members expressed concerns about what they perceived as the reputational damage wrought on banks by political corruption scandals, a number of which were widely publicized at the time.[25] The banks said that

[20] US Senate Permanent Subcommittee on Investigations, *Private Banking and Money Laundering: A Case Study of Opportunities and Vulnerabilities* (Washington DC 1999).

[21] Gemma Aiolfi and Hans Peter Bauer, 'The Wolfsberg Group' in Mark Pieth (ed), *Collective Action: Innovative Strategies to Prevent Corruption* (Dike 2012) 97.

[22] Mark Pieth and Gemma Aiolfi, 'The Private Sector Become Active: The Wolfsberg Process' (2003) 10 Journal of Financial Crime 359, 361.

[23] The October 2000 version of the Wolfsberg Group's Principles is not available on its website. The above principle was quoted in Kris Hinterseer's article 'The Wolfsberg Anti-Money Laundering Principles' (2001) 5 Journal of Money Laundering Control 25. Wolfsberg has subsequently noted (Wolfsberg PEP Guidance 2017, 1) that 'a focus on applying a consistent level of Enhanced Due Diligence (EDD) to all PEPs, irrespective of the risk of committing serious crimes against society, as well as the significant numbers of entries on PEP lists (including PEPs, their relatives and associates, close or otherwise), [has] considerably diluted both the application of [a risk-based approach] and the effectiveness of PEP screening'.

[24] Albeit a similar provision was previously included in domestic Swiss banking regulation—see n 18.

[25] See Pieth and Aiolfi (n 22).

they wished to ensure that they were not used as instruments of corruption or illegality.[26] For a group of private banks like Wolfsberg, the practical benefits of pre-empting the publication by norm-setters like FATF of anti-money laundering guidelines for financial institutions on how to deal with PEPs were manifold. Wolfsberg's members would be able to demonstrate that they were proactively engaged in the fight against corruption. The association with Transparency International and Professor Pieth was helpful, in that it projected an image of civil society-sanctioned legitimacy on Wolfsberg's recommendations. This ensured that it would be more difficult for third parties to criticize the guidelines developed by Wolfsberg generally or its PEP proposals specifically. Additionally, its members were able to craft and broadcast guidelines that would work well for them operationally before regulatory authorities had the opportunity to dictate an alternative system. Wolfsberg's ability to shape and influence FATF standards through its policy recommendations was a significant boon to the group—particularly in circumstances where, for example, its Recommendations form rules more akin to advisories or fall within the enforcement scope of a regulator rather than laws attracting harsher sanctions for breach.[27] Given the subsequent exposure of the systemic AML failings of some of Wolfsberg's members, acceptance of and adherence to the Wolfsberg recommendations in practice is questionable.[28]

The involvement of private institutions in setting standards which have subsequently become enshrined in public laws designed to counter the very practices facilitated by those institutions at the behest of their clients is obviously problematic. Aside from the conflict of interest, there is little transparency in the processes and rationales adopted in Wolfsberg's development of its October 2000 principles.[29] None of the financial institution participants involved in devising those standards was or is accountable to the public as policy-setters or lawmakers. They are only meaningfully accountable to their executive boards, their shareholders, and, depending on the jurisdiction, their regulatory bodies. There is thus no opportunity for critical scrutiny of the banks' decision to opt to apply enhanced due diligence measures against PEPs rather than adopting alternative risk mitigation processes. Options open to the banks regardless of whether or not account-holders are PEPs might have included applying enhanced due diligence only in circumstances where, for example and without limitation, particular financial products are used, when shell companies in particular jurisdictions or suspicious trust arrangements are involved, or where the legitimate sources of assets in

[26] Author interview with Gemma Aiolfi of Basel Institute on Governance, 6 February 2020.

[27] See eg Annex 1 of FATF *Guidance on the Risk-Based Approach to Combating Money Laundering and Terrorist Financing* (FATF June 2007), in which FATF acknowledges Wolfsberg as one of the organizations '*integrally involved in the development and finalisation*' of the publication.

[28] See Chapter 7, Section 3(b).

[29] No policy and consultation papers, agendas, guides, or internal policy documents shared in the discussions in which the original standards were formulated are publicly available.

transactions above a particular value cannot be adequately evidenced.[30] According to Wolfsberg Group facilitators, the decision to bring PEP family members and associates within scope of the rules was influenced by the US Senate Committee's criticisms of Citibank.[31] We do not know whether the potentially sweeping impact of bringing all family members and associates of high-ranking public officials within the measures' remit was discussed, nor whether negative aspects of such a wide conception of the 'PEP' were foreseen. Given the reputational concerns for banks which apparently catalysed the formation of Wolfsberg, we also do not know (though we can guess) if there was any discussion on whether individual banks who knowingly, recklessly, or negligently facilitate corrupt acts by PEPs, whether on a systemic basis or otherwise, should be subject to more stringent sanctions to incentivize good practice amongst the collective and to provide additional legitimacy to good actors. Even so, Wolfsberg's recommendations, which essentially were developed by private corporations as an expression of *their* preferences in dealing with grand corruption, were eventually adopted by various think-tanks and legislatures and are now enshrined in law.

c. PEPs and the FATF Recommendations

Various groupings of banking supervisory authorities from different countries coordinated efforts to publish suggestions for codifying PEP-specific rules quickly after the issuing of, and reflecting the principles espoused in, the Wolfsberg Principles.[32] Of these standards, guidelines, and recommendations, those published by FATF were to prove most consequential. FATF was founded as an ad hoc body in 1989 by the G7 to 'set standards and promote effective implementation of legal, regulatory and operational measures for combating money laundering', originally in the context of the war on drugs, but later with an expanded remit to take account of international developments in crime and terrorist financing.[33] Its membership has come to be recognized as 'the international standard-setter in the anti-money laundering field'.[34] FATF promulgates its message by periodic updates of its 'Forty Recommendations': a set of policy standards that is enormously influential

[30] For a discussion of more nuanced risk-based assessment criteria under discussion by the FCA, see Chapter 3, n 109 and accompanying text.

[31] See n 20.

[32] In October 2001, the Basel Committee for Banking Supervision published a report entitled *Consumer Due Diligence for Banks*; in November 2001, a PEPs Working Paper from a joint initiative of the banking supervisory authorities of the UK, France, Canada, Switzerland, and Germany was issued; and in 2003, FATF published both the 2003 version of its Recommendations and its *Report on Money Laundering Typologies 2003–2004*.

[33] See <www.fatf-gafi.org/about/>.

[34] Cecily Rose, *International Anti-Corruption Norms: Their Creation and Influence on Domestic Legal Systems* (OUP 2015) 178.

in shaping anti-money laundering law and policy.[35] The 2003 version of the Forty Recommendations provided that financial institutions should adopt enhanced customer due diligence and account approval measures in respect of PEPs,[36] who were defined as:

> individuals who are or have been entrusted with prominent public functions in a foreign country, for example Heads of State or of government, senior politicians, senior government, judicial or military officials, senior executives of state-owned corporations, important political party officials. Business relationships with family members or close associates of PEPs involve reputational risks similar to those with PEPs themselves. The definition is not intended to cover middle ranking or more junior individuals in the foregoing categories.[37]

Despite its status as the 'international agency principally charged with leading action against laundering',[38] in its capacity as a norm-setting body, FATF has been criticized for its set standards and membership, as well as for its lack of transparency and constitution.[39] It has been condemned by commentators for imposing ostensibly 'non-binding' standards (at times, historically, by coercion and blacklisting) on unrepresented and poorer states—often with little consideration of whether such standards are necessary or appropriate given the banking sector profiles of certain countries.[40] FATF also fails on 'the most basic element of normative legitimacy: the existence of State consent'[41] through its selective membership, resulting in 'the potential to privilege the interests of powerful States in ways that diminish the normative legitimacy of these norms and institutions'.[42] In questioning the legitimacy of FATF's rules, commentators have highlighted (without limitation) the absence of any evaluation of the performance of FATF itself, its status as a single-agenda body, and the fact that through its operations 'a specific agenda developed by technocrats and with limited scrutiny at the global level has been

[35] See Valsamis Mitsilegas, 'The European Union and the Global Governance of Crime' in Valsamis Mitsilegas, Peter Alldridge, and Leonidas Cheliotis (eds), *Globalisation, Criminal Law and Criminal Justice: Theoretical, Comparative and Transnational Perspectives* (Hart 2014) 153.

[36] The meaning of 'enhanced due diligence' within AML regulation depends on the context, region, and sector. Broadly, it requires regulated entities who provide financial and related professional services to customers in contexts that create higher money-laundering risks to obtain additional information to establish the customer's identity and using extra checks to ensure the legitimacy of that customer's sources of funds. For an explanation of how enhanced due diligence measures are required to be employed by law firms within the UK, for example, see Sarah Kebbell, *Anti-Money Laundering Compliance and the Legal Profession* (Routledge 2021) 47–48.

[37] FATF, The Forty Recommendations (FATF June 2003) 14.

[38] Peter Alldridge, *What Went Wrong with Money Laundering Law?* (Springer 2016) 11–12.

[39] See Alldridge (n 38) and Mitsilegas (n 35).

[40] See JC Sharman, *The Money Laundry: Regulating Criminal Finance in the Global Economy* (Cornell University Press 2011) 1–35, 37–66, 99–130 and, more generally, Dominic Thomas-James, *Offshore Financial Centres and the Law: Suspect Wealth in British Overseas Territories* (Routledge 2021).

[41] Sharman (n 40) 40.

[42] Sharman (n 40) 218.

legitimized'.[43] Despite its unrepresentative membership, lack of constitution, and scant transparency, FATF's influence on anti-money laundering standards internationally, at EU level, and domestically is beyond doubt.[44] Enthusiasm from countries for a positive result from FATF's periodic standard compliance reviews means that these standards end up having the status of norms which are ultimately codified into domestic statute.[45] Reservations about the legitimacy of FATF and its Recommendations have been largely ignored by its members.[46] Although reasonable criticisms have been levelled at FATF,[47] its procedure for developing PEP-specific due diligence rules for financial gatekeepers like banks is at least an improvement on the Wolfsberg process because the vested interests of the membership are not as baldly commercial in nature. Moreover, unlike Wolfsberg, it engages in public consultation and ongoing assessment and publishes guidance to accompany its Recommendations.

One of these guidance documents, FATF's *Report on Money-Laundering Typologies 2003–2004*, noted that revelations of PEP corruption 'occur frequently in the press',[48] that respondents to its typologies exercise had noted that PEPs sometimes use associates and family members to help conceal assets of illicit origin, and that PEPs use similar tactics to money launderers by moving wealth offshore and using shell companies.[49] The experts on the typologies panel considered that because of the special status of PEPs, 'there is often a certain amount of discretion afforded by financial institutions to the financial activities carried out by these persons or on their behalf' which has the effect of enabling PEP corruption and creating obstacles to its investigation and discovery.[50] The FATF experts concluded that:

> the techniques employed by PEPs to launder illegal proceeds were very similar to those of other criminal money launderers. If solely viewed from the perspective of the financial institution, these techniques look exactly the same.[51]

[43] Valsamis Mitsilegas and Niovi Vavoula, 'The Evolving EU Anti-Money Laundering Regime: Challenges for Fundamental Rights and the Rule of Law' (2016) 23 Maastricht Journal of European & Comparative Law 261, 266, 267. cf on FATF's lack of legitimacy more generally Rose (n 34) and Petrus C van Duyne, Jackie Harvey, and Liliya Gelemerova, 'Learning More about the FATF: Knowing the Tree by its Fruits' in Petrus C van Duyne, Jackie Harvey, and Liliya Gelemerova (eds), *The Critical Handbook of Money Laundering: Policy, Analysis and Myths* (Palgrave Macmillan 2018) 123.

[44] Rose (n 34) 178–216.

[45] Mitsilegas and Vavoula (n 43).

[46] House of Lords, European Union Committee, *Nineteenth Report: Money Laundering and the Financing of Terrorism*, 14 July 2009, paras 22–32 (Stationery Office 2009).

[47] See eg n 39.

[48] See FATF Report (n 8) para 75.

[49] FATF Report (n 8) paras 78 and 79.

[50] FATF Report (n 8) para 76.

[51] FATF Report (n 8) para 84.

If this is correct, it may be argued that (assuming they are actually effective to prevent financial crime), the non-PEP specific anti-money laundering measures devised by FATF and others should be sufficient by themselves to detect corrupt PEPs without the need for PEP-specific rules. It is acknowledged however that placing a duty on banks to ascertain whether their clients are those of a kind who are in a position to direct the movement of state resources may encourage more scrupulous vetting of potentially suspicious transactions undertaken by such individuals.

d. PEPs Become Part of EU and UK Anti-Money Laundering Law

The EU's Third AML Directive was introduced in 2005. It updated its money-laundering countermeasures to reflect the then-most recent iteration of the FATF Recommendations,[52] and so it introduced the concept of the PEP to EU law. The Council and the European Parliament agreed the text of the Directive on the first reading.[53] A Commission directive setting out implementing measures on the definition of 'politically exposed person' was published in August 2006.[54] Unsurprisingly, the use of comitology to clarify the measures relating to PEPs, thus removing any parliamentary scrutiny and opportunity for debate on the standards adopted, has been criticized.[55] Consequently and unsatisfactorily, FATF's limited drafting and consultation materials are all that are available for review to determine the reasoning behind the formulation of who is a PEP in the eyes of the EU.

In domestic UK legislation, the concept of a 'politically exposed person' first appeared in the 2007 Money Laundering Regulations,[56] which transposed the Third AML Directive into UK law by way of a copy-out strategy.[57] The Money Laundering Regulations were replaced in 2017 by way of negative resolution procedure[58] by

[52] Recitals 5 and 25 respectively of Directive 2005/60/EC of the European Parliament and of the Council of 26 October 2005 (the Third AML Directive). f Eur-Lex 52004PC0448: European Commission Explanatory Memorandum on Proposal for a Directive of the European Parliament and of the Council on the Prevention of the Use of the Financial System for the Purpose of Money Laundering, Including Terrorist Financing, COM (2004) 0448 final—COD 2004/0137.

[53] Valsamis Mitsilegas and Bill Gilmore, 'The EU Legislative Framework against Money Laundering and Terrorist Finance: A Critical Analysis in the Light of Evolving Global Standards' (2007) 56 International and Comparative Law Quarterly 119, 125.

[54] Commission Directive 2006/70/EC [2006] OJ L214, 29.

[55] See Mitsilegas and Gilmore (n 53) 129.

[56] The Money Laundering Regulations 2007, SI 2007/2157.

[57] This followed two public consultations which broadly supported the approach. See Explanatory Memorandum to the Money Laundering Regulations 2007, 2.

[58] As a consequence, the new regulations were not debated in full in Parliament. A parliamentary question in the Commons inviting representations on including domestic PEPs within scope was put to the then-Economic Secretary to the Treasury, Harriet Baldwin. The MPs who made representations all expressed, to varying degrees, their frustration with real-life consequences of enhanced due diligence. The Secretary advised that the UK would be implementing a risk-based approach in addressing the risks posed by domestic PEPs. See HC Deb 16 January 2016, vol 604, cols 1519–26. A similar discussion took place in the House of Lords on the same issue: HL Deb 14 October 2014, vol 756, cols 114–18, where, on the practical impact of financial institutions de-risking around PEPs, Lord Wright gave an example of his two sons who (at col 115): 'co-incidentally tried to open bank accounts in Singapore and

the AML Regulations.[59] These regulations directly implemented further EU law requirements relating to PEPs, amongst other matters, as introduced by the Fourth AML Directive in UK law. These provisions, insofar as they apply to PEPs, substantively remain in force.[60]

e. PEPs under the Proceeds of Crime Legislation

PEPs were an established feature of the domestic anti-money laundering landscape by the time they made their first appearance in the UK's proceeds of crime laws. The Criminal Finances Act 2017 amended the POCA to allow enforcement authorities to apply for unexplained wealth orders against PEPs (defined as inclusive of family members and associates) provided certain conditions were met.[61] The definition of PEPs provided under the POCA is in practical terms significantly different to the term as defined in the AML Regulations. This section identifies the discrepancies and evaluates whether the proceeds of crime legislation's definition of 'PEP' is more appropriate than its AML-based counterpart to the purpose it is designed to serve.

i. United Kingdom and EEA PEPs excluded from the POCA definition of 'PEPs'

Little distinction is made in the AML Regulations between domestic and foreign PEPs. That said, the Regulations were amended in 2023 to provide that for domestic PEPs, their family members, and their associates, 'the starting point for the assessment [of risk by financial institutions and other regulated services] is that the customer or potential customer presents a lower level of risk than a non-domestic PEP'.[62] By contrast, the PEP-specific provisions for unexplained wealth orders apply solely to PEPs entrusted with public functions by non-EEA or non-UK states or international organizations, and their family members and associates. When asked in debates preceding the introduction of the legislation making provision for unexplained wealth orders whether the definition of PEPs should be amended to encompass domestic and EEA PEPs,[63] the then-Minister for Security, Ben Wallace, responded:

in New York[.] In both cases they were asked who their father was, and on discovering that [he] was a Member of [the House of Lords], were both refused accounts.'

[59] The Anti-Money Laundering, Terrorist Financing and Transfer of Funds (Information on the Payer) Regulations 2017, SI 692/2017 (the AML Regulations).

[60] Directive (EU) 2015/849 of the European Parliament and of the Council of 20 May 2015 on the Prevention of the Use of the Financial System for the Purposes of Money Laundering or Terrorist Financing (the Fourth AML Directive).

[61] POCA, s 362B as inserted by s 1 of the Criminal Finances Act 2017.

[62] AML Regulations, reg 35(3A).

[63] Law Enforcement and Security (Amendment) (EU Exit) Regulations 2019, SI 742/2019, reg 107 clarified post-Brexit that the references previously made in the POCA to 'the United Kingdom or another EEA State' have been amended to 'the United Kingdom or an EEA State'.

> The amendment would cover us sitting in this room—all PEPs in the EEA. That is important because, if any of us were to face an unexplained wealth order, we would want to know that it had been issued on the basis of evidence linking us to serious crime; we would not want to give our authorities the ability just to slap one on without any evidential threshold. We have confidence that, within the EEA . . . there are the tools to find the evidence and the ability to work with fellow law enforcement agencies around Europe to meet the evidential threshold.[64]

The Minister apparently saw no double standard in observing that it would be unacceptable for enforcement authorities to 'slap [a UWO] on without any evidential threshold' linking EEA or UK PEPs to serious crimes. This outrage would apparently be dispensed with in circumstances where a non-UK or EEA PEP is involved. He alluded to pre-existing 'tools to . . . meet the evidential threshold' should an allegation arise in relation to an EEA or UK PEP. The Minister offered no details to support this. No similar distinction between PEPs based on their country of appointment is made in the AML Regulations, so it is unclear to what he was referring. An influential Transparency International UK paper calling on the government to consider introducing UWOs against PEPs made no distinction between foreign and domestic PEPs.[65] In this way, 'PEP' as defined for the purposes of UWOs discriminates between PEPs based on their geographic origin for no apparent reason. This is despite the anti-money laundering standard-setting bodies and commentators being more or less universally agreed that if measures are to apply to PEPs, they should apply to all foreign and domestic PEPs.[66]

It might of course be argued that it is inherently more suspicious for foreign PEPs to do business and hold assets in the UK compared to domestic PEPs. For example, foreign PEPs will assume exchange rate risk, and logistically it is less feasible for non-resident PEPs to enjoy the use of those assets. Chaikin and Sharman assert that 'PEPs are more likely to conceal their illicit funds by using banking services in foreign jurisdictions because they are not as well-known and have a greater opportunity of masking their identity and illicit gains'.[67] Moreover, unlike

[64] HL Deb 17 November 2016, vol 617, cols 84–85. In seeking to amend the definition of 'PEPs' to include all PEPs, regardless of the country in which they hold public office, Tristram Hunt MP noted that Slovenia's former Prime Minister Janez Janša was recently convicted for accepting bribes in a €278m arms deal. Mr Hunt also referred to recent cases involving PEPs in Cyprus and a proposed blanket immunity from prosecution for domestic PEPs in Hungary in arguing that official corruption was also an EEA phenomenon, and the definition of PEPs should be amended to take account of this. See HL Deb 17 November 2016, vol 617, col 84.

[65] Transparency International and Transparency International UK, *Empowering the UK to Recover Corrupt Assets: Unexplained Wealth Orders and Other New Approaches to Illicit Enrichment and Asset Recovery* (Transparency International and Transparency International UK March 2016).

[66] See David Chaikin and JC Sharman, *Corruption and Money Laundering: A Symbiotic Relationship* (Palgrave 2009) 84. Since their book was published in 2009, the European Parliament and Council and FATF have each expanded their definitions of PEPs to include domestic PEPs.

[67] Chaikin and Sharman (n 66) 103.

foreign PEPs who hold property in the UK but rarely if ever enter the UK, domestic PEPs are within easier jurisdictional reach of domestic criminal laws and law enforcement authorities. However, none of these reasons adequately explains why the UWO provisions, if they are to apply to PEPs, should not apply to PEPs of all nationalities. UWOs could still be useful against domestic PEPs in circumstances where enforcement authorities lack sufficient evidence to build a criminal case but wish to pursue a civil recovery investigation against their assets.

ii. Former and current PEPs

Under the Proceeds of Crime Act 2002, anyone who 'is or has been' entrusted with prominent public functions is a 'PEP' while only individuals who *are* holders of such functions under the AML Regulations qualify. The Treasury received a number of responses to its AML Regulations consultation noting that a 'large number of former PEPs were being treated as though they were still performing prominent public functions'.[68] The opprobrium energetically directed at banks in relation to their treatment of domestic PEPs, their family members, and their close associates during the parliamentary debates[69] and the consultation process[70] resulted in the AML Regulations adopting (i) a twelve-month period after which (absent any evident money-laundering risks) the heightened or enhanced levels of due diligence applicable to PEPs who had left public office would no longer apply; and (ii) a provision that family and close associates of senior public officials should no longer be subject to heightened due diligence processes when a PEP ceased to hold office.[71] It is of course appropriate that the principle of 'once a PEP, always a PEP' is not adopted in every case. The anecdotal evidence proffered during the parliamentary debates on UWOs was that financial institutions impose a high administrative burden on people connected with PEPs, who experience difficulties in opening accounts as a result of their status.[72] Allegations have been made that banks sometimes refuse to establish business relationships with PEPs as a means of insulating themselves from corruption risk,[73] even though this is not the law's

[68] HM Treasury, *Money Laundering Regulations 2017: Consultation Outcome*, 26 June 2017, para 8.3 <www.gov.uk/government/consultations/money-laundering-regulations-2017/money-laundering-regulations-2017>.

[69] See eg n 68.

[70] See the Treasury's *Consultation Outcome* (n 68) para 8.2.a.

[71] AML Regulations, regs 35(9) and 35(11) respectively.

[72] It is difficult to meaningfully quantify the impact of de-risking measures affecting PEPs as it is unlikely that financial institutions will maintain data on their refusal to provide account services to PEPs in contravention of the AML Rules. However, the Dispute Resolution: Complaints (Politically Exposed Persons and Pensions Ombudsman) Instrument 2018 (FCA 2018/13; FOS 2018/1) amended the Dispute Resolution: Complaints Sourcebook (DISP) part of the FCA Handbook to designate individuals who have been identified as PEPs as 'eligible complainants' in certain circumstances. Consequently, some data are now being collected because of complaints against financial institutions by PEPs to the Financial Ombudsman.

[73] See David Artingstall and others, *Drivers and Impacts of Derisking: A Study of Representative Views and Data in the UK* (John Howell & Co Ltd for the FCA 2016) para 32.33, where the 'significant shrinkage' in the number of personal accounts of PEPs compared to other personal accounts over the

intention.[74] On a practical level, there would be an exponential (and ungovernable) increase in the numbers of individuals subject to enhanced due diligence from regulated entities if people never lose their PEP status.

Nevertheless, this is a good example of the anti-money laundering laws being somewhat arbitrary insofar as they apply to PEPs.[75] Corrupt former PEPs can simply wait a year and see whether they are still considered risky prospects by the relevant banks before making their next move. The Stolen Assets Recovery Initiative (StAR) has noted that:

> Time limits are always artificial and pose problem[s]: They can impart a false sense of security that a customer no longer poses an increased risk of money laundering. Evidence suggests that corrupt PEPs do not cease to move proceeds of corruption after leaving office and some may continue to receive payments. Indeed, officials and their family members and close associates may wait until after leaving to move the funds.[76]

StAR, Wolfsberg, FATF, and various academic commentators advocate that risk-based approaches should be used to determine who should be regarded as a higher risk PEP (albeit in different ways). Yet in devising their AML rules, the EU and HM Treasury each have adopted provisions which, certainly at least for family members and close associates of PEPs, dispense with enhanced due diligence requirements for twelve months following an official's departure from office or any longer period which the regulated entity considers appropriate. The approach adopted under the proceeds of crime legislation which, by contrast, purportedly applies to all past and present PEPs in perpetuity is consequently more comprehensible, albeit the apparent indefinite temporal designation of *all* senior public office holders, their families, and their associates as PEPs is problematic in its own right.

iii. Individuals 'otherwise connected' with prominent public officials

The concept of who is 'connected' to a PEP and will therefore be subject to enhanced due diligence under the AML measures or to UWOs under the proceeds

four-study year period of 2011–14 at a large UK bank was observed. Note however the authors' caveat that these data are not reliable as a means of concluding that PEP accounts were necessarily closed for purely financial crime reasons. For more on StAR, see Chapter 1, n 129ff and accompanying text.

[74] Fourth AML Directive, Recital 33: 'Refusing a business relationship with a person simply on the basis of the determination that he or she is a politically exposed person is contrary to the letter and spirit of this Directive and of the revised FATF Recommendations.'

[75] For more on arbitrariness of PEP measures and in particular on the fact that such measures target only senior officials, and that the formulations of family members and 'close associates' in UK law are of questionable value, see Dennis Cox, *Handbook of Anti-Money Laundering* (John Wiley & Sons 2014) 208–12.

[76] Theodore S Greenberg and others, *Politically Exposed Persons: A Guide on Preventive Measures for the Banking Sector* (World Bank 2010) 31.

of crime legislation is, again, far more expansive under the Proceeds of Crime Act than under the AML Regulations. Section 362B(7)(d) of the POCA provides that PEPs include individuals who are 'otherwise connected' to an individual who is or has been entrusted with prominent public functions.[77] The interpretation of whether a person is 'connected' in this context is defined, amongst other things, by reference to section 1122 of the Corporation Tax Act 2010, and includes within the meaning of 'connected person' without limitation, companies, partnerships, and trust arrangements with which the relevant public official is connected. Curiously, the AML Regulations or the POCA definitions of individuals 'connected' to 'PEPs' do not include public officials' partners who are not either spouses or civil partners, or children who have not been publicly acknowledged.[78] These are noteworthy omissions. Some commentators argue that the ambit of who is regarded as 'connected' is too narrow, ignoring, for example, the cultural importance of kinship ties and the economic importance of charities in administering public funds, thus excluding individuals and bodies who are well positioned to act as proxies on behalf of relevant public officials.[79] The confinement of the laws to only higher-ranking public officials has also been criticized by some academic commentators.[80] The problem with these contentions, though, is that each time a broader net is cast over who should be subject to PEP measures, it imposes an increased administrative burden on financial institutions and widens the pool of individuals subject to more intense scrutiny. In any event, there is no clear rationale underpinning the discrepancy in scope of 'connected person' between the proceeds of crime regime and the narrower interpretation in the AML Regulations.

iv. Discrepancies in PEP definitions under UK legislation

Aside from domestic and EEA PEPs being excluded, the range of individuals who are eligible to be subject to PEP-specific unexplained wealth orders is broadly defined. This approach is surprising, because it ignores the prevailing trend adopted in the FATF Recommendations (and, to a lesser degree, in the EU anti-money laundering laws) towards more tailored risk-based approaches in determining who should be subject to PEP-oriented measures. The UK's AML Regulations were introduced into law two months after the legislation introducing unexplained wealth orders was passed. Care could have been taken to ensure that the scope of the concept of PEPs was harmonized on the statute books to provide certainty of the concept across domestic laws. If the intention was that a distinct, wider category of public officials and their associates was to be captured under

77 ie not a family member or a close associate.

78 See eg Vivian Salama and others, 'US Withholds Sanctions on a Very Close Putin Associate: His Reputed Girlfriend' *Wall Street Journal* (New York, 24 April 2022).

79 Chaikin and Sharman (n 66) 83–115.

80 See eg Paul L Lee 'A Renewed Focus on Foreign Corruption and Politically Exposed Persons' (2010) 127 Banking Law Journal 813.

the unexplained wealth laws, then a designation other than PEP could have been used. Furthermore, the proposition underpinning UWOs against foreign PEPs is that the 'measure reflects the concern about those involved in corruption overseas laundering the proceeds of crime in the UK'.[81] It would seem sensible therefore that the definition of PEPs for the purposes of unexplained wealth investigations should be generally consistent with the definition that the law has elsewhere recognized as appropriate for addressing money laundering.

The approach to the definition of PEPs adopted in the POCA is more coherent from a policy perspective than the narrower scope of the definition used in the AML Regulations. It recognizes the prevalence of the use of shell companies and trust arrangements in laundering illicitly acquired assets by including an expansive 'otherwise connected' entities limb in the definition and recognizes that illicitly acquired assets can be laundered after officials have left office at a time when the levels of due diligence scrutiny to which they are subject might be less intense. However, the reasons provided for the exclusion of domestic and EEA PEPs from the POCA definition are unconvincing. The EU AML Directive currently in force expressly provides: 'The international effort to combat corruption also justifies the need to pay particular attention ... to persons who are or who have been entrusted with prominent public functions domestically or abroad.'[82] It is perverse that the European Commission and Parliament (and the UK Parliament, in passing the AML Regulations) believed that measures aimed at European and UK PEPs are necessary to tackle money laundering but the UK Parliament did not hold the same view in circumstances where suspected illicitly acquired assets involving the same individuals are in dispute.

The absence of a clear consensus within the domestic law on what is meant by 'politically exposed', who constitutes a PEP, and for how long individuals should be considered to hold that status exposes uncertainty in the law. Beyond these difficulties, there exist more fundamental problems, not least the lack of evidence-based research published or sponsored by regulators establishing the effectiveness of such measures in impeding or deterring corruption, and/or the inherent risk that arises from *not* imposing special measures on PEPs.[83] Moreover, however widely they are defined, an unscrupulous, well-advised PEP intent on laundering can simply employ the services of a myrmidon who falls outside the ambit of the regulations to transact on his or her behalf, thus necessitating the creation of further categories of PEP, and so on. In this way, PEP-specific measures might be said

[81] Home Office, *Criminal Finances Bill—Explanatory Notes to Bill brought from House of Commons*, 22 February 2017, para 13.

[82] Fourth AML Directive, recital 32.

[83] See eg Lanier Saperstein, Geoffrey Sant, and Michelle Ng, 'The Failure of Anti-Money Laundering Regulation: Where is the Cost-Benefit Analysis?' (2015) 91 Notre Dame Law Review Online 1; cf Michael Levi, 'Money for Crime and Money from Crime: Financing Crime and Laundering Crime Proceeds' (2015) 21 European Journal of Criminal Policy Research 275.

to necessitate a widening of the circle of complicity, as corrupt PEPs are forced to enlist the services of more tenuously connected individuals to facilitate the commission of offences.

To the extent that a trend can be discerned between the definitions of PEPs under the AML Regulations and the proceeds of crime legislation, it seems that the definition that applies for unexplained wealth orders is, inexplicably, as expansive as possible (aside from the exclusion of domestic and EEA PEPs) whereas the AML Regulations are more limited. In circumstances where one of the specified objectives of UWOs is to address the proceeds of grand corruption,[84] given the limited cohort capable of committing the predicate crimes in that case, it would seem to make more sense to have had a more limited and nuanced definition of 'PEP' in the POCA. Within both the EU and the UK, aside from consultation responses, no public discussion took place when the relevant provisions were being passed into law on who or what constitutes or should constitute a PEP, the justification for those provisions, and/or the impact of the enactment of the measures affecting *all* PEPs, their families, and their close associates. In light of this, it is worth examining the key justifications commonly forwarded for introducing laws specifically targeting PEPs.

3. Why the Focus on PEPs?

Several rationalizations have been advanced to justify the imposition of PEP-specific requirements. In considering the legitimacy of the laws on PEPs, it is useful to examine some of them critically.

Premise 1: the enormity of the impact of grand corruption justifies the imposition of special measures against PEPs.

As corruption is covert in nature, it is impossible to quantify accurately its scale or impact.[85] Estimates vary, but the IMF asserts that 'between US$1.5tn and US$2tn are paid in bribes each year',[86] whilst the US Department of Justice has

[84] See Chapter 3, Section 4.

[85] Jason Sharman notes that in addition to the covert nature of the criminal activities involved, the 'serious methodological problems in the macro- and microeconomic estimates produced' have contributed to difficulties in quantifying the scale of money laundering globally. See Sharman (n 40) 18.

[86] IMF, 'Costs and Mitigating Strategies', SDN16/05, May 2016. The IMF bases this figure on an updated extrapolation by Daniel Kaufmann, Director for Governance at the World Bank Institute, of estimates originally made in 2005, suggesting that there has been no subsequent review of the methodology or data used to reach the 2005 estimate. The original estimate was calculated by drawing on data collected from 'two different enterprise surveys: the World Bank Enterprise Survey (WBES) carried out in the year 2000 in 81 countries, and drawing on 10,033 responses from firms (WBES 2000), and on the Global Competitiveness Survey in 104 countries, drawing on 8,729 responses (Survey 2004)'. The team also used the 'results from household surveys carried out by the World Bank in the context of 16

estimated that global cross-border flow of the proceeds of crime including corruption may be valued at as much as US$2.6tn per year.[87,88] Corruption has a disproportionately corrosive effect on the poor and vulnerable.[89] It is perceived globally, regardless of nationality or income bracket of the observers, as a serious problem,[90] constituting 'one of the biggest roadblocks to effective, lasting development'.[91] With regard to corruption specifically committed by PEPs, there are no reliable data or even any estimates available quantifying the aggregate scale and impact internationally. It is possible, as Transparency International have done, to roughly estimate the sums which may have been misappropriated from public coffers upon or following the fall of individual corrupt administrations.[92] It is not however possible to put a total value on assets stolen globally by high-ranking public officials on an ongoing basis. Consequently, it is also impossible to assess quantitatively the effectiveness of corruption countermeasures aimed specifically against PEPs, either in terms of repatriation of assets or by reference to deterrence rates. We know from case studies, however, that the impact of PEP corruption on the citizens of kleptocratic states in particular can be devastating. For example, Equatorial Guinea has been governed by the rapaciously corrupt Obiang family since 1977. The country has the same GDP as many industrialized nations yet over 60 per cent of its citizens subsist on US$1 or less per day in circumstances where other countries have repeatedly investigated the origins of the assets of its ruling parties and found them to be stolen.[93] Similar trends are evident in the

different Governance and Corruption Diagnostic Surveys'. The survey results were then extrapolated across non-surveyed countries and, in finalizing the estimate, an assumption was made that the overall population engaged in bribery patterns similar to the sampled populations. See Daniel Kaufmann, 'Myths and Realities of Governance and Corruption'. Available at *SSRN 829244* (2005) app 1. In the absence of recent data, such estimates should be approached with caution.

[87] See the speech delivered by the UN Secretary-General António Guterres to the UN Security Council on 10 September 2019 <www.un.org/sg/en/content/sg/statement/2018-09-10/secretary-generals-remarks-security-council-corruption-conflict>.

[88] Tanzi acknowledges that it is not possible to measure corruption—it is possible only to measure perceptions of corruption. This is a more realistic approach in establishing a sense of the scale of the problem. See Vito Tanzi, *Corruption around the World: Causes, Consequences, Scope, and Cures* (IMF 1988) 20.

[89] See Aline Rocha Menical and others, *Why Corruption Matters: Understanding Causes, Effects and How to Address Them: Evidence Paper on Corruption* (UK Department for International Development 2015).

[90] See Transparency International's Global Corruption Barometer, available at <www.transparency.org/gcb2013>.

[91] World Bank, *Governance and the Law: World Development Report 2017* (World Bank 2017) xiii.

[92] Transparency International, *Global Corruption Report* (Transparency International 2004) 13.

[93] See Human Rights Watch, '*Manna From Heaven*'?: *How Health and Education Pay the Price for Self-Dealing in Equatorial Guinea*, June 2017 <www.hrw.org/report/2017/06/15/manna-heaven/how-health-and-education-pay-price-self-dealing-equatorial-guinea>; and Alexander Cooley, John Heathershaw, and Ricard Soares de Oliveira, 'Transnational Uncivil Society Networks: Kleptocracy's Global Fightback against Liberal Activism' (2024) 30 European Journal of International Relations 382.

economies of other states with high levels of corruption in their upper political echelons.[94] The underlying theoretical claim is that special measures for PEPs are appropriate because the impact of official corruption is significant: it 'distorts the activities of the state and ultimately takes a toll on economic growth and the quality of people's lives'.[95]

What is not clear from the policy conversations around PEPs is what kind of corruption is sought to be addressed by PEP-specific measures. Policy papers will refer to despotic leaders stripping state resources, yet then advocate for a very broad scope of who falls within the 'PEP' ambit. They tend not to distinguish between grand corruption and pettier forms of official corruption. If the intention is to target *grand* corruption, then it seems logical that resources and attention should be focused on individuals with fiscally significant functions and heads of government, and possibly on those who beneficially own assets above a particular value threshold, rather than on *all* PEPs. The categories of individuals captured by the definitions of 'politically exposed person' in the POCA and in the anti-money laundering rules are so broad as to dilute the effectiveness of the concept as originally intended, namely: to address the problem of corrupt elites. This is counterproductive because it may result in countercorruption resources being misallocated and focus diverted or distorted, thereby undermining the effectiveness of the measures.[96]

Premise 2: As PEPs are often discovered to be corrupt, a risk-based approach to oversight of PEPs' financial transactions is necessary

A risk-based approach is a policy pursuant to which:

> competent authorities and financial institutions are able to ensure that measures to prevent or mitigate money laundering and terrorist financing are commensurate to the risks identified . . . The principle is that resources should be directed in accordance with priorities so that the greatest risks receive the highest attention.[97]

The approach allows financial institutions discretion to direct oversight resources toward the areas of their business representing the greatest risk of abuse for

[94] See n 89.
[95] IMF, *Fiscal Monitor: Curbing Corruption* (IMF April 2019) 39.
[96] Opinion expressed by Hans-Peter Bauer in an interview with the author, 6 February 2020. Mr Bauer was present at the earliest meetings of the Wolfsberg Group in 2000 in his capacity of Head of Global Compliance for the Swiss bank, UBS AG.
[97] FATF, *Guidance on the Risk-Based Approach to Combating Money Laundering and Terrorist Finance* (FATF 2007) 6.

criminal purposes, rather than using more prescriptive 'rules-based' approaches which fail to differentiate between different levels of risk.[98] The EU's anti-money laundering rules direct regulators to adopt risk-based approaches in devising policies and measures to address money laundering.[99] Such approaches are endorsed by FATF.[100] Their general adoption has not however triggered a shift away from the blanket imposition of PEP provisions in the international anti-money laundering recommendations. FATF, for example, continues to specify that 'foreign PEPs are always high risk'.[101] This implies that *all* business transactions undertaken by *all* foreign PEPs should continue to be subject to the most rigorous due diligence standards when opening bank accounts or using those accounts.

The definitions of 'PEP' as provided for under the UK's anti-money laundering regulations and its proceeds of crime laws each fail to take a risk-based approach because they fail to distinguish between public officials who are de facto capable of diverting large amounts of money or who are significantly influential in the allocation of public resources, on the one hand, and all other senior public officials on the other. Even Wolfsberg, which, as far as the author can tell, was largely responsible for broadening the scope of PEP provisions by recommending the imposition of measures on the families and associates of PEPs is on record as:

> disagree[ing] with the assertion that all PEPs (whether foreign or domestic) are high risk and note that even PEPs presenting increased risks may not create a high risk relationship if the products and services are inherently low risk.[102]

A more coherent and targeted risk-based approach could, without limitation, be revised to:

(i) focus on the *actual* functions of the individual PEP in acting on behalf of the state rather than operating on an assumption that *all* PEPs are worthy of scrutiny; and/or
(ii) focus primarily on the risk profile of transaction types which might raise red flags including, for example, transactions routed through several

[98] cf Petrus C van Duyne, Jackie Harvey, and Liliya Gelemerova. 'A "Risky" Risk Approach: Proportionality in ML/TF Regulation' in Colin King, Clive Walker, and Jimmy Gurulé (eds), *The Palgrave Handbook of Criminal and Terrorism Financing Law* (Palgrave Macmillan 2018) 345.
[99] The Fourth AML Directive, arts 2(9) and 4(1).
[100] FATF (n 97).
[101] FATF, *Politically Exposed Persons (Recommendations 12 and 22)* (FATF 2013) 5.
[102] See Wolfsberg Group's response to the consultation on revised FATF Recommendations dated 6 January 2011, s 3 <www.wolfsberg-principles.com/sites/default/files/wb/pdfs/comment-letters/22.%20Wolfsberg_Group_Comment_Letter_on_FATF_Consultation_Paper_Jan-6th-2011_unsigned.pdf>.

jurisdictions for no apparent reason, transactions involving large sums flowing from state-owned accounts to private accounts,[103] and transactions in particularly risky business sectors or involving jurisdictions with poor AML records;[104] and/or

(iii) impose PEP-specific provisions on particular individuals subject to a threshold being applied in relation to a minimum value of assets beneficially owned by a PEP or by reference to the value of sums passing through that PEP's accounts; and/or

(iv) to the extent that a PEP is subject to income and asset declaration requirements, target transactions apparently inconsistent with such mandated declarations.[105]

The Financial Conduct Authority (FCA) has recently published a series of criteria for consideration in risk-based analysis as part of a public consultation on the approach of financial institutions to PEPs. These are discussed further in the next chapter.[106]

Premise 3: All PEPs are capable of corruption.

StAR has stated that:

> Obviously, most PEPs do not actually engage in corrupt activities; however, all PEPs are potentially in a position to misuse their positions for personal gain—no matter their country of origin, nature of business activities, or seniority of position.[107]

The suggestion that *all PEPs* are able to misuse their positions to commit corrupt acts is manifestly incorrect. The ability of a PEP to commit grand corruption

[103] For a list of red-flag transaction proposals, see Anton De Klerk, 'The Importance and Relevance of Financial Institutions Doing Business with Politically Exposed Persons in the Global Fight against Money Laundering' (2007) Journal of South African Law 368, 379. Industry groups have also identified specifically low risk transaction types; for example, Eurofinas notes that the risk profile for consumer loans is inherently low, even where they are made to PEPs. See EuroFinas, 'Response to the FATF's Second Public Consultation on the Review of the Standards—Preparation for the 4th Round of Mutual Evaluation' September 2011.

[104] Sungyong Kang, 'Rethinking the Global Anti-Money Laundering Regulations to Deter Corruption' (2018) 67 International and Comparative Law Quarterly 695, 700.

[105] cf Ruta Mrazauskaite and Matthew C Stephenson, 'A Proposal for a Global Database of Politically Exposed Persons' (2020) 56 Stanford Journal of International Law 153.

[106] See Chapter 3, n 108ff and accompanying text.

[107] Theodore S Greenberg and others, *Politically Exposed Persons: A Guide on Preventive Measures for the Banking Sector* (World Bank 2010) 3.

offences is contingent on, amongst other factors, having the capability or influence necessary to access or divert significant public resources. Assuming that, to take an example of a category of PEP from the EU's anti-money laundering rules, all members of national parliaments have such powers or abilities is to fundamentally misunderstand the levels of power and influence that the majority of such individuals hold. By contrast, those holding administrative roles (but not necessarily overtly 'political' roles) including, for example, senior civil servants responsible for advising on who should be awarded licences to exploit natural resources, may be well placed to commit large-scale embezzlement and/or receive significant bribes from multinationals. Like StAR, Transparency International UK asserts that '[PEPs] have access to state money and government contracts and are therefore deemed to pose a potential corruption and money laundering risk'.[108] However, just because public office *might* afford certain individuals power and access, it does not logically follow that measures should therefore automatically be targeted against all PEPs. The scope of access to public resources or opportunity for misappropriation will vary from public official to public official, depending on their role. Sweepingly characterizing foreign PEPs as having a propensity for corruption is also unhelpful. The EU's anti-money laundering laws and the FATF Recommendations each expressly discourage banks from refusing banking services to PEPs simply because they are PEPs.[109] Anecdotally, however, there is evidence that PEPs risk being debanked or wholly unbanked as a result of their status.[110]

A more pragmatic response to imposing PEP-specific rules on a blanket basis would involve states clearly delimiting the functions and powers of categories of state employees, officials, and representatives. Application of PEP-specific measures could then be limited to those (i) directly responsible for public spending and procurement; and/or (ii) who realistically can use their influence and power to direct the transfer or allocation of public resources.

[108] Transparency International UK and Thomson Reuters, *London Property: A Top Destination for Money Launderers* (Transparency International UK and Thomson Reuters December 2016).

[109] Recital 33 of the Fourth AML Directive provides: 'Refusing a business relationship with a person simply on the basis of the determination that he or she is a politically exposed person is contrary to the letter and spirit of this Directive and of the revised FATF Recommendations.'

[110] HL Deb 14 October 2014, vol 756, cols 114–15. More recently, the English politician Nigel Farage alleged that Coutts Bank had closed his account as a result of his PEP status. See Siddharth Venkataramakrishnan, 'FCA Begins Probe into Banks and "Politically Exposed Persons" Rules' *Financial Times* (London, 14 August 2023).

Premise 4: By including PEPs in a specific risk category, it is easier to detect their crimes.

FATF suggested in 2011 that a distinct risk category was necessary for PEPs to aid detection of corruption:[111]

> [T]he stolen assets of a corrupt public official are useless unless they are placed, layered, and integrated into the global financial network in a manner that does not raise suspicion. In some ways, a [PEP] who gathers vast sums of money through corrupt means is far more vulnerable than some other criminals. A narcotics trafficker may reliably depend on being able to remain anonymous . . . a public official begins to draw unwanted attention as soon as he is associated with significant sums from unknown sources. Thus, the corrupt PEP's vulnerability presents an opportunity for those authorities engaged in both anti-money laundering/combating the financing of terrorism (AML/CFT) and anti-corruption (AC) enforcement.[112]

FATF implies that scope for detecting corrupt activity by PEPs is increased within the banking sector in circumstances where a bank is on notice that its customer is a PEP (and therefore, in theory at least, is more susceptible to graft). The theory is that in such circumstances, a bank will be better placed to recognize large transactions involving unknown sources or destinations as suspicious and report such transactions to enforcement authorities. Why policy-makers have chosen to focus on PEPs on that basis, but not impose similar requirements on other graft-susceptible parties whose potential malfeasance (whether as bribees or embezzlers) would have implications for public institutions (eg senior officials of non-publicly owned banks of systemic importance to the integrity of a country's economy,[113] or arbitrators enlisted to determine disputes around high-value public procurement contracts) shows inconsistency in applying anti-corruption measures. Furthermore, a 'true' risk-based approach would ensure that red flags are raised whenever *anyone* is associated with significant sums from unknown or suspicious sources. A relatively recent investigation by the FCA involving Barclays and Qatari PEPs demonstrated that if the financial incentives are sufficiently appealing, it can be a reasonably straightforward matter for bank officials to override PEP identification requirements.[114] This further undermines the argument in favour of PEP-focused measures.

[111] Prior to publishing the report cited at n 112, FATF had done little to explain the nexus between corruption and money laundering, and how implementing the FATF Recommendations would operate to combat corruption. See Rose (n 34) 189.

[112] FATF, *Laundering the Proceeds of Corruption* (FATF 2011) 6.

[113] Note eg the Bank of New York employees who were paid US$1.8m by Russian mobsters to launder US$7bn. See Chaikin and Sharman (n 66) 76.

[114] See FCA, *Final Notice to Barclays Bank plc*, 25 November 2015.

Premise 5: PEPs are the source of legal and reputational damage to financial institutions.

Some anti-corruption commentators suggest that corruption scandals expose financial institutions (and by extension, the integrity of a country's banking infrastructure) to reputational risk:

> Past scandals illustrate that financial institutions put themselves at high risk in reputation terms if they are misused by so-called 'potentates' to hide the bounty of 'graft' (be it the product of theft, embezzlement, fraud, corruption or other forms of misappropriation and abuse of their position).[115]

Other commentators have however disputed the idea that banks suffer damage following corruption scandals. Jason Sharman has noted that:

> there are few major financial institutions that have not been hit with a serious money-laundering scandal. Yet, in nearly every case, there seems to be little, if any, evidence of reputational damage beyond some transitory embarrassment.[116]

He notes that AML deficiencies apparently do not feed into private third-party assessments when new customers are choosing their banks, and that regulators tend to pull their punches in imposing sanctions, wishing to avoid crises of confidence in the banking sector, given their mandates to stabilize and safeguard financial systems.[117] The absence of economic impact is also clear from a survey of share prices of banks who have had significant fines levied against them. Table 2.1 below shows the market closing share prices on the London Stock Exchange of certain banks immediately before, at close of business on, a few days following, and four weeks following the issuance of, decision notices by the FCA, in each case imposing significant fines on the banks for anti-money laundering failings.[118] The data suggest that the markets are either oblivious to the fines or do not believe that those failings (and the attendant reputational fallout, if any) will adversely impact upon the profitability of the financial institutions in question, with share prices sometimes actually *increasing* in the aftermath of the issuance of some FCA decision notices.

[115] Mark Pieth and Gemma Aiolfi, *A Comparative Guide to Anti-Money Laundering* (Edward Elgar 2004) 32.

[116] Sharman (n 40) 50.

[117] Sharman (n 40) 50.

[118] Source London Stock Exchange <www.londonstockexchange.com>. Note that in the case of Deutsche Bank, no share price was available for the day of the FCA notice, and so the share price for the following day (31 January 2017) is included instead. A further bank, Santander UK plc, was subject to a significant FCA fine for money-laundering failings in December 2022 but does not trade ordinary shares on the London Stock Exchange so a like-for-like comparison is not possible.

Table 2.1 Impact of FCA fines on banks' share prices

Financial institution	Share price before FCA notice	Share price on date of FCA notice	Share price following FCA notice	Share price 4 weeks post-FCA notice
HSBC (HSBA)	13 December 2021: 421.25	14 December 2021: 424.57	15 December 2021: 422.22	12 January 2022: 489.52
Standard Chartered (STAN)	4 February 2019: 621.3	5 February 2019: 634.8	6 February 2019: 639.3	5 March 2019: 633.1
Deutsche Bank AG (0H7D)	27 January 2017: 16.65	31 January 2017: 16.71	1 February 2017: 17.02	27 February 2017: 16.37
Barclays (BARC)	23 November 2015: 219.2	25 November 2015: 220.2	1 December 2015: 223.8	22 December 2015: 217.7

Drawing conclusions from the above data should be approached with caution, because additional external factors may also impact on the share price, and it should be noted that where there is information available in advance regarding the expected fine or settlement amount, this may soften the consequences for the share price on the date on which the penalty is imposed. Even so, a sample of London Stock Exchange's share prices of a competitor bank, NatWest Group Limited, which was not subject to scandalous headlines on the same dates as those outlined above, followed similar share price trajectories as the prices for each of the banks referenced above. The data thus allow us to broadly determine that the imposition of fines for anti-money laundering non-compliance is hardly disastrous in terms of the impact on banks' share prices.

The 'retirement' of Riggs Bank in 2005 following a number of high-profile scandals, including the concealment of the assets of the former dictator of Chile, Augusto Pinochet, and the facilitation of embezzlement of oil revenues from Equatorial Guinea,[119] is sometimes held out as a salutary case study demonstrating that banks need to ensure PEP requirements are met to protect their financial well-being and, indeed, their existence.[120] Based in Washington DC, a significant part of its business was comprised of providing banking services to the diplomatic corps and politicians. It was the personal bank for twenty-one US presidents.[121] In other words, because of the diplomatically sensitive profile of much of the bank's

[119] Terence O'Hara, 'For Riggs Customers, an Uneven Transaction' *Washington Post* (Washington DC, 14 May 2005).

[120] Notably the case study cited at n 122, and see also eg Robert E Williams Jr, 'From Malabo to Malibu: Addressing Corruption and Human Rights Abuse in an African Petrostate' (2011) 33 Human Rights Quarterly 620; and John T McCormick and Nancy Paterson, 'The Threat Posed by Transnational Political Corruption to Global Commercial and Development Banking' (2006) 13 Journal of Financial Crime 183.

[121] Paul Lashmar, 'The Bank that Liked to Say Yes to the Dirty Cash of Third World Dictators' *Independent on Sunday* (London, 22 August 2004) Business, 3.

clientele, it was unsurprising that many of its clients swiftly withdrew their business from the bank when scandal hit. However, the Riggs experience is an exceptional case, especially because its client profile was atypical. Furthermore, the bank's provision of services to autocrats was not exposed as part of any regulatory AML process. Instead, it was revealed because of an investigation by a non-governmental organization, Global Witness, who asked the US Senate Permanent Subcommittee on investigations to look into rumours circulating about the mis-use of the bank's services.[122] Consequently, it cannot be said that the anti-money laundering regime insofar as it focuses on PEPs was in any way helpful in exposing Riggs' dubious practices. This widely cited instance of the damage inflicted by corrupt PEPs on banks is therefore a bad example. On close scrutiny, arguments that the imposition of requirements relating to PEPs will help banks avoid reputational, legal, and/or business risks are unconvincing.

Premise 6: PEPs own a lot of expensive property in London through offshore companies. There are concerns about the proceeds of foreign official corruption flooding the London property market. Therefore, the PEPs who own property in London may be corrupt.

In attempting to establish an empirical basis for claims of money laundering committed by PEPs in the UK property market, Transparency International UK and Thomson Reuters undertook a study of interests held by overseas companies in titles to London properties registered at the Land Registry. The authors were able to establish that just over 2 per cent of these properties were owned by overseas companies linked to PEPs or persons closely related to them.[123] They went on to note that '[o]ver half the land titles connected to PEPs are owned by companies based in secrecy jurisdictions, which are also typically used in money laundering schemes'.[124] To conclude that any PEP owning property in London might therefore be a money launderer is to stretch logic. So-called secrecy jurisdictions are used by money launderers, but interests in offshore-registered companies, based on leaks from a single Panamanian corporate service provider, are also owned by six members of the House of Lords and three MPs, none of whom were subsequently

[122] US Senate Minority Staff of the Permanent Subcommittee on Investigations, *Money Laundering and Foreign Corruption: Enforcement and Effectiveness of the Patriot Act: Case Study Involving Riggs Bank* (Washington DC 2004) 15.

[123] See Transparency International UK and Thomson Reuters (n 108) 5. This represented a total of 986 London properties. The authors noted that owing to gaps in the available data (with almost 50 per cent of the 44,022 properties identified as being owned by companies registered in countries where the company beneficial ownership is not publicly available), the true ownership of properties owned by PEPs is 'likely to be much higher'.

[124] See n 108.

charged with money-laundering offences.[125] There are a number of legal, if not wholly legitimate, reasons why an individual may wish to own properties via secrecy jurisdictions including, without limitation, for legal tax avoidance and estate planning purposes.[126] Even if we accept an argument that PEPs owning interests in offshore companies should raise suspicion, it is not clear that PEPs should be distinguished from all other individuals in making this proposition.

4. Conclusion

From the term's first use by the BCBS to the work of the banking industry in directing the focus in corruption discourse on the actions of PEPs, the evolution of the use of 'politically exposed persons' in the law has been largely led by organizations with expertise in finance, rather than expertise and a primary interest in tackling financial crime. The untransparent and unrepresentative character of FATF, and the lack of parliamentary discussion and scrutiny on the concept of the PEP at EU and domestic level have each been highlighted above. Based on the discussion above of six common justifications for PEP-specific measures, there is clearly some incoherence in the rationales underpinning their establishment. From the analysis in this chapter, a trend of input legitimacy deficit is evident in the historical development of corruption countermeasures addressed directly at PEPs. This conclusion is based, amongst other matters, on the lack of discussion, attention, and consistency of approach given in developing the concept of 'PEP' in the law and on the limited legitimacy of the norm-setters responsible for the introduction of PEP-specific measures. Whilst a limited focus on high-level PEPs may be justified, the contention that the 'PEP' concept is over-diluted seems sound. It is against this background that the question is raised as to whether UWOs against PEPs might be the product of a moral panic in response to the amplification of corruption-related events in society, rather as a response to an actual widespread and identifiable harm. The question is considered in Chapter 4.

[125] While holding offshore accounts is not illegal as a matter of UK law, it does raise a suspicion of potential tax avoidance or evasion. See Luke Harding, 'What Are the Panama Papers?' *The Guardian* (London, 6 April 2016) 3.

[126] See further Chapter 7, n 97 and accompanying text.

3

Responding to Grand Corruption

Unexplained Wealth Orders

1. Introduction

The focus of this chapter is on civil recovery of corruptly acquired assets in general, and on the unexplained wealth order (UWO) in particular. The nature and purpose of the order as a tool to recover the proceeds of grand corruption, its place within the proceeds of crime framework, and how it was intended to work in practice are each considered. Drawing primarily on doctrinal analysis, the discussion of civil recovery and UWOs including this Introduction comprises five sections. The second outlines the proceeds of crime regime in England and Wales. Key criticisms made of civil recovery are highlighted as part of this discussion. The third explains how the UWO is used within the proceeds of crime regime and critiques the statutory tests to be satisfied by enforcement authorities applying for the orders in the High Court. The fourth part identifies and assesses the legislative aims underlying the orders' inception by reference to contemporaneous Home Office policy documentation and parliamentary debates. The final substantive section evaluates the operation of the UWO in practice and queries the likely effectiveness of the mechanism, in the case of PEPs at least, in the longer term in meeting the statutory objectives underpinning its introduction.

Placing the PEP-specific UWO in context in this chapter informs analysis in the second half of this work on the limitations and potential of other legal routes to tackling grand corruption. It contributes to a wider conversation throughout this work on the legitimacy of anti-corruption measures from rights and procedural fairness perspectives and the efficacy of available asset recovery tools in dealing with the fruits of grand corruption. It asks whether, considering the conclusions drawn, some alternative approaches might be preferable for achieving similar ends. UWOs are helpful as a means of demonstrating the tensions which Herbert Packer identified in his classic work on the criminal process.[1] In this analysis, Packer proposed two models as a device to demonstrate the 'normative antinomy at the heart

[1] Herbert Packer, *The Limits of the Criminal Sanction* (Stanford University Press 1968). The 'criminal process', wrote Packer, is a 'compendious term that stands for all the complexes of activity that operate to bring the substantive claw of crime to bear (or to keep it from coming to bear) on persons who are suspected of having committed crimes', at 149.

Unexplained Wealth Orders and the UK's Anti-Corruption Regime. Áine Clancy, Oxford University Press.
 DOI: 10.1093/9780198907312.003.0004

of the criminal law'.[2] He dichotomized the criminal process into, on one end of the spectrum, a Due Process Model which privileges an accused's procedural rights and a rigorous adjudication as to culpability at trial over the greater efficiencies afforded by its inverse: the Crime Control Model. The latter emphasizes speed and finality within the criminal process and prefers informal 'administrative' means to reach a point at which sanctions can be imposed. The Crime Control Model is founded on a consequentialist idea that to maintain human freedoms by avoiding the breakdown of public order, 'the repression of criminal conduct is by far the most important function to be performed by the criminal process'.[3] It assumes that the preliminary screening processes adopted by enforcement authorities and prosecutors are reliable indicators of probable guilt, and that once those early stages are complete, the remaining criminal process should be relatively perfunctory.[4] Packer's model has been used in evaluations of non-conviction-based confiscation processes other than UWOs.[5] Liz Campbell has summarized the grounds on which critics have deservedly attacked Packer's thesis, but notes that it is 'heuristically valuable as an empirical tool'.[6] Packer's work provides a loose theoretical basis around which to consider the matters discussed in this chapter.

2. Asset Recovery in the United Kingdom

The Proceeds of Crime Act 2002 (POCA) sets out the legislative framework for asset recovery in the UK. The measures provided for thereunder can be broadly categorized into four separate processes. First, enforcement authorities can seek confiscation of assets from someone who has been convicted of a crime. Claims for conviction-based confiscation (hereafter 'confiscation') can be based on allegations either that the defendant has benefited from a specified predicate offence[7] or that the defendant has benefited from conduct forming part of a course of criminal activity.[8] Confiscation of UK-based assets following a criminal conviction in the context of overseas grand corruption is rare, for reasons which will be discussed in Chapter 5. Second, where enforcement authorities discover cash during the course of an investigation which they reasonably suspect represents the proceeds of crime or is intended for use in unlawful conduct, this cash can be seized and detained, subject to an order being made by a magistrate (or a sheriff in Scotland).[9]

[2] Packer (n 1) 153.
[3] Packer (n 1) 158.
[4] Packer (n 1) 160–61.
[5] Liz Campbell, 'Theorising Asset Forfeiture in Ireland' (2007) 71 Journal of Criminal Law 441, 447.
[6] Campbell (n 5) 455.
[7] As specified in sch 2 of the POCA. The relevant predicate offences include money-laundering offences.
[8] POCA, s 75.
[9] POCA, s 294.

Such sums can be forfeited subsequently without the need for a court-issued forfeiture order or a related criminal conviction provided that at least thirty days are first given to anyone who might be affected by a potential forfeiture and that period elapses without challenge.[10] There are similar powers available to allow for forfeiture of art, jewellery and watches,[11] crypto assets,[12] cash held in bank accounts,[13] and various other valuable goods.[14] In each case, the magistrates' court (or the sheriff in Scotland) must be satisfied on the balance of probabilities that the relevant assets represent recoverable property or are intended for use in unlawful conduct. Third, the POCA empowers the National Crime Agency (NCA) to exercise tax investigation powers and raise tax invoices in circumstances where 'chargeable gains' or other tax liabilities are suspected of having accrued as a result of criminal conduct.[15] The fourth and most potentially potent of all of the POCA powers in the context of the fruits of overseas corruption are those of civil recovery. Civil recovery orders allowing assets to be permanently seized without a prior criminal conviction are issued by the High Court where an enforcement authority proves on the balance of probabilities that those assets represent the proceeds of unlawful conduct.[16] UWOs were introduced specifically with the intention of facilitating enforcement authorities to obtain civil recovery orders against wealth which they suspect constitutes the proceeds of crime. To understand better the operation of UWOs in context, it is necessary first to appreciate how asset recovery powers in the UK have evolved over the past five decades.

The parliamentary approach to the development of asset recovery powers in the UK over the past half century is characterized by a philosophy of 'more is more'. This period has seen progressive expansion of both the categories of individual against whom the powers can be used, and the powers themselves.[17] The introduction of each new statutory power has tended to follow a court's refusal of recovery or confiscation on the basis that no power existed either at common law or in statute allowing for asset recovery under the circumstances.[18] The UK's

[10] POCA, s 297C(3)—provided a period of notice provided to parties with a potential interest in the cash has first elapsed without challenge.

[11] POCA, ch 3A.

[12] POCA, ch 3E.

[13] POCA, ch 3B.

[14] Other types of listed assets provided for in ch 3A of the POCA which may be subject to forfeiture include postage stamp collections and vouchers.

[15] POCA, pt 6. It is not intended to discuss tax powers in detail in this volume. For more on the taxation recovery powers under the POCA, see Peter Alldridge, 'Proceeds of Crime Since 2003—Two Key Areas' [2014] Criminal Law Review 171. On state powers to seize the suspected proceeds of crime, see generally Peter Alldridge, *Money Laundering Law: Forfeiture, Confiscation, Civil Recovery, Criminal Laundering and Taxation of the Proceeds of Crime* (Hart 2003) (*Money Laundering Law*).

[16] POCA, s 241. Cash forfeiture orders can also be made where the magistrates' court or sheriff is satisfied on the balance of probabilities that the cash the subject of an order is intended for use in unlawful conduct.

[17] See Chapter 6, Section 8.

[18] See Table 3.1.

confiscation regime was first introduced under the Drug Trafficking Offences Act 1986, for example, as a response to the House of Lords decision in the Operation Julie case.[19] In that case, the House of Lords reluctantly held that no forfeiture powers existed to allow enforcement authorities to seize £750,000 representing the proceeds of drug trafficking because the defendants were convicted of offences other than those provided for under the Misuse of Drugs Act 1971.[20] The powers allowing post-conviction confiscation of the proceeds of drugs crimes introduced in the Drug Trafficking Offences Act 1986 were later expanded pursuant to the Criminal Justice Act 1988 to allow for confiscation of the proceeds of various non-drugs offences. The requirements of the latter were later loosened in turn to provide that the question of whether a defendant had benefited from criminal conduct could be decided using the civil, rather than the criminal, standard of proof.[21]

Notwithstanding the significant expansion of asset recovery powers in the 1980s, Parliament's belief that insufficient recovery of criminal proceeds was being made resulted in the further widening of powers throughout the 1990s. This is illustrated by Table 3.1 below, which sets out the progressive removal of legal barriers to recovery of the suspected proceeds of crime. The most notable of these developments was the introduction of so-called 'lifestyle provisions', which allow the Crown Court to make assumptions about the origins of a convicted defendant's assets provided certain criteria are met.[22] These provisions in some circumstances *require* the Crown Court to assume that any assets obtained by a convicted defendant in the six years preceding that defendant's indictment represent the proceeds of the defendant's general criminal conduct.[23] The Crown Court's rulings on whether a defendant has a criminal lifestyle and on whether they have benefited from their criminal conduct are determined on the balance of probabilities.[24]

[19] Proceeds of Crime Act 2002 Explanatory Notes, para 3.

[20] *R v Cuthbertson* [1981] AC 470. Had the defendants been convicted of offences provided for under the Misuse of Drugs Act 1971, s 27 of that Act would have allowed for forfeiture of assets 'related to the offences'.

[21] s 71(7A) of the Criminal Justice Act 1988, as inserted by the Criminal Justice Act 1993, s 27 and now provided for pursuant to s 6(7) of the POCA.

[22] For discussion, see ch 7 of *Money Laundering Law* (n 15).

[23] What constitutes a 'criminal lifestyle' is set out in s 75 of the POCA. The criteria to be satisfied leading to the Crown Court being required to order confiscation are set out in s 6. The Crown Court is in some cases required to make confiscation orders either where a defendant has been convicted of one of the many offences listed under sch 2 of the POCA, which includes a wide range of offences including money-laundering offences under ss 328 and 329 of the POCA; drug, arms, and/or people trafficking; counterfeiting and intellectual property offences; and inchoate offences relating to any of those crimes. It must also make confiscation orders where a defendant has been convicted of an offence committed over the course of six months, or where the defendant has been convicted more than twice in the preceding six years.

[24] POCA, s 10. These assumptions can be defeated if the defendant shows otherwise or 'there would be a serious risk of injustice if [an] assumption were made'.

Table 3.1 Laws removing barriers to asset recovery

Issue	Identified in	Resulting legislation
No power to confiscate the proceeds of drugs trafficking	*R v Cuthbertson* [1981] AC 470	Drug Trafficking Offences Act 1986 introduced confiscation
Power to confiscate the proceeds of drug trafficking—but not other crimes		Criminal Justice Act 1998 expanded the range of applicable crimes
Power to confiscate the proceeds of crime—but must be proven to a criminal standard that the defendant has benefited	*R v Dickens* [1990] 2 QB 102	Criminal Justice Act 1993 changed the applicable standard to the civil standard
Power to confiscate the proceeds of crime—but the prosecution must prove to a civil standard that the defendant's assets obtained in the preceding six years are obtained through criminal conduct Confiscation considered only at the discretion of the court		Proceeds of Crime Act 1995 placed the burden on the defendant of *disproving* that their assets represent the proceeds of crime It also imposes an obligation on the court to consider confiscation where the prosecutor considers it necessary or desirable
No power to recover assets without a conviction		POCA, Part 5 introduced non-conviction-based asset recovery (ie civil recovery)
Insufficient powers to establish to a civil standard that assets are 'recoverable property'		POCA, Part 8 provided for new powers including powers for enforcement authorities to apply for production orders, disclosure orders, and search and seizure warrants
No proprietary remedies against overseas respondents to disclosure orders	*R v Perry* [2008] UKSC 35	Criminal Finances Act 2017—UWOs
No power to recover unexplained wealth, without some link to criminality, where property is held by PEPs	*R (Director of the ARA) v Green* [2005] EWHC 3168 (Admin)	Criminal Finances Act 2017—UWOs (insofar as they apply to PEPs)

The POCA expanded investigative and judicial powers to allow for recovery where no conviction had been secured in respect of an alleged crime in spite of concerns expressed by criminal law experts about the prospect of using non-conviction-based forfeiture to circumvent criminal procedural protections.[25] Mirroring a cycle evident in the development of confiscation powers, civil recovery powers were ushered in as a corrective following judicial decisions which confirmed that 'there is no statutory power to confiscate the proceeds of [crime] within the United Kingdom where the person entitled to possession of the money is not convicted of . . . [an] offence'.[26]

Whilst forfeiture and confiscation each existed in various forms prior to the 2002 Act, civil recovery was introduced as a novel concept in the POCA.[27] No prior conviction is necessary to trigger a cause of action in civil recovery. Instead, it is sufficient for the applicant authority to establish on the balance of probabilities to the High Court that an asset represents the proceeds of crime.[28] The High Court must make a civil recovery order in respect of any property that it is satisfied constitutes recoverable property.[29] By removing criminal conviction as a pre-condition to the permanent seizure of property, the introduction of civil recovery marked a shift towards the Crime Control Model end of Packer's spectrum as far as asset recovery was concerned, as it moved proceeds of crime matters away from the Crown Court and the protections accruing to criminal defendants.[30] Unlike confiscation, which is a value-based remedy, civil recovery proceedings operate *in rem*; that is, civil recovery operates as a proprietary remedy, with (in theory, at least) a focus on the criminal origin of an asset rather than the holder of that asset,[31] albeit the asset holder will be the named respondent in proceedings.

Notwithstanding the populist appeal of the 'tough on crime' New Labour mantra preceding the introduction of the POCA,[32] there was significant scepticism on civil recovery in some quarters—most notably in the House of Lords—during the discussion of the draft legislation.[33] A majority of the House voted in favour of an amendment to the civil recovery provisions that would entitle respondents

[25] See the discussion on the Hodgson Report: Howard League for Penal Reform, *Profits of Crime and Their Recovery: Report of a Committee Chaired by Sir Derek Hodgson* (Heinemann 1984). Peter Alldridge (n 15 (2003)) 226–28 and 240; and Johan Boucht, *The Limits of Asset Confiscation: On the Legitimacy of Extended Appropriation of Criminal Proceeds* (Bloomsbury 2017) 29.

[26] May LJ in *Webb v Chief Constable of Merseyside Police* [2000] QB 427, 446 (May LJ). The series of judgments include *Webb* and *Attorney-General v Blake* [2000] UKHL 45, [2001] 1 AC 268, in the latter of which the House of Lords considered whether a former member of the British secret service who became a Soviet agent was entitled to the payment of royalties from a memoir containing material written in contravention of the Official Secrets Act 1911.

[27] See Peter Alldridge and Ann Mumford, 'Tax Evasion and the Proceeds of Crime Act 2002' (2005) 25 Legal Studies 353.

[28] POCA, s 241(3).

[29] POCA, s 266(1).

[30] This is cause for deep concern among some commentators. See eg Colin King and Jennifer Hendry, *Civil Recovery of Criminal Property* (OUP 2023).

[31] Ian Smith, Tim Owen, and Andrew Bodnar, *Asset Recovery: Criminal Confiscation and Civil Recovery* (OUP 2003) para 1.145.

[32] Jackie Harvey, 'Asset Recovery: Substantive or Symbolic?' in Colin King and Clive Walker (eds), *Dirty Assets: Emerging Issues in the Regulation of Criminal and Terrorist Assets* (Ashgate 2014) 199.

[33] See eg Proceeds of Crime Bill HL Deb 11 July 2002, cols 840–59.

through whose alleged unlawful conduct relevant property was obtained 'to have the question [of whether the respondent benefited from crime] determined in a separate trial by the Crown Court'.[34] This was proposed because the civil recovery process amounted, in the view of some peers, to a de facto adjudication on the guilt of the respondent or the respondent's associates.[35] The proposed amendment and the suggestion that the use of a civil recovery process is analogous to a criminal trial were each rejected without debate in the House of Commons.[36] However, as a concession to the Lords' concerns, the then-Attorney General (Lord Goldsmith) acknowledged that 'prosecution [would] remain the priority, and that [enforcement authorities] will pursue civil recovery or taxation only where a prosecution is not appropriate'.[37] This policy is expressly reflected in the legislation.[38] In principle, therefore, civil recovery was intended to be targeted solely at individuals suspected of benefiting from criminality, but in respect of whom a prosecution cannot feasibly proceed whether for lack of evidence, on grounds of impossibility (eg where a suspect absconds or dies), or where the 'public interest [would] be better served' by pursuing civil recovery.[39]

Civil recovery was made available with the intention of disrupting the activities of organized crime groups by targeting their leaders, who, whilst directing crimes, were often thought to act at a remove from the actual commission of offences and were therefore less liable to prosecution.[40] This assumption has been criticized as 'plainly spurious' and based on the contemporaneous policy discourse's 'false conception of "organized crime" groups' as formal and rigid power structures.[41] Commentators have questioned the general efficacy of the asset recovery regime in the UK as a means of crime reduction or disruption, highlighting the lack of robust empirical evidence of its impact.[42] Others have noted that, in

[34] Proceeds of Crime Bill HL Deb 11 July 2002, col 858.

[35] Which provides: 'nor will [we] proceed against or prosecute any free man save by the lawful judgment of his peers'—quoted by Lord Lloyd of Berwick, Proceeds of Crime HL Deb 25 June 2002, col 1265. He went on to describe the 'distinction between a conviction and a finding of guilt by the High Court judge [in a civil recovery matter as] simply illusory'.

[36] Proceeds of Crime Bill HL Deb 22 July 2002, cols 57–70.

[37] Proceeds of Crime Bill HL Deb 22 July 2002, col 58.

[38] POCA, s 2A(4): '[Guidance to enforcement authorities] must indicate that the reduction of crime is in general best secured by means of criminal investigations and criminal proceedings'.

[39] Attorney General's Office, *Guidance—Asset Recovery Powers for Prosecutors: Guidance and Background Note 2009*, published 29 November 2012 <www.gov.uk/guidance/asset-recovery-powers-for-prosecutors-guidance-and-background-note-2009>.

[40] Home Office, *One Step Ahead: A 21st Century Strategy to Defeat Organised Crime* (Stationery Office 2004). See also Boucht (n 25) 73.

[41] Karen Bullock and David Lister, 'Post-Conviction Confiscation of Assets in England and Wales: Rhetoric and Reality' in Colin King and Clive Walker (eds), *Dirty Assets: Emerging Issues in the Regulation of Criminal and Terrorist Assets* (Ashgate 2014) 47, 58.

[42] For a survey of the views of a number of commentators, see Julia Chistyakova, David S Wall, and Stefano Bonino, 'The Back-Door Governance of Crime: Confiscating Criminal Assets in the UK' (2021) 27 European Journal on Criminal Policy and Research 495, 496–97.

practical terms, rather than the 'significant revenue flows' for the Treasury envisaged as the product of the civil recovery regime,[43] recovery has been limited and has tended to focus on lower-level criminals rather than the 'kingpins' whose apparent impunity the POCA sought to address.[44] From a jurisprudential perspective, commentators and the courts alike have observed that the rules governing asset recovery under the POCA are inflexible, offering little discretion for judicial responses tailored to specific circumstances, particularly in comparison with other countries' schemes.[45] There was no parliamentary discussion on how civil recovery might be used to recover the proceeds of grand corruption when it was first introduced. With the benefit of hindsight, some assumptions on the corrupt overseas activities of foreign PEPs map neatly onto the perceived criminal activities of the kingpins that civil recovery was introduced to target. Like some corrupt PEPs, organized crime gang leaders are assumed to 'organize or finance the criminal activity of others and profit from the results but remain at a remove from the actual commission of particular crimes', making prosecution difficult or impossible.[46]

Four criticisms made by commentators of civil recovery are especially noteworthy on a liberal rights analysis. First, in civil recovery processes, it is suggested that respondents typically face state-made claims that they are 'other than innocent' without the mediating effect of criminal procedural guarantees.[47] It is questionable whether the public at large appreciates to any sophisticated degree the differences in a respondent to a proceeds of crime process and a criminal defendant, but the nomenclature of the process (the proceeds of crime) and its enforcement machinery (enforcement by criminal law enforcement authorities) risks incorrectly and unfairly depicting civil recovery respondents as suspected criminals in the eyes of the public.[48] Second, the evidential threshold that enforcement authorities

[43] Karen Bullock, 'Criminal Benefit, the Confiscation Order and the Post-Conviction Confiscation Regime' (2014) 62 Crime, Law and Social Change 45, 47, citing a 2000 report from the Cabinet Office's Performance and Innovation Unit.

[44] Harvey (n 32) 200–01; Bullock and Lister (n 41); and King and Hendry (n 30) 52.

[45] See Boucht (n 25) fn 108. He notes in particular Lord Walker's comments in *R v Waya*, where it was observed that '[m]any of the complexities and difficulties of confiscation cases, arising from the extremely involved statutory language, would undoubtedly be avoided if a measure of discretion were restored' [2012] UKSC 51, 54.

[46] King and Hendry (n 30) 51.

[47] Liz Campbell, 'Criminal Labels, the European Convention on Human Rights and the Presumption of Innocence' (2013) 76 Modern Law Review 681.

[48] See Liz Campbell and Áine Clancy, 'The Principled and Practical Limits to Unexplained Wealth Orders' (2024) 52(1) University of Western Australia Law Review 29.

must meet to establish that property is 'recoverable property' and therefore ought to be subject to permanent seizure is low in a civil recovery context. Property is recoverable if it is established to a civil standard that it was obtained through unlawful conduct.[49] No 'link to any concrete criminal conduct' is required—which, Johan Boucht notes, 'means that the contextual assumption of the provenance of the assets in question may itself be weak'.[50] The fact that the state is not required to establish that a crime has been committed before expropriating assets from individuals on the basis that those assets represent the proceeds of crime is viewed by some as excessively draconian.[51] Third, everyone who engages with civil recovery is expected to conspire in the fiction that no adjudication of criminality is being made, yet simultaneously and paradoxically accept that assets are being 'recovered' by way of a court order because they represent the proceeds of crime. The idea is that the illicit origin of the asset is a matter entirely apart from the question of the possessor's (or the possessor's associates') culpability (or lack thereof) in acquiring the asset. Ostensibly, it is the property that is tainted with criminality rather than its possessor.[52] This proposition has been met with understandable incredulity by some judges and commentators.[53] Characterising the *property* as criminal—suggesting that static objects are somehow volitional and culpable—is tactically adroit because it allows enforcement authorities to sidestep the procedural counterbalances they would face in a criminal proceeding. It is also however, intellectually unconvincing, given that the social stigma of civil recovery and the significant financial costs that may be incurred in resisting civil recovery claims and applications will be borne by individual respondents.[54] The idea that civil

[49] POCA, s 304.

[50] Boucht (n 25) 71.

[51] This was the tenor of much of the academic discussion when civil recovery was first introduced, albeit some commentators with practical proceeds of crime experience welcomed the process. See King and Hendry (n 30) 165. Since civil recovery powers' initial 'bedding-in' period however, there is a tacit acknowledgement amongst some that whilst many aspects of civil recovery remain 'a mess', the 'results in the civil recovery cases . . . appear generally satisfactory'—see Alldridge (n 15) 187–88.

[52] See the discussion of how US enforcement authorities formally pursue the asset itself (and name it, rather than the putative asset holder as the formal counterparty to asset recovery proceedings): Áine Clancy, 'A Better Deal? Negotiated Responses to the Proceeds of Grand Corruption' (2022) 33 Criminal Law Forum 149.

[53] See Colin King, 'Using Civil Processes in Pursuit of Criminal Law Objectives: A Case Study of Non-Conviction-Based Asset Forfeiture' (2012) 16 International Journal of Evidence and Proof 337, 350–51

[54] The beneficial owners of the properties involved in *NCA v Baker* [2020] EWHC 822 (Admin) (*Baker*) claimed £1.5m in costs following the Court of Appeal's refusal of leave to the NCA to appeal the High Court's decision to discharge certain UWOs. See 'Ex-Kazakh President's Grandson, Others Seek 1.5 Million Pound Costs after UK Wealth Order Failure' *Reuters* (London, 29 June 2020).

recovery is a process instituted against property rather than the property holder has been characterized by King and Hendry as a 'legal fiction operationalised as a procedural shortcut', which they view, unsurprisingly, as 'damaging'.[55] Finally, given the ordinary English usage of the word 'recovery', meaning the regaining or taking back into one's control or possession,[56] even the term 'civil recovery' is a misnomer. 'Recovery' suggests that assets are reinstated to an earlier possessor and 'civil' suggests a benign process divorced from the criminal law paradigm. In non-proceeds of crime contexts, where parties litigate in the civil courts on the recovery of an asset, an original possessor will have a private claim against a subsequent holder of an asset if that asset is illegally acquired. Peter Alldridge notes in challenging the 'civil' and 'recovery' appellations that this is not what is contemplated at all by civil recovery. He observes that civil recovery is in fact 'state appropriation of property'. It is important to distinguish the inconsistency, he says, because 'the justifications that are offered for "civil recovery" frequently appeal to ordinary language notions of recovery and return' but in practice, civil recovery's use is almost wholly confined to proceeds of offences where there are no readily identifiable victims (drug trafficking, corruption, and money laundering) to whom such proceeds could be returned.[57] Rather than being 'recovered' on behalf of the victims of crime, the realized value of assets permanently seized are usually distributed to police forces and enforcement authorities as part of the Asset Recovery Incentivisation Scheme (ARIS).[58]

As should be clear from the foregoing, the availability of UWOs forms part of a longer-term pattern of ever-expanding asset recovery powers. The timeline set out in Table 3.2 shows a non-exhaustive expansion of UK enforcement authorities' statutory powers in relation to property suspected to be linked to crime from forfeiture of instrumentalities to confiscation to civil recovery.[59] Although common law powers of forfeiture pre-existed the Misuse of Drugs Act 1971, no powers existed for confiscation or civil recovery until they were introduced by statute.

[55] King and Hendry (n 30) 22.

[56] 'recovery, n' (*OED Online*, March 2022) <www.oed.com/view/Entry/159940>.

[57] Peter Alldridge, 'Civil Recovery in England and Wales: An Appraisal' in Colin King, Clive Walker, and Jimmy Gurulé (eds), The *Palgrave Handbook of Criminal and Terrorism Financing Law* (Palgrave Macmillan 2018) 515, 516.

[58] See Home Office, Asset Recovery Statistical Bulletin: Financial Years Ending 2018 to 2023 (7 September 2023) <www.gov.uk/government/statistics/asset-recovery-statistical-bulletin-financial-years-ending-2018-to-2023/asset-recovery-statistical-bulletin-financial-years-ending-march-2018-to-march-2023>.

[59] See also Table 5.1 in Chapter 5.

Table 3.2 Incremental expansion of asset recovery powers and diminution of evidential barriers to recovery

Legislation	Measure	Conviction necessary?
Misuse of Drugs Act 1971	Forfeiture of anything shown to be connected to particular drugs offences (albeit not extending to the proceeds of those offences)	Yes
Drug Trafficking Offences Act 1986	Confiscation of proceeds of drug trafficking offences	Yes
Criminal Justice Act 1988	Confiscation of proceeds of some offences beyond drug trafficking offences	Yes
Northern Ireland (Emergency Provisions) Act 1991	Northern Ireland only: confiscation of proceeds of various terrorism-related offences	Yes
Criminal Justice Act 1993	• Amended the Drug Trafficking Offences Act 1986 to allow the court to apply the civil standard of proof in determining whether a person has benefited from drug trafficking and the amount of the benefit in granting restraint orders (pending a conviction); and	No
	• Amended the Criminal Justice Act 1988 and the Northern Ireland (Emergency Provisions Act) 1991 to allow the court to apply the civil standard of proof in determining whether an offender has benefited from a particular offence	Yes
Proceeds of Crime Act 1995	• Empowered the courts to assume that all property that passed through a defendant's hands in the six years preceding criminal proceedings was criminal in origin; and	Yes
	• Extended the offences for which confiscation could be ordered	Yes
Terrorism Act 2000	Extended forfeiture powers to the suspected proceeds of terrorism funding arrangements and fundraising	Yes
Proceeds of Crime Act 2002	• Introduced civil recovery where it can be established on the balance of probabilities that property is 'recoverable property'; and • Introduced new restraint and investigations powers for civil recovery and confiscation investigations	No
Serious Crime Act 2015	• Imposed default sentences for failure to satisfy confiscation orders by due date; and • Extended restraint and investigation powers for confiscations	Yes
Criminal Finances Act 2017	Introduced presumption that those involved in serious crime and PEPs and who hold unexplained wealth hold recoverable property	No

Table 3.2 demonstrates a few pertinent points. First, it shows how confiscation powers were confined initially to drug trafficking and then to terrorism-related offences, and were subsequently and incrementally extended to all crimes. Second, it shows a progressive reduction in the evidential thresholds to be met before enforcement authorities become entitled to seize property. Prior convictions slowly became less necessary for the state to exercise asset recovery powers. Third, it offers a snapshot of the accretion of state investigation, restraint, and recovery powers over the space of fifty years. Incidentally, there is no recognition in English law of the doctrine of desuetude, a defence preventing unfair exercise by enforcement authorities of laws that are almost never enforced.[60] This US doctrine acts as a partial antidote to the '"pathological" proliferation of vague statutes that criminalise innocuous or marginally immoral misbehaviour',[61] allowing prosecutors in the US to charge for multiple offences on a single indictment in the hope that at least one prosecution will succeed. By contrast, in the UK, once a statutory power is created, even if its use proves misconceived in practice, and even if it has lain effectively obsolescent for decades, it remains available for reanimation at any time unless expressly repealed by statute.[62] The concern with this is the potential for the development over time of an ever-widening menu of investigative powers available for use by enforcement authorities, even if there is little or no concrete evidence of respondents' criminality.

There is no evidence to suggest that there has been a commensurate reduction in crime following the introduction of any of the measures, nor is it likely that enforcement authorities, having been granted these powers, will conclude that sufficient powers to recover criminal assets are now available.[63] Tables 3.1 and 3.2 above show that as far as the legislature is concerned, the asset recovery powers existing at any one point in time are never enough. Barriers to asset recovery must be constantly removed, and the Overton window for the acceptable limits of state powers for asset recovery purposes is constantly expanding. In this way, the equality of arms between enforcement authorities and respondents subtly becomes ever more attenuated, increasing the opportunity for state interference in individuals' lives. In

[60] Richard Albert, 'Constitutional Amendment by Constitutional Desuetude' (2014) 62 American Journal of Comparative Law 641, 651–53.

[61] Michael L Seigel and Christopher Slobogin, 'Prosecuting Martha: Federal Prosecutorial Power and the Need for a Law of Counts' (2005) 109 Penn State Law Review 1107, 1108.

[62] Where an enforcement authority exercises a power of dubious legitimacy, it is theoretically open to respondents to seek judicial review of the decision to use that power. However, where an investigative power such as a UWO has already been applied for, the aspersive damage created by an application, if publicized, may have already been suffered by the time a review is sought. Moreover, applications for judicial review in the context of enforcement authority decisions are rarely successful. See the decision of Stuart Smith LJ in *R v Inland Revenue Commissioners, ex p Mead and Cook* [1993] 1 All ER 772.

[63] Such powers might include eg increased surveillance powers or access to respondents' digital records. Senior officers in the NCA advised the author in an interview on 16 December 2020 that they had potential new powers in mind but preferred not to elaborate on what those new powers might be because it could confirm areas of weakness from an operational perspective.

principle, this is not necessarily objectionable where the measures are objectively justified and ultimately prove effective in meeting their legislative aims. However, where a measure is introduced (a) following an apparently relatively perfunctory discussion on its potentially adverse impact on individuals, (b) with little evidence demonstrating its necessity, and (c) on a substantively discriminatory basis, then the measure's legitimacy and the wisdom of its introduction must be questioned.[64]

Having outlined some key aspects and critiques of the asset recovery regime in general and civil recovery in particular, it is useful to turn attention to a tool which was expressly introduced with the intention of allowing enforcement authorities to investigate the proceeds of foreign corruption more easily: the unexplained wealth order.

3. Unexplained Wealth Orders

UWOs allow enforcement authorities to require property holders to account for how assets were acquired in circumstances where there is no obvious explanation for how those property holders could have afforded to acquire those assets through legitimate means.[65] Where a respondent fails without reasonable excuse to provide the information on the origins of assets sought pursuant to an order within the time frame set out therein, a presumption will arise that the relevant assets are recoverable property for the purposes of the POCA.[66] The High Court will take this (rebuttable) presumption into account where enforcement authorities subsequently apply for civil recovery orders against the relevant property.[67] The choice to make UWOs available reflected 'the fact that it may be difficult for law enforcement agencies to satisfy the evidential standard at the outset of an investigation given that all relevant information may be outside of the jurisdiction'.[68] Their introduction was the culmination of lobbying by civil society groups concerned about the impact of kleptocracy, including Transparency International UK,[69] and was expressly endorsed in Parliament by enforcement authority representatives as something that would facilitate pursuit of the proceeds of overseas political corruption.[70]

[64] See Sunstein (n 128) and accompanying text, and see Chapter 6, Section 8 for further discussion on the point.

[65] 'Enforcement authorities' in this context are, in England: the NCA, HM Revenue & Customs (HMRC), the Financial Conduct Authority, the Director of the Serious Fraud Office, and the Director of Public Prosecutions (DPP)—s 362A(7) of the POCA.

[66] POCA, s 362C(2).

[67] POCA, s 304(1).

[68] Explanatory Notes to the Criminal Finances Act 2017, para 13.

[69] Jeremy Carver and others, *Empowering the UK to Recover Corrupt Assets: Unexplained Wealth Orders and Other New Approaches to Illicit Enrichment and Asset Recovery* (Transparency International UK March 2016).

[70] Note eg the comments of the NCA's then-Director for Economic Crime, Donald Toon, giving evidence at the first sitting in the House of Commons discussing the legislation introducing UWOs at Criminal Finances Bill Deb 15 November 2016, col 5: 'A particular problem around international

Prior to the introduction of UWOs, it was understood that an assumption of criminality justifying a civil recovery order could not be sustained just because a respondent had 'no identifiable lawful income to warrant the lifestyle and purchases of that respondent'.[71] In *R v Green*, the High Court noted that Parliament had not allowed for civil recovery of property simply because it had been apparently 'obtained by or in return for some unspecified unlawful conduct'.[72] Something more had to be shown to indicate that the relevant property derived from criminality.

The PEP-specific UWO represents the latest chapter in the annals of asset recovery whereby new statutory powers are introduced to cure a 'deficiency' in the law. It is not necessary for enforcement authorities to show a nexus between a PEP's assets and criminality when applying for a UWO. The UWO requires respondents (or 'responsible officers' of respondents where the relevant asset-holder respondents are not individuals) to establish the legitimate origins of the assets held by them to avoid a presumption of recoverable property being raised against those assets. If a respondent fails to comply with all of the requirements of an order, the property that is the subject of an order will be automatically (albeit rebuttably) presumed to constitute recoverable property.[73] Where a presumption is raised, it facilitates enforcement authorities seeking civil recovery of assets: provided the High Court is satisfied that property constitutes recoverable property, it must issue a civil recovery order.[74] Upon compliance or purported compliance with an order, the applicant enforcement authority must determine 'what, if any, enforcement or investigatory proceedings it considers ought to be taken'.[75] It must make this determination within sixty days—extendable up to 186 days—and properties will remain frozen pending this decision being finalized.[76] What the legislation envisages by *purported* compliance is open to question. It is an offence to deliberately or recklessly provide false or misleading information in purporting to comply with a UWO.[77] Beyond that, however, there is no obligation

corruption has been the need to have evidence from overseas, often from a difficult jurisdiction if we are talking about political-level corruption, that is capable of being used in a UK court to take action to recover assets. From our perspective, the introduction of the unexplained wealth order is a particularly important step in response to that'.

[71] *R (on the application of the Director of the Assets Recovery Agency) v Green* [2005] EWHC 3168 (Admin) [1].

[72] Green (n 71) [42].

[73] POCA, s 362C. An example of this presumption automatically arising following the failure of a respondent—who was on the run when the orders were issued—to respond to UWOs issued in June 2023 is set out in NCA Press Release, 'Failure to Respond to Unexplained Wealth Order Sets Legal History' (15 September 2023) <www.linkedin.com/posts/national-crime-agency_earlier-this-year-the-nca-obtained-an-unexplained-activity-7108812080966684672-Wel3>.

[74] POCA, s 266.

[75] POCA, s 362D(4).

[76] POCA, s 362D(3).

[77] POCA, s 362E.

on respondents to use anything conceptually akin to what commercial lawyers might refer to as 'best endeavours' to furnish information allowing investigators to gain as complete a picture as possible as to the origins of the assets the subject of an order. Even if there were, it is difficult to see how this might be enforced. As it stands, purported compliance with an order is sufficient to avoid having a presumption raised against the relevant property, but it is plausible that future respondents might take this as an invitation strategically to disclose as little information as possible to allow them to formally comply with an order whilst revealing little about the financing of their assets. The legislation on UWOs allows wide scope to enforcement authorities on the type and format of the information they may seek. Applicant enforcement authorities may require a statement to be made orally or in writing,[78] and the legislation allows for a generous generalist capacity for orders to 'require the respondent to produce documents of a kind specified or described in the order'.[79] This non-specificity means that a respondent might be inclined to err on the side of over-disclosure to avoid falling foul of an accusation of failing to comply. This can offer its own benefits to enforcement authorities. In *NCA v Hussain*,[80] a UWO case against a non-PEP who was suspected of involvement in serious crime, the respondent's data dump of 127 lever arch folders explaining his sources of wealth 'inadvertently gave NCA investigators clues to make a bigger case against him'.[81]

Enforcement authorities' applications for UWOs are typically made *ex parte* to the High Court to prevent forewarned respondents from dissipating assets.[82] Interim freezing order applications in respect of the relevant property are generally heard contemporaneously with the UWO applications.[83] The resulting interim freezing orders and UWOs are served on respondents simultaneously. Unless otherwise directed by the presiding judge, all initial applications are held in private.[84] As is evident from the applications in respect of properties owned by PEPs to date,[85] subsequent challenges to UWOs tend to be highly publicized. Indeed, it is enforcement authority *policy* to actively 'publicise civil investigations to the maximum possible extent [. . . and . . .] inform the media (as we do in criminal cases) and relevant NGOs of upcoming civil investigation events such as open court

[78] POCA, s 362A(4).
[79] POCA, s 362A(5).
[80] *NCA v Hussain* [2020] EWHC 432 (Admin).
[81] This resulted in the parties entering into a settlement agreement in respect of, inter alia, forty-five properties and £583,950 in cash. See <www.nationalcrimeagency.gov.uk/news/businessman-with-links-to-serious-criminals-loses-property-empire-after-settling-10m-unexplained-wealth-order-case>.
[82] POCA, s 362I.
[83] POCA, s 362J.
[84] Ministry of Justice, *Practice Direction: Civil Recovery Proceedings*, updated as of 21 March 2018, para 11.1.
[85] *NCA v Hajiyeva* [2020] EWCA Civ 108, [2020] All ER (D) 34; *Baker* (n 54).

hearings'.[86] The positive public attention received by enforcement authorities following asset recoveries is something that was acknowledged by a representative of the National Police Chiefs Council whilst providing evidence on the potential impact of the then-yet to be formally introduced UWOs:

> What really hurts [serious and organized criminals] and their associates and family members is the denial and removal of the assets and the image that portrays to the public. It gets a lot of positive reception when we carry that out. From a public perception point of view, we know how much they appreciate the removal of assets.[87]

This high level of publicity is potentially unhelpful. Where UWOs involving overseas PEPs are highly publicized, the risk is that UWOs could impact on respondents' privilege against self-incrimination, particularly where the alleged predicate crimes were committed overseas.[88] This is because respondents risk being impugned with a connection to criminality, even if they subsequently successfully challenge the UWOs in question.[89]

Jurisdiction for matters relating to UWOs is vested in the High Court. Where an order is sought by an enforcement authority from the court, the judge must be satisfied that:

(i) the respondent is a PEP, or there are reasonable grounds for suspecting that the respondent or someone connected to them is, or has been, involved in serious crime (whether in the UK or elsewhere);[90]
(ii) there are reasonable grounds for suspecting either (i) 'that the known sources of the respondent's lawfully obtained income would have been insufficient for the purposes of enabling the respondent to obtain the property'[91] (the 'Income Limb') or (ii) that the property was obtained through unlawful conduct (the 'Recoverable Property Limb');[92]
(iii) there is reasonable cause to believe that the respondent holds the property the subject of the order;[93] and
(iv) the relevant asset is worth at least £50,000.[94]

[86] NCA, *Civil Financial Investigations and Associated Publicity: Policy*, 18 February 2021, para 5 <www.nationalcrimeagency.gov.uk/who-we-are/publications/496-nca-civil-financial-investigations-policy-and-associated-publicity/file>.
[87] Mick Beattie of the National Police Chiefs Council, Criminal Finances Bill Deb 15 November 2016, col 5.
[88] See Chapter 6, Section 5.
[89] Discussed in Áine Clancy, 'Proving the Dough: National Crime Agency v Baker & Ors' (2021) 84 Modern Law Review 168.
[90] POCA, s 362B(4)(a).
[91] POCA, s 362B(3)(a).
[92] POCA, s 362B(3)(b).
[93] POCA, s 362B(2).
[94] POCA, s 362B(2).

It bears repeating that the first test to be met is that a respondent must *either* be a PEP *or* someone who is, or is connected to, someone suspected of involvement in serious crime. It is submitted that little is gained by including the option of having a respondent who is a PEP. The rhetoric surrounding the introduction of UWOs was that inclusion of specific references to PEPs reflected the concern around foreign corrupt PEPs laundering the proceeds of corruption in the UK. If PEP-specific UWOs are designed to target those suspected of benefiting from official corruption, then surely the respondents to PEP UWOs are suspected of involvement in (or of being connected to someone suspected of involvement in) serious crime. This, it is submitted, renders a PEP-specific limb unnecessary.

These tests for PEP-specific UWOs will now be discussed under the headings 'PEP Requirement', the 'Source Requirement', the 'Holding Requirement', and the 'Value Requirement' respectively (collectively, the 'Statutory Tests').

a. PEP Requirement

UWOs can be sought either against (i) individuals suspected of involvement in serious crime or their family members or close associates (Serious Crime UWOs), or (ii) PEPs, in each case where the respondent holds wealth that is apparently unaccounted for. Limb (i) imposes some restraint on enforcement authority discretion, because applicants must demonstrate reasonable grounds for suspecting a potential respondent's involvement (or that of their family member or close associate) in serious crime. By contrast, PEPs are eligible by reason of their employment, social, or familial status, dependent respectively on whether the PEP is a current or former foreign senior public official, or is an associate or a family member of, or is 'otherwise connected' with such an official. One on level, this is an entirely sensible reflection of the fact that corrupt politicians often vest misappropriated wealth abroad in the names of their family members and close associates. This certainly appears to be the case in respect of assets held in the UK. The forfeiture orders served on a former president of Moldova's son in respect of £460,000 held in UK-based bank accounts he opened when he started university in London serve as a prominent example of this.[95] Other recent examples include in the UK include, without limitation, a bank account containing £25,000 being seized from the niece of Syria's former dictator Bashar al Assad,[96] a confiscation order for £2.6m being issued against the mistress of a former governor of a Nigerian state,[97] further

[95] David Pegg, 'Court Orders Son of Moldova's former PM to pay £466,000' *The Guardian* (London, 7 February 2019).

[96] NCA Press Release, 'al-Assad Family Cash Forfeited in London Court' (21 May 2019) <www.nationalcrimeagency.gov.uk/news/al-assad-family-cash-forfeited-in-london-court>.

[97] *Onuigbo v R* [2014] EWCA Crim 65.

orders being made against the same politician's wife and brother-in-law,[98] and a £4m asset forfeiture settlement made between the NCA and a married couple comprising the cousin of Azerbaijan's president and the son of a former Azerbaijan deputy energy minister, respectively.[99] There is an admittedly somewhat remote risk that a wholly innocent person could have their assets 'recovered' because they are not in a position to adequately explain or document the licit source of funds for a property. But this is only part of the principled objection to PEP-specific UWOs. The more pressing concern is the ability of law enforcement authorities to seek to hold someone to account based on criteria including their relationships to foreign senior public officials rather than based on any suspected link to criminality. This concern is more pronounced because rather than applying uniformly to PEPs of all nationalities (as the term 'PEP' is conceived under the anti-money laundering regulations), the POCA definition of PEP is instead limited in scope to PEPs holding public office in countries other than the UK or the EEA or their family members or associates.[100] Although it is not necessary for enforcement authorities to demonstrate an obvious (or even tenuous) nexus to criminal conduct in seeking a PEP-specific unexplained wealth order, this does not prevent a presumption that property is 'recoverable property' being raised against a PEP's assets.[101] Consistent with the Crime Control Model, without more, this is an unprecedentedly low threshold for allowing state authorities to (i) compel respondents to disclose their sources of wealth (outside a taxation context, at least); and (ii) raise a presumption against their property that it was unlawfully acquired.

b. Source Requirement

If relying on the Income Limb, enforcement authorities must establish that there is a discrepancy between a PEP's known licit sources of income and assets allegedly held by that PEP. This is a worryingly inexact test. It is unclear what metrics are being used to determine what constitutes 'income', and what sources enforcement authorities rely on in determining a potential respondent's legitimate or illegitimate income. Inheritances or capital acquired legitimately but outside the context of a foreign PEP's employment as a senior public official might each, for instance, generate income that might not be easily trackable by, or easily explicable

98 *R v Nakanda* [2016] EWCA Crim 2302.

99 John Simpson, '"Laundromat" Couple Hand Over £4m To Crime Agency' *The Times* (London, 7 July 2021) 23.

100 On the distinction between the definitions of 'PEP' under the AML Regulations and the POCA, see Chapter 2, Section 2(e).

101 It is acknowledged that the 'without reasonable excuse' specification in s 362C(1) will assist some respondents in this regard.

to, domestic enforcement authorities. Whilst enforcement authorities typically examine publicly available records to build a picture of a respondent's sources of wealth,[102] they are under no obligation to demonstrate that they have made (or sought to make) a thorough investigation of any such records prior to the application for a UWO. There is no statutory requirement to establish that granting a UWO is proportionate and/or is necessary to build a case for a civil recovery order,[103] nor is it necessary to establish that less intrusive measures might be used instead.[104] The reason for the use of the expression 'known sources' is not clear. It *might* be perceived as imposing an obligation on enforcement authorities to conduct a minimum level of due diligence through searches of public registers in relevant jurisdictions to verify an individual's source of wealth. However, the existence or scope of any such obligation has not been documented. The Attorney General's Guidance on the use of statutory powers in asset recovery investigations is limited to a single unilluminating paragraph providing that the courts should interpret 'known' sources to mean sources of income 'that are reasonably ascertainable from available information at the time of making an application, which will include open source material including from other jurisdictions.[105]

Income is considered 'lawfully obtained' if 'it is obtained lawfully under the laws of the country from where the income arises'.[106] This provision potentially dilutes the measure's efficacy as it applies to some kleptocratic regimes because it fails to consider the operation of kleptocracies in practice. Some descriptions of how wealth was acquired by individuals following the dissolution of the USSR, for example, suggest that whilst many of those acquisitions were not illegal per se, it is simultaneously difficult to describe them as wholly legitimate.[107] The challenge that lawmakers failed to meet in providing for PEP-specific UWOs was to establish how to deal with wealth falling through the cracks between the letter and the spirit of anti-corruption and asset recovery laws.

A holistic and altogether more practical list of criteria to assess the 'riskiness' of wealth held by PEPs has been developed and published by the Financial Conduct Authority for use by its regulatees in considering whether assets were potentially illicitly acquired. It cites factors including benefit from 'wealth derived from the granting of government licenses (such as mineral extraction concessions . . .)' and 'appointment to a public office that appears inconsistent with personal merit' as

[102] Author's observations from attendance at a High Court hearing for *Baker*.

[103] Albeit there is an expectation that the courts will ensure that measures are used by enforcement authorities in a fair and proportionate manner, as discussed in Chapter 6, Section 9.

[104] eg raising an assessment to tax as discussed in Chapter 7, Section 5.

[105] Attorney General, *Code of Practice issued under Section 377A of the Proceeds of Crime Act 2002* (April 2024) para 177.

[106] POCA, s 362B(6)(c).

[107] See eg Catherine Belton, *Putin's People* (William Collins 2020).

factors potentially indicative of wealth obtained through questionable means.[108] In assessing PEPs who are prospective customers, it suggests that regulatees look also at geopolitical factors where the individual holds or is associated with a prominent public function in a country that has, without limitation, the following characteristics: political instability, human rights abuses committed by the state, widespread organized criminality, and weak state institutions.[109] Using these objectively disquieting factors as gauges of potentially illegitimate wealth is perhaps a more realistic, and a less legalistic, reflection of the fact that not all illegitimate wealth is necessarily criminally acquired. Though somewhat amorphous, they might serve as the kind of factors that judges hearing unexplained wealth cases could usefully employ in future in considering the likelihood that wealth was amassed without the taint of impropriety.

An alternative test to the Income Limb was introduced in 2022 for enforcement authorities seeking UWOs.[110] It allows applicant enforcement authorities to instead demonstrate a reasonably held suspicion that property the subject of a potential order constitutes the proceeds of unlawful conduct.[111] The existence of the Recoverable Property Limb again raises the question of why a PEP-specific type of UWO is necessary at all. If enforcement authorities reasonably hold a suspicion that property is derived from unlawful conduct, then presumably seeking a UWO of the kind that is available for assets held by individuals who are reasonably suspected to be involved in serious crime, or who are connected with such individuals, would be as, if not more, appropriate.[112]

c. Holding Requirement

Section 362H of the POCA provides that a person will be taken to 'hold' a property if they have effective control over the property, if they are the trustee of a settlement in which the property is comprised, or if they are an actual or potential beneficiary in relation to such a settlement. The applicant enforcement authority's failure in *NCA v Baker* to establish clearly the named respondents' legal or beneficial ownership in, or their effective control over, certain properties proved fatal to certain

108 Financial Conduct Authority (FCA), FG 17/6: *The Treatment of Politically Exposed Persons for Anti-Money Laundering Purposes* 2017, para 2.32. At the time of writing (December 2024), this guidance is under review following consultation with PEPs and financial instructions, but the FCA has expressly pointed to the use of its holistic customer risk assessment factors as an example of good practice and is likely to retain this aspect of the guidance in any updated version.

109 FCA (n 108) paras 2.29–2.30.

110 Pursuant to the Economic Crime (Transparency and Enforcement) Act 2022, s 47.

111 s 242 of the POCA emphasizes that it is not necessary for enforcement authorities to 'show that the conduct was of a particular kind if it is shown that the property was obtained through conduct of one of a number of kinds'.

112 As provided for pursuant to s 362B(4)(b) of the POCA.

of the UWOs sought in that case.[113] The case involved unexplained wealth orders served against assets ultimately beneficially owned by the daughter and grandson of Kazakhstan's then de facto president-for-life, Nursultan Nazarbayev. The NCA alleged that these individuals had acquired the property using the proceeds of serious crimes committed by an individual who was their former husband and father respectively, and who was also a PEP. The NCA sought to rely on the PEP limb, or in the alternative, on the Serious Crime limb of the Statutory Tests in seeking the UWOs. On their initial application to the High Court for the orders, Supperstone J agreed with the NCA that both limbs of the Statutory Test applied.

The respondents in the *Baker* case successfully challenged the UWOs. In the High Court, Lang J found, amongst other matters, that the first-named respondent in the orders (the president of the remaining respondents, a number of Panamanian foundations registered as the owners of the properties) did not formally 'hold' or control the substantial London properties the subject of the orders, given the primarily administrative role of foundation presidents in Panama. The decision has been the subject of significant criticism from academic experts and civil society groups, not least because the presiding judge failed 'ask searching questions about the sources of wealth, setting back anti-kleptocracy efforts to before 2007, when the money laundering regulations introduced the concept of political risk'.[114]

d. Value Requirement

The property the subject of an order must be worth at least £50,000. The original proposal was a threshold of £100,000 but, owing to lobbying during the relevant legislation's passage through Parliament, this was decreased to reflect lower-value properties outside London being purchased through involvement in serious crime and to bring the threshold closer to the criteria used in other jurisdictions.[115] This is despite the fact that neither of the other jurisdictions cited in Parliament as having success in using unexplained wealth order-type mechanisms—Ireland and Australia—have anything resembling PEP-specific UWOs on their statute books. On the assumption that the measure was designed to deter grand corruption, such a low-value threshold seems inconsistent with that objective. A better option might have been to retain the £50,000 threshold for Serious Crime UWO respondents

[113] *Baker* (n 54) [114]–[124].
[114] Tom Mayne and John Heathershaw, *Criminality Notwithstanding: The Use of Unexplained Wealth Orders in Anti-Corruption Cases* (Global Integrity/Anti-Corrupt Evidence Research Programme, March 2022) 67, and see further Anton Moiseienko, 'The Limitations of Unexplained Wealth Orders' [2022] Criminal Law Review 230.
[115] Criminal Finances Bill HC Deb 17 November 2016, cols 79–95.

but reflect the legislative intention of deterring and disrupting grand corruption by providing for a higher threshold for actions against PEPs.

e. Recoverable Property

A respondent's failure to comply with an order will raise a presumption against the property the subject of the unexplained wealth order that it is 'recoverable property'.[116] Unless this presumption is satisfactorily rebutted the High Court must, if it is satisfied that the property in question is recoverable and subject to some limitations,[117] issue a recovery order against the property in question. The absence of a credible explanation for how the property was obtained allows for an inference to be drawn that the property can only be derived from crime.[118] A further problem (and one which apparently has not been highlighted to date in any of the commentary on UWOs) is that of the significance of applicable limitation periods. If property the subject of an order is deemed to be 'recoverable property', section 27A of the Limitation Act 1980 imposes a twenty-year limitation period running from the date on which that recoverable property was obtained. There is, in other words, a temporal limit to the restitution ostensibly offered in using UWOs after which corrupt PEPs can rest assured that unless they are convicted of an offence in their countries of origin or are prosecuted for a money laundering offence in the UK, they will enjoy the fruits of that corruption uninterrupted. Whilst there are no reported cases to date of asset recoveries having failed as a result of an expired limitation period, given (i) the tendency for corruption scandals to not be uncovered until years after the corrupt acts have been committed, and (ii) the lengths to which corrupt PEPs will go (use of complex webs of corporate vehicles and secrecy jurisdictions, etc.) to obscure the true ownership of illicitly acquired assets, this is something that might usefully be revisited.

As a process, the UWO is paradigmatic of the Crime Control Model when viewed through Packer's lens. Through its characterization as a civil process, it dispenses with the procedural safeguards afforded to criminal defendants.[119] Where initial applications for UWOs are made, it privileges expediency and efficiency over an exhaustive assessment of the evidence which would allow courts to conclude whether the provenance of assets is illegitimate on the basis of a high burden of proof first having been met.

[116] POCA, s 362C.

[117] s 266(3) of the POCA provides that if a civil recovery order would result in a contravention of ECHR rights, or if it 'would not be just and equitable' to make an order provided certain conditions relating to the good faith of, and potential detriment to, a respondent are met.

[118] *R v Anwoir* [2008] EWCA 1354.

[119] For a thorough critique of this characterization in the context of non-conviction-based asset confiscation more generally, see King and Hendry (n 30).

4. UWOs: Legislative Objectives

The UWO is 'an investigation tool . . . specifically designed to support the building of a case for civil recovery'.[120] The Home Office suggests its introduction was necessary because situations arise where enforcement authorities suspect that particular assets represent the proceeds of crime but other civil recovery tools provided for under the Proceeds of Crime Act 2002 are insufficient to allow them to gather evidence.[121] In a PEP-specific context, the Home Office pointed to the difficulties of gaining overseas evidence as one particular reason why UWOs may prove useful.[122] In circumstances where they are not challenged, UWOs represent a potentially fast, cheap, and effective means of establishing the sources of a respondent's assets, particularly when compared with production orders (which can be far more resource-intensive),[123] and are therefore an exemplar of the Crime Control Model's aspirations. The UK government expressed its aims in introducing UWOs in somewhat oblique terms, but it is possible to identify four overarching objectives, namely: (i) to deter criminality by depriving criminals of the proceeds of crime; (ii) to condemn corruption; (iii) to aid ease of investigations; and (iv) to return corruptly acquired assets to the states from which they were taken. The main contention made in this section is that PEP-specific UWOs were poorly designed and represent a crisis-driven and ineffectual response to the problem of the proceeds of overseas official corruption being laundered in the UK. This suggestion will now be examined through looking in turn at each of the stated legislative objectives underpinning the measure's introduction.

a. Crime Deterrence through Asset Recovery

The primary objective of UWOs is 'to deprive criminals from benefiting from the proceeds of unlawful activities'.[124] The expectation was that UWOs' availability would deter, disrupt, and prevent the commission of corrupt acts and the laundering of their proceeds in the UK. Notwithstanding the intention that UWOs would be used primarily in civil recovery investigations, this is clearly a crime control objective, as suggested by the Home Office's use of value-laden references to 'criminals' and 'unlawful activities'. The problem is that the policy assumption that corrupt PEPs will be deterred by a civil investigation measure does

[120] Attorney General's Office, *Code of Practice Issued Under Section 377 of the Proceeds of Crime Act 2002: Investigations* (June 2021) para 160.
[121] Home Office, *Criminal Finances Act—Unexplained Wealth Orders Impact Assessment No: HO0282*, 20 June 2017, 1.
[122] See n 136 and accompanying text.
[123] See case commentary on *NCA v Hussain* [2020] Lloyd's Rep FC 158, 177.
[124] Home Office (n 121) 5.

not hold up well to scrutiny. It appears to be based on rational choice theory: a framework popular amongst criminal law policy-makers who assume that decisions on whether to commit a crime are based primarily on a rational calculation of the relative costs and benefits of potentially engaging in the criminal act. If there is a heightened risk of proceeds being recovered, the theory suggests, criminals are disincentivized and thereby deterred from offending. The application of this theory to underpin the introduction of civil recovery measures has been widely criticized as unreliable, because it is based on a non-empirically verified assumption that corrupt actors' conduct is 'variously deterred or dis-inhibited by the manipulation of [primarily economic] incentives'.[125] Rational choice theory sceptics note that the theory largely disregards the complex sociological, environmental, psychological, and other factors that create the opportunity for and/or motivate (or de-motivate) individuals from offending.[126] It follows that measures aimed at deterring PEPs from holding the proceeds of corruption in the UK which are premised on the idea that those PEPs are acting on the basis of rational economics-driven choices are themselves worthy of scepticism.

b. Expressive Function

The measure's introduction is intended to perform an expressive function. UWOs were intended to:

> send a powerful message that the UK is serious about rooting out the proceeds of overseas grand corruption; and that we are taking the necessary steps to end the UK's reputation as a safe haven for stolen funds.[127]

This raises further questions: was the introduction of PEP-specific countermeasures proposed to be primarily *symbolic* of the UK's rejection of corruption? Or was the chief expressive motivation behind the measure's introduction informational: communicating to corrupt foreign PEPs that the consequence of laundering illicit assets in the UK will be enforcement of recovery powers and repatriation of the property? Examining the tenor of the above statement, one could argue that UWOs were designed merely to 'send a powerful message' to other 'upstanding' members of the international community of the UK's cultural and normative

[125] David Garland, *The Culture of Control: Crime and Social Order in Contemporary Society* (OUP 2001) 130. See, in the context of crime control generally, Garland, 129–32; and in the context of asset recovery more specifically, Harvey (n 32) 183–86.

[126] Harvey (n 32) 184–85.

[127] Speech delivered by the then-Home Secretary, Amber Rudd MP at the FCA's annual financial crime conference on 10 November 2016. Transcript available at <www.gov.uk/government/speeches/home-secretarys-speech-to-the-fcas-financial-crime-conference>

condemnation of corruption. This expression may be intrinsically valuable from a diplomatic and political perspective, but if the availability of UWOs against PEPs is primarily about symbolic statement-making and not bolstered by significant enforcement action (as has proven to be the case in practice so far), it seems unlikely that it will cultivate meaningful reluctance amongst corrupt foreign PEPs to hold their illicitly acquired assets in London.

Cass Sunstein has cautioned against support for laws which might be expressively attractive without first making a thorough consequentialist enquiry:

> [F]or purposes of law, any support for 'statements' should be rooted not simply in the intrinsic value of the statement, but also in plausible judgments about its effect on social norms and hence in 'on balance' judgments about its consequence.[128]

He warns against the dangers of expressively attractive laws which prove in their implementation to be futile, or counterproductive from a rights perspective.[129] In the context of UWOs against PEPs, quite apart from the implications for individual rights,[130] potential unintended consequences might include, for example, creating a demand for increasingly complex property ownership structures to impede investigators, thereby benefiting money-laundering facilitators. The only risks referred to by the Home Office in introducing UWOs were the state's (vastly under-estimated) expected costs in making applications and respondents' 'unknown costs such as legal fees, monetary and emotional costs of responding' being assessed.[131] There is a danger that, given their limited use to date, one unintended consequence of the introduction of UWOs is to draw attention to the poor resourcing both in terms of financing and expertise available to enforcement authorities tasked with tackling corruption.[132] The then-Home Secretary's reference to 'overseas grand corruption' in the quote cited at the beginning of this sub-section is significant. The aspiration was to target individuals benefiting from large-scale corruption. This supports a contention that the only PEPs intended to be targeted by the measure are those who have actual access to (or hold sufficient influence to direct the movement of) significant public monies. This in turn reenforces the argument made in the last chapter that the breadth of the definition of 'politically

128 Cass R Sunstein, 'On the Expressive Function of Law' (1996) 141 University of Pennsylvania Law Review 2021, 2045.

129 Sunstein (n 128) 2044–50.

130 See Chapter 6.

131 Home Office (n 121) para 20.

132 Commentators note the significant mismatch between the resources of enforcement authorities and those of allegedly corrupt PEPs. They cite by way of example the fact that the NCA's anti-corruption unit's annual budget has been just over £4m in recent years, whilst the costs claimed from the NCA by the respondents in the *Baker* decision alone came to £1.5m. See Tom Mayne and John Heathershaw, *Criminality Notwithstanding: The Use of Unexplained Wealth Orders in Anti-Corruption Cases* (Anti-Corruption Evidence Research Programme 2022) 30.

exposed person' as provided for in the POCA is excessive for the purpose of realizing the legislative objective.

Moreover, opting for PEP-specific UWOs as a symbol of the UK's rejection of corruption is a curiously insipid choice. Potentially more compelling deterrents could have included the possibilities of a stand-alone criminal offence where there is evidence of monies misappropriated from any foreign state having been invested in the UK, or simply providing for the Serious Crime UWO only, thereby emphasizing that corrupt PEPs found to hold illegitimate unexplained wealth in the UK are reasonably suspected of benefiting from a serious crime. The Home Office considered and rejected an offence of illicit enrichment for PEPs because of concerns around civil liberties.[133] By failing to either (i) criminalize PEPs holding assets of inexplicable provenance; (ii) take enforcement action against corrupt foreign PEPs using existing money-laundering offences provided for under the POCA;[134] or (iii) using Serious Crime UWOs against corrupt foreign PEPs, the messaging on the norms addressing misappropriated property laundered by overseas PEPs becomes incoherent. The introduction of the PEP-specific UWO attempted to convey the idea that the UK is serious about countering corruption whilst simultaneously suggesting that corrupt PEPs will not attract individual criminal liability for holding assets representing the proceeds of crime or corruption. Holding such property will be deemed unlawful *only if* an enforcement authority opts to seek a UWO against someone who then fails to respond to the order without reasonable excuse. Even then, only the property, not the actions of any individual, will be declared 'unlawful'.[135]

The tone-deafness of having expressive objectives in introducing a measure falling on the Crime Control Model end of Packer's spectrum to target and curtail the behaviours of corrupt PEPs from regimes with little interest in upholding the rule of law needs little discussion. Introducing criminal offences for holding the proceeds of overseas corruption, enforcing existing offences, or providing for a higher standard of procedural rights than are typically available for civil respondents would have heightened safeguards for those suspected of holding illegitimate

[133] art 20 of the UNCAC asks States Parties to consider criminalizing 'when committed intentionally, illicit enrichment' which is defined as 'a significant increase in the assets of a public official that he or she cannot reasonably explain in relation to his or her lawful income'. There was no public consultation on UWOs specifically against PEPs. A consultation applied solely to UWOs for assets derived from suspected serious crime, during which concerns were raised about the civil liberties implications deriving from individuals failing to give explanations about their wealth (see Home Office, *Action Plan for Anti Money-Laundering and Counter-Terrorist Financing: Government Response* (October 2016) para 4.21). We cannot know (though we can surmise) whether similar civil liberties concerns would have been raised for UWOs against PEPs.

[134] eg POCA, s 329(1)(c) provides that it is an offence for a person to 'have possession of criminal property', which is property which 'constitutes a person's benefit from criminal conduct or it represents such a benefit (in whole or part and whether directly or indirectly)'. It is immaterial who carried out the conduct (POCA, s 340).

[135] POCA, s 362C(2).

wealth, thereby demonstrating the UK's valorization of due process and the rule of law. Furthermore, it would have telegraphed clearly that benefiting from grand corruption bears criminal justice consequences. Alternatively, assuming that PEPs against whom UWOs are sought are indeed suspected of grand corruption offences, it was open to the legislature to make it clear that the Serious Crime UWO was being introduced as a means of addressing grand corruption proceeds laundering, amongst other matters. These opportunities were missed.

c. An Investigative Tool

That UWOs against PEPs are available:

> reflects the concern about those involved in corruption overseas, laundering the proceeds of crime in the UK; and the fact that it may be difficult for law enforcement agencies to satisfy the evidential standard at the outset of an investigation.[136]

The PEP-specific UWO is the first and only part of the UK's proceeds of crime architecture expressly introduced with the aim of addressing the proceeds of overseas grand corruption being laundered within the jurisdiction. The suggestion that extant investigative powers are insufficient is suggestive of Howard Becker's moral enterprise identification criteria, and the idea that, as part of the process, existing rules are often deemed by moral crusaders and rule enforcers as insufficient to tackle a particular harm being done. Each of these propositions is discussed in the next chapter. The measure was introduced to assist in building cases in civil recovery proceedings.[137] Because of territorial enforcement jurisdiction limitations and the difficulties involved in obtaining evidence from overseas, UK enforcement authorities encounter difficulties in instituting criminal prosecutions for corruption offences against foreign PEPs for crimes committed (or substantially committed) within other jurisdictions.[138] Limiting UWOs' use to civil recovery proceedings ostensibly justifies the absence of criminal procedural safeguards for respondents. However, the reference to 'the concern about . . . laundering the proceeds of crime in the UK' is vague and seems to contemplate that UWOs might be used as an investigative tool as a prelude to prosecuting money-laundering offences. This is confusing. If 'the reduction of crime is in general best secured

[136] Home Office (n 121) para 14.

[137] Home Office (n 121) 1. However, they may be also used to facilitate confiscation—see s 362D(8) of the POCA.

[138] Particularly given the UK's own tradition of defining criminal jurisdiction by reference to territoriality, though it has become recently more expansive—see Chapter 5, n 93 and accompanying text.

by means of criminal investigations and criminal proceedings',[139] then surely enforcement authorities should first pursue a criminal investigation, rather than having two opportunities to pursue a PEP, first using a civil mechanism and then through a criminal prosecution based on information derived from a civil investigation. Enforcement authorities are prohibited from using statements provided by a respondent during a UWO investigation in subsequent criminal investigations against the respondent (with some limited exceptions) as a result of 'use immunity' provisions in the POCA.[140] The concern from a self-incrimination perspective, however, is the risk that investigators will procure evidence indirectly derived from such statements. The policy preference for criminal rather than civil investigations and proceedings originated from parliamentarians' concerns around insufficient safeguards being in place for civil recovery respondents.[141] Introducing a criminal charge *after* civil recovery proceedings would seem to go against the spirit of the provision.

Beyond that, the *design* of the provision appears flawed. To obtain a PEP-specific UWO, enforcement authorities must prove that there are reasonable grounds for suspecting *either* that a PEP's licit income is incommensurate with their assets *or* that the PEP's 'property has been obtained through unlawful conduct'.[142] Assuming the second of these criteria can be satisfied, then it would surely make more sense for it to be dealt with as a Serious Crime UWO. With regard to the first option, if an enforcement authority constructs a theory that property for which there is no obvious explanation must be the proceeds of crime, this (as Johan Boucht notes) 'would seem to disregard too many alternative hypotheses even if the respondent remains silent'.[143] This will not of course be true of all cases, but the practical impact of Boucht's observation where enforcement authorities pursue an incorrect hypothesis in seeking UWOs is that they risk unfairly impugning potentially blameless respondents with state-made claims of benefit from corruption, and throwing away resources on ever-increasing legal costs if they err on the basis on which they suspect property to constitute recoverable property.[144]

[139] POCA, s 2A(4). This reflects the policy position that criminal prosecution is preferable to civil proceedings as a starting point is expressly set out in s 2A of the POCA, which notes that enforcement authorities must exercise their functions under the POCA in the way which they '[considers] is best calculated to contribute to the reduction of crime'.

[140] The use immunity provisions are set out in s 362F of the Proceeds of Crime Act 2002.

[141] See nn 33 to 39 and accompanying text above.

[142] POCA, s 362B(3).

[143] Johan Boucht, 'Non-conviction Based Confiscation: Moving the Confiscation of Criminal Proceeds from the Criminal to the Civil Sphere' in Vanessa Franssen and Christopher Harding (eds), *Criminal and Quasi-Criminal Enforcement Mechanisms in Europe* (Hart 2022) 415, 444.

[144] Amendments made to the POCA's provisions in 2022 sought to mitigate this potential costs issue where it arises for enforcement authorities by prohibiting the High Court from making costs orders in favour of UWO respondents unless the applicant enforcement authority were found to have acted unreasonably in seeking applications or progressing a UWO case, or where the enforcement authority acted dishonestly or fraudulently. See POCA, s 362U.

d. Repatriation

A fourth, less clearly articulated objective is identifiable. The prospect of returning corruptly acquired property to prior legitimate owners of those assets was expressly referred to in the parliamentary debates preceding the enactment of the Criminal Finances Act 2017 as an advantage afforded by UWOs.[145] The proposed inclusion of a provision expressly requiring the repatriation of corruptly acquired assets held by PEPs was narrowly defeated on the basis that repatriation by the UK of the proceeds of corruption to a state of origin is already an international law obligation applicable to it under Article 57 of the UNCAC.[146] As discussed in Chapter 1, however, the performance of that obligation is contingent on certain conditions first being met. Holding states like the UK that assist in recovering corruptly acquired assets are required to return the profits or proceeds of corruption to those assets' states of origin only where requested by the state of origin on the basis of a final judgment issued in that state of origin.[147] Where no such judgments and requests are made, holding states are required merely to give 'priority consideration' to returning the assets to the state of origin.[148] In discussing the repatriation aim of the UWO, it was successfully argued during the parliamentary debates that any legislative measures seeking to regulate this obligation could impact upon the government's flexibility on the form repatriation measures might take.[149] However, if the government had reservations about returning assets to corrupt regimes, it could have included broad statutory language evincing an intention to the effect that the assets would, for example, be administered for the benefit of the citizens of the state in question.[150] This would have preserved its discretion on to whom in the state of origin the assets would be returned. Furthermore, an argument made on behalf of the government suggesting that repatriation is already required pursuant to Article 57 of the UNCAC ignores that this provision imposes a positive obligation on States Parties to repatriate assets only in limited and specific circumstances.[151] The duty to repatriate under international law is confined to situations where it is unlikely that UWOs will be necessary because states of origin

[145] See eg Criminal Finances Bill HC Deb 22 November 2016, cols 189–94.

[146] To be made in consultation with NGOs, civil society actors, and the Department for International Development, and subject to certain repatriation restrictions or conditions in circumstances where there was a perception that repatriated assets might be subject to further misuse. See Criminal Finances Bill HC Deb 22 November 2016, cols 190–95. The proposed additional provision was defeated by a single vote.

[147] UNCAC, art 57(3)(b). This requirement may be waived at the discretion of the haven state. See Chapter 1, Section 4(a).

[148] UNCAC, art 57(3)(c).

[149] UNCAC, art 57(3)(c).

[150] See the BOTA Foundation-style mechanisms used to apply the funds for states of origins' citizenries discussed in Anton Moiseienko, 'The Ownership of Confiscated Proceeds of Corruption under the UN Convention Against Corruption' (2018) 67 International and Comparative Law Quarterly 669.

[151] See col 193 of the debate cited at n 146.

will already have taken action themselves to prosecute the relevant offences and seek recovery of the relevant assets through mutual legal assistance processes.

Moreover, as a matter of English property law, it seems inconsistent with basic principles of good title that misappropriated assets recovered by English authorities are not returned to states of origin. Where assets recovered by enforcement authorities are distributed using ARIS,[152] this might be viewed as an (indirect) application of the *bona vacantia* doctrine. Where assets are viewed by the law as ownerless, they pass under the doctrine to the Crown. Where assets are recovered as part of a foreign official corruption civil recovery investigation, enforcement authorities in essence are disputing the PEP asset holder's good title to the assets the subject of the investigation. Assuming those assets are recovered but then kept by the UK for itself, then it follows that the Crown *knows* that it is not entitled to an interest in the assets as ultimate beneficiary because the relevant state of origin (or its citizenry, or, where relevant, the entity within the state of origin from which the assets were misappropriated) holds a superior property interest. The Home Office has published a policy framework setting out what it describes as principles designed to 'ensure consistency, transparency, and accountability' in the return of assets, in which it notes that each case will receive case-specific treatment and that ultimately any decision about repatriation is to be taken by the UK government.[153] But commentators have highlighted the disparity in the value of proceeds *recovered* and those *repatriated* by the UK: 'the amount of proceeds of grand corruption recovered and returned to foreign governments totalled just over £95 million and £240,610 respectively in FY 2022–23'.[154] Maria Nizzero notes that much of the recovered but unreturned assets remain in the UK pending agreement of Memoranda of Understanding between HM Government and the relevant states of origin pursuant to which the countries agree how the assets are to be returned and applied.[155] All of this is to say that depending on the circumstances, repatriation of recovered assets should not be taken for granted, notwithstanding the requirement in the UNCAC to give 'priority consideration' to the return of those assets and the questionable title of the Crown to any such property. In any event, as of the date of writing, no assets representing the proceeds of foreign corruption recovered using UWO processes have been reported as having been returned to states of origin, suggesting that the mechanism has failed or largely failed to satisfy the statutory objective of repatriation.

[152] See n 58 and accompanying text.

[153] Home Office, 'Framework for Transparent and Accountable Asset Return' (13 January 2022). The Framework covers assets recovered in England, Wales, and Northern Ireland.

[154] Maria Nizzero, 'Exploring Mechanisms for the Return of Proceeds of Corruption' (RUSI Emerging Insights, December 2023) 4.

[155] Nizzero (n 154).

5. Do UWOs Targeted at PEPs Meet Their Stated Legislative Objectives?

Based on the performance of the PEP-specific UWO since it was first made available in January 2018, the measure largely has failed to achieve those objectives which Parliament stated that it wished to meet through its introduction. Measuring the impact of UWOs against PEPs in achieving the first objective, that of crime deterrence by 'depriv[ing] criminals from benefiting from the proceeds of unlawful activities',[156] is challenging for the same reasons that determining the deterrence effect of crime control measures more generally is difficult. Because of the clandestine nature of crime, the extent of the problem sought to be addressed cannot reliably be established.[157] There is no quantitative baseline for proceeds of corruption in the UK from which an 'improvement' might be observed, and there are doubts on whether deterrence as a crime control measure is effective at all. It is not inherently unlawful for foreign PEPs to own properties in the UK whether directly or through corporate vehicles and trusts (whether organized under the laws of other countries or under domestic law), and so undertaking a property ownership survey akin to Transparency International UK's will not yield a verifiable indication of the number of *corrupt* foreign PEPs holding interests in property in the UK.[158] On a practical level, corrupt PEPs, if they have acquired the proceeds of corruption from their states of origin, are already presumably undeterred by the criminal law in their jurisdictions of origin. It is difficult to see how an increased detection risk in holding assets in the UK will impact on their decisions to commit acts of corruption in their home countries. Corrupt PEPs have the option of simply moving or holding their illicitly acquired assets elsewhere. Thus, at best, UWOs have the potential to divert the proceeds of crime to jurisdictions other than the UK, as opposed to the ability to deter crime. The fact that corrupt PEPs can shop around for jurisdictions which will best facilitate their theft and laundering is a strong argument in favour of the introduction of grand corruption offences which can be prosecuted globally, rather than continuing reliance on the domestic criminal laws currently used to tackle transnational crimes of kleptocracy.[159]

As to laundering in the UK, an unintended but practical consequence of UWO proceedings is that they may expose shortcomings in enforcement authorities' investigation capabilities and capacities in terms of both expertise and resourcing. Even UWO advocates have commented in the past on the relative lack of

[156] See n 124.

[157] See JC Sharman, *The Despot's Guide to Wealth Management: On the International Campaign Against Grand Corruption* (Cornell University Press 2017) 120.

[158] Transparency International UK and Thomson Reuters, *London Property: A Top Destination for Money Launderers* (Transparency International UK and Thomson Reuters 2 December 2016).

[159] See eg arguments in favour of this proposition forwarded by Mark Wolf, 'The World Needs an International Anti-Corruption Court' (2018) 147(3) Daedelus 144.

sophistication of the NCA's team in the field of complex financial crime.[160] In *Baker*, in discharging a UWO on the grounds that the NCA had failed in meeting the Statutory Tests, Lang J criticized a series of assumptions made by the NCA as unreliable and questioned its investigative rigour in preparing its application for the UWO.[161] As highlighted in Chapter 1, one claim for costs made against the NCA in 2020 was the equivalent of a third of its International Corruption Unit's entire budget for that year.[162] The risk here is that a perceived inequality of financial arms between enforcement authorities and individuals whom they suspect of having benefited from corruption may deter potential recovery investigations from proceeding. For completeness, it should be noted that senior officials from the NCA have said that they are aware of certain intelligence (unverifiable by the author) suggesting that the availability and the threat of potential enforcement of the UWO measure has dissuaded apparently corrupt PEPs from investing the proceeds of corruption in the UK.[163] This claim of the measure's success in deterring putative corrupt PEPs from holding their assets in the UK should however be taken with a grain of salt if we accept contentions made by critical deviance theorists that rule enforcers typically claim that 'by reason of their efforts the problem they deal with is approaching solution'.[164]

Furthermore, even if it is accepted that putative launders *might* be deterred by UWOs, any deterrence impact is undermined by the fact that UWOs are rarely used in practice. Deterrence, even if we assume that it is in fact an effective form of crime control, is conditional on the following two causal links, as neatly summarized by Alejandro Chehtman:

> First, the visitation of punishment needs to result in actual deterrence of potential offenders. Secondly, the deterrence of potential offenders should cause a reduction in the overall number of offences.[165]

Commentators note the 'substantial evidence' available to suggest that, for deterrence, certainty of punishment (or apprehension probability) matters more than severity of punishment.[166] As there has only been a single successful set of

[160] See the comments of Tom Keatinge of the Royal United Services Institute: 'We are quite good at what the NCA might call drugs and thugs . . . but on what they call high-end money laundering, with the best will of the world, your average NCA officer is not going to understand the kinds of structures that we used to put together at JP Morgan', House of Commons Foreign Affairs Committee, *Moscow's Gold: Russian Corruption in the UK Eighth Report of Session 2017–19* (Stationery Office 2018) para 55.

[161] *Baker* (n 54). Note the report cited at n 173 which sets out arguments on what the authors suggest are the High Court's failings in reaching the conclusions in that decision.

[162] Oliver Bullough, *Butler to the World* (Profile Books 2022) 202.

[163] Author interview with senior NCA officials, 16 December 2020.

[164] See Chapter 4, n 56 and accompanying text.

[165] Alejandro Chehtman, *The Philosophical Foundations of Extraterritorial Punishment* (OUP 2010) 44.

[166] Daniel Nagin, 'Deterrence in the 21st Century' (2013) 42 Crime and Punishment 199.

UWOs against a PEP to date, it follows that the deterrent impact of the measure is likely to be negligible. Based on the (admittedly not empirically verified) significant amounts of Russian 'dirty money' reportedly flowing through 'Londongrad', at least before the sanctions imposed against Putin's allies in March 2022, notable deterrence seemed to be absent. Furthermore, if we assume that corrupt PEPs employ rational choice in deciding to use the UK as the location in which to hold the proceeds of their illicitly acquired assets, the insights into enforcement authorities' operational limitations and resourcing weaknesses, far from providing a deterrence effect, might empower corrupt PEPs to make a more informed assessment of their likelihood of avoiding detection.

The efficacy of UWOs as an expressive measure—the second objective—is similarly difficult to quantify. One somewhat unsatisfactory means of doing this is by reference to Transparency International's (oft-criticized)[167] annual Corruption Perceptions Index report. Early indications from the Index suggest that the expressive function of UWOs in showing the UK as a bastion of anti-corruption activism may be ineffective. The UK has actually slipped in the corruption rankings since UWOs were introduced.[168] Furthermore, it is possible that the operation of UWOs will undermine their expressive value by undermining the UK's 'remarkable reputation for the rule of law'.[169] First, the PEP Requirement—the ability to impose a measure on a category of the population by reference to their social, familial, or employment status—is, absent any reliable data that foreign PEPs are more corrupt than the population at large, an arbitrary criterion. Second, the availability of a presumption that unexplained assets are recoverable property without evidence of criminality raises serious questions of proportionality. This will be discussed in more detail in Chapter 6. It is sufficient for now to note that these procedurally problematic aspects of UWOs against PEPs may besmirch rather than enhance the UK's reputation for upholding the rule of law and countering autocracy.

The measure has failed to meet the third objective, namely, ease of investigation for civil recovery proceedings for the suspected proceeds of foreign corruption given the lack of successful enforcement actions to date. Even in the single successful case—*Hajiyeva*[170]—the decision on the NCA's part to apply for UWOs using the PEP limb rather than the Serious Crime iteration may have been based

[167] See eg Paul M Heywood and Jonathan Rose, '"Close But No Cigar": The Measurement of Corruption' (2014) 34 Journal of Public Policy 507, 510. In addition to ideological objections raised on the Corruption Perceptions Index, the inexactness of the methodology employed suggests that its conclusions should not be slavishly relied upon.

[168] Transparency International, *Corruption Perceptions Index 2023* (January 2024) <www.transparency.org//en/cpi2023>. In 2016 and 2017, the UK was, according to the Corruption Perceptions Index, the tenth least corrupt country in the world. As of 2024, it is the twentieth.

[169] Criminal Finances Bill HL Deb 9 March 2017, col 1483 (Lord Faulks).

[170] [2020] EWCA Civ 108, [2020] 1 WLR 3209.

more on the expressive usefulness of successfully obtaining a PEP-specific UWO than it was on using the most appropriate measure. The respondent's husband had already been convicted of a serious crime in Azerbaijan. Consequently, satisfying the tests necessary to obtain a Serious Crime UWO, to the extent that using the measure was necessary at all, would have been more straightforward and perhaps more apt. The fourth objective—asset repatriation—is something that can be quantified. Based on the information available from the Home Office, the measure has proven wholly ineffective in meeting this objective. There is no available evidence of any assets yet having been returned to Azerbaijan as a result of the action against Mrs Hajiyeva, and it is unclear whether there ever will be.

6. Conclusion

The policy justification for making PEP-specific UWOs available is one that is unfalsifiable.[171] If a foreign PEP who is a respondent to a UWO admits to holding illicitly acquired assets, then it proves that such PEPs are likely to be corrupt. If a foreign PEP denies holding assets of illegitimate origin, then that is expected, because corrupt PEPs targeted with UWOs are suspected of (at least benefiting from) dishonesty and are allegedly excellent at obscuring the origins of their assets.

The classic justification for valorizing the Due Process Model in crime control matters is that formal fact-finding processes with high burdens of proof on state authorities are important to avoid innocent accused parties being wrongfully convicted. As to where on the spectrum between Crime Control and Due Process the courts will allow UWOs to rest, it is entirely likely that they will continue to demand exacting standards of enforcement authorities in meeting the Statutory Tests before applications for UWOs are allowed. The High Court's approach so far to UWOs recalls Packer's observations on the importance of the judiciary's role as the validating authority for the Due Process Model, 'asserting limits on official power'.[172] In UWO matters to date, the High Court has embraced—at times, some persuasively argue, overzealously[173]—its role as the guardian of the Due Process Model. It initially looked as though UWOs would represent a victory for pragmatism at the expense of principle, for the Crime Control Model over the Due Process Model. In the abstract at least, it is a positive development that enforcement authorities can exercise powers in respect of individuals who, for diplomatic,

[171] ie where a theory is couched in terms which makes it amenable only to confirmation. Karl Popper, *The Logic of Scientific Discovery* (tr of *Logik der Forschung*, Hutchinson 1959).

[172] See Packer (n 1) 158.

[173] Commentators have criticized Lang J's decision in *Baker* as inter alia ignoring corruption in Kazakhstan more generally. See the publications cited in n 114.

jurisdictional, or evidentiary reasons, may never otherwise be held accountable.[174] Instances where UWOs are uncontested or not complied with are beginning to arise in non-PEP contexts already, generating easy wins for enforcement authorities. In September 2023, the High Court refused an application to replace the respondent named on a Serious Crime UWO with his son in circumstances where the alteration was sought because the respondent was on the run from returning to prison in breach of licence. As the respondent was unable to respond to the terms of the UWO within the time frame set out therein, a presumption of recoverable property was automatically raised against the assets specified in the order.[175] All of this suggests an exemplar of efficiency, and the measure's availability is perhaps intuitively laudable as a counterbalance to the impunity potentially enjoyed by corrupt PEPs.

Nevertheless, concerns remain. Whilst repatriation to 'victim' states is a worthy intention, this objective has not been met in practice. The expressivist benefit to the UK as an aspiring anti-corruption champion is rendered largely meaningless for so long as the UK simultaneously adopts or retains policies apparently acquiescent to corrupt practices in other respects,[176] and fails to adequately resource enforcement authorities in pursuing existing powers. The failure to meet these statutory objectives suggests that the 'necessity' of introducing the measure to allow enforcement authorities to meet the stated legislative aims was overstated. In any event, it would be perhaps more expressively potent to obtain UWOs against PEPs on the basis that the relevant PEP respondents are suspected of benefiting from involvement in serious crime. This would allow clearer narratives to emerge on *why* those PEPs are ordered pursuant to UWOs to account for their sources of wealth.

Second, the availability of UWOs against PEPs is also of some concern from broader individual rights perspectives, particularly given the incremental and under-examined expansion of enforcement authority civil recovery powers and the discrimination inherent in legislatively targeting a specific section of society based on demographics. This is considered in more detail in Chapter 6.

[174] It is acknowledged that this conclusion might be premature and over-optimistic given the well-reasoned conclusions drawn by Heathershaw and Mayne in the aftermath of the *Baker* case on the invulnerability of 'incumbent elites' from post-Soviet kleptocratic states to questioning in the UK on the legality of their wealth. See John Heathershaw and Tom Mayne, 'Explaining Suspicious Wealth: Legal Enablers, Transnational Kleptocracy, and the Failure of the UK's Unexplained Wealth Orders' (2023) 26 Journal of International Relations and Development 301.

[175] The refusal of the application was made on an unreported basis. See LNB News, 'NCA Reports First Recoverable Property Presumption under an UWO' *Lexis+ UK Regulatory Materials Summaries* (London, 18 September 2023) 27.

[176] See eg the report from the House of Commons Foreign Affairs Committee cited at n 160. This report noted the inconsistency of having various Russian banks the subject of sanctions being openly involved in a company floatation on the London Stock Exchange (LSE). Trading on the LSE in the company the subject of the Initial Public Offering in question, En+, was suspended in March 2022, some weeks after the Russian invasion of Ukraine and eventually commenced a delisting process on the orders of the Kremlin in April 2022.

Finally, and as will be discussed in the next chapter, critical deviance theorists have taught us that enforcement authorities tread a fine line between proclaiming their success at managing crime on one hand, and the ongoing need for new tools to ensure that crime doesn't pay on the other. Further enhanced civil investigative powers may be sought over the next few years, with attendant risks of further obscuring the circumstances in which criminal procedural protections should be correctly employed. The tendency towards relentless lobbying for new powers is vexing in circumstances where extant powers, or potentially less intrusive alternative powers, are currently under- or unenforced. A selection of these are described in Chapter 5, and might provide in many cases sufficient scope for enforcement authorities to achieve the results sought.

4
PEPs and Panic

1. Introduction

The first draft of the legislation introducing UWOs against foreign PEPs was issued following the publication of a number of official studies and policy documents flagging concerns about PEPs as 'high risk' potential participants in money laundering.[1] The documents evinced an intention on the UK government's part to focus resources 'on higher risk individuals in line with international best practice'.[2] Characteristic of all policy documentation discussing PEPs, these papers offered no hard data on the scale of the 'PEP problem' in the UK,[3] albeit one report tantalizingly made reference to unspecified

> analysis of ongoing and recently concluded investigations undertaken by the [SFO and the now-NCA which] highlight[s] that . . . sums of money [constituting proceeds of crime which] were significant and linked to cases of international corruption and specifically to corrupt PEPs.[4]

No further information was offered on these investigations. In any event, in the period 2015–2016, foreign PEPs were expressly identified as a category of interest for anti-corruption policy purposes. The first draft of the Bill introducing UWOs against PEPs was published soon after the occurrence of some major

[1] The measure was introduced in Parliament pursuant to the Criminal Finances Bill 2016. The relevant policy publications include, without limitation, the risk assessment document cited at the end of this footnote, and HM Government, *National Security Strategy and Strategic Defence and Security Review 2015* (Cm 9161, 2015). In using the term 'high-risk', the literature asserts that PEPs are particularly susceptible to involvement in corruption: 'A PEP generally presents a higher risk for potential involvement in bribery and corruption by virtue of their position and the influence that they may hold'. See Home Office and HM Treasury, *UK National Risk Assessment of Money Laundering and Terrorist Financing* (October 2015) 101 <assets.publishing.service.gov.uk/government/uploads/system/uploads/attachment_data/file/468210/UK_NRA_October_2015_final_web.pdf>.

[2] Home Office and HM Treasury, *Action Plan for Anti-Money Laundering and Counter-Terrorist Finance* (April 2016) <assets.publishing.service.gov.uk/government/uploads/system/uploads/attachment_data/file/517992/6-2118-Action_Plan_for_Anti-Money_Laundering__web_.pdf>.

[3] This is something the publications' authors sometimes acknowledge: 'there are significant intelligence gaps, in relation to 'high-end' money laundering . . . particularly relevant to major frauds and serious corruption'. Home Office and HM Treasury (n 1) 5.

[4] Home Office and HM Treasury (n 1) 36.

Unexplained Wealth Orders and the UK's Anti-Corruption Regime. Áine Clancy, Oxford University Press.
 DOI: 10.1093/9780198907312.003.0005

corruption-related events in British public life. In March 2016, Transparency International UK re-issued a report detailing the findings of a taskforce comprised of academics and NGOs.[5] The report highlighted London's status as a popular destination for politically exposed persons investing illicitly acquired assets in real estate. It advocated for the imposition of UWOs against PEPs as a means of increasing the recovery of corruptly acquired assets and to deter corrupt foreign elites from holding the proceeds of corruption in the UK.

In April 2016, the Panama Papers were leaked. The resulting stories repeated and amplified the message on the prevalence of corruption so recently broadcast by Transparency International UK. Twelve national leaders and a total of 143 known PEPs were disclosed as holding interests in offshore corporate vehicles—and this was the revelation from only one firm.[6] Embarrassingly for the then-UK Prime Minister, David Cameron, who was hosting a major global anti-corruption summit in London the following month, he was found to be a beneficiary of an off-shore trust established in the Bahamas.[7] In the foreword to a publication of essays compiled to mark the anti-corruption summit, Mr Cameron wrote: 'we in the UK are looking closely at the potential of Unexplained Wealth Orders, and . . . I urge other countries to do the same'.[8] This confluence of highly publicized events placed UWOs firmly on the legislative agenda. By the time draft legislation was published five months later, the cross-party support with which it was received provided the UK Parliament, then grappling with the divisive outcome of the Brexit referendum, with a welcome respite from the increasing acrimony of debates on contemporaneous matters. Just over six months were available in which to finalize the new laws from the date of their first introduction. Deliberation on its contents was therefore relatively hurried.[9] To date, utilization of UWOs against PEPs has been markedly limited.[10] The second and third sections of this chapter use a critical deviance studies analysis to determine whether the measure might be viewed reasonably as a 'panic-induced' statutory measure. It is argued that the process surrounding the introduction of the PEP-specific UWO mechanism conformed to tropes typical of

[5] Transparency International and Transparency International UK, *Empowering the UK to Recover Corrupt Assets: Unexplained Wealth Orders and Other New Approaches to Illicit Enrichment and Asset Recovery* (Transparency International and Transparency International UK March 2016).

[6] See Luke Harding, 'What Are the Panama Papers?' *The Guardian* (London, 6 April 2016) 3.

[7] Lucy Fisher, 'Cameron: I Held Shares in Offshore Tax Haven' *The Times* (London, 8 April 2016) 1, 6, 7.

[8] Prime Minister's Office, *Against Corruption: a Collection of Essays* (12 May 2016) <www.gov.uk/government/publications/against-corruption-a-collection-of-essays/against-corruption-a-collection-of-essays>.

[9] The previous significant amending statute to the POCA, the Serious Crime Act 2015, was a significantly shorter piece of legislation and received royal assent nine months following its first reading.

[10] As of 1 January 2025, reportedly only five sets of UWOs—including only one involving a PEP-specific investigation—have ever been successfully applied for and survived appeals processes in the UK. This is notably less than the twenty UWOs per year anticipated by the Home Office's Impact Assessment for UWOs: Home Office, *Criminal Finances Act—Unexplained Wealth Orders Impact Assessment No: HO0282* (20 June 2017) 1.

moral panics. In making this contention, the chapter draws on the work of critical deviance theorists, including Howard Becker and Stanley Cohen, and uses media surveys and reviews parliamentary debates in assessing the public and political discourse surrounding the introduction of both UWOs and newer sanctions measures. This chapter urges caution in adopting rhetorically useful but practically ineffective means of pursuing kleptocratic spoils, arguing in the fourth section that lessons could be drawn from a more tailored approach of the kind represented by targeted sanctions. It cautions, however, that while the imposition of sanctions is a politically popular move, this popularity may be bolstered by public misconceptions of how sanctions work in practice.

2. Panic and Entrepreneurialism Around PEPs

Throughout the 1960s and 70s, a movement of criminologists and sociologists known as the 'critical deviance school' steered discussion on crime away from the act of perpetrating criminal offences per se and towards an examination of why particular acts are designated as criminal acts.[11] Francis Fukuyama has described the movement's underlying philosophy:

> [B]ecause of the frequent arbitrariness of crime definitions . . . [it is] a school of criminology that holds that crime is simply whatever the dominant elites in a given society choose to label as crime and what is deviant for one group is normal for another.[12]

The theory provides a useful framework to understand why particular groups of individuals are designated as 'deviant' in the law. It is appropriate to consider the introduction of UWOs against PEPs through the use of a critical deviance theoretical lens because (i) the process bears the hallmarks of a moral panic—a recurring phenomenon in case studies examined in critical deviance writing; and (ii) the imputation of delinquency to an entire 'high risk' category of individuals as a result of the wrongdoing of an unquantified number of PEPs recalls the legislative hand-wringing in the late 1960s and early 70s with regard to the bored youths and jazz musicians discussed in two celebrated studies of critical deviance theory published

[11] This movement can be broadly categorized as critical deviance studies. It comprised writers from the Chicago School movement in the US (a number of the leading thinkers including Howard Becker and Joseph Gusfield completed their doctoral studies in and/or worked at the University of Chicago) and the National Deviancy Conference movement in the UK (named after the eponymous series of conferences hosted by the University of York at the time).

[12] Francis Fukuyama, *The Great Disruption: Human Nature and the Reconstitution of Social Order* (Profile Books 1999) 265.

by Stanley Cohen[13] and Howard Becker,[14] respectively. Using what Cohen describes as an 'interactionist or transactional approach to deviance' as an analytical framework allows us to better pinpoint the socio-political impetus for the introduction of UWOs against PEPs.[15] This is particularly useful in circumstances where new legislation cannot, perhaps, be clearly categorized as a rational and proportionate response to a specifically defined threat posed by a distinct group of people. The following discussion shows how the introduction of UWOs against PEPs may be fairly characterized as a response to a moral panic.

3. PEPs and Moral Panic

The series of events culminating in the introduction of UWOs against PEPs is an object lesson in demonstrating the features common to moral panics. Concerns around corrupt PEPs being broadcast to the public resulted in an eruption of media and political sentiment demanding that 'something must be done' which in turn resulted in the swift enactment of new laws targeting the 'problem group' in a quintessential example of a moral panic.[16] In understanding the concept, it is worth setting out Cohen's seminal definition:

> A condition, episode, person or group of persons emerges to become defined as a threat to societal values and interests; its nature is presented in a stylized and stereotypical fashion by the mass media; the moral barricades are manned by editors, bishops, politicians and other right-thinking people; socially accredited experts pronounce their diagnoses and solutions; ways of coping are evolved or (more often) resorted to; the condition then disappears, submerges or deteriorates and becomes more visible . . . Sometimes the panic [has] . . . serious and long-lasting repercussions and might produce such changes as those in legal and social policy or even in the way the society conceives itself.[17]

The imputed threat the subject of the panic may be genuine and harmful but, Cohen's thesis argues, the reaction to it tends to be disproportionate to the level of identifiable harm.

[13] Stanley Cohen, *Folk Devils and Moral Panics: The Creation of Mods and Rockers* (3rd edn, Routledge 2003).

[14] Howard S Becker, *Outsiders: Studies in the Sociology of Deviance* (The Free Press 1963).

[15] Cohen (n 13) 4.

[16] See further David Garland, *The Culture of Control: Crime and Social Order in Contemporary Society* (OUP 2001) 126.

[17] Cohen (n 13) 1.

Erich Goode and Nachman Ben-Yehuda, developing Cohen's theory further, identify five criteria which, they contend, are consistent with moral panics; namely:[18]

(a) **concern:** concerns are heightened in relation to the behaviour of a distinct category of person and the consequences and impacts of that behaviour upon society as a whole;
(b) **hostility:** whereby members of that category are collectively designated as: 'the enemy of respectable, law-abiding society; their behaviour is seen as harmful or threatening to the values, interests, way of life [of "respectable" society]'[19] resulting in a dichotomization between 'them' and 'us' or, to use Cohen's formulation, in the creation of 'folk devils';[20]
(c) **consensus:** a critical mass of sentiment develops in segments of society (not necessarily society as a whole) that something must be done to address the perceived threat;
(d) **disproportionality:** the level of concern in response to the imputed harm is disproportionate to any objective harm (assuming it is even possible to measure such harm); and
(e) **volatility:** the idea that there will be a temporal limitation to the scale of the fervour created around the concern.

Goode and Ben-Yehuda's taxonomy of moral panic criteria provides a useful basis on which to structure a discussion on the introduction of UWOs against PEPs. Section 362C of the POCA provides that unless shown otherwise, property the subject of an UWO will be presumed to be 'recoverable property' for the purposes of enforcing civil recovery powers. Unless a PEP satisfactorily complies with an UWO made against their property, broadly, a presumption is raised that the property in question represents the proceeds of crime. On that basis, it is appropriate to utilize a criminological framework in discussing the development of the law because it conduces to determining whether a PEP-specific measure is legitimate or whether, in the alternative, it might reasonably be regarded as a politically expedient move unjustified by reference to any relevant applicable data as to whether (i) PEPs are more likely to launder the proceeds of crime than anyone else; and/or (ii) the measure was necessary given the availability of pre-existing and analogous powers.[21]

[18] Erich Goode and Nachman Ben-Yehuda, *Moral Panics: The Social Construction of Deviance* (2nd edn, Wiley-Blackwell 2009) 37–43.
[19] Cohen (n 13) 11–12.
[20] Erich Goode and Nachman Ben-Yehuda. 'Moral Panics: Culture, Politics, and Social Construction' (1994) 29 Annual Review of Sociology 149, 157.
[21] Such analogous measures are discussed in more detail in Chapter 5.

a. Concern

From a policy-making perspective, Cohen notes that the occurrence of exceptional and dramatic events have the capacity to '[coalesce] into more organized opinions and attitudes. These opinion and attitude themes correspond roughly to . . . generalized belief systems: the cognitive beliefs or delusions transmitted by the mass media and assimilated in terms of audience predispositions'.[22] Cohen describes this process as 'sensitization'.[23] In other words, repeated exposure to major grand corruption scandals or periodic public conversations about such scandals result in (segments of the) public taking greater notice of grand corruption events, allowing foreign PEPs to be re-characterized as corrupt PEPs—or at least allowing for associations to be made linking foreign politically exposed persons with corruption in the minds of the public. Media reportage is fundamental to sensitization. Exposed corruption involving political elites tends to be well-publicized because its protagonists are typically individuals holding prominent public functions. Consequently, stories involving financial crime perpetrated by PEPs are likely to have higher degrees of name-recognition factor, are highly newsworthy, and therefore are reported widely. PEPs became the subject of regulatory activism and a feature of anti-money laundering regulation contemporaneously with and immediately following high-profile revelations involving a swathe of ultra-high-value-corruption scandals in the 1990s and the early 2000s.[24] The evolution of the 'PEP' concept thus coincided with a time of heightened public consciousness of unscrupulous rulers stealing from their countries.[25] The scale of corruption highlighted by lurid details in cases like the Zairean president Mobutu Sese Seko with his shopping trips to Paris on Concorde sharply contrasted with the poverty of victim states' populaces and unsurprisingly provoked outrage.[26]

In examining the situational contexts in which rules around deviance are developed or expanded, widely publicized scandals or outrages are a recurring feature. In some circumstances, the advancement may be catalysed or hastened by a

[22] Cohen (n 13) 47, citing Neil J Smelser, *Theory of Collective Behaviour* (The Free Press 1963).

[23] Cohen (n 13) 86.

[24] Jason Sharman provides detailed case studies on grand corruption scandals including, inter alia, in respect of UK-linked examples, the cases of Nigeria's de facto former president General Sani Abacha; three former Nigerian Governors; former President Chiluba of Zambia; and the post-Arab Spring recovery of assets misappropriated from Libya, Egypt, and Tunisia: JC Sharman, *The Despot's Guide to Wealth Management: On the International Campaign Against Grand Corruption* (Cornell University Press 2017). cf Radha Ivory, *Corruption, Asset Recovery, and the Protection of Property in Public International Law: The Human Rights of Bad Guys* (CUP 2014).

[25] Commentators have identified the timing of Wolfsberg's first meeting to grapple with the issues presented by corruption in 1999 as 'particularly apposite as abuses of private banking by corrupt officials had been revealed in the 1990s': Mark Pieth and Gemma Aiolfi, 'The Private Sector Become Active: The Wolfsberg Process'. (2003) 10 Journal of Financial Crime 359, 362. See the discussion on the Wolfsberg Group in Chapter 2, Section 2.

[26] Kevin Fedarko, 'Zaire: Waiting for Kabila' *Time* (24 March 1997) 56.

particular occurrence or series of occurrences ranging from, for example, at one end of the spectrum of gravity, mild delinquent behaviour in a seaside resort over a bank holiday weekend[27] to, at the other end, the 9/11 attacks in New York.[28] Major scandals are not necessarily the sole precipitating factor for each milestone. However, many of the milestones in the historical development of the concept of PEPs followed swiftly on the heels of highly publicized scandals, typically involving corrupt politicians (see Table 4.1 below).

Table 4.1 Scandals and PEP development milestones

Time period	Precipitating event(s)	Subsequent regulatory milestone	Rule makers
1989	Concerns about money laundering as part of the failure of the 'War on Drugs'	Financial Action Task Force (FATF) established; FATF Recommendations published	FATF members (currently thirty-nine members and nine associate members)
1993–1999	Scandals involving Mexican, Pakistani, and Chinese public officials	US Senate Investigations Committee Report on Citibank[29]	US Senate Investigations Committee and the Dept of Justice
1999	US Senate Investigations Committee Report on Citibank—see above	Wolfsberg Principles	Wolfsberg Group
1998–2001	Abacha Scandal	BCBS Working Paper	BCBS
Sept/Oct 2001	11 September 2001 attacks	USA PATRIOT Act	US President/US Congress
1999–2003	- US Senate Investigations Committee Report on Citibank; - Fujimori and Montesinos scandals revealed in Peru	Negotiations commence on the draft UNCAC (passed in 2015)	UN Ad Hoc Committee for the Negotiation of the UNCAC (US and Peru developed Chapter V)

[27] See Cohen (n 13) 162–200 on events precipitating the introduction of the Malicious Damage Bill 1964 in the UK Parliament.

[28] The USA PATRIOT Act (Public Law 107-56) was passed on 26 October 2001.

[29] US Senate Committee on Governmental Affairs, Permanent Subcommittee on Investigations, *Report on Private Banking and Money Laundering: A Case Study of Opportunity and Vulnerabilities* (26 January 2000).

Table 4.1 Continued

Time period	Precipitating event(s)	Subsequent regulatory milestone	Rule makers
Sept 2001–Oct 2006	11 September 2001 attacks	FATF expanded its mandate to include terrorist financing; in turn reflected in the AML Directives	FATF and EU
2002–2010	Scandals involving Equatorial Guinean, Angolan, Nigerian and Gabonese PEPs	US Permanent Subcommittee on Investigations publish report[30]	US Senate
2010–2015	Publication of US Permanent Subcommittee on Investigations report in 2010	FATF (2012, 2013) .and EU (the Fourth AML Directive—2015) require legal professionals to employ enhanced due diligence processes against PEPs	FATF, EU
2014–2017	- 1MDB scandal[31] and Petrobras/Brazilian car wash scandal uncovered;[32] - Release of the Panama Papers; and - UK hosts anti-corruption summit in London	Introduction and enactment of the of Criminal Finances Act 2017	UK Parliament[33]

These events triggered, amongst other things, concerns around the developmental integrity of states (predominantly in the Global South), concerns around the financial stability of and reputational risks to financial institutions, and public

[30] US Committee on Homeland Security and Governmental Affairs, Permanent Subcommittee on Investigations, *Report on Keeping Foreign Corruption out of the United States: Four Case Histories* (4 February 2010).

[31] 'Malaysian Taskforce Investigates Allegations $700m Paid to PM Najib' *The Guardian* (London, 6 July 2015).

[32] Jonathan Watts, 'Operation Car Wash: Is This the Biggest Corruption Scandal in History?' *The Guardian* (London, 1 June 2017).

[33] Note too lobbying by Transparency International UK on UWOs prior to the introduction of the Criminal Finances Bill—see n 5.

condemnation of the acts committed. In response to these concerns, standards or laws were swiftly introduced aimed at preventing future corrupt acts being perpetrated by the 'folk devil' subjects spotlighted by the media: corrupt PEPs. The increase in policy concern in 2015 and 2016 in the UK referred to earlier in this chapter corresponded to an incremental increase in media interest in official corruption in the preceding decade. While this was not determinant, it is at least suggestive of heightened public concern around PEPs (see Figure 4.1 below). As with so much folk-devilment preceding laws targeted at specific cohorts, the media (and subsequent legislative) opprobrium was aimed at a societal segment ill-organized to protest increased regulation of a group of people, most of whom do not have voting rights in the UK, and who would not generally be the subject of much public sympathy. Consequently, proposals introducing UWOs potentially impacting on PEPs met little resistance, even though aspects of the measure might be regarded as harsh when compared with measures available against the general population.[34]

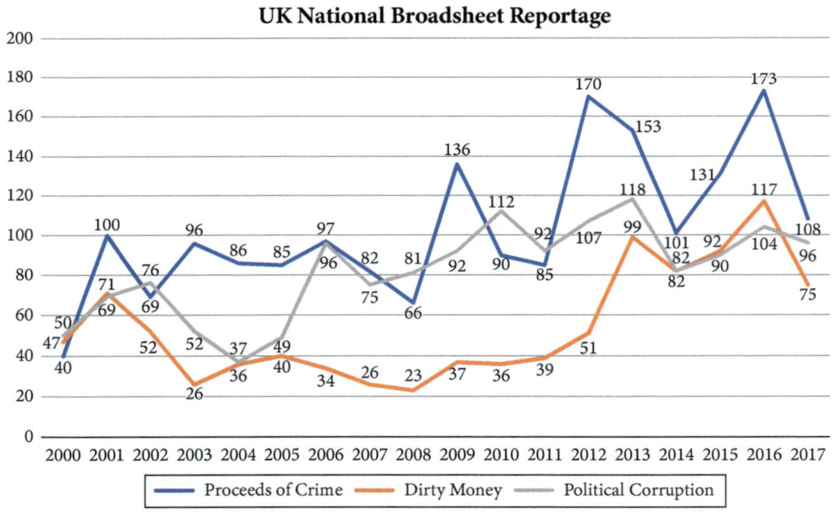

Figure 4.1 Media interest in proceeds of crime and official corruption, 2000–2017

Figure 4.1 shows the search results of the occurrence of the terms 'Proceeds of Crime', 'Dirty Money', and 'Political Corruption'—terms which are frequently used in corruption-related news items—based on a search of UK national

[34] Akin to the 'deviants' identified by critical deviance theorists and discussed in n 49 and accompanying text below, and measures targeted at 'others' discussed by Lucia Zedner (see Chapter 6, n 228 and accompanying text).

broadsheet newspapers for the years 2000–2017.[35] It shows a general upward trend in media reportage of corruption in the years preceding the enactment of the UWOs legislation in 2017, culminating in a spike in 2016—the year in which the draft legislation was introduced. Similar spikes can be observed in 2001: the year in which the legislation introducing civil recovery was introduced in draft form in Parliament,[36] in 2009 when the draft Bribery Bill was introduced,[37] and for the period 2012–2013, ahead of the Courts and Crime Act establishing the NCA being enacted.[38] Figure 4.1 demonstrates a trend of increased corruption reportage (and, perhaps, increased public concern about corruption) being followed shortly thereafter by laws targeting the behaviour triggering that concern. Media reportage focusing particularly on money laundering and which included references to corruption involving senior politicians and their families spiked around the period in which the Panama Papers revelations were made. A survey of media articles searched by reference to the search term 'money laundering' shows that references to official corruption or corrupt PEPs are commonly made in such articles. Figure 4.2 below illustrates (i) that the proportion of articles which refer to the search term 'money laundering' and also referring to corrupt PEPs or official corruption published on the *Financial Times* website in 2016 remained consistent throughout the year;[39] and (ii) that there was a pronounced spike in reportage on money laundering around the time of the publication of the Panama Papers, a few months before the introduction of the draft UWOs legislation in Parliament in October 2016.[40]

[35] These data were collected by undertaking a search of the Lexis®Library News Search function, which allows users to search all UK national broadsheet publications with the exception of the *Financial Times* (FT) (which is not searchable on that database). Duplicate results were excluded from the search outcomes. The searches were made on 1 October 2024.

[36] POCA, pt 5.

[37] Bribery Act 2010.

[38] Courts and Crime Act 2013.

[39] The FT's reportage on corruption was selected for analysis because (i) of its focus on business and economics reporting; (ii) of the ability to search by reference to date-range on its website; (iii) of a perception that its media bias rating skews relatively centrist; and (iv) that the FT is the preferred broadsheet of the UK's financial sector, key stakeholders in the PEP discussion. On the third of these contentions, see <www.allsides.com/news-source/financial-times-media-bias>, a media analysis website which claims to be staffed by individuals from a range of political biases. It is acknowledged that any such rating will always be somewhat imperfect because it will be informed by biases of the individuals responsible for compiling such ratings.

[40] The Panama Papers were not a one-off leak of confidential information on companies registered offshore, but in terms of UK-based revelations were perhaps the most prominent because they revealed assets in which both the Queen and the Prime Minister held beneficial interests in assets through Panama-registered vehicles. The International Consortium of Investigative Journalists, who published the Panama Papers, have subsequently revealed the offshore financial activities of a number of powerful people in leaks including (but not limited to) the Paradise Papers, the FinCEN Files, the Pandora Papers, and the Mauritius Leaks. Incidentally, since then, further spikes are observable around the publication of further leaks.

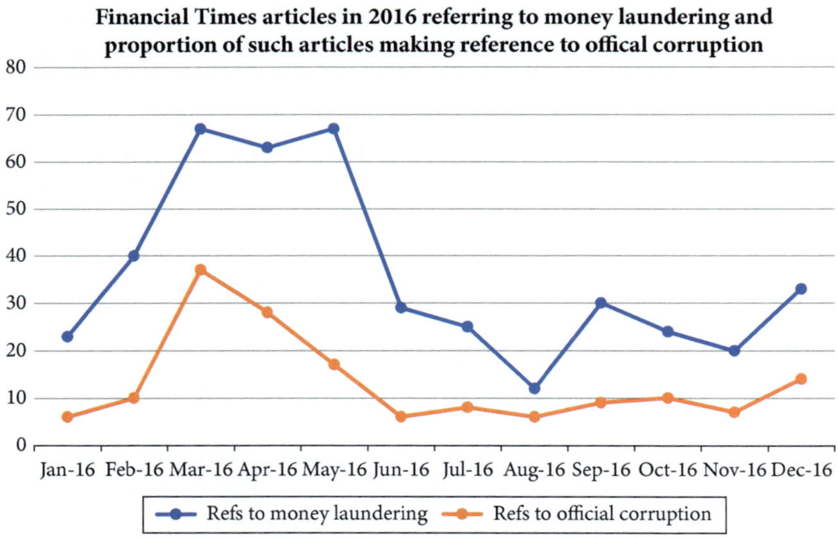

Figure 4.2 *Financial Times* reports referencing money laundering and official corruption, 2016

The confluence of increased media reportage and the publication of policy papers by ministerial departments and civil society is suggestive of an increased unease in some segments of society around corruption involving PEPs at the relevant times. However, while broad assertions were made by the government, NGOs, and the media around (i) PEPs owning property in London; (ii) PEPs being susceptible to corruption; and (iii) the prevalence of money laundering necessitating special measures to be imposed on PEPs to deter further crime; at no point did anyone explain in detail why pre-existing criminal justice powers were incapable of addressing such perceived harm. Moreover, there was no discussion on why a Serious Crime UWO would not be sufficient to deal with unexplained wealth acquired corruptly by foreign PEPs. It is noteworthy that of the *Financial Times* articles surveyed which referred to official corruption, exactly 50 per cent were articles dealing either with the 1MDB sovereign wealth fund scandal, in which the Malaysian prime minister was implicated, or with the Petrobras scandal which involved large-scale corruption on the part of Brazilian officials.[41] Neither of these scandals had particularly strong links to the UK. In other words, the breadth of the news coverage was out of proportion to the actual scale of the foreign PEP corruption problem insofar as it affected London and the UK, potentially contributing to a perception that PEP corruption may be more pervasive than it is. This suggestion

[41] Seventy-nine out of 158 articles.

is supported by a review of the number of prosecutions for money laundering committed by foreign PEPs in the UK in the same period.

Table 4.2 below shows data provided by the UK's Solicitor General in response to a written parliamentary question on the number of prosecutions by the Crown Prosecution Service of offences where money laundering was the principal offence in the years 2015–2017 (no individuals were successfully prosecuted by the Serious Fraud Office for money laundering as the primary offence in the same period). The Solicitor General was unable to respond on how many of those offences involved high-end money laundering or money laundering involving foreign politically exposed persons. In the analysis of the FT articles in 2016 in which the term 'money laundering' was mentioned, official corruption was frequently mentioned in such articles, but none of those articles dealt with UK investigations on or prosecutions for money laundering with links to official corruption (whether perpetrated by foreign or domestic PEPs).

Table 4.2 Money-laundering prosecutions undertaken by the CPS

Relevant Offences	2015–2016	2016–2017
Sections 327 to 330—Proceeds of Crime Act 2002[42]	4,542	4,866

From the above analysis, it is possible to conclude:

1. There are many prosecutions for money laundering in the UK annually (or at least there were in the years where the UWOs legislation was introduced in, and subsequently passed by, Parliament).
2. Money laundering and reports of official corruption are often referred to in the same media articles in the UK.
3. In the year in which laws specifically targeting money laundering by corrupt foreign politically exposed persons were introduced in Parliament, no money laundering prosecutions in the UK involving PEPs were, as far as the writer can tell, reported in the media (and certainly, none were reported in the *Financial Times*).
4. Much of the reporting on official corruption and money laundering can be linked to a small number of scandals, often having negligible links to the UK, which receive (disproportionately) heavy media coverage.

[42] Money Laundering: Convictions and Prosecutions: Written question—194669, answered on 27 November 2018 <www.parliament.uk/business/publications/written-questions-answers-statements/written-question/Commons/2018-11-22/194669/>.

The Home Office's *Explanatory Notes to the Criminal Finances Act 2017* explained that UWOs against PEPs were introduced in the UK in response to 'the concern about those involved in corruption overseas, laundering the proceeds of crime in the UK'.[43] The analysis above, while not suggesting that no UK prosecutions for money laundering by PEPs were considered in 2016, does suggest that the incidence of established PEP-linked money laundering in the UK may be somewhat overstated.

b. Hostility

Moral panics typically feature an increased level of hostility towards—and a singling out of—the grouping deemed responsible for the specified behaviour of concern.[44] As of the introduction of the draft legislation providing for UWOs, usefully, the pre-existing anti-money laundering laws had provided a clear definition of PEPs to distinguish that cohort from the rest of society.[45] Any references to PEPs in the law were made in the context of categorizing PEPs as individuals at 'high risk' of committing corrupt acts: an imputation of potential criminality on an entire group of people, notwithstanding the lack of data to support that aspersion. The ability to characterize foreign PEPs as both 'foreigners' and 'elites' belonging to a ruling class provided comprehensible and comprehensive criteria with which to 'other' foreign PEPs from the population at large. Amplifying mistrust of both foreigners and elites had recently proven a politically expedient move in international politics.[46] It is not suggested that such mistrust was a primary motivation for the introduction of measures impacting specifically upon foreign PEPs, but there may have existed insufficient political appetite or energy to muster dissent against the measures.[47]

Howard Becker, in writing about the development of legislation targeting marijuana users (a group categorized by the law as deviants in one of his case studies) found that the segment of society designated as deviants were 'powerless, unorganised and lacking publicly legitimate grounds to attack, sent no representatives to [participate in a deliberation process relating to the drafting of the new law]

[43] Explanatory Notes to the Criminal Finance Act 2017, para 22.

[44] As Goode and Ben-Yehuda (n 20) put it at 39: 'a clearly identifiable group in or segment of the society must be seen as responsible for the threat'.

[45] Though, confusingly, the statutory definition of PEPs for UWO purposes differs to the one used for anti-money laundering purposes—see Chapter 2, Section 2(e).

[46] Fear-mongering and contempt aimed at each group had recently proven effective for Trump, Orbán, Bolsonaro, and others.

[47] In a post-Brexit edition of the London Review of Books, thinkers Ross McKibbin, Pankaj Mishra, and Neal Ascherson each attributed the outcome of the Brexit referendum, at least in part, to mistrust within the electorate of either or both foreigners and elites: 'Where Are We Now?: Responses to the Referendum' (2016) 38(14) London Review of Books 8–18.

and their point of view found no place in the record'.[48] This is a common trend in the creation of deviance and categories of deviants.[49] Foreign PEPs in the UK might similarly be characterized as a group insufficiently organized to represent, and consequently incapable of representing, their collective interests. In the moral panic reinforced by the release of the Panama Papers, foreign PEPs were potentially far more straightforward to categorize as deviants than, say, the banking industry, service professionals in the City of London, estate agents who facilitate money laundering, or the offshore jurisdictions with poor corporate transparency thus allowing corporate vehicles registered in their jurisdictions to act as conduits for dirty money. There exists a well-established media narrative linking foreign PEPs to corruption—and it is, after all, difficult to argue with the righteousness of a law targeting corruption.[50] In any event, media and official narratives accompanying the legislation in law of UWOs applicable to foreign PEPs might fairly be categorized as hostile.

c. Consensus

Consensus is reached where there is substantial agreement (or little dissent) amongst significant segments of society that the deviants identified are responsible for the perceived threatened harm to society, and that action of some sort is needed to address that harm. The advocacy of stakeholders including David Cameron, the Home Office, and Transparency International UK; the narratives contributed by the media; as well as the revelations set forth in the Panama Papers, each provided further political urgency to the progression of an anti-corruption agenda.

Becker notes that rule-making related to deviance is often characterized by:

a. a harm needing to be discovered and pointed out, and a class of people 'responsible' for the 'deviance' must be created and treated as outsiders for committing the act—usually by a 'moral crusader';[51]
b. the crusader arguing that the existing rules are insufficient to tackle the harm being done and that new rules are required;

[48] Becker (n 14) 145.

[49] cf bored youths designated as 'mods and rockers' by the UK media in Cohen's original work; the numerous categories of 'folk devils' in the third edition of his book (2002, fn 13) including single mothers, welfare cheats, Satanists and asylum seekers; and the residents of the economically deprived Easterhouse area of Glasgow identified by law enforcement as deviants as recorded by Gail Armstrong and Mary Wilson in 'City Politics and Deviancy Amplification' [1973] Politics and Deviance 61.

[50] On the growth of civil/criminal procedural hybrid mechanisms the product of 'normatively motivated political expediency', see Jennifer Hendry and Colin King, 'Expediency, Legitimacy, and the Rule of Law: A Systems Perspective on Civil/Criminal Procedural Hybrids' (2017) 11 Criminal Law and Philosophy 733.

[51] Becker (n 14) 147–63.

c. the offending act being formally classified as deviant by professional 'rule creators' responsible for creating the new rule, who will create that rule in a professional forum. The moral crusader will often leave the rule creators to create the rules, thereby opening 'the door for many unforeseen influences. For those who draft legislation for crusaders have their own interests, which may affect the legislation they prepare'.[52]

In other words, lawmakers will introduce rules on deviance in response to pressure from moral entrepreneurs and with the acquiescence or support of the public rather than necessarily as a direct response to a pressing and proven thereat. The steps above broadly align with Cohen's description of the development of a moral panic, albeit Cohen's thesis does not expressly spell out the involvement of moral crusaders and rule creators.

In the case of PEPs, political pressure to introduce measures came from at least two directions; namely (i) the perception that corrupt PEPs purchasing property through offshore ownership vehicles are at least partially responsible for the lack of affordable housing, especially in London;[53] and (ii) the government's own commitment made at the May 2016 anti-corruption summit, following the Panama Papers leak, to address official corruption.[54] Moreover, enforcement authorities pressed on an ongoing basis for further investigative powers more generally in the fight against corruption.[55] The approach of enforcement authorities is explicable by reference to Becker's observation that the enforcers of the rules introduced in moral crusades:

> typically oscillate between two kinds of claims. First, they say that by reason of their efforts the problem they deal with is approaching solution. But, in the same breath, they say the problem is perhaps worse than ever (though through no fault of their own) and requires renewed and increased effort to keep it under control.[56]

By May 2016, a general anti-corruption consensus was clear, but was apparently not strong or unanimous, as evidenced by the fact that measures against foreign PEPs were privileged over, for example, a clamp-down on *all* PEPs or on some obvious grand corruption facilitators including banks and offshore jurisdictions.[57] In

[52] Becker (n 14) 152.

[53] See eg Transparency International UK, *Faulty Towers: Understanding the Impact of Corruption on the London Property Market* (Transparency International UK March 2017).

[54] See n 8.

[55] Author discussion with senior NCA officials, 16 December 2020.

[56] Becker (n 14) 157.

[57] For criticism of the differentiation between UK and EEA PEPs and all other PEPs, see Chapter 2, Section 2(e).

Becker's study of the introduction of marijuana laws, he notes that in introducing new offences 'care is taken not to interfere with what were regarded as the legitimate interests of other groups in the society'.[58] Parallels might be drawn with the PEPs case, in which UWOs could only be sought against officials of countries other than EEA countries or the UK: excluding from their ambit a more 'respectable' class of domestic and European PEPs. As well-organized groups capable of (i) advocacy on their own behalf; and (ii) implementing measures showing willingness to target corrupt practices (effective or otherwise), banks,[59] and the UK's Overseas Territories and Crown Dependencies have seemingly, for now, avoided the 'folk devil' label in a way that foreign PEPs have not.

d. Disproportion

The discrepancies between (i) reportage of PEP corruption with the actual incidence of reported grand corruption; and (ii) the number of prosecutions of PEPs for money laundering in the UK with reports in the UK press about PEPs involved in money laundering were highlighted earlier in this chapter.[60] Goode and Ben-Yehuda contend that:

> if the attention paid to a given condition at one point in time is vastly greater than that paid to it during a previous or later time, without any corresponding increase in objective seriousness, then the criterion of disproportion may be said to have been met.[61]

Figures 4.1 and 4.2 earlier in this chapter illustrate this phenomenon in action in relation to anti-corruption measures. While general public awareness of grand corruption may be said to have increased in the period prior to the introduction of the legislation providing for UWOs, there is nothing to suggest that the number of incidences of such corruption increased in that time.

The discussion on the premises used to justify measures against politically exposed persons in Chapter 2 shows that how 'PEPs' are conceptualized in the law is inconsistent with, and incoherent in relation to, the objectives purportedly pursued by the framers of the concept. Chapter 3 discussed how UWOs against PEPs grant unprecedented powers to the state to require PEPs to account for the legitimate origins of their assets without the necessity to establish first any suspicion of crime associated with such individuals or assets. In principle, one would

[58] Becker (n 14) 137.
[59] Who were already subject to the anti-money laundering regime.
[60] See Section 3(a) (*Concern*).
[61] Goode and Ben-Yehuda (n 20) 46.

expect a clear and pressing need for UWOs against PEPs to be demonstrated before foreign politically exposed persons were singled out in the UWO legislation. However, the interest groups instrumental in introducing the measure into the law failed to demonstrate a strong justification for any such unprecedented burden, at least in the context of those PEPs who hold little influence with regard to the distribution or allocation of public resources or assets but who are nonetheless captured within the broad definition of 'politically exposed person' provided for under the POCA.

One prominent American critical deviant theorist, Troy Duster, noted the inconsistencies in societal perceptions of identical behaviours in the context of housewives and drug addicts as cohorts each relying on sedatives. He observed that the sedated housewives provoked no major reaction from wider society, which simultaneously regarded drug addicts using sedatives as 'morally' deviant.[62] An analogy may be drawn with the inconsistency in responses to foreign PEPs on the one hand, and domestic investors on the other, using offshore ownership vehicles to achieve tax 'efficiencies' on their respective investments in London property. Such behaviour is a cause of suspicion in respect of the former group,[63] but goes relatively unremarked upon for the latter: the late Queen Elizabeth II was revealed by the Panama Papers to have availed of a Cayman Islands investment vehicle.[64] One would expect that measures would be introduced to address identical behaviours by all PEPs, regardless of origin—but instead, suspicion is raised where one segment of society engages in such behaviour but not others. The 'moral' complexion of the activity is apparently altered and requires further attention if it is engaged in by foreign PEPs rather than by the UK's royal family. On proportionality of response more generally, Duster warns against assuming a moral posture against a 'total moralistic interpretation' of a particular class of deviant until there is a 'firm, adequate knowledge of the . . . effects'.[65] Noting the detrimental consequences arising from labelling individuals as deviant, he has advocated for a principled determination of *actual* harm, and has suggested that 'an empirical test of the theoretical propositions offered . . . leads one to seek practical solutions'.[66] This kind of formal analysis was markedly absent from, and certainly germane to a discussion on, the labelling of foreign PEPs as deviants, and indeed, to a discussion more generally of the efficacy of the anti-money laundering rules which first introduced the concept of the PEP.[67]

[62] Troy Duster, *The Legislation of Morality* (The Free Press 1970) 237.

[63] See Harding (n 6). Her son, King Charles III, the UK's current head of state was found in the subsequently published Paradise Papers to have invested millions of pounds in funds and companies organized under the laws of 'secrecy' jurisdictions.

[64] Hayley Dixon, 'Leak Reveals that the Queen Kept Money in Offshore Funds' *The Daily Telegraph* (London, 6 November 2017) 1–2.

[65] Duster (n 62) 236.

[66] Duster (n 62) 249.

[67] For a comprehensive consideration of this, see JC Sharman, *The Money Laundry: Regulating Criminal Finance in the Global Economy* (Cornell University Press 2011) 37.

e. Volatility

Goode and Ben-Yehuda advise that 'by their very nature, moral panics are volatile: they erupt fairly suddenly (although they may lie dormant or latent for long periods of time, and may reappear from time to time) and, nearly as suddenly, subside'.[68] As will be discussed in Chapter 7, notwithstanding what was apparently at the time the imperative introduction of UWOs against PEPs in combatting the problem of the UK's status as a foreign corruption proceeds laundry, the subsequent introduction of a broader range of measures and practices that might usefully address the issue has been remarkably slow in coming to pass. Figure 4.1 earlier in this chapter shows a coincidence of media reportage with key developments in the proceeds of crime laws every three to five years. It is a habitual occurrence within the realm of moral enterprise that successful 'moral crusaders'—those who canvass for and achieve the introduction of innovative and unprecedented new measures to tackle perceived harms—are essentially out of a job if their crusade is successful, and therefore must find new crusades to which to devote their energies.[69] This may at least partially explain the periodic introduction of new asset recovery or anti-corruption measures on something approaching the same timescale.

4. Panic and Sanctions?

Some of the tropes of panic-induced rules are similarly evident in the recent discourse around the imposition of targeted sanctions in the UK against individuals connected to Putin's regime in the UK. These tropes, some of which had been evident for years, crystallized into panic upon Russia's invasion of Ukraine. As with UWOs, there are clear and justifiable reasons for concern around the imputed threat the subject of the panic, and these will be discussed shortly, but first, it is necessary to explain the policy rationales for and the impact of sanctions targeted against named individuals.

Circumstances may arise where an official from an endemically corrupt country or someone connected to them is suspected of holding property in, say, London but (i) UK enforcement authorities cannot satisfy the statutory tests necessary to obtain an UWO or any other investigation tool; and (ii) there is insufficient evidence to bring criminal proceedings in the UK. In any event, the wealth under suspicion, whilst perhaps acquired in questionable circumstances, may have been obtained with the approval of the state of origin (eg where such state is a kleptocracy), so it is possible that double criminality conditions allowing for a prosecution

[68] Goode and Ben-Yehuda (2009) (n 18) 41.
[69] Becker (n 14) 152–55.

may not be met,[70] and the state of origin will have no interest in pursuing the assets. Judicial remedies will be unavailable, so recourse against the officials involved will only be available at an executive level, meaning that the government can either (a) do nothing—thereby facilitating impunity; or (b) act against the relevant individual or kleptocracy by using targeted sanctions. The use of targeted sanctions against individuals or entities has been described as a 'milder, humanitarian alternative' to more comprehensive sanctions against states because their use does not indiscriminately impact upon an entire citizenry but instead enables holding states to impose asset restraint measures and (sometimes) entry bans on targeted individuals as a means of condemning their or their country's acts.[71]

The Sanctions and Anti-Money Laundering Act 2018 (SAMLA) expanded the reach of Magnitsky provisions[72] to allow the UK to unilaterally impose sanctions against individuals and companies to 'provide accountability for or be a deterrent to gross violations of human rights'[73] or 'promote respect for democracy, the rule of law and good governance'.[74] The UK has subsequently imposed a series of targeted sanctions against named individuals from a number of jurisdictions who are suspected of direct involvement in or facilitation of grand corruption and gross human rights abuses.[75] The provisions of SAMLA were updated following the Russian invasion of Ukraine to allow the Home Secretary or the Chancellor of the Exchequer to designate individuals or organizations allied to the Putin administration as subject to sanctions on an 'urgent' basis without first having to be satisfied, subject to a number of conditions, that there are reasonable grounds to suspect that the sanctioned individual or entity is an 'involved person' in the actions sought to be condemned by the sanctions, or is related to or connected to an 'involved person'.[76]

In this way, the amendments to SAMLA introduced following the invasion of Ukraine achieve some of the same expressive purposes sought to be achieved by PEP-specific UWOs. Unlike the latter, however, targeted sanctions are not intended to facilitate the ease of investigation and asset repatriation aims that UWOs purportedly enable. Nor are sanctions designed as a deterrent to crimes. They are intended to operate primarily as administrative measures with a distinctly political

[70] For accounts of such wealth acquisition in Russia, see Catherine Belton, *Putin's People* (William Collins 2020).

[71] Anton Moiseienko and Saskia Hufnagel, 'Targeted Sanctions, Crimes and State Sovereignty' (2015) 6 New Journal of European Criminal Law 351.

[72] See Chapter 5, Section 2(b).

[73] SAMLA, s 1(2)(f).

[74] SAMLA, s 1(2)(i).

[75] Pursuant to the the Global Anti-Corruption Sanctions Regulations 2021, SI 2021/488 and the Global Human Rights Sanctions Regulations 2020, SI 2020/680.

[76] SAMLA, s 11(2B)(ii) and s 12(5A)(ii) as inserted by pt 3 of the Economic Crime (Transparency and Enforcement) Act 2022. For completeness: the designation of a person subject to targeted sanction using the urgent sanction procedure lapses within fifty-six days unless certain conditions are met.

valence rather than as crime control measures.[77] The UK's sanctions regime largely replicates and is modelled on the EU's. In introducing targeted misappropriation sanctions against individuals, the EU has expressly remarked that its objectives are primarily political, stating that they are a means of ensuring stabilization of new governments and post-revolutionary leaderships in relevant countries, coercing transgressors towards better behaviour,[78] as well as preventing capital flight and preserving assets for future recovery.[79] Individuals who are made the subject of targeted sanctions are typically banned from dealing with their assets held in the sanctioning state—a de facto asset freeze—and their leave to enter or remain in the sanctioning state is withdrawn for so long as the relevant sanctions remain in place.[80] In practical terms, this can make life uncomfortable or inconvenient for sanctioned parties but constitutes, in theory, an incentive to sanctioned individuals to improve their behaviour or seek to positively influence the behaviour of others with the prospect of potentially having restored access to their assets in future.

Sanctions are not particularly useful or effective as a means of recovering assets from kleptocrats on a case-by-case basis. They prevent sanctioned individuals from selling or otherwise dealing with their assets, and from using the UK's financial system (including accounts in UK-based banks) or otherwise engaging in financing with UK companies so long as sanctions issued by the government remain in place. Crucially, however, they do not by themselves entitle the UK's authorities to seize those assets (albeit breach of sanctions may provide bases on which to freeze assets).[81] If the UK-based assets of those sanctioned were to be seized, this would need to be the subject of separate judicially supervised processes (whether through domestic civil recovery, enforcement of foreign mutual legal assistance confiscation requests, or otherwise). There have been some commitments made at executive level in the US, the EU, and the UK around using income generated by assets frozen as a result of sanctions (albeit not the proceeds of sale or lease of the assets themselves) to fund reconstruction efforts in Ukraine, for example, with the intention that the underlying assets remain untouched, albeit practical progress on this proposal has moved at a glacial pace.[82] Thus, rather than providing a viable means of ensuring that the spoils of kleptocracy are seized, sanctions typically operate more effectively as a political response to wrongdoing by signalling the

[77] See Moiseienko and Hufnagel (n 71) 354.

[78] Clara Portela, 'Are European Union Sanctions "Targeted"?' (2016) 29 Cambridge Review of International Affairs 912.

[79] See Clara Portela, *Sanctioning Kleptocrats: An Assessment of EU Misappropriation Sanctions* (CiFAR—Civil Forum for Asset Recovery 2019).

[80] See eg regs 11 and 20 respectively of The Russia (Sanctions) (EU Exit) Regulations 2019, SI 2019/855.

[81] See eg reg 19 of The Russia (Sanctions) (EU Exit) Regulations 2019, SI 2019/855.

[82] See Claire Mills and Philip Brien, *Post-Conflict Reconstruction Assistance to Ukraine*, House of Commons Library: Research Briefing 9728, 15.

sanctioning state's condemnation of conduct.[83] For now, in the absence of concrete plans to move from 'freeze' to seize' of assets subject to sanction more generally, the discussion on the utility of the sanctions regime as a feasible mechanism for recovering the proceeds of foreign corruption is largely moot.

Returning to the question of moral panics in the context of the recent discourse around sanctions, numerous individuals connected to Vladimir Putin's regime hold properties in the UK, and there are strong policy justifications for imposing targeted sanctions against those individuals.[84] In the response adopted by parts of its media and body politic, the UK's recent imposition of sanctions against named Russian nationals bore some signs of meeting Goode and Ben-Yehuda's criteria for identifying moral panics. In response to the Russian invasion of Ukraine the UK government used an expedited procedure (though perhaps not expedited enough)[85] to sanction individuals and organizations with links to Russia. There was long-held *concern* about the provenance of wealth used by Russian nationals viewed as Putin's allies to purchase expensive property in London and elsewhere.[86] Immediately following the invasion of Ukraine, a mixture of peaceful protests and more overtly violent protests outside London's Russian embassy signified a growing public *hostility* towards the Putin regime.[87] There was increased evidence of *consensus* within society that 'something must be done' about the flow of Russian 'dirty money' through the UK and ensuring that any individuals who had profited illegitimately from their ally-ship with Putin were duly held accountable.[88]

[83] See Andreas Boogaerts, 'Short-Term Success, Long-Term Failure? Explaining the Signalling Effects of EU Misappropriation Sanctions following Revolutionary Events in Tunisia, Egypt, and Ukraine' (2020) 23 Journal of International Relations and Development 67, where sanctions imposed by the EU against members of certain overthrown regimes are characterized as succeeding in providing quick signals of support to the relevant countries, but not especially effective in aiding repatriation or deterring PEP misappropriation more generally.

[84] Rowan Moore, 'How London Became the Place to Be for Putin's Oligarchs' *The Observer* (London, 6 March 2022).

[85] Russia invaded Ukraine on 24 February 2022. Prominent oligarchs with assets in London including Roman Abramovich were not designated on UK sanctions lists until 10 March 2022, allowing for plenty of time to dissipate UK-based assets in the intervening period. Savvy PEPs will quickly remove their assets from a jurisdiction where sanctions are a possibility, taking advantage of potentially slow administrative processes. Infamously, the UK failed to take action for thirty-seven days following the toppling of Hosni Mubarak's regime in Egypt to freeze his, and eighteen of his associates' assets.

[86] See eg House of Commons Foreign Affairs Committee, *Moscow's Gold: Russian Corruption in the UK. Eighth Report of Session 2017–19* (HC 932, 2018).

[87] Zoe Tidman, 'Eggs Thrown at Russian Embassy as Hundreds Protest against Ukraine Invasion in London' *The Independent* (London, 26 February 2022) 3.

[88] See Figure 4.3. Based on a media search of the UK's national newspapers available on Lexis®Library undertaken on 26 April 2023. The newspapers in question are *The Daily Star Online, The Daily Mirror, The Sunday Mirror, The Express, The Sunday Express, The Daily Mail, The Mail on Sunday, The Sunday Telegraph, The Daily Telegraph, The Sunday Times, The Sun, The Observer, The Times, The Guardian, The People*, and *The Independent*. A search was undertaken for all articles published from 3 February 2022 to 17 March 2022 which contained all of the following words: 'sanctions', 'Russia', 'Ukraine', and variations of the word 'seizure'. The search yielded 913 results. 205 of those results were removed from the analysis because they were duplications of other results. Of the remaining results, 238 specifically dealt with UK targeted sanctions imposed against Russians. Of those results, 203 articles referred to sanctions allowing enforcement authorities to 'seize' the UK-based assets of sanctioned individuals

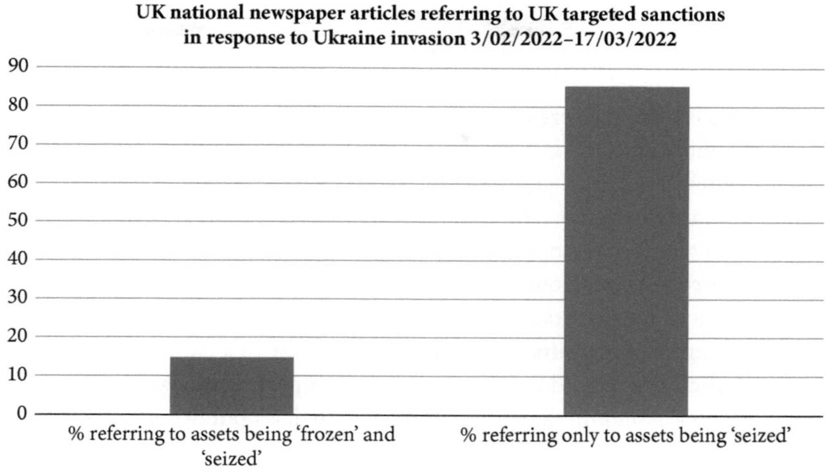

Figure 4.3 UK national newspaper articles referring to UK targeted sanctions in response to Ukraine invasion

The *proportionality* of sanctions against some of those individuals is open to debate. As of the date of writing, over 2,000 individuals and organizations with links to official corruption or pro-Kremlin associations have had sanctions imposed against them by the UK.[89] However, a great number of these people will have no assets in the UK—many of them are public administrators, Putin allies, or people connected to such individuals including some 400 parliamentarians in the Duma who voted in favour of the measures leading to the 2022 invasion of Ukraine. This is not particularly a ground for concern, given the primarily expressive tenor of targeted sanctions. More concerning from a *disproportionality* perspective was the disconnect between the public's understanding of the impact of sanctions and the actuality of that impact. Whilst there was significant public and political clamour in the UK for measures to be taken against individuals associated with Putin's regime, the practical operation of targeted sanctions was apparently lost on both the media and some legislators in the UK in the aftermath of the invasion. Figure 4.3 shows articles in UK national newspapers published in the three weeks preceding and

without explaining that sanctions merely freeze sanctioned parties' interests in assets rather than permanently depriving them of those interests. The remaining thirty-five articles made reference to 'freezing' as well as 'seizing' assets of sanctioned individuals, and some seventeen of those articles also referred to UWOs as a means of recovering the assets of sanctioned individuals.

89 This number represents the number of individuals and entities who, as of 1 December 2024, are sanctioned by the UK under the Russia (Sanctions) (EU Exit) Regulations 2019, SI 2019/855. This number does not include other individuals linked with the Putin regime and sanctioned pursuant to the Global Anti-Corruption Sanctions Regulations 2021, SI 2021/488 and the Global Human Rights Sanctions Regulations 2020, SI 2020/680.

the three weeks following Russia's invasion of Ukraine. Most of those articles referred directly to or alluded to the prospect of the UK-based assets of those subject to sanctions being seized. Very few clarified or explained outright that the impact of sanctions is only to freeze assets—that sanctions would not be determinative of the proprietary rights to assets. Prominent politicians and journalists exacerbated this problem by referring to the assets of sanctioned parties being 'seized' by, rather than temporarily frozen by, the UK.[90] Finally, the *volatility* associated with panics is evident in terms of the media and political coverage devoted to the problem of allegedly corrupt Russian oligarchs laundering their assets in the UK. As discussed earlier in this chapter, Goode and Ben-Yehuda noted a temporal limitation to the outcry surrounding measures introduced in response to a panic. In a comparison of media articles published in UK national newspapers in the six-week period surrounding the Russian invasion of Ukraine and articles published in the same period a year later, articles using the expression 'Russian oligarch' had decreased by over 90 per cent, notwithstanding the fact that the war in Ukraine continued and no London properties belonging to sanctioned individuals had been permanently seized.[91] Media (and by extension, perhaps, public and political) attention towards the problem of Russian 'dirty money' had demonstrably waned over time.

The take-aways from this discussion on sanctions following the discussion of PEP-specific measures in this chapter are three-fold. First, targeted sanctions operate with a far higher degree of precision than more generically applicable measures (eg measures capable of being deployed against 'foreign PEPs'). In the UK, ministers designating the imposition of sanctions are required to provide reasons justifying the imposition of sanctions against the named individuals targeted. If anything, the ability to sanction individual family members and associates of those against whom targeted sanctions have already been imposed in order to obstruct those best positioned to facilitate sanctions evasion is sometimes underemployed.[92] Sanctions avoid much of the diffusion of focus that is a feature of the wide net-casting of PEP-specific measures, and their imposition therefore represents a pragmatic means of flagging to enforcement authorities

[90] And, in some cases, speaking about either selling London properties used by Russian oligarchs to fund Ukrainian refugees and/or the Ukrainian war effort or housing Ukrainian refugees in those properties. Either of those options is predicated on an assumption that properties are permanently confiscated from the property holders, not merely temporarily frozen. The politicians were drawn from across the political spectrum including the Mayor of London, Sadiq Khan; the Secretary of State for Justice, Dominic Raab MP; Labour party politician Chris Bryant MP; and Conservative party politician Michael Gove MP.

[91] Based on a media search of the UK's national newspapers available on Lexis®Library undertaken on 26 April 2023. The newspapers in question are the same as those listed in n 88. A search was undertaken for all articles published from 3 February 2022 to 17 March 2022 which contained the term 'Russian oligarch'. The search yielded 508 results. A search of the same term for the period 3 February 2023 to 17 March 2023 yielded fifty results.

[92] See eg the comments of Tom Keatinge, a sanctions expert at the Royal United Services Institute in Miles Johnson, 'Horses, Art and Private Jets: The Charmed Life of Russian Warlord's Family' *Financial Times* (London, 26 April 2023).

those whose finances may be of interest. This is a point which might be borne in mind by policy-devisers when considering alternatives to PEP-specific measures. Second, it is nevertheless important to understand that targeted sanctions are not designed as a viable means of recovering the proceeds of kleptocracy from those who may have laundered those proceeds in the UK. There exists, in theory, the possibility for policy-creators to engage in a significant re-imagining of how sanctions *should* operate (by introducing, for example, the expropriation of UK property of the main players in corrupt and sanctioned regimes). In practice, however, this would be a fraught process which could undermine the political rationales underpinning sanctions and trigger reprisals against assets owned by UK-based interests overseas. Third, as with the circumstances preceding the introduction of PEP-specific UWOs before them, the recent amendments to SAMLA were precipitated by a widely reported public scandal or crisis and were a useful means of demonstrating to the public at large that legislators were 'doing something' about the problem in question. In each case, there was evidence of the public at large not quite grasping how the availability of the relevant measures would impact on the proceeds of kleptocracy in practice, and there was perhaps little public understanding that the imposition of each of these measures would not automatically involve the seizure of the proceeds of kleptocracy. On each occasion, it was politically expedient to introduce the relevant measures. In the aftermath of each relevant measure's introduction, there is evidence of public and political over-expectation and/or under-delivery in terms of the practical impact of how the new measures work in practice.[93]

5. Conclusion

As Becker sees it, the broad problem with rules created as a response to crises stimulating moral enterprise is that rules following a crusade are typically primarily emotionally motivated. They tend to be made without reliance on any meaningful data in relation to the class of deviants created, and with insufficient research into the deviants' behaviour underpinning the justification for the creation of the rules. He argues that the trouble with creating a deviant class is that it presupposes deviance on the part of all members of the class.[94] This is a pitfall avoided through the use of targeted sanctions, but Becker's arguments can be made in relation to the responses to deviance comprising, first, the establishment of PEP-related norms by the Wolfsberg Group, FATF, et al, which filtered their way into anti-money laundering laws and second, the introduction of UWOs to be

[93] And, as with other anti-kleptocracy measures, this under-delivery might be attributed at least partially to enforcement authorities being under-resourced—see Chapter 7.
[94] Becker (n 14) 165.

applied against PEPs. There are no data on the efficacy of anti-money laundering measures insofar as they apply to PEPs, nor is there any information available on the proportion of PEPs who commit corrupt acts. Consequently, there has been no meaningful evaluation on the part of policy-makers of the actual efficacy of PEP-specific measures, nor has any study been made on whether the corrupt act of a foreign politically exposed person could be captured by a well-functioning anti-money laundering system without having to resort to PEP-specific measures. All we *do* know is that creating PEP-specific measures in the law has the effect of imposing upon foreigners with political connections an aspersion of untrustworthiness. More recent anti-corruption legislation might be said similarly to adhere to the tropes surrounding panic-induced legislation. Significant public concern preceded and motivated the long overdue enactment of the Economic Crime (Transparency and Enforcement) Act 2022, which inter alia finally provided for the Registry of Overseas Entities, and the Economic Crime and Corporate Transparency Act 2023, which amongst other matters conferred increased verification powers on the Registrar of Companies.[95] Each followed swiftly in the wake of the Russian invasion of Ukraine and heightened public concern around Russian oligarchs buying trophy properties in London with the perceived spoils of corruption. These two later pieces of legislation do not fit as neatly into the analysis in this chapter on panic-induced law-making, however, because rather than creating 'folk devils' of specified cohorts, the law instead reacted to introduce systemic change on a value-neutral basis that would impact on everyone equally, and the transparency proposals had been in development for several years before the legislation was introduced in Parliament.

In practical terms, the focus on 'PEPs' when investigating kleptocracy is unhelpful. A focus on *all* senior public officials, all of their family members, and all of their close associates diffuses focus from individuals who hold positions which allow them the ability and the opportunity to use illegitimately their political offices for personal gain. Simply ascribing a label of deviance to a particular group based on their nationality and employment status might be a politically valuable means of responding to a public concern, but it is of dubious substantive value as a means of addressing the problem of the proceeds of corruption being laundered in the UK. Unless the government is willing to invest political and financial capital in meaningful enforcement of existing measures and a more thorough analysis of the empirical causes and harms of the proceeds of grand corruption, the sincerity of its messaging will remain in question, and these causes and harms will persist. In the meantime, the more focused model afforded by the targeted sanctions regime offers policy-makers useful food for thought.

[95] This legislation is discussed further in Chapter 7.

5
Responding to Corruption
Alternative Legal Routes to Asset Recovery

1. Introduction

Notwithstanding the principles espoused in the UN Convention Against Corruption (UNCAC), the UK is under no general obligation as a matter of international or domestic law to investigate reasonably held suspicions raised about the provenance of assets owned by overseas elites. Even where UK enforcement authorities have compelling reasons to doubt the legitimacy of the origins of those assets, jurisdictional barriers, difficulties in obtaining evidence, immunities, and realpolitik considerations can operate to prevent investigations being instituted or progressed. One of the rationales put forward for requiring foreign PEPs to provide evidence establishing the legitimacy of their assets pursuant to unexplained wealth orders (UWOs) is the difficulty in securing admissible evidence from overseas.[1] As the previous chapter made clear, however, in practice the orders have not lived up to the hope invested in them at their conception when it comes to investigating the alleged proceeds of foreign grand corruption. The purpose of this chapter is to survey over Sections 2 to 5 inclusive options other than the UWO available (i) to enforcement authorities in England and Wales; and (ii) to representatives of other states in seeking to recover corruptly acquired assets held in the jurisdiction. The second section examines alternative potential responses to overseas official corruption available under the civil recovery regime in England and Wales,[2] the third looks at relatively recent innovations in account freezing and forfeiture, the fourth considers criminal law options, and the fifth assesses private law routes to recovery. The chapter assesses the viability of each in facilitating recovery of the proceeds of grand corruption.

[1] See Home Office, *Criminal Finances Act—Unexplained Wealth Orders Impact Assessment No: HO0282* (20 June 2017) para 14.

[2] Scotland and Northern Ireland have substantially similar civil recovery regimes in place.

Unexplained Wealth Orders and the UK's Anti-Corruption Regime. Áine Clancy, Oxford University Press.
 DOI: 10.1093/9780198907312.003.0006

2. Civil Recovery Investigation Tools

Part 8 of the POCA provides for numerous investigative measures for use by enforcement authorities undertaking civil recovery investigations.[3] The most potent of these is the disclosure order, which requires any person who an enforcement authority 'considers has relevant information' to answer questions, provide information, or produce documents relating to an individual or property the subject of an investigation.[4] Others include the production order, which requires specified individuals (including third parties not under investigation) to produce or give access to materials relating to the person or property the subject of a civil recovery investigation,[5] and the customer information order, which compels financial institution recipients to provide to enforcement authorities 'any such customer information as it has relating to the person specified in the application'.[6] These tools are accompanied by ancillary powers allowing for asset freezing on an interim basis pending the outcomes of investigations,[7] and by more far-reaching search and seizure powers in some instances.[8] In discussing investigative tools, this section focuses on the disclosure order, because it is the mechanism which most closely resembles the UWO in terms of its operation and the kind of information obtainable through its use.[9]

a. Disclosure Orders

As with UWOs, disclosure order respondents are required to answer questions and/or produce information and documents relevant to an investigation at a time and place or within a time limit specified in the order.[10] The forms of information sought can be requested in relatively generic terms. Consequently, disclosure orders can 'potentially greatly reduce the need for multiple production orders [and]

[3] Each of the investigative tools referenced in this section is also available for use in confiscation investigations and money-laundering investigations.

[4] POCA, s 357(4).

[5] POCA, s 345.

[6] POCA, s 363(5).

[7] POCA, s 245.

[8] eg s 352(6)(a) of the POCA allows enforcement authorities to apply for search and seizure warrants where there is non-compliance with a production order and there are reasonable grounds for believing that the material sought is on the premises specified in the application for the warrant.

[9] For completeness, it is worth acknowledging that criminal administration and regulatory routes to information-gathering and powers under the banking regulatory regimes are available to the Financial Conduct Authority (FCA). Given the FCA's non-enforcement of grand corruption matters in practice, these will not be considered in this work.

[10] POCA, s 357(4).

potentially yield up more in terms of recoverable relevant information than [may] be achieved by production orders'.[11] By design, they are a mechanism that allows enforcement authorities to require individuals to provide information or access to documents without the need for those authorities to return to the courts for further orders each time new people who might be in possession of relevant information are identified.[12] These orders have been successfully used to gather information from individuals holding unexplained wealth originating overseas.[13] The tests to be satisfied by enforcement authorities applying for disclosure orders are substantively similar to those for UWOs. A disclosure order will be issued for a civil recovery investigation where there are reasonable grounds:

- for suspecting that an individual specified in the application for the order holds or at any time has held recoverable property, or that any property specified in the order is recoverable property;[14] and
- for believing that the information sought is likely to be of substantial value to the investigation and there is a public interest in the information being provided.[15]

The first limb of the test described above resembles the Source Requirement for UWOs.[16] The second limb is de facto something that also applies to UWOs owing to the proportionality requirements implicit in applications for them.[17] Table 5.1 shows the tests to be satisfied by applicant enforcement authorities when applying for each type of order.[18]

[11] *In re the NCA* [2020] EWHC 268 (Admin), [2020], 1 WLR 3224 [60] (Davis LJ).

[12] *National Crime Agency v K* [2018] EWHC 3531 (Admin), [2018] 11 WLUK 629. In that case, Ouseley J upheld a disclosure order extending to 'any person whom the appropriate officer considered had relevant information'.

[13] *NCA v K* (n 12) applying the criteria set out in POCA, s 357.

[14] POCA, s 358(2).

[15] POCA, s 358(3) and (4).

[16] See Chapter 3, n 92.

[17] See the Attorney General's Office, *Code of Practice Issued Under Section 377 of the Proceeds of Crime Act 2002: Investigations* (June 2021) para 18, which emphasizes the need for ensuring investigative orders are necessary and proportionate, and para 167, which encourages enforcement authorities to consider whether alternative tools or powers could be used instead of UWOs to obtain the same information. See also Lang J's decision in *NCA v Baker* [2020] EWHC 822 (Admin) [61]–[65].

[18] Note that the application criteria for a 'serious crime' UWO are slightly different than those applicable to PEPs. For a 'serious crime' UWO, an enforcement authority will need to establish that there are reasonable grounds for suspecting that a respondent is or has been involved in serious crime or is connected to a person so involved—POCA, s 362B(4)(b).

Table 5.1 Application criteria for disclosure orders and UWOs

Standard of evidence	UWO	Disclosure order
Respondent:	- must be a PEP; or - an individual who is, or has been, involved in serious crime (whether in a part of the UK or elsewhere) or is connected with such a person.	- N/A
Reasonable grounds for believing:	- the respondent holds the relevant property; and - the property has a value of at least £50,000.	- it is in the public interest to grant the order; and - the information to be provided is likely to be of substantial value to the investigation.
Reasonable grounds for suspecting:	- the property specified in the application is recoverable property; or - the known sources of the respondent's lawfully obtained income would have been insufficient for the purposes of enabling the respondent to obtain the property.	- the respondent holds or has held recoverable property; or - the property specified in the application is recoverable property; or - (for confiscation investigations) the respondent has benefited from their crimes; or - (for money-laundering investigations) the respondent has committed a money-laundering offence.

In short, the information available from, and the difficulty in obtaining, disclosure orders and UWOs are appreciably alike. This raises the question: why was it necessary to introduce the UWO at all? The answer may lie in the potential *outcomes* of each type of order. Where a respondent fails to respond to an unexplained wealth order without reasonable excuse within the time frame specified in the order, the property the subject of an order will be presumed to be recoverable property for civil recovery purposes.[19] By contrast, where a respondent fails without reasonable excuse to comply with a disclosure order, they will be guilty of an offence and potentially liable to six months' imprisonment and/or an unlimited fine.[20] With regard to *property* the subject of a disclosure order, the legislation sets out no express consequences for failure to comply with a disclosure order. It is possible that in addition to a criminal conviction, a failure to comply with the

[19] POCA, s 362C.

[20] POCA, s 359(2). Where a respondent knowingly or recklessly makes a false or misleading statement in response to a disclosure order, they will also be guilty of an offence.

order may hold some evidential consequences by allowing inferences perhaps to be drawn as to the provenance of the relevant property. This might in turn aid a recovery application. A relevant property may remain the subject of an accompanying freezing order pending the discharge of a disclosure order. However, no automatic presumption of the property's recoverability arises.

The disclosure order's criminal law consequences apply only insofar as the individuals who are subject to it are physically within the jurisdiction. The Supreme Court has ruled that seeking to enforce disclosure orders overseas would empower domestic enforcement authorities to impose positive obligations on individuals outside the UK under threat of criminal sanction, which 'would be a particularly startling breach of international law'.[21] Where a disclosure order is issued to an individual overseas, the obligation the order seeks to impose is transformed into a mere request to provide information on a voluntary basis. It was clarified in *Faerman v SFO* that it remains possible in principle to serve investigative orders on someone outside the UK provided that no information notice suggesting that the respondent will be subject to a penal sanction if they fail to comply is attached.[22] Consequently, there is an enforcement gap where disclosure orders are used against individuals who are abroad, albeit the orders may still provide enforcement authorities with some negotiation leverage, especially where accompanied by interim freezing orders.[23] Where a disclosure order is made against a respondent who maintains addresses in multiple countries and opts not to respond to the order whilst they remain abroad, should they fail to respond, the respondent may not be able to deal in the relevant property but will not face other consequences.

UWOs are thus distinguishable from disclosure orders in terms of outcome. A presumption of recoverable property will arise against the UK-based assets specified in an unexplained wealth order where the respondent fails without reasonable excuse to comply, even if the order was served on the respondent abroad. This was established in a case where unexplained wealth orders were served on Irish-resident respondents whilst they were in Ireland (with the cooperation of Irish enforcement authorities) in respect of their Northern Ireland properties.[24] If the disclosure order process had been amended to 'fix' the absence of any long-term proprietary disincentive for respondents outside the jurisdiction to ignore disclosure orders, then UWOs targeting PEPs might not have been necessary.

[21] *Serious Organised Crime Agency v Perry* [2012] UKSC 35, [2013] 1 AC 182 [94] (Lord Phillips).

[22] *Faerman v Director of the Serious Fraud Office* [2020] EWHC 1849 (Admin).

[23] In *Faerman* (n 22), the Serious Fraud Office agreed in a settlement with the respondent to seek discharge of its disclosure order and a freezing order against a London property owned by the respondent reportedly worth £4.25m, and forbear from seeking civil recovery of the property on condition of the respondent's payment of a sum of £1.2m plus costs. See Charles Hyman, 'SFO Secures £1.2m from Sale of London Flat Linked to Brazilian Bribery Scandal' *The Daily Telegraph* (London, 13 November 2020) Business, 3.

[24] *NCA v Grew (No 1)* [2023] NIKB 77.

b. Civil Recovery Using Magnitsky Provisions

Although not an investigative tool per se, it is worth highlighting a further amendment made to the POCA allowing for civil recovery of the UK-based proceeds of foreign official corruption. The 'Magnitsky' provisions are so named for a Russian tax lawyer, Sergei Magnitsky, who discovered and testified about enormous tax fraud against the private company for whom he worked, committed by Russian public officials. After refusing to withdraw his testimony against them, he died in prison having suffered serious mistreatment there.[25] The provisions were introduced into the law under the same legislation that introduced UWOs following vigorous and very public campaigning by Sergei Magnitsky's friend and employer, Bill Browder. The Magnitsky provisions amend the definition of 'unlawful conduct' as a ground for civil recovery under the POCA to include conduct outside of the UK 'that constitutes (or is connected with) the commission of a gross human rights abuse or violation'.[26] 'A gross human rights abuse or violation' includes the torture of an individual by or at the instigation of or at the consent or acquiescence of a public official operating or purporting to act in their official capacity in response to the tortured individual either obtaining, exercising, defending, or promoting human rights and fundamental freedoms or exposing illegal activity carried out by a public official.[27] Provided that the High Court is satisfied on the balance of probabilities that any matter alleged to constitute a gross human rights violation has occurred anywhere in the world and that property in the UK was obtained as a result of that conduct, it must make a recovery order for that property.[28]

When it was introduced, the amendment represented a departure for the UK's asset recovery regime because it allows enforcement authorities to take civil recovery action where the alleged misconduct is a criminal offence in the UK but not in the jurisdiction where the crime was committed, thereby removing a dual criminality requirement.[29] The Magnitsky provisions were designed, in theory at least,

[25] The Magnitsky provisions are set out in s 241A of the POCA and were introduced in the Criminal Finances Act 2017. Similar provisions have been introduced in a number of jurisdictions, including the US. See Bill Browder, *Red Notice: How I Became Putin's Number 1 Enemy* (Bantam Press 2015). These provisions are distinct from Magnitsky sanctions, albeit based on the same general principle. Magnitsky sanctions are a form of targeted sanctions that can be imposed on individuals suspected of corruption or gross human rights abuses.

[26] POCA, s 241(2)(a).

[27] POCA, s 241A.

[28] POCA, s 241(2A) and (3) (location of unlawful conduct) and POCA, s 266(1) (obligation on court to make a recovery order).

[29] The dual criminality requirement in transnational criminal cooperation can operate as a technical route to impunity for corruption. It is, per Radha Ivory, 'criticized as an unnecessary and outmoded barrier to cooperation; it is increasingly omitted from or curtailed in domestic and international instruments on international cooperation in criminal matters', Radha Ivory, *Corruption, Asset Recovery, and the Protection of Property in Public International Law: The Human Rights of Bad Guys* (CUP 2014) 11. cf Robert Cryer, Darryl Robinson, and Sergey Vasiliev, *An Introduction to International Criminal Law and Procedure* (4th edn, CUP 2019) 93.

to aid the recovery of the UK-based proceeds of corruption from the officials of so-called pariah states. Even though the sentiment behind the measures is creditable, the likelihood of establishing an obvious throughline from (i) conduct which occurred in another (uncooperative) jurisdiction, (ii) resulting in a respondent obtaining proceeds, which (iii) are used to acquire specified property in the UK seems prima facie likely to be insurmountably challenging. It is reasonable to conclude that the primary impetus for its introduction was as a rhetorical measure aimed at expressing opprobrium towards kleptocratic state practices in Russia rather than something that will be actually used in practice.[30] Since it was introduced in early 2018,[31] the measure has not been used by enforcement authorities even though, like UWOs, it offers enforcement authorities a means of pursuing the proceeds of foreign official corruption held in the UK, albeit in limited circumstances. A separate set of legal rules known as Magnitsky sanctions were introduced in 2020 allowing the UK to unilaterally impose sanctions, including travel bans and asset freezes, on individuals involved in serious human rights violations.[32] Individuals including those involved in the mistreatment and death of Mr Magnitsky and in the death of the Saudi journalist Jamal Khashoggi are amongst those who have been sanctioned by the UK under this human rights-oriented sanctions regime to date. It is unknown whether the individuals sanctioned under the Magnitsky sanctions actually own any assets in the UK, but the ability for the government to impose targeted sanctions against named members of a particular regime and their associates achieves in a clearer way the expressive objectives sought in introducing the Magnitsky civil recovery provisions.

The Magnitsky civil recovery provisions do not aid investigation of the origins of a misappropriated asset per se—they merely widen the scope of conduct allowing for civil recovery. Adopting such provisions as an expressive manoeuvre is a double-edged sword. It is a useful means of signalling condemnation of human rights abusers and allows the government to avoid further full-throated and highly publicized criticism from the broader media or campaigners like Bill Browder for *not* implementing such measures. At the same time, enacting laws which are unlikely to have much practical impact risks creating a misleading impression to both the legislature and the public that something significant has been done to address the underlying problems of human rights abuses and/or the laundering of illegitimate wealth in the UK. In other words, passing such laws runs the risk of being counterproductive as a response to overseas corruption.

[30] Other jurisdictions have introduced their own versions of the law since Magnitsky measures were introduced in the US in 2012. See Ben Smith and Joanna Dawson, *Magnitsky Legislation*, Briefing Paper No CBP 8374, House of Commons Library, 13 July 2020.

[31] Effective from 31 January 2018—The Criminal Finances Act 2017 (Commencement No 4) Regulations 2018, SI 2018/78.

[32] Global Human Rights Sanctions Regulations 2020, SI 2020/680.

Disclosure orders and other practical civil recovery investigative tools are an altogether more compelling proposition. They offer similar flexibility in terms of the type and scope of information available under unexplained wealth orders, albeit the latter offer a (formally non-penal) asset-based disincentive to respondents overseas who might be disinclined to respond to orders. Disclosure orders therefore constitute a viable alternative to UWOs—but only where the respondents are physically present in the UK.

3. Account Freezing, Account Forfeiture, and Cash Forfeiture Powers

While unexplained wealth orders were the marquee asset recovery introduction under the Criminal Finances Act 2017, two further innovations provided for thereunder—the account freezing order (AFrO) and the account forfeiture order (AFO)—have proven significantly more successful for enforcement authorities in terms of the numbers of orders issued and the value of assets recovered.[33] Enforcement authorities can make applications to the magistrates' courts for AFrOs where they have reasonable grounds for suspecting that money held in a bank account is recoverable property.[34] These are typically made *ex parte*.[35] Similar powers are available for freezing and forfeiting crypto wallets administered by UK-connected crypto asset service providers.[36] Like unexplained wealth orders, AFrOs and AFOs are granted at the discretion of the relevant court, which in the context of account freezing and forfeiture powers are the magistrates' courts in England, Wales, and Northern Ireland and the sheriff in Scotland.[37] AFrOs may remain in force for up to two years. Any person affected by an account freezing order may apply to the court to have it set aside or varied.[38] Enforcement authorities will have a right of hearing at such applications.[39] Where such orders are not set aside,

[33] Now provided for under ss 303Z4 and 303Z9 of the POCA, respectively.

[34] s 316 provides that 'recoverable property' is to be understood having regard to the provisions of ss 304 to 3010 of the POCA. Section 304(1) of the POCA provides that '[p]roperty obtained through unlawful conduct is recoverable property', and the remaining referenced provisions provide formal definitions of 'unlawful conduct' for the purpose of the POCA and provide some carve-outs.

[35] POCA, s 303Z1(4) provides that applications may be made without notice where 'if the circumstances of the case are such that notice of the application would prejudice the taking of any steps . . . to forfeit money that is recoverable property'.

[36] Introduced pursuant to the Economic Crime and Corporate Transparency Act 2023 inserting POCA, s 303Z36.

[37] POCA, s 303Z1.

[38] POCA, ss 303Z4(1)(b) and 303Z17A. Rachel Barnes and Ryan Dowding have suggested that grounds for discharge of AFrOs may include, without limitation: 'the lack of any reasonable grounds for suspicion [and] the funds are not recoverable property', Rachel Barnes and Ryan Dowding, 'Account Freezing Orders: Part 2—in Practice' (2020) Archbold Review 2, 7, 8. Section 303Z17A allows third parties and true owners of funds subject to an AFO or an AFrO to apply to the magistrates' courts to seek the release of their money.

[39] POCA, s 303Z4(3).

enforcement authorities may apply to the magistrates' courts to have the money held in the frozen accounts forfeited using account forfeiture orders.

Whilst to date only the NCA and the SFO have applied to the courts for unexplained wealth orders, a full range of enforcement authorities including the FCA and HMRC have made use of AFrOs and AFOs. The reasons for the measures' popularity include practical and procedural factors. Applications to magistrates' courts are less expensive than unexplained wealth order applications to the High Court, and thus less financially risky for applicant authorities. To succeed in obtaining an account freezing order, it is necessary to satisfy a magistrates' court that there are reasonable grounds for suspecting that the contents of a particular account are recoverable property.[40] A magistrates' court may issue an account freezing order where it is satisfied that the money held in the relevant frozen account represents recoverable property or is intended for use in unlawful conduct.[41]

There are two points of special note about AFrOs and AFOs. The first is that, where they are used in tandem, they are an immensely efficient means of freezing and ultimately seizing the proceeds of crime. The average annual value of cash made subject to forfeiture orders in the five years prior to those measures' introduction was £40m.[42] The per annum value of cash recovered in the five years following their introduction was £95.7m.[43] In the financial year 2022/2023, just under 50 per cent of the total value of assets subject to forfeiture orders were the result of account freezing orders.[44] A second surprising aspect of AFrOs and AFOs is the fact that they have garnered so little of the kind of judicial, academic, and media attention that unexplained wealth orders have attracted. Given the potential for the fabric of respondents' lives to be rended by the removal of access to their bank accounts, the relative paucity of commentary on the mechanisms is curious. Similar rights concerns around, inter alia, the impact on individual privacy rights, the burden of disproof of the unlawful origins of assets falling on respondents, and the lack of procedural safeguards afforded to respondents apply to both unexplained wealth mechanisms and account forfeiture powers.[45] The evidential threshold to be met by enforcement authorities seeking account freezing orders is relatively low. They must establish on the balance of probabilities 'reasonable grounds to suspect' that accounts contain recoverable property. Given the correlation between lower evidential burdens to be met by enforcement authorities and a heightened risk of error accompanying low burdens, this is of

[40] The statutory tests to be satisfied in obtaining an AFrO are set out in s 303Z(2) of the POCA.

[41] PCOA, s 303Z9(2).

[42] Home Office, *Asset Recovery Statistical Bulletin 2012/13—2017/18 England, Wales and Northern Ireland*, Research Report 18/18 (September 2018) 3 <https://assets.publishing.service.gov.uk/media/5b9794b8ed915d66720a706d/asset-recovery-financial-years-2013-to-2018-hosb1818.pdf>.

[43] Home Office, *Asset Recovery Statistical Bulletin: Financial Years ending March 2018 to March 2023 England, Wales and Northern Ireland* (September 2023) <https://shorturl.at/0yW7v>.

[44] See the Home Office *Asset Recovery Statistical Bulletin* (n 43).

[45] See the individual rights discussion in Chapter 6.

particular concern.[46] Practitioner commentators have noted that because AFrOs are available at the very earliest stages of an investigation, whether for criminal confiscation, civil recovery, money laundering, or other purposes, enforcement authorities are often working off very little information.[47] The same writers have noted that the 'reasonable grounds to suspect' test appears to have been borrowed from the POCA's cash forfeiture provisions,[48] but that while holding large quantities of physical cash might be regarded in many contexts as inherently suspicious, the same cannot be said for large amounts of money being held in bank accounts.[49] It follows that the justifications for a relatively low evidential bar for cash forfeiture are less applicable for AFrOs yet, in an incidence of apparently unthinking policy transfer, the same test applies for both.

We can only speculate on the reasons why UWOs have captured the public and academic imagination in a way that AFrOs and AFOs have not. One may be that notwithstanding the prevalence of AFrOs and AFOs,[50] published decisions specifically concerning individuals seeking to challenge, vary, or discharge those orders are rare.[51] Magistrates' courts decisions tend not to be reported on in the media or constitute the subject of published judgments unless they are legally significant in some way. For AFrOs there are no legislative grounds for appealing to a higher court: appeals to the High Court must be by either case stated or judicial review.[52] Another reason is that aesthetically, the facts surrounding the mechanisms are less sensational and consequently less newsworthy than those surrounding unexplained wealth orders. The first ever unexplained wealth order case in the High Court concerned a respondent who had reportedly blown £16.4m in Harrods, including almost £5m pounds in its jewellery concessions and a further £250,000 in its toy department.[53] This kind of story is narratively more interesting (and more

[46] For a detailed discussion on risk allocation through the criminal burden of proof, see Alex Stein, *Foundations of Evidence Law* (OUP 2005) 173–213.

[47] Rachel Barnes and Ryan Dowding, 'Account Freezing Orders: Part 1 – An Introduction' [2020] Archbold Review 3, 8.

[48] POCA, ss 295, 297C, and 297D.

[49] Barnes and Dowding (n 47).

[50] It is difficult to gain an up-to-date and accurate picture of how many AFOs have been issued to date because the Home Office does not publish these numbers, but by way of illustration, responses to an FOI request submitted by Hickman Rose Solicitors at the end of 2023 showed that a combined total of 1,100 AFOs had been issued to the NCA, HMRC, the FCA and various local police authorities in England, Wales, and Northern Ireland during the financial year 2021/2022.

[51] Based on a search of the term 'Account Freezing Order' using Westlaw UK's cases search function on 1 October 2024, the author found only three decisions referring to the mechanism in proceeds of crime investigative contexts, one of which was a judicial review and the other two of which dealt with procedural issues in relation to the hearing of the relevant AFrO applications. A search for the term 'Forfeiture order' on the same date resulted in a total of two reported decisions concerning AFOs: each of those cases involved applications by enforcement authorities seeking judicial reviews of decisions of lower courts.

[52] Barnes and Dowding (n 47).

[53] The relevant case is *NCA v Hajiyeva* [2018] EWHC 3524 (Admin), [2018] 1 WLR 5887 (QBD). Her expenditure was reported in Rupert Neate, '"McMafia" Banker's Wife Will Have £22m Seized Unless She Reveals Source of Wealth' *The Guardian* (London, 21 December 2020).

capable of inciting outrage) than rather less glamorous accounts of how, for example, a back office anti-money laundering compliance team in a bank noticed unusual account activity and issued a suspicious activity report leading to an enforcement authority seeking an AFrO.

4. Domestic Criminal Law

The proposition that jurisdiction for crimes that occur on a state's territory lies primarily with that state is a cornerstone of sovereignty in public international law. This idea becomes complicated when the impact of crimes is felt beyond the borders of a particular state, or when an offence is committed across the territories of multiple states. The classic means of recovering the proceeds of crimes, as endorsed by the UNCAC, is through conviction-based confiscation.[54] The chief difficulty in pursuing this option where the relevant crimes are those of grand corruption committed overseas lies in challenges in establishing enforcement and adjudicative jurisdiction over the predicate offences generating those proceeds.[55] There are three logical categories of offences open in some cases for consideration by UK enforcement authorities contemplating criminal action against overseas corrupt elites. These sets of offences offer some measure of flexibility in challenging the relatively rigid limits of criminal territorial jurisdiction. Where enforcement authorities in the UK succeed in prosecuting kleptocrats for any of them, they may apply for conviction-based confiscation orders against the defendants' assets. First and most plausibly where the proceeds of overseas corruption are concerned is the possibility of a prosecution for money-laundering offences. Second, where bribery is involved, prosecutors can seek in some limited instances to prosecute pursuant to the Bribery Act 2010.[56] Third, enforcement authorities can consider whether any of the underlying offences are theft or fraud offences with a connection to the UK that would bring those offences within jurisdictional scope for prosecution under the Criminal Justice Act 1993. For completeness, it is worth noting that, in theory, aggrieved states of origin may also institute private prosecutions in the English courts pursuant to the Prosecution of Offences Act.[57] A key reason motivating complainants to resort to private prosecutions—a theme which recurs throughout public commentary on approaches to corruption in the UK—was set out in a Court of Criminal Appeal decision as follows:

[54] UNCAC, art 57.

[55] For more on jurisdictional challenges to criminal prosecution for overseas corruption, see Áine Clancy, 'Unexplained Wealth Orders against Politically Exposed Persons as a Response to Jurisdictional Limitations: Problems and Potential' in Micheál O'Floinn, Lindsay Farmer, and others (eds), *Transformations in Criminal Jurisdiction: Extraterritoriality and Enforcement* (Hart 2023) 293.

[56] Bribery Act 2010, s 3(6).

[57] Prosecution of Offences Act 1985, s 6(1).

> [T]here is an increase in private prosecutions at a time of retrenchment of state activity in many areas where the state had previously provided sufficient funds to enable state bodies to conduct such prosecutions.[58]

Where the Director of Public Prosecutions is satisfied that there is sufficient evidence to progress a prosecution and it is necessary and in the public interest to do so, the Crown Prosecution Service (CPS) subsequently may take over a case initiated by privately prosecuting parties.[59] It is not intended to consider the private prosecution route in any detail in this volume. Where overseas corruption is alleged, there are already significant evidential and jurisdictional challenges for public prosecutors to overcome, as discussed later in this chapter. It is worth noting however that making applications to institute private proceedings is potentially a strategically adroit means by which states of origin can bring key evidence to the CPS's attention and encourage it to investigate matters. The potential availability of money-laundering, theft and fraud, and bribery offences as routes to recovery of the fruits of kleptocracy by enforcement authorities through confiscation will now each be discussed in turn.

a. Money Laundering

The introduction of UWOs reflected the concern about those involved in corruption overseas, laundering the proceeds of crime in the UK.[60] Given the reported prevalence of the proceeds of foreign official corruption laundered in the jurisdiction,[61] it is therefore worth examining the plausibility of using the money-laundering regime to recover the proceeds of kleptocracy. Where a defendant is convicted of a money-laundering offence, they face a prison sentence of up to fourteen years and/or an unlimited fine.[62] A criminal conviction for a money-laundering offence in the UK will allow enforcement authorities to confiscate assets the subject of that offence in accordance with Part 2 of the POCA, and at the discretion of the government, the proceeds of those assets may be returned to the

[58] Per the then-Lord Chief Justice, Lord Thomas of Cwmgiedd in *R (Virgin Media) v Zinga* [2014] EWCA Crim 52, [2014] 1 WLR 2228, 2232.

[59] Prosecution of Offences Act 1985, s 6(2) and CPS, *The Code for Crown Prosecutors: Private Prosecutions* (updated October 2019) <www.cps.gov.uk/legal-guidance/private-prosecutions>.

[60] Explanatory Notes to the Criminal Finances Act 2017, para 13.

[61] There is a distinct lack of empirical data on this: Michael Levi, 'Money for Crime and Money from Crime: Financing Crime and Laundering Crime Proceeds' (2015) 21 European Journal of Criminal Policy Research 275, but even HM Government sources acknowledge the scale of the problem: Patrick Wintour, 'Nearly 40% of Dirty Money is Laundered in London and UK Crown Dependencies' *The Guardian* (London, 14 May 2024).

[62] POCA, s 334(1).

relevant country of origin.[63] Even though the UK fares well in the Financial Action Task Force's evaluation of its anti-money-laundering systems and prosecution incidence,[64] reports of prosecutions for money-laundering offences against foreign politically connected elites being instituted anywhere in the UK are rare.[65] The money-laundering offences set out in Part 7 of the POCA are stand-alone offences, meaning that it is not necessary for prosecutors to prove that predicate offences have been committed before seeking to prosecute. The three headline money-laundering offences are (i) concealing, disguising, transferring, or converting criminal property, or removing such property from the UK;[66] (ii) facilitating the acquisition, retention, use, or control of criminal property by or on behalf of another person;[67] and (iii) possessing, acquiring, or using criminal property.[68] 'Criminal property' is defined as property constituting a 'person's benefit from criminal conduct'[69] provided the alleged offender 'knows or suspects that it constitutes or represents such a benefit'.[70] 'Criminal conduct' is defined as activity which 'constitutes an offence in any part of the United Kingdom' or 'would constitute an offence in any part of the United Kingdom if it occurred there'.[71]

For an enforcement authority to obtain a money-laundering conviction where it suspects that a foreign elite holds and is using the proceeds of corruption in

[63] For more on the obligation (or lack thereof) to return assets to states of origin see Maria Nizzero, *Exploring Mechanisms for the Return of Proceeds of Corruption* (Royal United Services Institute December 2023).

[64] The Financial Action Task Force (FATF) is the global body which develops and oversees the implementation of anti-money laundering (AML) policy. Its role and its activities relating to overseas corruption, PEPs, and AML policy are discussed in Chapter 2. In its most recent evaluation of the UK's AML performance, the FATF wrote approvingly of the '7,900 investigations, 2,000 prosecutions and 1,400 convictions annually for standalone ML or where ML is the principal offence'—FATF, *Anti-Money Laundering and Counter-Terrorist Financing Measures: United Kingdom Mutual Evaluation Report* (December 2018) Executive Summary <www.fatf-gafi.org/media/fatf/documents/reports/mer4/MER-United-Kingdom-2018.pdf>.

[65] An exception is the arrest by London's Metropolitan Police of three former Governors of federal states in Nigeria in separate money-laundering investigations in the 2000s. Each arrest was precipitated by Nigerian Economic and Financial Crimes Commission investigations as part of a crackdown on official corruption in Nigeria. See Julius Olatunde and others, 'The Role of Financial Intermediaries in Elite Money Laundering Practices: Evidence from Nigeria' (2012) 15 Journal of Money Laundering Control 58, and Tim Daniel and James Maton, 'Is the UNCAC an Effective Deterrent to Corruption?' in Jeremy Horder and Peter Alldridge (eds), *Modern Bribery Law: Comparative Perspectives* (CUP 2013) 299, 305–14. Of the three, two left for Nigeria shortly after they were each arrested on bail. A third, James Ibori, pleaded guilty to a number of offences including fraud, theft, and money laundering. He was sentenced to thirteen years in prison, a term which he subsequently unsuccessfully appealed. See *R v Ibori* [2013] EWCA Crim 815. A confiscation order to the value of over £100m was issued by the High Court on the application of the CPS against Mr Ibori in July 2023. See the CPS press release: 'A former Governor of Nigeria's Delta State Has Been Ordered to Pay Over £100 Million and His Solicitor over £28 Million' <www.cps.gov.uk/cps/news/former-governor-nigerias-delta-state-has-been-ordered-pay-over-ps100-million-and-his>.

[66] POCA, s 327.

[67] POCA, s 328.

[68] POCA, s 329.

[69] POCA, s 340(3)(a).

[70] POCA, s 340(3)(b).

[71] POCA, s 340(2).

the UK, it will be necessary for it to establish beyond reasonable doubt that the suspect: (i) has acquired, uses, or has possession of certain property; (ii) that is criminal property; and (iii) that the suspect knows or suspects that the property represents the proceeds of criminal conduct.[72]

The test's first part is akin to the Holding Requirement to be fulfilled by enforcement authorities in obtaining an unexplained wealth order, where the High Court must be satisfied that there is 'reasonable cause to believe' that a 'respondent holds the property' the subject of an order.[73] Obviously, the burdens of proof differ between the (civil) UWO and (criminal) money-laundering measures. However, the question of whether an individual holds property is generally an objectively ascertainable fact. It is the second part of the test to obtain a money-laundering conviction—demonstrating beyond a reasonable doubt that property comprises 'criminal property'—that presents more evidential difficulty for enforcement authorities. The decision in *R v Anwoir* established that for money-laundering offences, the burden of proving criminal property can be satisfied by presenting evidence establishing either (i) that the property derived from crime; or (ii) that the property the subject matter of the investigation was handled in such a way that the only logical conclusion—or 'irresistible inference'—that can be drawn is that the property constitutes the product of crime.[74] Admissible circumstantial evidence allowing a court to draw such an irresistible inference might include, without limitation, the use of complex audit trails, the unlikelihood of the assets being of legitimate origin, or 'social media entries demonstrating a lavish lifestyle which is not supported by legitimate income'.[75] On the evidence required to draw an irresistible inference that an asset constitutes criminal property, a number of principles have crystallized:

- it is not necessary for enforcement authorities to point to any specific criminality as the source of the laundered assets,[76] or present any evidence of any criminal conduct (other than the laundering itself);[77]
- credible evidence as to the legitimacy of allegedly laundered wealth will operate as a defence;
- where an individual holds significant sums of unexplained cash without documentation supporting its origin, and where any explanations offered for those sums can be rejected as untruthful, it is correct to infer that the cash constitutes the proceeds of crime;[78] and

[72] POCA, s 329(1).
[73] POCA, s 362B(2).
[74] [2008] EWCA Crim 1354, [2009] 1 WLR 980.
[75] CPS, *Legal Guidance, Proceeds of Crime: Money Laundering Offences* (version last updated 2 April 2024).
[76] *R v F* [2008] EWCA Crim 1868, [2009] Crim LR 45.
[77] *R v Kuchhadia* [2015] EWCA Crim 1252.
[78] *ARA v Olupitan* [2007] EWHC 162 (QB).

- in some circumstances (eg where an individual with no history of employment and no visible means of support holds a substantial amount of unexplained cash), unexplained wealth *simpliciter* entitles a jury to infer that the only reason why someone in the accused's position would have been entrusted with it was that the assets represent the proceeds of crime. It is not for the prosecution to exclude every other possible inference as to the origins of the cash.[79]

The critical difference between civil recovery proceedings and money-laundering prosecutions is that for the latter, the strength of the inference must be such as to place the criminal origins of the asset beyond reasonable doubt.[80] The third limb to be satisfied in a money-laundering prosecution is a *mens rea* requirement establishing that the defendant knew or suspected that the relevant assets represented the proceeds of criminal conduct. 'Suspicion' is interpreted broadly.[81] It is difficult to contemplate circumstances arising where assets are held in a way which for a jury almost unavoidably points to the assets' criminal origins yet arouses no suspicion in the holder of those assets as to the provenance of their origins. By contrast, civil recovery operates *in rem*, so the state of mind of the respondent is irrelevant: the court is interested only in whether the asset is tainted by criminality.

FATF, in evaluating the UK's performance in anti-money laundering regulation noted that investigations of what it refers to as 'high end' money-laundering cases 'generally take years to progress to prosecution and conviction and limited statistics are available on high-end [money-laundering] investigations, prosecutions and convictions'.[82] However, Lang J's reference in the *Baker* decision to the NCA's failure to produce sufficient evidence to draw an 'irresistible inference' in the context of a UWO application suggests that the courts in practice may require—in civil investigative tool applications at least—a standard of evidence to be satisfied akin to that applicable to money-laundering convictions before granting orders.[83] On this analysis, a policy emphasis on seeking money-laundering convictions to address grand corruption might be an apt alternative to civil recovery notwithstanding the disadvantage for enforcement authorities of the higher standard of proof. The range of activities capable of forming offences—from holding or using criminal property, to disguising it, converting it into different forms, or

[79] *R v Gillies* [2011] EWCA Crim 2140.

[80] POCA, s 340(3).

[81] *R v da Silva* [2006] EWCA Crim 1654, [2007] 1 WLR 303 [16] (Longmore LJ): 'It seems to us that the essential element in the word "suspect" and its affiliates, in this context, is that the defendant must think that there is a possibility, which is more than fanciful, that the relevant facts exist. A vague feeling of unease would not suffice. But the statute does not require the suspicion to be "clear" or "firmly grounded and targeted on specific facts" or based upon "reasonable grounds"'.

[82] FATF, *Mutual Evaluation Report: Anti-Money Laundering and Counter-Terrorist Financing Measures in the United Kingdom* (2018) 3.

[83] *NCA v Baker* [2020] EWHC 822 (Admin) [99].

transferring it covers a wide spectrum of activities.[84] A complementary strategy would be to increase focus on prosecuting UK-based professional facilitators of money laundering, discussed further in Chapter 7.

b. Prosecutions for Theft or Fraud

Typically, a state cannot exercise enforcement jurisdiction in respect of criminal offences committed in another state without the consent of the state in whose territory the offence was committed. As a matter of public international law, generally only the jurisdiction of the territory where the corrupt acts allegedly occurred can establish enforcement jurisdiction over such offences.[85] Territorial jurisdiction for criminal enforcement is not, however, absolute. James Crawford observed that for states to assert territorial jurisdiction over an offence, 'if there is a cardinal principle emerging, it is that of genuine connection between the subject matter of jurisdiction and the territorial base or reasonable interests of the state in question'.[86] Increasingly, enforcement jurisdiction may lawfully be established on the basis of objective territoriality and the identification of a territorial nexus with the offence depending on the type of offence involved.[87]

Acceptance of this principle is expressed in section 2 of the Criminal Justice Act 1993, which was introduced amongst other reasons 'in order to address the number of transborder interactions and transactions through electronic data interchanges and the internet, and the concomitant economic and financial crimes'.[88] The 1993 Act specifically contemplates an exercise of extraterritorial enforcement jurisdiction in relation to fraud and theft offences provided that at least one constituent element (or 'relevant event') of the offence takes place in England or Wales. 'Relevant event' in this context is defined as 'any act or omission or other event (including any result of one or more acts or omissions) proof of which is required for conviction of the offence'.[89] Section 3 provides that in relation to fraud and theft offences, a person may be guilty of fraud or theft regardless of 'whether

[84] It is an offence to inter alia hold or use criminal property pursuant to s 329 of the POCA. Disguising, converting, or disguising criminal conduct are offences under s 327. 'Criminal property' is defined under s 340 as property constituting or representing all or part of the benefit derived from criminal conduct. 'Criminal conduct' is defined as conduct which would be an offence if performed in any part of the UK or would constitute an offence in any part of the UK if it occurred there.

[85] On the bases of jurisdiction under public international law, see James Crawford, *Brownlie's Principles of Public International Law* (9th edn, OUP 2019) 440–47.

[86] Crawford (n 85) 442.

[87] See generally Cedric Ryngaert, *Jurisdiction in International Law* (2nd edn, OUP 2015) chs 3 and 4.

[88] Julia Hörnle, *Internet Jurisdiction Law and Practice* (OUP 2021) 137. The CJA 1993's provisions were informed by the work of the Law Commission in *Criminal Law: Jurisdiction Over Offences of Fraud and Dishonesty with a Foreign Element* (Law Com No 180, 1989).

[89] CJA 1993, s 2(1). For the constituent elements approach in practice, see eg *R v Pogmore* [2017] EWCA Crim 925, [2018] 1 WLR 3237.

or not . . . he was in England or Wales at the relevant time'.[90] It follows that if, for example, an individual 'dishonestly appropriates property belonging to another with the intention of permanently depriving the other of it' in contravention of section 1 of the Theft Act 1968, provided the property is received in England and Wales, it is irrelevant that the act of misappropriation took place overseas. Section 4 of the 1993 Act provides that 'there is an obtaining of property in England and Wales if the property is either despatched from or received at a place in England and Wales'.[91] Though reported cases are few, foreign PEPs have been investigated for, and have been prosecuted successfully in England and Wales for, extraterritorial theft, handling of stolen goods and fraud offences linked to acts of official corruption.[92]

Beyond theft and fraud offences, recently, the English courts have become significantly less conservative about assuming jurisdiction for other crimes partially committed overseas, endorsing a 'substantial measures' test in accepting adjudicative jurisdiction over criminal offences. Where a substantial measure of the criminality has occurred within England and Wales, this allows the English courts to 'accept jurisdiction unless it can be argued that another country is better placed to assume jurisdiction according to the principles of international comity'.[93] This further expands the scope of prosecutions potentially available to enforcement authorities to pursue. The development of a more expansive jurisdiction for fraud offences is significant when read together with enhanced powers available to enforcement authorities investigating certain types of crimes. The Criminal Justice Act 1987 (CJA 1987) was introduced directly in response to recommendations of the Fraud Trials (Roskill) Committee, the purview of which was to consider the investigation of, and procedures relating to, the investigation and prosecution of complex fraud offences.[94]

In investigating suspected offences involving serious or complex fraud, section 2 of the CJA 1987 empowers the Serious Fraud Office's Director to:

> by notice in writing require the person whose affairs are to be investigated ('the person under investigation') or any other person whom he has reason to believe has relevant information to answer questions or otherwise furnish information with respect to any matter relevant to the investigation at a specified place and either at a specified time or forthwith.[95]

[90] CJA 1993, s 3(1)(a).
[91] CJA 1993, s 4(a).
[92] See eg the investigation of corrupt Nigerian PEPs discussed at n 65.
[93] Hörnle (n 88), citing the Court of Appeal's decision in *R v Sheppard and Whittle* [2010] 1 WLR 2779.
[94] Fraud Trials Committee Report (HMSO 1986).
[95] CJA 1987, s 2(2).

By being required to 'otherwise furnish information', an individual under investigation can be required to account for specific questions, including how they obtained property. There are, however, three critical differences in the exercise of this power when compared to the use of a civil investigative order like an unexplained wealth order. First, the power is exercisable at the discretion of the Director of the SFO, not at the discretion of a court. Consequently, the concerns around reputational damage faced by, say, UWO or AFrO respondents in publicized hearings do not apply.[96] Second, it is a criminal offence to fail to comply with the Director's notice.[97] Third, as the power is exercised in the context of a criminal investigation, the usual criminal procedural protections apply. The upshot of all of this is that there exist criminal investigative powers of similar potency and greater flexibility. Furthermore, from a rights perspective, they enjoy arguably greater legitimacy when compared to civil recovery investigative mechanisms or forfeiture processes where there is a UK nexus, even if the alleged offence was committed largely outside of the UK. The section 2 power provided for under the CJA 1987 was originally limited to use in serious or complex fraud cases, but was extended subsequently, first in limited circumstances (specifically, at pre-investigation stage) to certain bribery investigations,[98] and subsequently to all investigations.[99]

The SFO's case reporting form invites cases meeting the following criteria to be reported:

> serious or complex fraud, bribery or corruption (affecting several victims/harming the wider public/impacting on the UK as an international financial centre, and/or likely involving large sums of money in the tens of millions of pounds or higher).[100]

The cases likely to meet these criteria are limited in number, and/or may prove too politically fraught to investigate,[101] and/or might have been jettisoned as the outcome of a Shawcross exercise and/or simply may have insufficient evidence to support them.[102] These reasons might explain the dearth of reported cases of the

[96] Discussed in Chapter 6. See eg the application by respondents to AFOs for a judicial review of a magistrates' court decision to hear their matter in public in *R (Javadov) v Westminster Magistrates' Court* [2021] EWHC 2751 (Admin), [2022] 1 WLR 1953.

[97] CJA 1987, s 2(13). It is also an offence (s 2(14)) to knowingly or recklessly provide false or misleading information.

[98] CJA 1987, s 2A.

[99] CJA 1987, s 2A, as amended by s 211 of the Economic Crime and Corporate Transparency Act 2023.

[100] Serious Fraud Office, SFO Case Acceptance: Statement of Principle <www.sfo.gov.uk/publications/guidance-policy-and-protocols/sfo-statement-of-principle/>.

[101] See eg the allegations of bribery by BAE Systems of Saudi Arabian officials the subject of *R (Corner House Research) v Director of the Serious Fraud Office* [2008] UKHL 60.

[102] See Chapter 1, n 151 and accompanying text.

power being used in a foreign corruption context, but at the same time, given the alleged scale of the proceeds of corruption in the UK, it is surprising that those powers are not more widely used to investigate how wealthy foreign elites have succeeded in laundering their ill-gotten gains in the UK. The SFO is highly selective in the cases it accepts. The Director's Statement of Principle provides:

> In considering whether to authorise an investigation the Director will take into account the actual or intended harm that may be caused to:
> - the public, or
> - the reputation and integrity of the UK as an international financial centre, or
> - the economy and prosperity of the UK.[103]

It is open to the SFO to use its section 2 powers when investigating allegations of crimes leading to the laundering of dirty money in the UK, which fall squarely within the investigations of the sort contemplated by the Statement of Principle. The tenor, for example, of the public and media reaction to certain high-profile and wealthy Russians holding some of their allegedly ill-gotten gains in 'Londongrad' following the invasion of Ukraine suggests that, at a minimum, the UK's reputation and integrity as an international financial centre was impugned by its perceived failure to curb laundering of the proceeds of corruption within its borders. Whether this reputational impact directly resulted in quantitative harm in the sense that legitimate investors who would otherwise have used London as a financial centre opted to go elsewhere cannot be ascertained. It is, however, reasonable to suggest that public confidence in the integrity of the UK as a financial centre was damaged and that, on that basis, allegations of corruption against relevant oligarchs would have fallen within the SFO's bailiwick.

The POCA expressly provides that guidance issued to enforcement authorities thereunder must provide that 'the reduction of crime is in general best secured by means of criminal investigations and criminal proceedings'.[104] In principle, therefore, the policy approach is to contemplate a criminal prosecution in the first instance and then 'downgrade' to a civil recovery proceeding for reasons of either insufficient evidence or jurisdiction.[105] It is impossible to know whether any UK enforcement authority's civil recovery investigations into the proceeds of grand corruption started off as criminal investigations, but it is not beyond the bounds

[103] Serious Fraud Office, *SFO Case Acceptance: Statement of Principle* <www.sfo.gov.uk/publications/guidance-policy-and-protocols/sfo-statement-of-principle/>.

[104] POCA, s 2A(4).

[105] It has been observed elsewhere that 'in the field of acquisitive crime, it seems that if reduction of crime is really "in general" secured at all well by means of criminal investigations and criminal proceedings, the Proceeds of Crime Act 2002 would have been unlikely to have been brought forward in the first place'—Peter Alldridge, 'Bribery and the Changing Pattern of Prosecution' in Jeremy Horder and Peter Alldridge (eds), *Modern Bribery Law: Comparative Perspectives* (CUP 2013) 244.

of possibility that section 2(2) powers have already been used to investigate allegations of overseas grand corruption.

c. Prosecutions for Bribery

On a first appraisal, offences under the Bribery Act 2010 offer limited scope for prosecuting recipients of bribes in the context of overseas grand corruption and recovering the proceeds of those crimes using confiscation powers. Section 6 provides for a specific offence of bribing foreign public officials—an offence more explicitly tailored to official corruption scenarios than the offences provided for under the theft and fraud legislation.[106] The offence only covers the offering, promising, or giving of bribes. Where a foreign public official *accepts* bribes in those circumstances while they are still physically overseas, they are usually not committing an offence under the Bribery Act. To the extent that a corrupt foreign public official improperly performs their public functions in anticipation of their later receipt of a bribe which is delivered at a time that coincides with their presence in the UK, they could be liable under section 2 of the Act. It is acknowledged that the likelihood of this scenario is remote, albeit not impossible. Of course, on the rare occasion where a corrupt foreign public official commits a bribery offence *within* the UK's territory, all jurisdictional impediments to prosecution are removed. This was demonstrated in a 2024 case where a former chief of staff of the Madagascan Prime Minister was convicted at Southwark Crown Court and sentenced to three and a half years' imprisonment for soliciting bribes in London in the course of her official duties.[107] A further possibility for the UK prosecution of a corrupt foreign PEP is where they accept or agree to receive bribes for improperly performing their functions in circumstances where they have a 'close connection' with the UK, regardless of where the crime is committed.[108] To the extent therefore that a foreign public official receives a bribe overseas at the time they have a 'close connection' with the UK, whether because, for example, they are ordinarily resident in the UK[109] or because they hold British citizenship or citizenship of a British overseas territory, they may be prosecuted in the UK.[110]

Prosecutions of corrupt foreign public officials for bribery offences are thus possible in very limited circumstances. Prosecution of any bribery offences committed

[106] This offence was introduced to comply with the Paris Convention—see Explanatory Notes to the Bribery Act 2010, para 35.

[107] NCA, 'Press release: Audio Released as Former Chief of Staff to Madagascan President Sentenced' 10 May 2024 <www.nationalcrimeagency.gov.uk/news/audio-released-as-former-chief-of-staff-to-madagascan-president-sentenced#:~:text=Romy%20Andrianarisoa%2C%2047%2C%20from%20Madagascar,with%20the%20Government%20of%20Madagascar>.

[108] s 12 of the Bribery Act provides for nationality jurisdiction over bribery offences.

[109] As will be the case for many foreign diplomats and representatives of international organizations.

[110] Bribery Act, s 12.

abroad can be challenging for enforcement authorities from evidence-gathering and jurisdictional perspectives, and because the consent of the Director of Public Prosecutions or the Director of the SFO is required to institute proceedings.[111] Indeed, the Organisation for Economic Co-operation and Development (OECD) observed in 2019 that the UK's enforcement of overseas bribery cases relative to the size of its economy 'remains relatively low'.[112] For completeness, it is worth noting that UK enforcement authorities maintain that they monitor ongoing overseas bribery investigations and incoming mutual legal assistance requests from foreign law enforcement authorities to determine whether UK connections exist that might render appropriate the commencement of bribery or other investigations within the jurisdiction.[113] The NCA unilaterally initiated an account forfeiture order investigation, for example, against a national of the UK and their bank accounts on the suspicion that those accounts held the proceeds of bribery. The individual's involvement in a corporate bribery case overseas was what triggered the NCA's investigation.[114] Despite the low prosecution rate for bribery offences in the UK, the possibility of extraterritorial enforcement and the international co-operation processes engaged in by domestic enforcement authorities mean that the bribery laws offer potential in some cases for holding those involved in grand corruption overseas criminally liable for their crimes.

d. Cooperation on Investigating Transnational Crimes

Law enforcement agencies cannot lawfully engage in investigations within another state's territory without the latter's consent.[115] Where a state of origin suspects that one of its public officials or some other politically connected elite has misappropriated its resources and laundered the proceeds abroad, one of three outcomes will typically eventuate.

First, if grand corruption is generally tolerated as part of the state of origin's operating apparatus, it is possible that the suspect will suffer no consequences domestically. No final judgments will be handed down allowing for a request for asset return to be made to a holding state in accordance with the United Nations Convention Against Corruption (UNCAC). In the absence of a suspect being investigated and held accountable for their actions by the state of origin, it may be

[111] Bribery Act, s 10.

[112] OECD Working Group on Bribery, *Implementing the OECD Anti-Bribery Convention: United Kingdom Phase 4 Written Follow-Up* (OECD 6 March 2019) 4.

[113] OECD Working Group on Bribery (n 112) 19.

[114] OECD Working Group on Bribery (n 112) 19.

[115] See Neil Boister, *An Introduction to Transnational Criminal Law* (2nd edn, OUP 2018) 281, where he discusses this principle being emphasized both in the *Lotus* decision (*France v Turkey* (1927) PCIJ Rep Series A No 10 and subsequently in art 4 of the United Nations Convention against Transnational Organized Crime.

open to the holding state depending on the types of offences alleged (as discussed above) to pursue its own criminal actions against the suspect. Second and alternatively, the state of origin's law enforcement authorities may opt to investigate a suspect for alleged crimes of grand corruption. Should this investigation fail to result in a domestic criminal prosecution, the state of origin may nevertheless opt to pursue the defendant's assets in the holding state through the civil courts. This option is discussed further in Section 5 of this chapter. A third potential scenario arises where the state of origin's law enforcement authorities institute a criminal investigation and seek the holding state's assistance in gathering evidence and freezing assets pending the outcome of a criminal investigation. This may be done through informal cooperation with the holding state's law enforcement agencies and/or through a formal mutual legal assistance (MLA) process (this process is also known as judicial cooperation). This is a further means by which the UK's enforcement authorities can prospectively assist states of origin in recovering the proceeds of overseas grand corruption and holding the corrupt to account.

i. Mutual legal assistance

Several international and regional legal instruments dealing with transnational crimes require their signatories to cooperate and provide assistance to one another in the investigation of crimes and, in many instances, both conviction-based and non-conviction-based recovery of assets.[116] The UNCAC obliges States Parties to 'afford one another the widest measure of mutual legal assistance in investigations, prosecutions and judicial proceedings in relation to the offences covered by this Convention'.[117] There is no customary international law obligation requiring states to satisfy MLA requests. It is instead premised on a principle of reciprocity,[118] with many states entering into bilateral agreements formalizing the scope of their respective rights and obligations to their co-signees.[119] States Parties to corruption suppression conventions can alternatively rely on the 'mini-MLA treaties' embedded in the texts of those conventions to regulate the process,[120] or agree ad hoc arrangements.

Mutual legal assistance is typically used for 'obtaining material that cannot be obtained on a police cooperation basis and particularly for enquiries that require coercive measures'.[121] It is generally used in a mature stage of investigations and

[116] Discussed in more detail by Cryer and others (n 29) 108–10.

[117] UNCAC, art 46.

[118] The UK's position on reciprocity for MLAs is somewhat Delphic: 'The UK does not generally require reciprocity but would expect assistance from countries which are parties to relevant bilateral or international agreements with the UK. The UK would also expect reciprocity from countries to which we give assistance without a treaty or an international agreement'. Home Office, Requests for Mutual Legal Assistance in Criminal Matters—Guidelines for Authorities Outside of the UK (2022) 8. See generally Boister (n 115) 311–12.

[119] At the time of writing, the UK is a party to forty-nine such bilateral agreements.

[120] See eg UNCAC, art 46. The UK is also party to a number of agreements embedding mini-MLAs at Commonwealth and regional levels.

[121] Home Office MLA Guidelines (n 118) 6.

involves formal requests for assistance from the authorities or the courts of one state to another state, usually through the latter's courts. To succeed, MLA requests require a high level of preparation and underlying evidence. For example, where a state of origin seeks to enforce a confiscation order issued by its courts through the UK's courts, it typically relies on mutual legal assistance measures. In so doing, it must inter alia demonstrate to the Home Office's UK Central Authority that a dual criminality requirement is met, that the person named in the confiscation order has been convicted with no appeal outstanding, and that the relevant order (an original or duly authenticated copy of which must be produced to the English court) is enforceable outside the requesting state. It must also set out the material facts of the case, the link between the accused and the property, and details of property held by the accused *outside* the UK.[122] For requests for enforcement of restraint orders, similar conditions apply, save that a criminal investigation can be ongoing, but the request must explain why there is reasonable cause to believe that the defendant named in the request has benefited from the alleged misconduct.[123] There is a significant demand from the UK's enforcement authorities for mutual legal assistance: in 2023, for example, the Central Authority received an estimated 5,955 MLA requests (not including requests for service of process).[124] The Central Authority does not publish data on how many requests are granted per annum.

The stringency of the requirements to be fulfilled in requesting mutual legal assistance discourages fishing expedition applications and goes some way to allay concerns around requests having political rather than criminal justice motivations.[125] The main downside of the level of specificity required is that MLA processes can be exceptionally time-consuming. It reportedly took four years for example for the Home Office to transmit information requested through mutual legal assistance in the Sani Abacha corruption investigations to Nigeria.[126] The difficulties in obtaining formal cooperation from other states in asset retrieval cases have been felt most acutely in transitional or post-conflict states—often the states most vulnerable to large-scale official misappropriation—where there may not be sufficient institutional capacity to pursue criminal proceedings domestically and/or issue MLA requests, even where crimes of grand corruption have been committed in public sight by heads of state or other high-ranking public officials. The institutional capacity problem is well illustrated by Haiti's difficulties in recovering

[122] Home Office's MLA Guidelines (n 118) 55.

[123] Home Office's MLA Guidelines (n 118) 31–32.

[124] Home Office, MLA Guidance <www.gov.uk/guidance/mutual-legal-assistance-mla-requests>. The UK's financial intelligence unit is the NCA.

[125] Additionally, the Home Office has discretion to refuse MLA requests if it suspects that an investigation is politically motivated (n 118) 15.

[126] Tim Daniel and James Maton, 'Is the UNCAC an Effective Deterrent to Corruption?' in Jeremy Horder and Peter Alldridge (eds), *Modern Bribery Law: Comparative* (CUP 2013) 299, 299–300. The authors note that the applications were subject to two judicial review applications from Abacha's team and numerous technical objections raised by Home Office lawyers. And see more generally Cryer and others (n 29) 107–09.

assets hidden in Swiss bank accounts by its former president, Jean-Claude 'Baby Doc' Duvalier in Switzerland. He was deposed as leader in 1986 and action to retrieve the assets commenced soon thereafter, yet no proceeds had yet been repatriated by the time Switzerland passed a new law some twenty-five years later enabling it to hand over assets to states lacking sufficient resources or capacity to pursue pending MLA requests in respect of the assets of notoriously corrupt PEPs.[127]

For asset recovery and repatriation, therefore, MLA can prove a cumbersome and time-consuming process with uncertain outcomes. However, where mutual legal assistance processes are successful, states are entitled to repatriation of assets (less reasonable expenses) pursuant to Article 57 of the UNCAC. The limited information available from the Stolen Asset Recovery Initiative's (StAR) asset recovery database shows that the proceeds of many corruption cases returned overseas by the UK to date have been recovered using these processes.[128]

ii. Informal police and agency cooperation

Assistance in earlier stages is usually dealt with using more informal police-force-to-police-force processes (also known as mutual administrative assistance), facilitated by Interpol where required. The less intrusive or coercive a request for assistance, the more likely it can be provided on an informal basis, thereby avoiding the pitfalls frequently encountered with MLA requests.[129] Informal cooperation is used, for example, in 'matters like locating witnesses or suspects, conducting interviews, sharing police files or documentation on a person or assessing whether a witness would be prepared to speak with investigators'.[130] It is a significantly less potent alternative to mutual legal assistance, and information gleaned from it may not equal the quality of evidence admissible in court, but it can be adopted as an efficient means of aiding preliminary investigations, and the intelligence generated can be used to bolster subsequent applications for formal assistance. It can be used as a gateway to establish joint investigation teams comprised of police forces from different countries.[131] The Home Office's Guidance provides that all asset tracing should be done in the first instance on an informal cooperation basis through the relevant countries' financial intelligence units.[132]

[127] The Federal Act on the Restitution of Illicit Assets (SR 196.1). The Act has retroactive application. See Ivory (n 29) 43–46, and Mark Vlasic and Greg Cooper, 'Repatriating Justice: New Trends in Stolen Asset Recovery and Fighting Corruption' (2011) 12(2) Georgetown Journal of International Affairs 98.

[128] See Chapter 1, nn 134–35 and accompanying text.

[129] United Nations Office on Drugs and Crime (UNODC), *Manual on Mutual Legal Assistance and Extradition* (2012) 66.

[130] UNODC (n 129) 67–68.

[131] See Boister (n 115) 290–93.

[132] Home Office MLA Guidelines (n 118) 50.

e. Conclusions on Criminal Prosecutions for Overseas Grand Corruption

A formal criminal conviction fundamentally bears more expressive weight than a civil recovery matter in communicating societal censure and condemnation for acts of grand corruption. Recalling that the PEP-specific unexplained wealth order was introduced in response to the concern about those involved in grand corruption overseas laundering the proceeds of crime in the UK,[133] money-laundering prosecutions are, perhaps, the most feasible potential domestic prosecution options available for institution against kleptocrats who launder the proceeds of their crimes in the UK. However, where it is open to enforcement authorities to instead consider charges for theft, fraud, or other forms of corruption, prosecutions for such offences may be preferable. They hold stronger expressive value because they involve, from the general public's perspective, more clearly comprehensible wrongs with more identifiable victims than those inherent in the comparatively esoteric money-laundering crimes. It is more desirable still for the relevant state of origin to prosecute successfully someone who has committed a crime against that state and its citizenry than it is for a foreign jurisdiction to undertake criminal proceedings.[134] If a domestic prosecution in a state of origin appears unlikely, whether because of lack of evidence or for reasons of politics or cronyism, a criminal prosecution in a foreign state that can establish some territorial nexus to the offence may be the next best means of ensuring that a corrupt elite faces individual criminal accountability for their crimes. It is clear from a review of English criminal law that there are however significant jurisdictional and evidential challenges in exercising criminal jurisdiction over transnational crimes. As a practical matter, therefore, the introduction of measures like the PEP-specific UWO as an alternative means of responding to those crimes is laudable and pragmatic, at least in theory, provided that the relevant measure is proportionately applied and robustly and properly enforced. It presents one potential means of ensuring that foreign public officials or their associates who hold stolen wealth of corrupt origin in the UK face at least *some* consequences for their actions.

[133] Home Office, *Criminal Finances Act—Unexplained Wealth Orders Impact Assessment No: HO0282* (20 June 2017) para 14.

[134] Some of the reasons a domestic prosecution is important for the public from an expressive perspective are set out in Joel Feinberg's 'The Expressive Function of Punishment' (1963) 49 The Monist 397. On why it is important in terms of a sovereign state's populace's well-being and self-respect: Alejandro Chehtman, *The Philosophical Foundations of Extraterritorial Punishment* (OUP 2010) 27. Prosecutions by jurisdictions other states of origin also risk attracting claims of jurisdictional overreach or even neo-colonialism.

5. States of Origin: Independent Civil Actions in the Courts of England and Wales

Where a foreign politically connected individual holds assets allegedly representing the proceeds of grand corruption in the UK, in circumstances where a successful criminal prosecution in any jurisdiction is unlikely and where UK enforcement authorities demur from investigating the origins of those assets, or where an investigation reaches a dead end, the state of origin may opt to institute its own civil proceedings to recover assets through the UK's courts. Article 53(a) of the UNCAC requires State Parties to 'take such measures as may be necessary to permit another State Party to initiate civil action in its courts to establish title to or ownership of property acquired through the commission of an offence established in accordance with [the] Convention'. The scope of that obligation, when read with the more general obligation on States Parties to the UNCAC to 'afford one another the widest measure of cooperation and assistance' in the return of assets, is unclear.[135] It could embrace anything from simply requiring holding states to refrain from interfering in the judicial process in question right up to unilaterally encouraging and actively assisting relevant states of origin in gathering evidence. Although expensive,[136] private civil actions instituted by states of origin are potentially useful because they allow those states to (i) apply to courts in the UK to freeze the relevant assets before they can be dissipated; (ii) direct the legal strategy underpinning the pursuit of the contested assets; and (iii) seek disclosure of evidence and information through civil proceedings which could subsequently prove useful for criminal prosecutions in the state of origin. This section focuses on the civil asset retrieval options where those assets are in England and Wales.

The path to asset recovery may be smoother in some cases for states of origin unilaterally making civil claims through the English courts rather than waiting for enforcement authorities in the UK to act. The UK's domestic enforcement

[135] UNCAC, art 51. It is worth noting that these provisions represented a marked watering down of earlier drafts of the UNCAC, which referred to 'the recovery of assets, including funds, of illicit origin by the affected countries of origin [being] an inalienable right'—UNODC, *Travaux Préparatoires of the negotiations for the elaboration of the United Nations Convention against Corruption* (United Nations, New York 2010) 438–39.

[136] By way of illustration, costs in favour of the claimant for a single (unopposed) High Court application by the State of Libya in the *Capitana Seas* case (see n 148) were summarily assessed by Popplewell J (as he then was) at £120,000. States of origin can have their litigation funded by private litigation financiers—see Jean-Pierre Brun and others, *Public Wrongs, Private Actions: Civil Lawsuits to Recover Stolen Assets* (World Bank 2015) 36—but litigation funders may end up directing the course of the litigation and would be entitled to a cut of any proceeds recovered, thereby indirectly profiting from corruption. Addressing this, Jason Sharman and Anton Moiseienko have each endorsed the view that even if corruption proceeds are not returned in their entirety to the state of origin, depriving corrupt PEPs of ill-gotten assets is a desirable end in itself. See JC Sharman, *The Despot's Guide to Wealth Management: On the International Campaign Against Grand Corruption* (Cornell University Press 2017) 196, and Anton Moiseienko, 'The Ownership of Confiscated Proceeds of Corruption under the United Nations Convention against Corruption' (2018) 67 International and Comparative Law Quarterly 669, 688–89.

authorities, whether because of insufficient resourcing, lack of what they believe to be sufficient evidence, or otherwise, may be reluctant to act to recover the suspected proceeds of corruption. Further, where a holding state unilaterally recovers the proceeds of grand corruption without first being prompted by an MLA request or other input from a state of origin, that holding state can retain control or supervision over how the recovered funds are disbursed.[137] Notwithstanding the UNCAC's general intention that the proceeds of grand corruption (less reasonable costs) be returned to states of origin,[138] holding states cannot be compelled to return the assets if the conditions set out in Article 57 of the UNCAC are not met. States of origin have a range of civil remedies available to them depending on the actions pursued, albeit recoveries by this route are unusual in practice. The reasons for this might include, without limitation, political reasons like institutional incapacity, state capture in the state of origin by kleptocrats, and/or evidential problems where the location and/or the ownership of the suspected proceeds of corruption have been effectively obscured.

a. Causes of Action

States of origin can claim through causes of action in tort or equity in the English courts, provided they can establish jurisdiction by demonstrating a sufficient nexus between England and Wales and the cause of action. The bar to be met in establishing that nexus is relatively low. When the Attorney General of Zambia pursued Zambia's former president Frederick Chiluba through the High Court in London for the proceeds of his alleged graft, for example, the court accepted jurisdiction on the basis that the relevant funds had been laundered through English bank accounts operated by a London law firm.[139] The most likely tortious claims against allegedly corrupt foreign senior public officials will be through the tort of deceit (ie the civil law equivalent of fraud) or through economic torts (as in the *Chiluba* case, where the claims included the tort of conspiracy to injure by unlawful means). Alternatively, the relevant public officials' alleged breach of the obligations they owe to a state as a representative or employee of that state may form the basis of an equitable claim. Acting in an official capacity on behalf of a state can give rise to a relationship of trust and confidence between the state and the

[137] eg the Department for International Development (as it then was) in 2017 identified key established projects in Chad to invest the proceeds of official corruption originating there, which the SFO recovered in the UK. See <www.sfo.gov.uk/cases/chad-oil>.

[138] The UK has committed (though notably *not* on a legislative basis) to returning the recovered proceeds of official corruption to the victim states in line with its obligations under art 55 of the UNCAC: Home Office, *Asset Recovery Action Plan* (July 2019) para 57.

[139] *Attorney General of Zambia v Meer Care & Desai (A Firm)* [2005] EWHC 2102 (Ch). In seeking to have the matter heard in London, the plaintiff noted that it would be easier to enforce orders of an English court rather than a Zambian court against the defendants' English assets.

official, thereby imposing on the public official fiduciary duties in favour of its state principal pursuant to which 'the principal is entitled to the single-minded loyalty of his fiduciary'.[140] In circumstances where a public official misappropriates their state's wealth or accepts a bribe, that state may be entitled to equitable remedies or to claims for monies had and received. In the *Chiluba* matter, for example, Zambia claimed inter alia for the defendant's breach of duties to the state. The reasoning used by the judge in finding in favour of Zambia (in a subsequently overturned judgment, though it was overturned on a different point) echoes the language used in UWO applications:

> [T]he only inference to be drawn from [certain substantial monetary transfers to which Mr Chiluba was a party] given his modest background is that these represent Government monies which have been misappropriated for his and his family and friends [sic] personal benefit. He is therefore accountable in full for these amounts as they have been paid in breach of his fiduciary duties.[141]

b. Remedies

Strictly speaking, tracing is not a remedy,[142] but rather a 'process of identifying assets; it belongs to the realm of evidence'.[143] It allows claimants to recover property which has been taken from them illegally, and any profits generated through the use of that property.[144] When tracing misappropriated assets, claimants 'follow' the asset to demonstrate that property represents the proceeds of assets originally belonging to them, even if that property has been converted into another form (eg from cash into real estate).[145] Where a state of origin successfully does this, it will have a proprietary claim over the substituted property, which will be deemed to be held for that state's benefit under a constructive trust.[146] The rightful owner's interest in the property will bind everyone who takes the property or its traceable proceeds except a bona fide purchaser for value without notice.[147] The State

[140] *Bristol and West BS v Mothew* [1998] Ch 1, 18 (Millett LJ (at the time)).

[141] *Attorney General of Zambia v Meer Care & Desai (A Firm)* [2007] EWHC 952 (Ch) [471].

[142] *Foskett v McKeown* [2001] 1 AC 102, 127 (Lord Millett): 'Tracing is thus neither a claim nor a remedy. It is merely the process by which the claimant demonstrates what has happened to his property'.

[143] *Foskett v McKeown* (n 142) 113 (Lord Steyn).

[144] For a comprehensive explanation of and discussion on tracing, see Alastair Hudson, *Equity and Trusts* (9th edn, Routledge 2017) 845–902.

[145] Note that different criteria will apply as between equitable tracing and common law tracing, the latter of which cannot 'follow assets' into mixed funds. See Warren Barr and John Picton, *Pearce & Stevens' Trusts and Equitable Obligations* (8th edn, OUP 2022) 842.

[146] See *Attorney General for Hong Kong v Reid* [1994] 1 AC 324, [1993] UKPC 2, [1994] 1 All ER 1. Note that notwithstanding the outcome of *Reid*, a constructive trust will not automatically be imputed where the proceeds of bribery were acquired in breach of fiduciary duty.

[147] *Westdeutsche Landesbank Girozentrale v Islington LBC* [1996] 2 WLR 802. In which case, the claimant instead will pursue the payee of the purchase price of the relevant property.

of Libya, for example, successfully obtained a declaration in the English courts to the effect that a particular London property was 'wrongfully and unlawfully purchased with funds' belonging to Libya and was held under a constructive trust for the benefit of Libya by the property's registered legal owner, a British Virgin Islands-incorporated company beneficially owned by Muammar al-Gaddafi's son.[148] Where the property into which the proceeds have been traced has appreciated in value, the state of origin is entitled to any profit made.[149]

Where proprietary remedies are unavailable, whether because there is insufficient evidence available to trace assets or because the claimant never held a proprietary interest in the relevant assets (eg as is the case where the defendant has received cash bribes), personal actions may be available. The main advantage of personal actions when compared to proprietary claims is that no evidential link between the relevant property and the defendant's alleged misconduct need be established. It is sufficient that the elements of the relevant tort or equitable wrong (as the case may be) are established to a civil standard. Successful claims against fiduciaries, for example, will result in a fiduciary being liable to account in equity for their breach of trust through a disgorgement of proceeds,[150] a constructive trust over unauthorized profits, and/or damages for the claimant's loss (including consequential damages) in tort.[151] Additionally, claimants can pursue corrupt officials or other kleptocrats for exemplary damages where a deliberate tort (eg deceit) can be established. Claimants will need to establish before pursuing any such personal claims whether a defendant has sufficient assets capable of recovery to make those claims financially worthwhile.

If a proprietary interest can be established, where the relevant asset (or its substitute) has depreciated in value, the claimant can seek damages for the difference between the misappropriated property and the value of the claimed asset.[152] Whether pursuing non-proprietary measures in England is tenable or desirable will obviously be contingent on whether countries of origin can establish jurisdiction when seeking to use the English courts.[153] As *Chiluba* demonstrates, the courts will take into consideration the fact that misappropriated assets or their proceeds are or were held in England,[154] and/or have passed through English law

[148] *Libya v Capitana Seas Ltd* [2012] EWHC 602 (Comm).

[149] *Foskett v McKeown* [2001] 1 AC 402.

[150] *Sinclair Investments (UK) Ltd v Versailles Trade Finance Ltd* [2011] EWCA Civ 347, [2011] 3 WLR 1153. cf Sarah Worthington, 'Fiduciary Duties and Proprietary Remedies: Addressing the Failure of Equitable Formulae' (2013) 72 Cambridge Law Journal 720.

[151] Jonathan Fisher, 'Fraud in Civil and Criminal Law' in Barry Rider (ed), *Research Handbook on International Financial Crime* (Edward Elgar 2015) 315.

[152] *Foskett v McKeown* [2001] 1 AC 402.

[153] For discussion on choosing a forum, see Brun and others (n 136) 39–48.

[154] See *Federal Republic of Nigeria v Dariye* [2007] EWHC 708 Ch, in which Lindsay J ruled that the expense and delay involved in seeking judgment against the defendant in Nigeria and then attempting to enforce that Nigerian judgment in England militated in favour of the matter being heard instead in the English courts.

firms and banks.[155] In addition, where the relevant defendant has insufficiently deep pockets to make a claim viable, states of origin can consider claims against those English intermediaries who may have facilitated corruption. The Nigerian state, for example, recently unsuccessfully attempted a claim of US$1.7bn against JP Morgan at the High Court in London. Nigeria alleged that JP Morgan was in breach of its Quincecare duty (a duty imposed on banks not to follow a customer's instructions where the relevant bank is put on enquiry that it may be facilitating a fraud) by allegedly facilitating the misappropriation of funds by a former Nigerian government minister.[156] The claim failed on the basis that, in the court's view, Nigeria had not established that a fraud leading to the alleged misappropriation had taken place. While the action was unsuccessful for Nigeria, it is a useful illustration of claimants looking for recourse beyond primary actors to those who allegedly facilitated their principals' corrupt activities. Action against facilitators is discussed further in Chapter 7.

c. Investigative Tools

The obvious disadvantage for states of origin in seeking to recover assets through civil proceedings in the UK's courts is having to invest in potentially lengthy and expensive processes to exercise any claim, the outcomes of which are not guaranteed. However, even if a claim is ultimately unsuccessful, the process can yield valuable information. As should be clear from Table 5.2, there are a number of investigative tools available to enforcement authorities pursuing civil recovery and criminal confiscation actions under the POCA for which broad analogues are available as discovery tools to private litigants pursuing fraud and recovery claims.

Table 5.2 Investigative tools available to civil litigants and enforcement authorities

Civil litigants	Enforcement authorities	Effect
Disclosure orders[157]	UWOs, disclosure orders	Disclosure of documents sought by the applicant from the other party to the proceedings.

[155] See n 139 and accompanying text above.
[156] *Federal Republic of Nigeria v JP Morgan Chase Bank NA* [2022] EWHC 1447 (Comm) [2].
[157] Provided for pursuant to CPR 31.17 and 31.18 and permitted under s 33 of the Senior Courts Act 1981 or s 52 of the County Courts Act 1984.

Table 5.2 Continued

Civil litigants	Enforcement authorities	Effect
Norwich Pharmacal orders[158]	UWOs, disclosure orders, customer information orders	Disclosure of information and documents sought by the applicant. Note: Norwich Pharmacal orders are not available against defendants—only against third parties who are in some way connected to the dispute.
Bankers Trust orders[159]	Production orders,[160] customer information orders	Require recipients to produce or provide access to material of a description specified in the application.
Freezing orders (Mareva injunctions[161]), proprietary injunctions and Chabra injunctions[162]	Property freezing orders[163] Account freezing orders[164]	Prohibit any person to whose property or account the orders apply from dealing with such property or account pending the outcome of proceedings.
Search orders[165]	Search and seizure orders[166]	Allow applicants to search premises and seize evidence without prior notice.
Disclosure orders ancillary to Mareva injunctions, proprietary injunctions and search orders[167]	Disclosure orders and UWOs	Require respondents to provide information in relation to the assets or matters the subject of primary orders.

The closest analogue in civil litigation to the disclosure orders and UWOs available under the POCA are disclosure orders (including disclosure orders made

[158] Provided for pursuant to CPR 31.17 and 31.18 and permitted under s 34 of the Senior Courts Act 1981 or s 53 of the County Courts Act 1984.

[159] Equitable jurisdiction for Banker's Trust orders was established in *Bankers Trust Co v Shapira* [1980] 1 WLR 1274, [1980] 6 WLUK 22, and the applicability of such orders to claims for stolen or misappropriated money was confirmed by the High Court in *Miles Smith Broking Ltd v Barclays Bank plc* [2017] EWHC 3338 (Ch), [2017] 12 WLUK 425.

[160] POCA, s 345.

[161] CPR 25.1(1)(f).

[162] The courts' jurisdiction to order the freezing of the assets made in pursuit of the enforcement of a judgment, or anticipated judgment, against a co-defendant to proceedings against whom the applicant does not have a direct and substantive cause of action was confirmed in *TSB Private Bank International SA v Chabra* [1992] 1 WLR 231.

[163] POCA, s 245Aff.

[164] POCA, s 303Z1ff.

[165] CPR 25.1(1)(h) and s 7 of the Civil Procedure Act 1997.

[166] POCA, s 352.

[167] Provided for pursuant to CPR 23 and 25 and permitted under s 37 of the Senior Courts Act.

ancillary to freezing and search orders). Applicants for the lay-litigant versions of disclosure orders and freezing orders face high barriers to their award. For proprietary injunctions, applicants must show first that there is a serious issue to be tried on the merits; second, that the balance of convenience is in favour of granting an injunction; and third, that it is just and convenient to grant the injunction.[168] Those seeking freezing injunctions must in addition show a substantial risk of dissipation of the assets.[169] The key difference between the types of discovery tools available for use by enforcement authorities and those used by lay litigants is that the sanction for failure to respond to the latter is a fine or, in cases where breaches of orders are more clearly intentional and obstructive, up to two years of imprisonment for contempt of court.[170] Fines or imprisonment for contempt of court are *civil* sanctions, albeit lay claimants seeking to commit respondents for failure to respond must prove the contempt to the criminal standard.[171] This differs from the failure to respond to or intentionally or recklessly providing misleading information in response to a disclosure order made pursuant to POCA powers, each of which can attract a *criminal* conviction.[172] Notwithstanding the 'criminal' and 'civil' classifications of the sanctions for failure to respond to orders instituted by enforcement authorities and civil litigants respectively, there does not seem to be much disparity in real terms in the consequences for failure to comply. That said, the criminal offence as a result of a failure to respond to an enforcement authority order will impact on respondents' criminal records, with all of the negative outcomes that can ensue.

Civil litigants can also seek Norwich Pharmacal orders, which can be sought against third parties *not* parties to litigation but who are involved in or connected to the dispute in some way to require them to disclose pertinent documents or information. Those seeking Norwich Pharmacal orders will need to establish that there is a good case to be made to suggest that a wrong was committed, and that the respondent is likely to hold the information sought.[173] Like disclosure orders used by enforcement authorities, applicants for Norwich Pharmacal orders might encounter enforcement difficulties where a witness is outside of the jurisdiction.[174]

[168] *American Cyanamid v Ethicon* [1975] AC 396.

[169] *Polly Peck International plc v Nadir (No 2)* [1992] 4 All ER 769. The criteria to be satisfied by enforcement authorities seeking disclosure orders and UWOs under the POCA are set out in Table 5.1.

[170] eg Mann J recently sentenced a respondent who was in 'serious and contumacious breach' of disclosure orders made against him to one year's imprisonment (unsuspended) for contempt of court in *Isbilen v Turk* [2024] EWHC 565 (Ch).

[171] *Daltel Europe Ltd v Makki* [2005] EWHC 749 (Ch).

[172] POCA, s 359.

[173] *Hickox v Dickinson* [2020] EWHC 2520 (Ch). In that case, the High Court emphasized that Norwich Pharmacal orders remain an 'exceptional jurisdiction' and mere 'fishing exhibitions' will be refused.

[174] In *AB Bank v Abu Dhabi Commercial Bank* [2016] EWHC 2082, for example, the judge refused service out of the jurisdiction because, inter alia, the respondent sought a search within the United Arab Emirates, and it therefore could not be said that the court was ordering an act 'within the jurisdiction' in accordance with the applicable Practice Direction.

To summarize, there exist tools available to civil claimants designed to compel respondents and defendants to provide information (including explanations as to how a defendant obtained an asset) as part of a disclosure process. Wide powers are not reserved to the use of enforcement authorities. In each of civil recovery investigations and (for example) civil tracing exercises and/or proprietary claims, it is claimed that the property being pursued has been tainted by its connection to wrongdoing. A state of origin pursuing assets through the courts may however have different calculi from enforcement authorities in mind in instituting proceedings. It may be principally interested in signalling a disavowal of impunity to its citizenry, and evidence gathered may be used for potential domestic criminal prosecutions. But in a more general sense, the key objectives of deterrence, ease of investigation, repatriation, and—to varying extents—expression of approbation will be achieved through both civil recovery proceedings undertaken by enforcement authorities and civil litigation undertaken by states of origin. If the courts are not satisfied that an order is proportionate and/or that the relevant tests for each type of order have been satisfied, or if they suspect that an application is frivolous or vexatious or tantamount to a fishing expedition, they may refuse to grant an order at their discretion in each scenario.

Pursuit of the proceeds of grand corruption through the civil courts may represent a viable option for asset recovery for states of origin in some circumstances. Discovery powers available to lay litigants are potent. Given that the UK is under no legal obligation to return assets representing the proceeds of foreign corruption to states of origin unless and until the requirements of Article 57 of the UNCAC have first been satisfied, recovery of assets through the civil courts potentially offers states of origin more access and control of assets misappropriated from them than they might otherwise enjoy. The use of civil proceedings might also be wielded by states of origin as a political tool to exert pressure on holding states to act more decisively in preventing dirty money from being held in their territories. That said, recovery through private civil cases taken in foreign courts is perhaps less expressively satisfactory for the citizenries of states of origin than conviction-based confiscation. Moreover, where there is insufficient evidence to sustain a criminal prosecution in either the state of origin or the holding state, it is difficult to avoid the conclusion that states of origin should not *have* to resort to making private claims in the civil courts of a holding state if they can make a viable case that they suspect that assets allegedly stolen from them are held in that holding state and should be investigated by that holding state's enforcement authorities.

6. Conclusion

Examining multiple potential means of recovering the proceeds of grand corruption in the UK and repatriating them to their states of origin move aspects of both policy and legal mechanism design into clearer focus. In seeking to recover misappropriated assets, enforcement authorities and states of origin will have varying motivations, and these will inform the policy approach of each. States of origin pursuing UK-held proceeds of corruption through its courts, in addition to being motivated by the retrieval of assets they believe to be theirs, are desirous of reasserting to their own populations and to the international community their agency over matters impacting on their citizens. On a policy level, by assisting states of origin to retrieve their assets, the UK gives effect to its stated desire to 'close down London as a centre for corrupt elites to launder money and enhance their reputations' and to strengthen its 'institutional integrity'.[175]

For countries of origin looking for mutual legal assistance from the Home Office, it is difficult, perhaps by design, to grasp how willing and effective both it and the UK's various domestic enforcement authorities are in responding to requests to investigate allegations that stolen assets originating overseas are held in the jurisdiction. Aside from the seemingly incomplete and somewhat inconsistent information available on the StAR database,[176] there is little information published allowing observers to form a sense of how actively cooperative the UK's authorities are in responding to such requests. The mismatch between the perceived scale of the 'Londongrad' problem relative to the ambition of visible enforcement activity against it through the courts has been highlighted.[177] If the Home Office and enforcement authorities are working diligently behind the scenes through mutual legal assistance and more informal cooperation processes to assist countries in recovering UK-based assets, at the very least a broad overview of that work should be published to burnish claims that efforts are being made proactively to deter the laundering of assets misappropriated from other states within the jurisdiction.

It is fundamentally more difficult to hold someone accountable for transnational crimes of the kind typified by asset misappropriation in one foreign jurisdiction followed by asset laundering in another jurisdiction than it is for a domestic crime. Establishing jurisdiction, relying on the goodwill and competence of multiple enforcement authorities, gaining access to witnesses and defendants, and gathering admissible evidence, the existent complexity of these tasks and others becomes more profound where attempting to prosecute crimes committed across multiple jurisdictions. On a liberal rights analysis, commentators have expressed persuasively their reservations on certain aspects of the civil recovery regime, including, without limitation, the apparent bypassing of the presumption of innocence,

[175] HM Government, *Integrated Review Refresh 2023: Responding to a more contested and volatile world* (CP 811, 2023) 49.

[176] See Chapter 1, Section 3.

[177] See eg the OECD Working Group's comments (n 112 and accompanying text above) and those of Transparency International UK, and comments from anti-corruption experts in the Royal United Services Institute and REDRESS, quoted in Eleanor Myers 'Londongrad Forever? Why the UK May Never Seize Russian Assets' *Politico* (London, 15 April 2024) <www.politico.eu/article/londongrad-forever-uk-never-seize-russia-assets-ukraine-war-sanctions/>.

amongst other criminal procedural safeguards.[178] Accepting these criticisms to be valid, there is nevertheless a case to be made that transnational financial crimes of grand corruption constitute special cases that justify special measures. Factors justifying such special treatment include the obstacles to, and the rarity of any forms of, criminal accountability for such crimes, and the fact that where state resources are misappropriated, those crimes are in a very real sense crimes which victimize societies. Kleptocratic acts as a rule abuse public trust in some way, because senior public officials or other individuals who have explicitly or implicitly committed to serving the public good abuse that public trust. These factors may collectively justify a departure from a rigid insistence on adherence to criminal procedural protections to assure *some* kind of liability for such crimes, even if that liability is civil rather than criminally punitive. To that end, and especially when assessed against other civil recovery powers, mechanisms like the AFO and the PEP-specific unexplained wealth order represent plausibly pragmatic responses to addressing kleptocratic impunity. The fact that such measures are not formally criminal in nature allows the UK to pursue unilateral action against corrupt elites without impediment by overseas evidence or territorial criminal jurisdiction enforcement limitations.

That said, where anti-corruption measures are introduced in response to panic, the risk is that the impetus to 'do something' about the reasons for that panic will obscure the focus on individual rights that should accompany new crime control measures, potentially eroding the strength of those rights in the process. It follows that for certain anti-corruption measures, concerns from a liberal rights perspective remain. These concerns are discussed in the next chapter.

[178] See eg Andrew Ashworth, 'Four Threats to the Presumption of Innocence' (2006) 10 International Journal of Evidence and Proof, 241, 250; and Colin King and Jennifer Hendry, *Civil Recovery of Criminal Property* (OUP 2023) 112–22.

6

Procedural and Human Rights Implications of Anti-Corruption Legislation

1. Introduction

This chapter uses a liberal human rights analysis to examine the human rights implications arising from the use of investigative measures targeting the proceeds of grand corruption. Where new legal mechanisms are suggested to tackle particular social ills, a tension typically arises between those who privilege pragmatism over principle and vice versa. One disquieting impact of attempting to address the harbouring of the proceeds of grand corruption is that states deem it necessary to resort to enacting laws that lower the thresholds at which they can require members of the populace to account to the state for their activities and/or that subtly erode or reshape human rights standards. Some commentators have argued that the individuals against whom civil recovery mechanisms are used are being subjected to state-made claims of criminal guilt without benefiting from a presumption of innocence or any other procedural protections.[1] These concerns are particularly acute where the measures impact on quiet enjoyment of property or where their use is widely publicized. This is because of their potentially unfair impact on respondents' privacy and reputations. A broader criticism relates to the under-scrutinized development of mechanisms reactively introduced by the state for reasons of political expedience. Where relatively draconian laws are introduced against a specified cohort of the population on an exceptional and limited basis and their operation subsequently becomes normalized, similar measures applicable against society more generally can be introduced later with little dissent.

Pragmatists generally accept these criticisms,[2] but argue that legislators have little choice but to introduce tools like the UWO given the evidential challenges implicit in establishing that assets represent the proceeds of overseas corruption. To date, the PEP-specific unexplained wealth order is the most prominent measure introduced specifically to tackle the problem of the proceeds of overseas

[1] Liz Campbell and Áine Clancy, 'The Principled and Practical Limits to Unexplained Wealth Orders' (2024) 52(1) University of Western Australia Law Review 29.

[2] Colin King and Jennifer Hendry, *Civil Recovery of Criminal Property* (OUP 2023) 163–65.

Unexplained Wealth Orders and the UK's Anti-Corruption Regime. Áine Clancy, Oxford University Press.
 DOI: 10.1093/9780198907312.003.0007

grand corruption being held in the UK.[3] To the extent that further mechanisms will be introduced given the limited impact of the orders to date, they are likely to be similarly civil in nature and similarly involve lowered evidential barriers and procedural protections. The chapter examines the human rights implications of the PEP-specific UWO with the intention of ensuring that greater caution be exercised when considering the unintended consequences for human rights that may eventuate when adopting future anti-corruption measures.

The discussion is conducted within three broad themes. First, the UK's increased resort to so-called 'hybrid' civil measures as a means of addressing wrongs is examined. The second part of this chapter highlights the problems implicit in the rigid binary employed in the European Convention on Human Rights (the ECHR, or the Convention) when it comes to the rights afforded to parties subject to civil processes and those available to criminal defendants. The European Court of Human Rights' (ECtHR) inflexible dichotomization of the application of those rights exacerbates these problems. The third, fourth, and fifth parts of the chapter respectively assess significant aspects of criminal procedural safeguarding, namely, the presumption of innocence, the rules around reverse burdens, and the privilege against self-incrimination. The conclusion to the chapter discusses whether these protections should be extended to 'civil' anti-corruption measures including UWOs.

The second broad theme examines challenges posed by anti-corruption measures to specific individual rights other than criminal procedural rights. The chapter's sixth and seventh parts doctrinally appraise how using UWOs against PEPs might impact on the rights to protection of property and to respect for private and family life, as provided for under Article 1 of the First Protocol (A1 P1) and Article 8 of the Convention, respectively. The third theme looks at parameters imposed on lawmakers, courts, and enforcement authorities when respectively enacting, interpreting, and enforcing laws in a liberal democracy. Part 8 assesses the discriminatory nature of laws targeting specific groups—in this case, foreign elites. The final substantive part analyses proportionality and fairness requirements imposed by UK law on enforcement authorities seeking UWOs.

Some might argue that if an anti-corruption asset recovery measure is used even once successfully to restore assets to a victim state which otherwise would not have had those assets returned, then its existence is justified and it has achieved output legitimacy. This chapter seeks to establish that this suggestion takes an unrealistically narrow view of output legitimacy, because it ignores the adverse and potentially disproportionate impact those measures can have on the individuals subject

[3] Other measures include legislative changes to the rules governing transparency around the ultimate beneficial owners of overseas private companies holding properties in the UK and the PEP-specific provisions in the anti-money laundering legislation, but unlike the PEP-specific UWO, these changes have broader application than merely to PEPs from outside the UK, European Economic Area (EEA), and EU and their family members and associates.

to them. Moreover, this approach risks ignoring the potential longer-term influence of those measures on the law and domestic society in terms of the precedents established by the measures' introduction and use.

2. Procedural Rights

Like other civil recovery mechanisms, the UWO is a hybrid measure because it enables enforcement authorities to employ the machinery of the civil courts using civil standards of evidence to recover the proceeds of suspected crime. Because of its designation as an investigative tool to aid *civil* recovery, UWO respondents do not formally benefit from criminal procedural safeguards protected, inter alia, under the criminal limb of Article 6 of the ECHR. As with other hybrid measures, UWO processes do not involve the adjudication of guilt of individuals per se. UWO respondents are consequently not formally entitled to rely on the presumption of innocence, on a prosecutorial obligation to establish guilt beyond reasonable doubt, or on any other criminal procedural safeguard. Critics suggest that the use (and proliferation) of hybrid mechanisms like the UWO adversely impacts on procedural rights and that they are detrimental to the relationships between states and their citizens, recalibrating the level of power accruing to the state in those relationships.[4] This section looks at these criticisms in the context of the UWO.

a. Are the Procedural Rights Accruing to Respondents Sufficient?

Before embarking on a more detailed discussion of due process rights, the main reasons for which civil recovery proceedings give criminal justice commentators pause should be highlighted. In the past thirty years, the UK's Parliament has appeared notably sceptical of the criminal trial's fitness to achieve its purposes, leading to an increased reliance on suppression tactics not always formally designated as criminal law measures. Lucia Zedner and Andrew Ashworth have pointed to the increased use of summary proceedings, fixed penalty notices, and strict liability offences as symptomatic of the pursuit of 'greater regulation, an emphasis on prevention and an authoritarianism linked closely with penal populism'. This increased use of hybrid measures tends to be made, they argue, at the expense of liberal conceptions of criminal justice, the criminal trial, and its attendant due process protections.[5] Hybrid mechanisms involve aspects of both criminal and civil measures in their operation, usually to enforcement authorities' procedural advantage.

[4] See eg Andrew Ashworth and Lucia Zedner, 'Defending the Criminal Law: Reflections on the Changing Character of Crime, Procedure, and Sanctions' (2008) 2 Criminal Law and Philosophy 21.

[5] Ashworth and Zedner (n 4) 44.

Like criminal laws, hybrid measures are utilized by enforcement authorities to pursue crime control objectives including deterrence. Unlike with criminal law mechanisms, the sanctions imposed are conceived and presented as primarily for preventative purposes rather than for punitive (crime control-centric) purposes.[6] Examples of hybrid processes targeting criminal behaviour include domestic violence protection orders, injunctions targeting anti-social behaviour, terrorism prevention measures, and civil recovery orders.[7] Common to the introduction of each, commentators argue, 'is a degree of normatively motivated political expediency'.[8] I observed similar motivations underpinning the introduction of UWOs against PEPs in Chapter 4. The key concern around hybrid measures in crime control is that they normalize the 'legislative privileging of expediency over considerations of human rights and due process'.[9] They are therefore archetypical of the Crime Control Model in action.

The leading justification provided for civil recovery's designation as a 'civil' measure and its consequent avoidance of criminal law safeguards is that its outcomes are not punitive. Joachim Vogel, for example, has postulated that 'recovery' of the proceeds of crime as a response to criminality is not founded on measures designed to correct and prevent crime.[10] He argues that civil recovery instead represents a 'third track' *sui generis* measure of a kind that is non-punitive in nature, aimed at preventing criminal unjust enrichment.[11] On this analysis, civil recovery is a restitutionary measure rather than a genuinely criminal sanction.[12] Vogel states that where the proceeds of crime are recovered, rather than traditional punitive measures being imposed, 'the worst that can happen to a criminal is that he or she will be deprived of the profits—which will result in the same economic situation as if the crime would not have been committed'.[13]

This analysis is problematic. It ignores the non-economic outcomes of civil recovery for respondents. A distinctive characteristic of criminal prosecutions is that

[6] See eg the ECHR's decision on civil recovery orders in *Walsh v UK* App no 43384/0 (ECtHR, 21 November 2006).

[7] For a detailed discussion of the due process implications of civil recovery as a hybrid measure, see King and Hendry (n 2).

[8] Jennifer Hendry and Colin King, 'Expediency, Legitimacy, and the Rule of Law: A Systems Perspective on Civil/Criminal Procedural Hybrids' (2017) 11 Criminal Law and Philosophy 733, 734.

[9] Hendry and King (n 8) 734.

[10] As distinct from the forfeiture of contraband or instrumentalities of crime.

[11] Joachim Vogel, 'The Legal Construction that Property Can Do Harm' in Jon Petter Rui and Ulrich Sieber (eds), *Non-Conviction-Based Confiscation in Europe: Possibilities and Limitations on Rules Enabling Confiscation without a Criminal Conviction* (Duncker & Humblot 2015) 225, 232.

[12] Vogel (n 11). Fried constructs a similar argument, contending that forfeiture merely reinstates the *status quo ante* and cannot therefore be regarded as punitive: David J Fried, 'Rationalizing Criminal Forfeiture' (1988) 79 Journal of Criminal Law & Criminology 328. Note Peter Alldridge's discussion of how, in English law, there were repeated attempts to establish a common law basis for the state to acquire the proceeds of crime but no such basis was found to exist: Peter Alldridge, *Money Laundering Law: Forfeiture, Confiscation, Civil Recovery, Criminal Laundering and Taxation of the Proceeds of Crime* (Hart 2003) 52–54 and more generally 45–69.

[13] Vogel (n 11) 236.

they attract a degree of societal condemnation usually absent from civil proceedings. Conviction by a state's law enforcement authorities of a criminal offence attracts a particularly potent kind of public opprobrium. Henry Hart noted that 'the judgment of community condemnation' which accompanies and justifies findings of criminal guilt is the one and only sanction which is peculiar to criminal law.[14] He observed that without that condemnatory aspect, a convicted criminal given a suspended sentence would be regarded as going unpunished, suggesting that the societal censure derived from a conviction is the element that is essential to a criminal sanction.[15] Elsewhere, it is observed that 'there is at least something to the idea that someone who has committed a serious wrong should not be able to live a life of "freedom and contentment"',[16] and that 'blaming' distinguishes the innocent from the guilty.[17] The problem with civil recovery processes is that unlike 'normal' civil proceedings, they involve an implicit element of blaming for criminal wrongs.

In the debates preceding the legislation introducing the unexplained wealth order, legislators recognized the non-economic outcomes which respondents might face:

> We need to be careful that [PEPs . . .] are sufficiently protected from the making of an application that could trash their reputation and that, even when that is not acceded to by the High Court judge, none the less still leaves him or her exposed to the allegations made against them.[18]

This statement reflects the uneasy relationship between the UWO's and civil recovery's characterizations as civil processes and the impugnation of (at least a benefit from) corruption cast by enforcement authorities on respondents, even if inadvertently.[19]

It is arguable that society at large is not equipped to appreciate the legal differences between, and peculiarities of, an action in pursuit of the alleged proceeds

[14] Henry M Hart, 'The Aims of the Criminal Law' (1958) 23 Law & Contemporary Problems 401, 404. In the civil sphere, he notes that restitutionary and punitive damages are available for tortious and contractual disputes; and that the insane, aliens, and recalcitrant witnesses are still imprisoned, and debtors used to be. In each case, he notes, the absence of societal condemnation is the 'vital difference' between a criminal and civil sanction.

[15] Hart (n 14) 405.

[16] RA Duff, *Punishment, Communication, and Community* (OUP 2001) 26.

[17] CS Steiker, 'Twenty-Sixth Annual Review of Criminal Procedure: Foreword: Punishment and Procedure: Punishment Theory and the Criminal-Civil Procedural Divide' (1997) 85 Georgetown Law Journal 775, 804.

[18] Edward Garnier KC, MP, Criminal Finances Bill Deb 25 October 2016, col 207.

[19] eg one of the ultimate beneficial owners of the properties the subject of *Baker* was dismissed as leader of the Kazakh senate shortly after the High Court confirmed the discharge of the UWO applicable to her London property, even though the National Crime Agency's (NCA) case against her property had failed. Analysts attributed the dismissal to the unwelcome publicity generated by the case. Marc Bennets, 'Heir to Kazakh Leadership Sacked after Property Row' *The Times* (London, 5 May 2020) 29.

of crime as a civil matter versus a criminal confiscation action.[20] The distinction is certainly not clarified by media coverage dealing with UWOs, which tends to have a distinctly aspersive flavour.[21] As a consequence, respondents to civil recovery proceedings and more particularly to UWOs, which are publicized, suffer adverse labelling akin to 'blaming'. This publicity is capable of impacting upon the 'freedom and contentment' of respondents in general, in partly the same way as for convicted criminals, but without the benefit of the protections designed to counterbalance procedural unfairness or the availability of 'not guilty' rulings. The significantly disparaging character of a publicized unexplained wealth order, and the fact that for PEPs, no link to criminality need first be shown to obtain an order, each support a proposition that enhanced procedural rights for respondents may be appropriate. It is acknowledged that the full range of criminal-limb safeguards available to criminal defendants may not be required for UWO respondents given the relatively less punitive consequences where courts find against their assets. However, given the quasi-criminal character of the measure, more significant protections than those that accrue to parties in normal civil matters should be considered.

b. The Inflexibility Problem

A significant development in the later twentieth century leading to greater emphasis on the distinction between criminal and civil laws in the UK was the enactment of the Human Rights Act 1998, which incorporated the rights protected by the ECHR into domestic law. The Act binds the UK, amongst other matters, to adopt the Convention's minimum human rights standards in criminal cases. Its adoption has likely contributed to the increased use of hybrid measures. Lawmakers, cognizant of the ECtHR's distinction between 'criminal' and 'non-criminal' measures, now legislate to expressly designate measures as 'civil' in line with ECtHR tests developed to distinguish between 'civil' and 'criminal' measures,[22] notwithstanding that such measures are employed by crime enforcement authorities and potentially hold punitive outcomes. Whilst in principle the early development by the ECtHR of a procedural rights jurisprudence was a promising step towards strengthening

[20] See Johan Boucht, 'Non-conviction Based Confiscation: Moving the Confiscation of Criminal Proceeds from the Criminal to the "Civil" Sphere' in Vanessa Franssen and Christopher Harding (eds), *Criminal and Quasi-Criminal Enforcement Mechanisms in Europe* (Hart 2022) 428–30.

[21] The perception of links between respondents to UWOs and criminality is hardly surprising given the tenor of the media reportage on UWOs. In a survey conducted on 16 May 2022 of the UK national broadsheet publications, with the exception of the FT, using Lexis®Library News Search function, over 25 per cent of the 551 articles making reference to 'unexplained wealth orders' published up to that date also used the term 'McMafia' as a descriptor for the measure.

[22] The test was originally set out in *Engel v The Netherlands*, App nos 5100/71, 5101/71, 5102/71, 5354/72, and 5370/72 (ECtHR, 8 June 1976).

the Due Process Model across the Convention's member states, in practice, the Court has shown both itself and the Convention to struggle with the nuances of more recent hybrid crime control measures incorporating aspects of both criminal and civil procedure.[23] The Convention strictly bifurcates due process rights into (i) those which apply only where an individual has been charged with a criminal offence (with the notion of 'criminal' being strictly construed), and (ii) other rights.

In determining whether a measure constitutes a criminal charge, the ECtHR typically relies on the *Engel* test, which requires the Court to consider the following three criteria:

(i) the classification of the measure under the internal law of the state in question;
(ii) the nature of the offence; and
(iii) the degree and severity of the penalty which the person concerned risks incurring.[24]

This is at variance with the more nuanced 'context and objectives' criteria used in the English courts to determine whether something comprises a criminal cause or matter.[25] In commenting on the *Engel* test, Stefan Trechsel laments the ECtHR's apparent inability to distinguish the concepts of 'criminal charges' and 'criminal proceedings'. It has applied the same *Engel* criteria to both questions.[26] The Court has rarely departed from its tripartite test, but it is applied unevenly,[27] and the ECtHR's explanation of the rationales underlying the criteria has been criticized as 'obscure, if not incoherent and inconsistent'.[28]

The first *Engel* criterion is to provide 'no more than a starting point' to the analysis.[29] It would be more appropriate if the first test (to which, as Trechsel has observed, the Court has never attached any weight)[30] were to look behind a measure's appellation to analyse the parliamentary objectives behind its introduction or, better yet, that it be dispensed with altogether as it does not employ a substantive evaluation of the type of proceeding involved. The second and third parts of the

[23] The ECtHR has repeatedly rejected the suggestion that art 6(2) rights should be available to respondents to non-conviction-based recovery proceedings. See *Walsh v UK* App no 43384/0 (ECtHR, 21 November 2006) and *Arcuri v Italy* App no 52024/99 (ECtHR, 5 July 2001).

[24] *Engel* (n 22) para 82.

[25] s 31(1)(a) of the Supreme Court of Judicature (Consolidation) Act 1925 as amended by the Criminal Appeal Act 1968. See Shaw LJ's discussion in *R v Board of Visitors of Hull Prison, ex p St Germain (No 1)* [1979] 1 QB 425.

[26] Stefan Trechsel, *Human Rights in Criminal Proceedings* (OUP 2005) 19.

[27] Trechsel (n 26) 17.

[28] Radha Ivory, *Corruption, Asset Recovery, and the Protection of Property in Public International Law: The Human Rights of Bad Guys* (CUP 2014) 250.

[29] *Engel* (n 22) para 82.

[30] Trechsel (n 26).

test are 'alternative and not necessarily cumulative' albeit this apparently should not preclude a cumulative approach being adopted where necessary.[31]

The Court's approach to the second, more important, criterion similarly suggests that it is asking the wrong questions. In examining the nature of proceedings, the Court does not contemplate the existence of measures which may not de facto fully fall within either the criminal or civil sphere, nor does it take a more holistic approach by examining societal or respondent perceptions, or the level or type of state condemnation implied in imposing a particular measure. On the third criterion—whether the penalty involved suggests that a measure belongs to the criminal sphere[32]—the Court again fails to appreciate contemporary discourse, this time on types of punishment. Whilst it recognizes that a measure does not require the imposition of criminal fines or imprisonment to be punitive in character,[33] it has so far not considered the societal condemnation implicit in, for example, the imposition of a civil recovery order on an individual's assets for that person.[34]

A key deficiency in the drafting of Article 6 that has led to the development of the *Engel* test and its jurisprudential progeny is that the engagement of criminal procedural protections is viewed in binary terms. A proceeding is either criminal—so the full suite of criminal procedural protections apply—or it is civil, and none applies. This is frustrating in circumstances where the ECtHR *has* accepted that less serious criminal offences may attract a less stringent application of the Article 6 criminal-head guarantees, showing that the Court recognizes some value in stratifying applicable safeguards.[35] The Convention's binary approach has informed the ECtHR's refusal to categorize criminal confiscation as a criminal proceeding. A pertinent example in this regard is its ruling in *Phillips v United Kingdom*, which confirmed that use of confiscation laws that assumed that all of the applicant's assets acquired in the six years prior to his conviction for drugs offences would not attract the presumption of innocence as provided for under Article 6(2) of the Convention[36] The Court's refusal to recognize conviction-based confiscation processes as forms of criminal proceedings in turn has impacted on how the Convention's member states approach asset recovery. Radha Ivory notes that '[t]he court's willingness to exclude confiscation orders from the scope of Art 6(2) and (3) has afforded ECHR state parties considerable latitude in legislating on confiscation at national, supranational and international levels'.[37] Given the

[31] *Jusilla v Finland* App no 73053/01 (ECtHR, 23 November 2006) para 31.

[32] *Öztürk v Germany* (21 February 1984) Series A no 73.

[33] eg in *Jussila* (n 31) it recognized the imposition of tax surcharges as attracting criminal procedural rights.

[34] Briefly discussed in Section 7.

[35] *Marčan v Croatia* App no 40820/12 (ECtHR, 10 July 2014).

[36] *Phillips v UK* ECHR 2001-VII 29.

[37] Ivory (n 28) 249. It is not uncommon in UK parliamentary debates to make reference to whether proposed measures will withstand an ECHR challenge. In the House of Lords debates on the introduction of civil recovery pursuant to the POCA, peers suggested amendments to make the legislation 'less

timings of the *Phillips* decision (July 2001) and the introduction of the Proceeds of Crime Bill introducing civil recovery in the UK Parliament (October 2001), it is not unreasonable to speculate that the ECtHR's blessing of criminal confiscation as 'non-criminal' allayed UK legislators' concerns on potential contests to civil recovery in Strasbourg.

The ECtHR has been consistent in its contention that civil recovery proceedings do not engage the criminal limb of Article 6.[38] In *Walsh v United Kingdom*, the Court found, applying the *Engel* criteria, that given civil recovery's civil classification and its apparently restitutionary (rather than deterrence-focused) purpose and effect, it should not be characterized as a criminal process.[39] The UK Supreme Court reached the same conclusion on civil recovery in *Serious Organised Crime Agency v Gale* on the basis of the ECtHR's jurisprudence.[40] The ECtHR's reliance on the *Engel* criteria and its jurisprudence in determining whether a process engages criminal procedural rights under Article 6 more generally is unsatisfactory because it has been consistently 'found wanting in terms of clarity, consistency or coherence'.[41] The reasons for this apparent lack of discursive rigour or clarity are not obvious, but may speak to the disparate criminal procedural common law (adversarial) and civil law (inquisitorial) traditions from which the Court's judges hail. Significant also, perhaps, are more prosaic factors like the fact that majority judgments are written by committee and therefore have to tread a line that is acceptable to all in that majority. The judges face a sometimes Procrustean task in seeking to establish broad-brush principles capable of operating harmoniously within the legal systems of all of the Convention's signatories. Additionally, it is possible that some decisions are influenced by matters of political or social expediency rather than strictly legal principles. It is difficult, for example, to imagine that the Italian state would have welcomed the imposition by the Strasbourg Court of criminal procedural protections in respect of its *confisca di prevenzione* process—a hybrid criminal/administrative measure which allows Italian law enforcement authorities to remove the suspected proceeds of (the ever-politically contentious) mafia crime.[42]

More fundamentally, the Court is constrained by the provisions of the Convention itself. It is the Convention, which largely predates the introduction

vulnerable to attack under the Human Rights Act': Proceeds of Crime Bill HL Deb 11 July 2002, cols 840–59.

[38] Most recently in *Gogitidze* (Chapter 5, n 152).

[39] *Walsh* (n 6).

[40] *Serious Organised Crime Agency v Gale* [2011] UKSC 49, [2011] 1 WLR 2760.

[41] Ian Dennis, 'The Human Rights Act and the Law of Criminal Evidence: Ten Years On' (2011) 33 Sydney Law Review 333, 337. Dennis includes relevant decisions dealing with reverse burdens of proof and the privilege against self-incrimination in his critique.

[42] See Michele Panzavolta, 'Confiscation and the Concept of Punishment: Can There Be a Confiscation Without a Conviction?' in Katalin Ligeti and Michele Simonato (eds), *Chasing Criminal Money: Challenges and Perspectives on Asset Recovery in the EU* (Hart 2017) 25–26.

of concepts of hybrid or administrative sanctions in common law jurisdictions at least, which silos rights into those which are 'criminal' and 'non-criminal'. The Convention's conceptually absolutist bifurcation of the law fails to accommodate the law's evolution since the ECHR came into force in 1953. Although hybrid measures are now common in the English legal landscape, the Strasbourg Court has not yet made (and, owing to the way in which the Convention is drafted, perhaps cannot make) a finding that there is any middle ground of laws or procedures deserving of heightened procedural protection where those measures should not be categorized definitively as either civil or criminal in nature. This entrenched dichotomization of due process rights fails to take account, without limitation, of matters which incorporate aspects of *both* criminal and civil procedure, of the objectives underpinning particular measures, of the gravity of harms sought to be addressed, or of the condemnatory impact on participants. It operates to calcify the level of procedural protection available to *civil* respondents and defendants by refusing to countenance the expansion of criminal procedural safeguards beyond formal criminal proceedings and laws.

The impact of the Human Rights Act 1998 therefore is to counterintuitively and counterproductively undermine the scope of, or create an artificial ceiling on the level of, procedural protections available to respondents to *quasi*-criminal measures. When the draft POCA was first being discussed in parliamentary debates, an amendment proposed to introduce a standard of evidence above the ordinary civil standard for civil recovery proceedings was defeated.[43] Given the condemnatory qualities inherent in unexplained wealth orders against PEPs, it may be time to legislatively revisit the issue around enhanced procedural protections for respondents to hybrid mechanisms in general, and to civil recovery respondents in particular.

3. The Presumption of Innocence

To situate the fundamental importance of the presumption of innocence in English criminal law, we begin with a near-compulsory quote of Viscount Sankey's creation of the principle in *Woolmington v DPP*:

> [T]hroughout the web of English Criminal Law one golden thread is always to be seen, that it is the duty of the prosecution to prove the prisoner's guilt . . . No matter what the charge, or where the trial, the principle that the prosecution must prove the guilt of the prisoner is part of the common law of England and no attempt to whittle it down can be entertained.[44]

[43] See Chapter 3, Section 2.
[44] *Woolmington v DPP* [1934] AC 462, 481.

The principle of innocence until guilt is proven is endorsed by and promulgated in various regional and international human rights conventions as a minimum standard of criminal procedural fairness.[45] It is invoked by many commentators as a fundamental human right.[46] The principle comprises two key components: that an accused will be presumed innocent until proven guilty and that the prosecution must prove guilt beyond a reasonable doubt.[47] In civil law jurisdictions, the criminal standard is proof of guilt to a degree that the judge is personally convinced of a person's guilt (*conviction intime*) to secure a conviction.

The arguments supporting the principle broadly fall into two overlapping categories. First, and more fundamentally, the presumption that an individual is innocent unless and until they are proven guilty is linked to the Kantian notion of each person's innate right to freedom: the idea that 'in the absence of wrongdoing, the liberal legal order has no reason for punitive interference with an individual's freedom'.[48] This conceptualization of the individual's rights is clearly linked to ideas around personhood, emphasized by the recognition of values including individuals' rights to privacy, dignity, and autonomy. Second, the presumption putatively operates to shield individuals from the exercise of arbitrary and/or intrusive state powers. It operates as a check on state authority by imposing what some scholars describe as a *mental* obligation on states to keep an open mind in their treatment of individuals within the adjudicative process.[49] This is founded on the idea that 'the conviction and punishment of an innocent person is deemed to cause more harm than the avoidance of liability by a guilty person'.[50] On this liberal rights account, the presumption's importance is not limited to criminal proceedings but applies more broadly in terms of how societies function and how states interact and co-exist with their populaces. It instils values of mutual trust that individuals will not be subject to unjust treatment by the state,[51] and that the state can assume that its populace by and large will act lawfully.

[45] eg and without limitation: art 14(2) of the International Covenant on Civil and Political Rights; art 11 of the United Nations Declaration on Human Rights; and art 6(2) of the ECHR.

[46] Hock Lai Ho, 'The Presumption of Innocence as a Human Right' in Paul Roberts and Jill Hunter (eds), *Criminal Evidence and Human Rights* (Hart 2012) 259.

[47] Although, as Andrew Ashworth observes, notwithstanding the 'beyond reasonable doubt' standard widely assumed, 'it is certainly possible to conceive of a presumption' demanding a lower standard. Andrew Ashworth, 'Four Threats to the Presumption of Innocence' (2006) 10 International Journal of Evidence and Proof 241, 250. The text of the ECHR is silent on standard of proof, but, as Campbell notes, 'numerous interpretations see it as encompassing "beyond reasonable doubt"': Liz Campbell, 'Criminal Labels, the European Convention on Human Rights and the Presumption of Innocence' (2013) 76 Modern Law Review 681, 683.

[48] Hamish Stewart, 'The Right to be Presumed Innocent' (2014) 8 Criminal Law & Philosophy 407, 409.

[49] Ferry de Jong and Leonie van Lent, 'The Presumption of Innocence as a Counterfactual Principle' (2016) 12 Utrecht Law Review 32.

[50] Campbell (n 47) 683.

[51] This is of course a somewhat imperfect assumption, especially in the context of magistrates' courts exercising criminal jurisdiction, see Rod Morgan, *Summary Justice: Fast—But Fair?* (Centre for Crime and Justice Studies 2008).

Antony Duff observes that this mutual trust is normatively subverted where someone gains the status of a criminal defendant.[52] Such an individual is someone against whom plausible evidence of wrongdoing has been laid, and who consequently assumes a number of obligations and burdens. A PEP respondent to a UWO against whom, potentially, no such plausible evidence of, or connection to, wrongdoing has been established will assume many similar burdens and obligations to those of criminal defendants. They will, for example, need to engage and instruct legal counsel, potentially at great expense. They may face default judgment and/or contempt proceedings for failure to respond to an order. They face potentially intrusive speculation and/or investigation by the state into their private arrangements. Their property will likely be frozen pending completion of the investigation.

In other words, a UWO (or an account freezing order or any other orders used to facilitate civil recovery investigations) transforms a respondent from a normal member of society to someone who, to use Duff's description of criminal suspects, 'is someone who simply cannot be trusted' and who is no longer entitled to what he terms the 'civic presumption of innocence'.[53] Admittedly, compared to respondents to civil recovery investigative orders, the burdens assumed are typically greater and the stakes are higher for criminal defendants. But even if it is accepted that UWOs are substantively civil rather than criminal mechanisms and therefore that respondents should not benefit from the presumption of innocence, it is not clear why the principles underpinning a general right to be presumed innocent, or free from liability or state intervention without good cause, should not apply.

Liz Campbell writes that '[w]here state agents describe a person as suspect, as problematic, as risky or as criminal, an official view is being conveyed that separates her from a "law-abiding majority"'.[54] This characterization might reasonably be made of UWO respondents. Even if an order is discharged by a respondent's full compliance, where its existence against a named respondent is publicized, the damaging aspects of a state-made assertion of suspicion implicit in the application for that order may have damaging consequences for a respondent.[55] In support of Campbell's argument, it is notable that the Supreme Court has recently held that, in general, a person under a *criminal* investigation has, prior to being charged, a reasonable expectation of privacy in respect of information relating to that investigation.[56] They are entitled to sue for misuse of private information if this expectation is not met. Given their potentially damaging character, it is curious

[52] Antony Duff, 'Who Must Presume Whom to Be Innocent of What' (2013) 42 Netherlands Journal of Legal Philosophy 170.

[53] Duff (n 52) 184.

[54] Campbell (n 47) 688. cf discussing themes of societal censure and stigmatization in the context of individuals the subject of targeted sanctions, Anton Moiseienko, *Corruption and Targeted Sanctions: Law and Policy of Anti-Corruption Entry Bans* (Brill 2019) 188–91.

[55] See eg n 19.

[56] *Bloomberg LP v ZXC* [2022] UKSC 5. Discussed further at n 198ff and accompanying text below.

that no protection apparently accrues to individuals involved in civil recovery investigations.

The principle that someone's guilt should be established beyond a reasonable doubt before they are found guilty or liable is admittedly an untenable position in a civil context, and possibly also within some financial crime contexts. Tackling financial crime requires strong investigative powers precisely because so much financial and beneficial ownership information is confidential or secret. The state's ability to compel holders or owners of private financial data to disclose financial or beneficial ownership information represents a practical check on the public's ability to exploit privacy or secrecy for illicit ends. The proliferation of various mechanisms developed and designed to conceal corruptly acquired assets has catalysed the introduction of investigative measures at a domestic and transnational level which might be regarded simultaneously as 'holistic and inventive' and running 'the risk of being uneven in coverage and unprincipled in purpose'.[57] That is not to say however that the relevant state should be entitled to compromise individuals' rights when investigating suspected benefit from the proceeds of crime without first showing that they have good reasons for holding those suspicions.

One of the problems with UWOs against PEPs is the absence of any threshold of plausibility to be met by enforcement authorities in establishing that the origins of property the subject of an application and/or the holders of that property are inherently worthy of suspicion. This differentiates it from all other civil recovery or criminal investigation mechanisms.[58] In discussing the civil standard of proof, Mike Redmayne noted that there is a case to be made in favour of insisting on an emphatic adherence to, and/or a strengthening of, the balance of probabilities standard where the imputed liability is serious.[59] Around the time the POCA was introduced, a number of commentators mused that given the potential adverse consequences of civil recovery proceedings for a respondent (in particular, the stigmatizing impact of such proceedings), the evidential burden on enforcement agencies should be increased to offset the potential risk of injustice.[60] Even the UK's government confirmed its view that civil recovery ought to attract an implicitly higher standard of evidence than other civil matters,[61] albeit this was not expressly

[57] Liz Campbell, 'The Organisation of Corruption in Commercial Enterprise: Concealing (and Revealing) the Beneficial Ownership of Assets' in Liz Campbell and Nicholas Lord (eds), *Corruption in Commercial Enterprise: Law Theory and Practice* (Routledge 2018) 82, 96.

[58] See the discussion in Section 2 of this chapter.

[59] Mike Redmayne, 'Standards of Proof in Civil Litigation' (1999) 62 Modern Law Review 167 (fn 257).

[60] Note the pre-POCA common law principle identified by some commentators to the effect that civil proceedings having a 'criminal content' required a higher degree of proof. See Ian Smith, Tim Owen, and Andrew Bodnar, *Asset Recovery: Criminal Confiscation and Civil Recovery* (OUP 2003) paras 1.51–1.52 citing, inter alia, *Khawaja v Secretary of State for the Home Department* [1984] AC 74, in which the (then) House of Lords identified the need for 'probability of a high degree' or 'convincing proof'.

[61] In fact, s 241(3) of the POCA expressly provides that 'the court must decide on the balance of probabilities whether it is proved that any matters alleged to constitute unlawful conduct have occurred'. Smith and others (n 60) note that this was included to distinguish the standard of proof in civil recovery

provided for in the POCA. Since then, however, the courts have made it clear that the applicable standard is the balance of probabilities, albeit they have acknowledged that the more improbable the alleged event or matter, the more evidence will be necessary to prove that it more probably occurred or existed than not.[62]

Campbell has suggested that a threshold of 'clear and convincing' evidence might be a more appropriate standard for civil recovery proceedings than the current civil standard considering the proceedings' potential outcomes which, she says, fall short of the 'hard treatment' necessitating a criminal standard of proof,[63] but which nevertheless might be regarded as punitive. Johan Boucht similarly suggests a standard of proof for civil recovery proceedings sitting between the criminal and civil standards. He proposes using the Norwegian 'clear balance of probabilities model' as a means of narrowing the margin of potential error on the court's part in such proceedings.[64] Mary Cheh notes that with regard to the Racketeer Influenced and Corrupt Organizations Act (RICO) in the United States, part of which similarly employs civil procedures to achieve criminal law objectives, both critics and supporters have accepted an argument in favour of a 'clear and convincing' evidential standard, based on a recognition that 'the stakes are higher in a civil RICO action than they are in a conventional civil lawsuit'. She suggests that there is scope for that standard to be employed more widely.[65] There is an analogous case to be made for civil recovery processes (including UWOs) given the stakes for respondents, even accepting a suggestion that civil recovery falls short of a substantive criminal proceeding. To realize the apparent original legislative intention that a more rigorous standard of proof than the ordinary civil standard should be imposed in civil recovery proceedings, this could be enshrined in statute.

4. Reverse Burdens

Once issued, UWOs impose obligations on respondents to provide details of how they acquired their properties or, put another way, to show that their assets were

contexts from the standard used in contempt of court proceedings, in which a standard of beyond reasonable doubt is applied. They highlight that in the parliamentary debates preceding the POCA, the government's intention was nevertheless to require a standard higher than is required in 'normal' civil proceedings. Per the Minister (John Denham MP) at the Bill's second reading: 'The standard is flexible, the more serious the allegation, the greater the degree of proof required by the courts under the balance of probabilities'. HC Deb Proceeds of Crime Bill 30 October 2001, col 764.

62 See Lord Hoffman's judgment in *In re B (Children)* [2008] UKHL 35.
63 Campbell (n 47) 706.
64 Boucht (n 20) 441.
65 Mary M Cheh, 'Constitutional Limits on Using Civil Remedies to Achieve Criminal Law Objectives: Understanding and Transcending the Criminal-Civil Law Distinction' (1990) 42 Hastings Law Journal 1325, fn 373.

not funded using the proceeds of unlawful conduct. Reverse burdens are not unusual in either of the civil or criminal law paradigms. They exist as creatures of both statute and common law.[66] As a general rule, in civil proceedings, some harm or fault must be first be demonstrated by a plaintiff before a rebuttable presumption can be raised.[67] In criminal law, in a frequently cited 1995 study of all triable offences in the Crown Court recorded in the then-current edition of *Archbold*, Andrew Ashworth and Meredith Blake found that some 40 per cent of offences involved legal burdens being raised or presumptions imposed against the defendant.[68] Notably, the offences investigated by Ashworth and Blake universally require the prosecution to first establish a case for the accused to answer before it can resort to raising a presumption against them.[69] The statutory obligation imposed upon a UWO respondent de facto to rebut a presumption of recoverable property is therefore not especially unusual. Looking at the recent history of asset recovery, for example, in a confiscation context, the 'lifestyle provisions' allowing the courts to assume the recoverability of all property obtained by a convicted defendant in the six years preceding their indictment have received the blessing of the courts, who have confirmed that Article 6(2) and (3) rights engaged are not engaged by those provisions.[70]

Although reverse burdens are permissible and common, the ECtHR has insisted that the presumption of innocence protected pursuant to Article 6(2) means that it:

> does not regard presumptions of fact or law with indifference. It requires states to confine them within reasonable limits which take into account the importance of what is at stake and maintain the rights of the defence.[71]

As to the principles that apply in determining whether a reverse burden unjustifiably infringes the presumption of innocence, the key question, per Lord Bingham in *Sheldrake*, is whether its application in a 'particular situation is a proportionate and justifiable legislative response to an undoubted problem'.[72] For the presumption raised by PEP-specific UWOs, although it is not quantifiable, there are

[66] Contract law provides eg for reverse burdens to disprove duress in some circumstances at common law, and to disprove misrepresentation pursuant to s 2(a) of the Misrepresentation Act 1967.

[67] Albeit there are some limited exceptions to this, which are primarily found in administrative contexts, eg the presumption of death and the presumption of regularity.

[68] Andrew Ashworth and Meredith Blake, 'The Presumption of Innocence in English Criminal Law' [1996] Criminal Law Review 306.

[69] See *Salabiaku v France* (7 October 1988) Series A no 141-A, para 30, and *R v Galbraith* [1981] 1 WLR 1039.

[70] POCA, s 10. Confirmed by the Privy Council in *McIntosh v Lord Advocate* [2001] 3 WLR 107, [2003] 1 AC 1078 and subsequently by the House of Lords in *R v Benjafield* [2002] UKHL 2, each of which considered confiscations made pursuant to statutory confiscation provisions broadly equivalent to those in the POCA.

[71] *McIntosh v Lord Advocate* [2001] 3 WLR 107 [28].

[72] *Attorney General's Reference (No 4 of 2002) and Sheldrake v DPP* [2004] UKHL 43, [2004] 3 WLR 976 [50].

a number of indicators suggesting that property in the UK has been purchased using the proceeds of overseas grand corruption,[73] and so we can assume that the requirement of an 'undoubted problem' is satisfied. It is whether the measure is 'proportionate and justifiable' as a response to this problem which is at issue. The absence of a component constituting a prima facie case (in a criminal law context), a harm, a liability or a fault (in a civil law context), or some reasonable basis for suspicion (in an investigative powers context) differentiates and particularly problematizes the operation of UWOs against PEPs when viewed alongside other legal reverse burdens. A rebuttable presumption is typically imposed by the law only where something *more* than a mere allegation of criminal or civil liability is shown. This lies in the Kantian idea raised earlier that a relationship of mutual trust between a state and its populace requires that state not to require individuals to account for themselves unless it has strong reasons for doing so.[74] With UWOs against PEPs, however, the weight of evidence presented by satisfaction of the Statutory Tests means that the imposition of the reverse burden can be made in response to something amounting to barely more than an allegation (ie a politically exposed person simply holding wealth the origins of which are not readily apparent).

Ashworth has examined a number of justifications advanced by the courts where reverse onuses are employed in a criminal law context. He concludes that there are instances 'internal to proof' that might be persuasive on a liberal rights reading where imposing an evidential burden (but not a persuasive burden) on a respondent might be justified.[75] Only two of them are likely to usefully apply in this context. The first relates to ease or difficulty of proof. Ashworth observes that an ease of proof argument might be justifiable in circumstances where a respondent is in the best position to resolve the question of whether or not a crime has been committed, because it places little strain on the fundamental right not to be unjustifiably punished.[76] Provided a case for accountability is first made, this seems a reasonable proposition in both a criminal and a civil context. The *Hajiyeva* matter provides a helpful case study of this principle in action. The evidential difficulties in proving public-sector corruption are often highlighted by commentators, including in parliamentary literature on UWOs.[77] In *Hajiyeva*, the respondent had previously confirmed on a Home Office visa application that she owned the

[73] See eg Transparency International UK and Thomson Reuters, *London Property: A Top Destination for Money Launderers* (Transparency International UK and Thomson Reuters 2 December 2016).

[74] cf R Kent Greenawalt, 'Silence as a Moral and Constitutional Right' (1981) 23 William & Mary Law Review 15.

[75] Andrew Ashworth, 'Four Threats to the Presumption of Innocence' (2006) 10 International Journal of Evidence and Proof 241, 270. He suggests that 'strong and specific reasons' would be necessary before an accused's burden of proof is raised to a persuasive standard.

[76] Ashworth (n 75) 266–67.

[77] See eg House of Commons Library, *Briefing Paper: Unexplained Wealth Orders* (CBP 9098, 8 January 2021) 2 and 7.

company which was registered as the legal owner of her residence.[78] It was reasonable for the NCA to assume that the information requested in the relevant UWO on how the respondent's company paid for that residence would be easily verifiable by the respondent. Furthermore, the NCA had a strong basis on which to seek the information. The respondent's husband had been found guilty of the theft of US$100m in Azerbaijan, inspiring reasonable questions around how the respondent could afford her London property and Surrey golf course without an apparent lawful income. Thus, on the facts of the case, there existed both compelling reasons for asking the respondent to account for her wealth and it was reasonable to surmise that the requested information was easily accessible to her.[79] Reversing the burden in such circumstances was justified.

The other relevant justification posited by Ashworth is where an accused must discharge an *evidential* (as opposed to persuasive) burden in circumstances where they seek to raise an issue or a defence.[80] This is, at first glance, a potentially attractive proposition in the context of UWOs. The legislation provides that property is presumed to be recoverable property 'unless the contrary is shown'.[81] The standard of evidence to be met to 'show' that property is *not* recoverable property is not specified in the legislation. In a criminal law context, prior to the introduction of the Human Rights Act 1998, commentators observed that it was 'widely assumed' that a statutory requirement to 'show' something imposes a persuasive burden.[82] This assumption has been tempered subsequently by the courts reading down persuasive burdens so that only evidential burdens apply where Article 6(2) is infringed.[83] Whether an infringement will be found will depend however on the nature of a particular measure and its application in practice. Per Lord Hope in *Ex parte Kebilene*:

> [T]his is not an exact science. The provisions vary so widely in their detail as to what prosecutors must prove before the onus shifts and their effect on the presumption of innocence depends so much on circumstances[84]

Consequently, in criminal matters, to the extent that it is up to a defendant to raise an issue (eg that a particular defence applies), it is increasingly incumbent upon the defendant only to meet an evidential rather than a persuasive burden in making that case. It seems likely (albeit not certain) that the UK courts would

[78] *Hajiyeva v NCA* [2020] EWCA Civ 108 [4].

[79] Something which she has denied. See Martin Bentham, 'Banker's Wife Says £15m Knightsbridge Home Bought Legitimately' *Evening Standard* (London, 9 June 2024).

[80] Ashworth (n 75) 269.

[81] POCA, s 362C(2).

[82] Ashworth and Blake (n 68) 311. This appears to be the tendency in the civil sphere too.

[83] In accordance with s 3 of the Human Rights Act 1998. *R v Lambert* [2001] UKHL 37; cf Lord Bingham's decision in *Sheldrake* (n 72).

[84] [1999] 3 WLR 972, 980.

similarly read down the burden on UWO respondents to minimize the adverse impact on respondents of an exercise of the measure.

One application of Ashworth's suggestion is demonstrated by case law dealing with (the since repealed) section 2(1) of the Public Bodies Corrupt Practices Act 1889, a measure which was broadly analogous in its operation to the presumptions raised pursuant to UWOs. The law in question provided that any gift or payment provided to a domestic public official acting *qua* public official would raise a presumption that the gift or payment was given or received corruptly.[85] In the parliamentary debates considering the presumption, it was noted that in those circumstances, it should be reasonably straightforward for the public official to explain why the gift or payment was made, but it was very difficult for a prosecution to establish that the gift was being made as a 'corrupt inducement'.[86] In other words, a public official's testimony in this case would be 'internal to proof'. The law was subsequently challenged following the enactment of the Human Rights Act 1998 in an appeal to a conviction which was decided inter alia based on the presumption. The Court of Appeal found that there had been an unjustified infringement of the defendant's Article 6(2) rights through the raising of the presumption. It held that the trial court should have read down the provision so as require the appellant to discharge an evidential burden rather than the legal burden of proving that the gift was not made 'corruptly'.[87]

If we accept Ashworth's (reluctant) suggestion that reversing the onus of proof may in some circumstances be justifiable where something is far easier for a respondent to disprove than it is for an enforcement authority to prove,[88] or specify in the context of UWOs that the respondent need only meet an evidential burden as in the example just cited, this may be a rather more palatable operation of UWOs against PEPs than the imposition of a persuasive reverse burden. Respondents would only have to introduce some credible evidence to the effect that either (i) there is something inherently incorrect with an enforcement authority's application, or (ii) that evidence rebutting a presumption sufficiently to discharge an evidential burden applies.

None of this should distract from the principle that before any burden can be imposed upon a respondent, enforcement authorities should first establish that there is a clear case to answer. This suggestion is supported by Antony Duff in discussing section 2 of the Public Bodies Corrupt Practices Act.[89] He, like Hamish Stewart,[90] appeals to the notion of the presumption of innocence as a totem of what

[85] Public Bodies Corrupt Practices Act 1889, s 2(1).

[86] For discussion of the legislation and relevant case law, see Amanda Pinto and Martin Evans, *Corporate Criminal Liability* (3rd edn, Sweet & Maxwell 2013) 196–99.

[87] *R v Webster* [2011] 1 Cr App R 16.

[88] Ashworth (n 75) 270.

[89] Prevention of Corruption Act 1916, s 2. The Act was repealed and replaced by the provisions of the Bribery Act 2010, pursuant to which no presumptions arise where public servants receive gifts.

[90] See n 48 and accompanying text.

he describes as 'the most minimal civil trust' that fellow citizens owe to each other by refraining from treating each other as 'suspicious strangers and potential enemies who must prove their bona fides'.[91] He argues that a logical extension of this civic-mindedness is that where they are in a position to offer appropriate evidence, individuals should be willing to respond to accusations of wrongdoing—but only 'once the prosecution offers evidence that generates a reasonable suspicion of guilt'.[92] It is that offering of plausible evidence that can be absent in a UWO context where the mechanisms are employed against PEPs.

5. Privilege against Self-Incrimination

Respondents to UWOs have three options. First, they can refuse to respond to an order. Should a respondent fail to comply with an order's requirements without what the High Court deems to be a 'reasonable excuse',[93] their property will be presumed to be recoverable property for civil recovery purposes. Furthermore, where an order is issued with a penal notice attached, non-complying respondents found to be in contempt are liable to prison sentences of up to two years and/or a fine.[94] Second, the respondent may choose to respond to an order by perjuring themselves and potentially expose themselves to criminal liability for knowingly or recklessly providing false or misleading information in response to an order.[95] Third, the respondent may opt to provide an honest account of how they obtained the property the subject of an order. This may reveal an innocent explanation as to the provenance of the respondent's assets or it could result in the respondent disclosing their benefit from crime.

The privilege against self-incrimination is a doctrine which protects a defendant (or someone who may become a defendant) in a criminal trial from the 'cruel trilemma' of perjury, contempt of court, or potential self-condemnation described above.[96] It prohibits the use against defendants of information that has been elicited from them by coercive or oppressive means, including through the threat of imprisonment for being in contempt of court.[97] The privilege only applies to 'evidence obtained through methods of coercion or oppression in defiance of

[91] RA Duff, 'Presuming Innocence' in Lucia Zedner and Julian Roberts (eds), *Principles and Values in Criminal Law and Criminal Justice: Essays in Honour of Andrew Ashworth* (OUP 2012) 57.

[92] Duff (n 91) 56–57.

[93] POCA, s 362C(1).

[94] Contempt of Court Act 1981, s 14. The notice affixed to Mrs Hajiyeva's UWO read as follows: 'If you disobey this order you may be held to be in contempt of court and may be imprisoned, fined, or have your assets seized'.

[95] POCA, s 362E.

[96] The unwillingness of courts to subject defendants to the 'cruel trilemma' by requiring them to give evidence against themselves was perhaps most notably referred to by Goldberg J in the US Supreme Court Fifth Amendment case of *Murphy v Waterfront Commission* 378 US 52 (1964).

[97] *Saunders v UK* [GC] ECHR 1996-VI (17 December 1996).

the will of the accused'.[98] The Strasbourg Court has confirmed that the privilege against self-incrimination can be invoked by anyone who has been accused of a criminal offence, no matter how minor.[99] In England, the privilege was also historically available in civil proceedings because in both criminal and civil proceedings, it was thought to discourage 'the ill treatment of a suspect . . . and the production of dubious confessions'.[100] There now appears to be a judicial consensus that the privilege has 'had its day' in civil matters.[101]

Although some of the ECtHR's case law has thrown doubt on the kinds of evidence covered by the privilege,[102] the Court seems to have settled on a position that any evidence existing independently of the will of an individual will not be protected (including, for instance, any physical evidence including documents of any kind that could alternatively be obtained through executing compulsory powers such as search warrants).[103] Given that the evidence substantively sought by enforcement authorities in obtaining UWOs is likely to be financial and therefore already existing in published or publishable format, the privilege may have limited application to respondents to those orders. Nevertheless, it is worthwhile considering the privilege here for two reasons. First, evidence gathered in response to an order, although likely inadmissible in a subsequent criminal prosecution against the respondent because of use immunity provisions under section 362F of the POCA, may inform derivative evidence used by enforcement authorities in subsequent criminal prosecutions against the respondent. Second, the position on the use of information provided in response to a UWO in *foreign* proceedings is unclear.

a. Origins of the Privilege

There are two prevailing and vigorously divergent schools of historical scholarship on the common law origins of the privilege against self-incrimination.[104] The first is typified by common law scholars darkly alluding to the abuses of the Star Chambers and the High Commission in England, where defendants were forced to take *ex officio* oaths. Trials often proceeded without defendants first being told of the charges proffered and the evidence against them, or of the identities of their

[98] *Saunders* (n 97) para 68.
[99] *O'Halloran and Francis v UK* (2008) 46 EHRR 21.
[100] *Istel v Tully* [1993] AC 45, 53.
[101] See decision of Lord Neuberger MR (as he then was) in *Coogan v News Group Newspapers Ltd* [2012] 2 WLR 848, 857. And as to why, see n 108 and accompanying text below.
[102] See eg *Funke v France* (1993) 16 EHRR 297, in which the privilege was found to apply to the applicant's financial records.
[103] *Saunders* (n 97) paras 68–69.
[104] Some legal historians trace the origins of the principle back even further, to Talmudic law. See Trechsel (n 26) 341.

accusers, and without access to defence counsel.[105] The theory was that the privilege developed in the common law courts as a reaction to intrusive or procedurally one-sided questioning, and that it had its roots in the canon law principle of *nemo tenetur prodere seipsum*.[106] The second school, led by John Langbein, offers an alternative and perhaps more plausible account. Langbein suggests that the privilege expanded more concretely in the eighteenth century in tandem with restrictions on the use of defence counsel in adversarial trials being relaxed. With that development, the emphasis on the defendant's involvement in the trial process moved from defendants (generally unsuccessfully) speaking on their own behalf (relying on judges to act as sometimes-helpful interlocutors) to defence lawyers testing the strength of the prosecution's case on behalf of their clients.[107]

The English courts have rejected the privilege in civil law matters on the basis that it is 'an archaic and unjustifiable survival from the past' based around (now apparently redundant) concerns about the risks of untrue extrajudicial confessions.[108] If Langbein's thesis is correct, however, the privilege against self-incrimination was not developed as a safeguard against confessions elicited through maltreatment, but rather as a means of ensuring that the prosecution case of an accused's guilt stands up to reasonable scrutiny independently of the accused's testimony. It follows that the basis on which the English courts have rejected the privilege in civil matters may be mistaken, and that there is scope for a reappraisal by them of the applicability of the privilege where the state makes a claim against a party, whether in a civil or a criminal context.

There are a number of arguments to be made in opposition to extending a privilege against self-incrimination to respondents to UWOs. The difficulties in obtaining evidence on financial crime and the instrumental undesirability of allowing corrupt PEPs to exploit fair procedure rules as a route to impunity have already been highlighted.[109] There has been some discussion both in the academy and by the judiciary to the effect that where there is a pressing social problem to be addressed, or where it is reasonable for an individual to provide information as a duty of citizenship,[110] then an individual should not be able to insist on recourse to

[105] For a summary of the main accounts of the origins of the privilege against self-incrimination, see Albert W Alschuler, 'A Peculiar Privilege in Historical Perspective: The Right to Remain Silent' (1996) 94 Michigan Law Review 2625.

[106] Broadly, 'No one is bound to betray oneself'. See Pat McInerney, 'The Privilege against Self-Incrimination from Early Origins to Judges' Rules: Challenging the Orthodox View' (2014) 18 International Journal of Evidence & Proof 101.

[107] See John H Langbein, 'The Historical Origins of the Privilege Against Self-Incrimination at Common Law' (1994) 92 Michigan Law Review 1047. Langbein observes that prior to the removal of restrictions on defence counsel at common law criminal trials, defendants relied primarily on themselves to provide exculpatory testimony. Given the capital punishment awaiting those convicted, to invoke a right to silence at trial would be 'literally [to invoke] the right to commit suicide' (at 1084).

[108] *Istel v Tully* [1993] AC 45, 53.

[109] See n 57 and accompanying text above.

[110] cf Peter Alldridge, *Criminal Justice and Taxation* (OUP 2017) 95–96.

the doctrine. However, these arguments are not particularly relevant to the principle apparently underpinning the operation of the privilege both in criminal law and civil law contexts; that is, the privilege is there to ensure that prosecutors or enforcement authorities establish a convincing case for a defendant or respondent to answer.

b. Use Immunity

With regard to the privilege against self-incrimination, the ECtHR's *Saunders v United Kingdom* ruling is probably the most relevant decision to the operation of UWOs. This case involved a matter where statements originally provided under compulsion as part of a regulatory investigation by the Department of Trade and Industry, as it then was, and admitted into the applicant's subsequent criminal trial were found to have attracted the privilege under European human rights law. Interestingly for the purposes of the current discussion, the ECtHR did 'not accept the Government's argument that the complexity of corporate fraud and the vital public interest in the investigation of such fraud and the punishment of those responsible could justify such a marked departure . . . from one of the basic principles of a fair procedure'.[111] In *Saunders*, the Department of Trade and Industry had worked with the police to facilitate criminal charges that potentially would be brought against the plaintiff in the future.[112] The ECtHR held that, under the circumstances, the use in criminal proceedings of information compelled under threat of a contempt of court finding was inconsistent with the conduct of a fair trial, even if that information was compelled in a context formally other than one involving a criminal investigation.

In response to *Saunders*, the government started including use immunity provisions in its legislation where enforcement authorities are afforded inquisitorial powers. Section 362F of the POCA, for instance, provides that statements made by respondents to UWOs cannot (subject to some exceptions) be used against them in subsequent criminal trials.[113] Nevertheless, concerns remain because, unhelpfully for respondents, the provision does not expressly preclude the admissibility of *derivative* evidence (ie evidence that can be independently sourced by enforcement authorities based on a disclosure made by a respondent in their response to an order) in a subsequent prosecution. The Canadian courts appear to

[111] *Saunders* (n 97) para 74.
[112] *Saunders* (n 97) para 23.
[113] The relevant exceptions are: for use in perjury prosecutions and offences under pts 2 or 4 of the POCA, in circumstances where a respondent has wilfully or recklessly provided false or misleading statements in response to a UWO, or where the respondent's statement contradicts evidence they provide as part of a defence in a prosecution for any other offence (where the contradictory evidence is led by the accused's counsel).

distinguish between evidence that is subject to use immunity and evidence derived from it, dismissing suggestions that to use the latter would be indirectly equivalent to using information subject to privilege.[114] Its conclusion that only 'testimonial' evidence attracts the privilege would doubtless, if expressly applied by the English courts, disincentivize UWO respondents from making full and frank disclosures. To the extent that it was intended that information derived *indirectly* from statements made in response to UWOs could be admissible, this should have been expressly provided for by statute.[115] Some legislative elucidation would be helpful on this point.

c. Incrimination in Overseas Prosecutions

If a PEP makes a statement in which they admit to holding misappropriated assets, a risk arises that the statement could be disclosed for use as evidence in overseas criminal prosecutions. The use immunity provision specifies that UWOs may not be used in evidence against a respondent 'in criminal proceedings'.[116] As far as the writer can tell, there is no general statutory definition of 'criminal proceedings' for the purposes of the POCA, but the term has been legislatively defined in connection with bad character evidence and hearsay evidence as 'criminal proceedings in relation to which the strict rules of evidence apply'.[117] This would seem to limit the protection against self-incrimination to UK prosecutions only, albeit in *Brannigan v Davison* Lord Nicholls acknowledged that the court may have some discretion at common law to excuse a respondent from making a statement on the ground of incrimination overseas.[118]

Section 14 of the Civil Evidence Act 1968 confirms '[t]he right of a person in any legal proceedings other than criminal proceedings to refuse to answer any question or produce any document or thing if to do so would tend to expose that person to proceedings for an offence or for the recovery of a penalty'. In *Hajiyeva*, the respondent argued that the requirement to furnish a statement under a UWO breached this provision on the basis that information submitted might prove incriminatory in potential future proceedings overseas. The High Court dismissed this claim. Supperstone J observed that in creating UWOs, the UK Parliament had 'necessarily intended' that the privilege against self-incrimination and the

[114] *Thomson Newspapers Ltd v Canada (Director of Investigation and Research, Restrictive Trade Practices Commission)* (1990) 54 CCC, 417 (La Forest J); subsequently upheld by the Canadian Supreme Court.

[115] eg in a criminal context, s 76(4) of the Police and Criminal Evidence Act 1984 clarifies that '[t]he fact that a confession is wholly or partly excluded in pursuance of this section shall not affect the admissibility in evidence ... of any facts discovered as a result of the confession'.

[116] POCA, s 362F.

[117] Criminal Justice Act 2003, ss 112 and 134 respectively.

[118] *Brannigan v Davison* [1997] AC 238, [1996] 3 WLR 859.

related privilege against spousal incrimination be abrogated by providing for use immunity provisions. Rosemary Pattenden argues that *Brannigan* is persuasive authority for the proposition that respondents facing the trilemma of contempt, perjury, or self-incrimination should be treated more humanely by the courts.[119] She suggests that unless in the court's view an overseas prosecution is unlikely or the domestic court receives a non-prosecution undertaking from foreign prosecutors, then the witness should not be compelled to give evidence.[120] In *Hajiyeva*, Supperstone J acknowledged the *Brannigan* discretion, but declined to excuse the respondent from providing her statement as he was not satisfied that the risk of prosecution overseas had been established.[121] The subsequent institution of extradition proceedings against Mrs Hajiyeva by Azerbaijan shows the limitations of this approach.[122]

The consultation documentation and the explanatory memoranda accompanying the legislation introducing the measure made no mention of whether the UK government considered whether a successful application for a UWO against a respondent could be so prejudicial as to jeopardize that respondent's right to a fair trial overseas. Given the publicity attending unexplained wealth actions against PEPs to date, the issue is not insignificant. The extradition proceedings brought against Mrs Hajiyeva suggests that the courts should carefully consider the self-incrimination implications in terms of potential overseas prosecutions, especially where proceedings are not anonymized.

d. Right of Silence

The right of silence relates to the right of a defendant in a criminal proceeding not to have adverse inferences drawn against them for refusing to speak when questioned.[123] It is a separate but cognate procedural protection to the privilege against self-incrimination. Section 38(3) of the Criminal Justice and Public Order Act 1994 expressly provides that an accused shall not 'have a case to answer or be convicted of an offence' solely because of inferences drawn from a failure to provide information.[124] English criminal law therefore statutorily prohibits a finding of guilt or even a prosecution based solely on an individual's invocation of their right of silence, albeit this does not preclude adverse inferences being drawn from

[119] Rosemary Pattenden, 'Self-Incrimination and the Threat of Prosecution under Foreign Law: Brannigan v Davison' (1998) 2 International Journal of Evidence & Proof 44.

[120] Pattenden (n 119) 48.

[121] *Hajiyeva* (n 78) [104]–[116], citing *R (CPS) v Bolton Magistrates' Court* [2004] 1 WLR 835.

[122] Jane Croft, 'Extradition of Azeri Banker's Wife Blocked by UK Court' *Financial Times* (London, 26 September 2019) 3.

[123] For a more comprehensive discussion on the distinction, see Trechsel (n 26) 341.

[124] This provision extends to refusals both to testify at trial and to answer when questioned by enforcement authorities.

a defendant's silence where other inculpatory evidence is available. The principle set out in the legislation is compatible with ECtHR's decision in *John Murray v United Kingdom*, where it found that inferences could be drawn from silence in situations which clearly call for an explanation from a suspect.[125] In that case, adverse inferences were drawn against the applicant, who had invoked his right of silence when he was found in the same house at the same time as an alleged kidnapping victim. In finding the adverse inferences drawn in that case admissible, the Strasbourg Court reiterated the general principle that 'it is incompatible with the immunities under consideration to base a conviction solely or mainly on the accused's silence or on a refusal to answer questions or to give evidence himself'.[126]

Andrew Ashworth observes that a reference in the decision to the 'persuasiveness of the evidence adduced by the prosecution' presupposes that the prosecution has first established a case against the accused sufficiently convincing to 'call for an explanation'.[127] The case is authority for the principle that in a criminal context, adverse inferences may be drawn from a refusal to speak provided that the prosecution has first made out a sufficient case against the accused. Defenders of the right of silence argue that there may exist plausible (and even excusable) reasons why a defendant might refuse to testify.[128] They suggest that the right encourages enforcement authorities to seek information from other sources, thereby ensuring more trustworthy evidence.[129] Moreover, it is not at all empirically clear that drawing adverse inferences aids in convicting the guilty and/or deterring putative offenders.[130] Allowing inferences to be drawn *before* the prosecution has made out a case, it has been argued, defeats the whole purpose of the prosecution having a burden of proof at all.[131] It allows the state, on the basis of very little, to presume the accused's guilt as its starting point.

In civil recovery investigations and proceedings, no right of silence exists and as a practical matter, adverse inferences *are* drawn from a respondent's silence because should a respondent refuse to comply with a UWO, 'the property is to be presumed to be recoverable property for the purposes of any proceedings taken in

[125] [1996] ECHR 3, para 47.

[126] [1996] ECHR 3, para 47.

[127] Andrew Ashworth, 'Self-incrimination in European Human Rights Law—A Pregnant Pragmatism' (2008) 30 Cardozo Law Review 751, 754–55, citing *Telfer v Austria* 34 Eur HR Rep 207 (2002).

[128] See Mike Redmayne, 'Re-thinking the Privilege against Self-incrimination at Common Law' (2007) 27 Oxford Journal of Legal Studies 209, 221–24.

[129] Hannah Quirk, 'The Right of Silence in England and Wales: Sacred Cow, Sacrificial Lamb or Trojan Horse' in J Jackson and S Summers (eds), *Obstacles to Fairness in Criminal Proceedings: Individual Rights and Institutional Forms* (Hart 2018) 78. This echoes Langbein's explanation as to the reasons for the development of the privilege against self-incrimination.

[130] See John Jackson, 'Reconceptualising the Right of Silence as an Effective Fair Trial Standard' (2009) 58 International and Comparative Law Quarterly 835, at 847, drawing on unchanged conviction rates in Northern Ireland after the law was changed to allow the courts to draw adverse inferences from defendants invoking their rights to silence in certain cases.

[131] Trechsel (n 26).

respect of the property under Part 5 [of the POCA—civil recovery of the proceeds of unlawful conduct] unless the contrary is shown'.[132] Contrary to the position in a criminal context, a UWO by its operation essentially allows for an inference to be raised against PEP respondents without enforcement authorities first establishing a case that the property's origins are linked to criminality. Clearly, judgments made against civil respondents are in principle less punitive than those handed down against criminal defendants, and so it is harder to justify a right of silence in civil recovery proceedings. On a first principles view, however, the concept of the state drawing inferences on the guilt of a person (or the 'guilt' of a property) without having something reasonably concrete on which to base those inferences subverts the notion that absent evidence to the contrary, individuals should be entitled to a presumption that they have not committed any wrongdoing.

Section 362C(3) of the POCA provides that once a presumption is raised against property as a result of a failure to comply with a UWO, 'it is for the court hearing [subsequent civil recovery order proceedings] in relation to which reliance is placed on the presumption to determine the matters in this subsection'. Given their duties to ensure fairness and proportionality,[133] the courts should tread cautiously in placing much weight on a presumption raised on the basis of silence with slim or no evidence on the criminal origins of assets.

6. Peaceful Possession of Property

On the publication of the draft legislation introducing UWOs to Parliament in October 2016, the Home Office and HMRC published a memorandum on that legislation's compatibility with rights protected under the ECHR (the ECHR Memorandum).[134] The ECHR Memorandum observed that the draft legislation engaged rights including those protected under Article 8 (respect for private and family life) and A1 P1 (peaceful enjoyment of possessions without arbitrary state interference) of the Convention. In the ECHR Memorandum, the Home Office advised that with regard to unexplained wealth orders, because 'the extent of any possible interference is restricted to the requirement for the [respondent] to provide an explanation of the origin of the property',[135] the measures are incapable of violating property rights. It explains that this is because a UWO is 'not the mechanism by which property is finally recovered',[136] since any eventual asset recovery

[132] POCA, s 362C(2).
[133] See Section 9.
[134] Home Office and HMRC, *Criminal Finances Bill: European Convention on Human Rights: Memorandum by the Home Office and HMRC* (19 October 2016).
[135] The ECHR Memorandum (n 134) para 65.
[136] The ECHR Memorandum (n 134) para 64.

will be the subject of a separate application for a civil recovery order or a consent order, as the case may be.

This position ignores two important aspects of how unexplained wealth orders operate. First, section 266(1) of the POCA provides that if 'the court is satisfied that any property is recoverable, the court *must* make a recovery order' [emphasis added]. It specifies that if a respondent fails to comply with any or all of the requirements of a UWO without reasonable excuse, '[t]he property is to be presumed to be recoverable property for the purposes of any proceedings taken in respect of the property under Part 5, unless the contrary is shown'.[137] The ECHR Memorandum suggests that 'presumptions' raised under UWOs do not impact on property rights. This is correct insofar as the presumptions do not *directly* or *immediately* impact on property rights, but the upshot of an unrebutted presumption is that enforcement authorities can seek a civil recovery order. The legislative intention seems to have been that, without more, a court hearing a subsequent civil recovery order application could treat non-compliance with a UWO as satisfying the requirement that the property is recoverable property, and that where this requirement is satisfied, the court must make a recovery order. This conclusion is based on (i) the Explanatory Memorandum accompanying the Criminal Finances Act 2017;[138] (ii) the views of parliamentarians presenting the Criminal Finances Bill;[139] and (iii) the courts' comments in dealing with UWOs.[140] It is difficult to understand how Parliament would have provided for the presumption *without* intending that property interests might be impacted upon by unexplained wealth orders.

Second, the government's view is that 'the UWO does not interfere with the individual's possession or use of the property, as the requirement to explain the origin of the property does not curtail or restrict those aspects of ownership'.[141] Whilst this is strictly speaking correct, it ignores the fact that enforcement authorities typically apply for interim asset freezing orders at the same *ex parte* hearings at which they apply for UWOs and both sets of orders are granted together.[142] Assets can be frozen for a significant amount of time as part of the process. The flow chart below shows where in the process respondents have the opportunity to provide evidence (both in response to an initial UWO, and at any subsequent

[137] POCA, s 362C(2).

[138] para 65 of which notes: 'if a respondent [to a UWO] fails to comply without reasonable excuse, the property concerned is to be *treated as* "recoverable property"'. [emphasis added]

[139] Criminal Finances Bill Deb 25 April 2017, col 1305, per Baroness Williams of Trafford (Minister of State, Home Office): 'If you do not comply with [a UWO], the property is presumed to be recoverable in any subsequent civil recovery proceedings. This is without the need for the enforcement authority to provide evidence that the property is the proceeds of crime'.

[140] See Lang J's decision in *NCA v Baker* [2020] EWHC 822 (Admin), where she observes of UWOs that (at para 63) 'the power is supported by the threat of forfeiture of the property itself in the event of non-compliance'.

[141] ECHR Memorandum (n 134) para 77.

[142] POCA, s 362J. Note that this has been the process employed with all reported UWO applications as of the date of writing.

civil recovery order proceedings, where applicable), and the points upon which the ability of property holders to deal with properties the subject of an order are impacted. The bold text shows points in time during a UWO process at which property can be permanently seized. The italicized text shows when property may be released to a respondent and unexplained wealth and freezing orders are discharged, or circumstances where those orders are not issued at all.

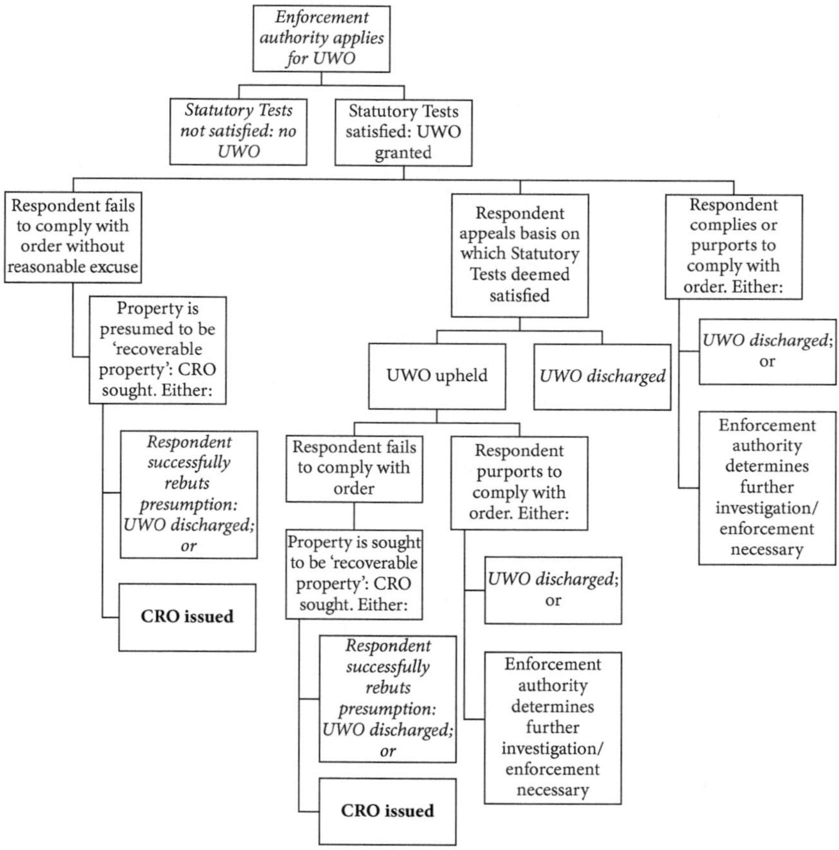

Figure 6.1 Impact of the UWO process on property interests

The stages in normal (not bold or italicized) text in Figure 6.1 show the parts of the process during which property is typically frozen on an interim basis. Formally, interim freezing orders can remain in place for a period of up to 186 days following a PEP respondent's purported compliance with a UWO (which, depending on the deadline for a response to an order, will likely aggregate to an even longer period of time) to allow enforcement authorities time to verify responses and consider their next moves.[143] If a respondent appeals the imposition of a UWO, the freezing period is further extended pending consideration of the appeal. This can impact significantly upon the right to peaceful disposal of property.[144] For example, the time period from the date of issue of Mrs Hajiyeva's UWOs to the eventual agreement of a settlement with the NCA and the issuance of civil recovery orders against her properties was six and a half years.[145]

A1 P1 rights are qualified rights. The Convention confirms a general right to peaceful possession of property but provides that this is subject to the rights of the state 'to control the use of property in the general interest' or to secure the payment of taxes or penalties. Interference with the right can be justified 'in the public interest and subject to the conditions provided for by law and by the general principles of international law'. These 'interests' qualifications represent 'the test of proportionality that pervades the Convention's consideration of interferences'.[146] It is generally accepted by the courts both domestically[147] and in Strasbourg[148] that civil recovery does not, as a rule, violate A1 P1 because it meets proportionality tests. So far, the English courts have avoided much substantive discussion on whether UWOs are proportionate for A1 P1 purposes in the PEP cases. In *Baker*, the issue was not relevant to the grounds on which the respondents sought to have the orders discharged. In *Hajiyeva*, Supperstone J noted that issuing unexplained wealth orders in that case was proportionate because there were 'grounds to believe that the property has been obtained through unlawful conduct'.[149] Supperstone's judgment seems to confirm that issuing an order is proportionate where links to suspected criminality are established—but this does not address proportionality (or the lack thereof) where, as in the case of PEPs, no suspected link is necessary. In the Serious Crime UWO case of *National Crime Agency v Hussain*, Murray J agreed that the impact, if any, of the requested order on A1 P1 rights, 'pursued a legitimate aim, would be in accordance with the law and would be justified and proportionate in all the circumstances'.[150] The aim pursued in issuing the order was legitimate because it improved 'the ability of the authorities to investigate and, where appropriate, recover the proceeds of crime'.[151] Although not discussed in

[143] POCA, s 362DA.

[144] *Marckx v Belgium* App no 6833/74, Series A no 31 (ECtHR, 13 June 1979), (1979–1980) 2 EHRR 330, para 63: 'the right to dispose of one's property constitutes a traditional and fundamental aspect of the right of property'.

[145] The UWOs were originally issued in February 2018, and the civil recovery orders were issued in August 2024.

[146] Bernadette Rainey, Elizabeth Wicks, and Clare Ovey, *Jacobs, White and Ovey: The European Convention on Human Rights* (7th edn, OUP 2017) 547.

[147] eg *Sanam v NCA* [2015] EWCA Civ 1234.

[148] *Gogitidze v Georgia* App no 36862/05 (ECtHR, 12 May 2015), discussed in detail below, and in *Arcuri* (n 23).

[149] *NCA v Hajiyeva* [2018] EWHC 2534 (Admin), [2018] 1 WLR 5887 [103].

[150] *NCA y v Hussain* [2020] EWHC 432 (Admin) [110] and [111].

[151] *NCA v Hussain* [2020] EWHC 432 (Admin) [107].

any depth, presumably the judge was more comfortable in that case in determining that the impact on A1 P1 rights was proportionate because the NCA had established the respondent's connections to serious criminality in obtaining the order.

As to how the ECtHR might approach the A1 P1 implications of UWOs against PEPs, an early indication may have been provided in the case of *Gogitidze and Others v Georgia*.[152] This case concerned an application disputing on A1 P1 grounds a measure which allowed Georgian enforcement authorities to pursue the proceeds of official corruption. The first applicant held, amongst other official roles, the office of President of the Audit Office of the semi-autonomous Georgian region of Ajaria. Together with some family members, he owned a number of properties the value of which was far higher than would have been commensurate with the owners' collective known incomes.[153] Subpoenas were served ordering the applicants to appear before the Ajarian Supreme Court to explain how they obtained the properties. The applicants failed to appear, and the Supreme Court ordered confiscation of their properties on the basis that the first applicant's income over the previous decade 'could not have sufficed to acquire the property in issue, and that the other applicants did not earn enough either'.[154]

Under the laws of that jurisdiction, evidence of a public official, their close relatives, or 'connected persons' holding unexplained wealth together with a failure to respond to the court's subpoena allowed the court to order a civil *in rem* recovery order without first having to obtain a criminal conviction. Unlike UWOs against PEPs, the measure could only be employed where the relevant public official had first been charged with a corruption or misappropriation offence committed in the course of holding public office. The ECtHR dismissed the applicants' claims that the recovery orders constituted disproportionate, illegitimate, and arbitrary infringements of their property rights and found that there had been no violation of A1 P1. There are a couple of takeaways from the judgment. First, the ECtHR is generally satisfied with and supportive of provisions from the UNCAC,[155] the Council of Europe's anti-corruption conventions,[156] and the Financial Action Task Forces' (FATF) Forty Recommendations. Each endorses the introduction of 'measures that allow [proceeds of official corruption] . . . to be confiscated without requiring a criminal conviction, which require an offender to demonstrate the lawful origin of the property, to the extent that such a requirement is consistent with the principles of their domestic law'.[157] Second, the Court confirmed that the

[152] *Gogitidze* (n 148). Michele Simonato has described the decision as an attempt by the ECtHR to 'put forward a more comprehensive vision concerning non-conviction-based confiscation regimes'—Michele Simonato, 'Confiscation and Fundamental Rights Across Criminal and Non-Criminal Domains' (2017) 18 ERA Forum 365, 366.

[153] *Gogitidze* (n 148) para 27. The first applicant's earnings over a decade from his official posts totalled €7,723. The applicants together owned properties with a value of €450,000.

[154] *Gogitidze* (n 148) para 27.

[155] *Gogitidze* (n 148) paras 55–57.

[156] *Gogitidze* (n 156) paras 58–64.

[157] FATF, The FATF Recommendations (FATF 2012) recommendation 4.

use of non-conviction-based confiscation measures can be a proportionate interference with property rights for A1 P1 purposes. In doing so, it reiterated its own 'well-established case law'[158] confirming the lawfulness of: (i) shifting the onus of explaining the legitimate origin of assets to respondents; (ii) *in rem* civil recovery of assets linked to serious crimes without requiring a conviction; and (iii) recovery measures against family members and close associates who are presumed to hold the impugned property on behalf of alleged offenders.[159] These factors bode well for UK enforcement authorities if UWOs are ever challenged in Strasbourg.

Notwithstanding this, the facts surrounding *Gogitidze* are distinguishable from the use of UWOs against PEPs in a couple of important ways. First, in *Gogitidze*, the civil recovery mechanism was only available where a respondent had first been charged with a crime.[160] The ECtHR emphasized, drawing analogies with its previous rulings on non-conviction-based confiscations for the suspected proceeds of drug trafficking and organized crime activities, that 'proof on a balance of probabilities or a high probability of illicit origins, combined with the inability of the owner to prove the contrary, was found to suffice for the purposes of the proportionality test under Article 1 of Protocol No. 1'.[161] This is a conjunctive test. It is doubtful that satisfaction of the Statutory Tests in a UWO against PEPs context will be sufficient to satisfy the first limb. 'Proof' or a 'high probability' that assets are of illicit origin seems to be required to engage the 'general interest' requirement.

In this way, the ECtHR's jurisprudence aligns with (but goes no further than) the decision in *Green*, in which Sullivan J ruled that '[a] claim for civil recovery cannot . . . be sustained upon the basis that a respondent has no identifiable lawful income to warrant his lifestyle'.[162] Something more—evidence establishing the 'illicit origins' of the relevant property to at least a civil standard *coupled with* the respondent's unexplained wealth—is necessary for the Strasbourg Court to deem that an interference in the respondent's property interest is proportionate. On this analysis, whilst a Serious Crime UWO would probably satisfy the A1 P1 proportionality requirement, a PEP-based UWO may not. The ECtHR in *Gogitidze* found that 'reasonable suspicion' on the part of prosecutors as to the illicit provenance of an asset was an acceptable threshold to meet to shift the burden to respondents to explain the provenance of an asset or face its recovery.[163] There is nothing (yet) in

[158] *Gogitidze* (n 148) para 121.

[159] *Gogitidze* (n 148) para 107 citing *Raimondo v Italy* (22 February 1994) Series A no 281, 16-20; *Arcuri* (n 23); *Morabito v Italy (dec.)* App no 58572/00 (ECtHR, 7 June 2005); *Butler v UK (dec.)* App no 41661/98 (ECtHR, 27 June 2002); *Webb v UK (dec.)* App no 56054/00 (ECtHR, 10 February 2004); and *Saccoccia v Austria* App no 69917/01 (ECtHR, 18 December 2008) paras 87–91.

[160] Gogitidze (n 148) para 55.

[161] *Gogitidze* (n 148) para 107.

[162] *R (on the application of the Director of the Assets Recovery Agency) v Green* [2005] EWHC 3168 (Admin) [33]. See Chapter 3, n 71 and accompanying text.

[163] *Gogitidze* (n 148) para 52. In the law under dispute, once public prosecutors held a reasonable suspicion that unexplained wealth might have been acquired unlawfully, they were entitled to file a civil action for recovery which had to 'be substantiated with sufficient documentary evidence'.

the Court's jurisprudence suggesting that unexplained wealth *simpliciter*, which is the standard applicable to PEP-based UWOs when issued where a court is satisfied that there are reasonable grounds for suspecting 'that the known sources of the respondent's lawfully obtained income would have been insufficient for the purposes of enabling the respondent to obtain the property'[164] is sufficient to ground an action for civil recovery. Some link to criminality, even if not proven to a criminal standard, has always hitherto been necessary to establish to the ECtHR that civil recovery satisfies the A1 P1 proportionality requirement. The test for proportionality is whether the recovery is 'in line with the general interest of the community, because the forfeiture of money or assets obtained through illegal activities or paid for with the proceeds of crime is a necessary and effective means of combating criminal activities'.[165] It is hard to reconcile the ECtHR being satisfied that PEP-specific UWOs meet this general interest in circumstances where it is not necessary to show a link to criminal activity in applying for the orders.

Perhaps significantly, the Court in *Gogitidze*, in confirming the legitimacy of the measure, observed that the civil recovery power in dispute in that case comprised one facet of a larger legislative package introduced in Georgia for the purposes of intensifying the fight against official corruption.[166] It referred, amongst other matters, to periodic monitoring from the Organisation for Economic Co-operation and Development's (OECD) Anti-Corruption Network for Transition Economies on Georgia and the wider impact of the suite of anti-corruption legislation introduced there. Prior to the introduction of the relevant laws, a number of monitoring reports observed that Georgia had a pervasive and highly visible corruption problem.[167] The ECtHR noted the OECD's reports, observing that the legislation, of which the contested measure formed a part, had achieved 'impressive results in eradicating administrative corruption',[168] citing 'studies confirm[ing] that corruption has been widely eradicated from the citizens' daily life'.[169] The Court found it 'important to emphasise that those legislative measures considerably helped Georgia to move in the right direction in combating corruption'.[170] It noted indicators including the World Bank's *Doing Business* survey and Transparency

[164] POCA, s 362B(3)(a).
[165] *Raimondo v Italy* (n 159) para 71.
[166] *Gogitidze* (n 148) paras 101–03.
[167] *Gogitidze* (n 148) para 73.
[168] OECD Anti-Corruption Network, *Istanbul Anti-Corruption Action Plan: Third Monitoring Report on Georgia*, adopted 23 September 2013.
[169] *Gogitidze* (n 148) para 73. Unhelpfully, not much detail was provided in the OECD ACN's Report (n 168) on the form this research took, other than to refer to two 2009 studies undertaken by the government of Georgia in conjunction with the Council of Europe among (i) the general public, assessing the degree of integrity of various service providers, the existing corruption reporting system, prevailing attitudes, and the role of the Georgian legal system; and (ii) public officials, addressing their perceptions of corruption and their experiences of various aspects of the institutions in which they work. The ACN also sent monitoring teams for on-site visits to Georgia to interview stakeholders.
[170] *Gogitidze* (n 148) para 107.

International's Corruption Perceptions Index, comparing the country's status in both sets of rankings before and after the introduction of the legislation.[171]

Given the low rate of use of UWOs against PEPs, it is difficult to imagine the ECtHR ever attributing perceptible reductions in the amount of property representing the proceeds of corruption being held in the UK to the measure's success. The fact that the impugned measure in the Georgian case formed part of a broader suite of legislation bolsters the credibility of the parliamentary intent behind its introduction—a claim that may not be as readily available for the politically convenient but largely unused PEP-specific UWO that was introduced on a piecemeal basis rather than as part of a broader anti-corruption strategy. The state's ability to seize property without first having to demonstrate evidence of criminality is central to the legitimacy deficit from which PEP-specific UWOs suffer and risks appearing to approximate somewhat arbitrary interference with property rights. On this account, it is difficult to see the Strasbourg Court being quite as quick as it was with the measure in *Gogitidze* to give the PEP-specific version of the UK's UWO its blessing.[172]

7. Privacy and Right to a Good Name

Commentators discussing theoretical justifications for privacy almost universally refer to how inexactly the concept of privacy is defined under the law.[173] Even so, the classic liberal human rights formulations recognize that the right to privacy is an intrinsic value that overlaps with other concepts at the core of individuals' humanity including personal freedom, autonomy, integrity, and dignity.[174] Charles Fried posits that 'ends and relations of the most fundamental sort: respect, love, friendship and trust', are inconceivable without privacy, and that part of the morality which underlies these relations is respect for individuals' privacy 'by state and citizen alike'.[175] Fried's expansive conception of the necessity for privacy is reflected in the ECtHR's jurisprudence, where privacy is described as a 'broad term not susceptible to exhaustive definition',[176] embracing multiple aspects of the

[171] *Gogitidze* (n 148) para 73. A caveat should be applied that the methodology, data sources, and precision of each of these sets of rankings as empirical indicators are widely criticized. On Transparency International's Corruption Perception Index, see Chapter 3, n 167 and accompanying text. On the World Bank's survey, the ease with which UK companies (prior to reforms introduced in 2024, at least) could be established (one of the main positive markers in the Doing Business survey) has been criticized as facilitative to corruption.

[172] Incidentally, the *Gogitidze* measures are less likely to offend art 14 than UWOs against PEPs, because they target domestic, not foreign, public officials.

[173] For further discussion on this, see Adam Thimmesch, 'Tax Privacy' (2017) 90 Temple Law Review 375, 396–97.

[174] Law Reform Commission (Ireland), *Report on Privacy* (LRC 57–1998) paras 1.09–1.16.

[175] Charles Fried, 'Privacy' (1968) 77 Yale Law Journal 475, 477, and 480.

[176] *Denisov v Ukraine* [GC] App no 76639/11 (ECtHR, 25 September 2018) para 95.

person's physical and social identity. Significantly for the purposes of the current discussion, the right extends to a right to a good name.[177] One classic articulation of the right to conduct one's personal correspondence and business dealings free from public scrutiny placed emphasis on an individual's right to 'inviolate personality' or 'a right to be let alone'.[178] This notion has been embraced in Europe, where the principle encompasses a right to live 'away from unwanted attention'.[179]

Interferences by public authorities with Article 8 rights to a private life and to a good name can be justified if they:

- are made 'in accordance with the law' (meaning they must be provided for under domestic law and compatible with the rule of law);[180]
- are 'necessary in a democratic society', meaning that there must be a 'pressing social need for the interference'[181] to underpin the proportionality of the measure; and
- further a legitimate aim. Such aims include 'the interests of national security, . . . the economic well-being of the country, [or] the prevention of disorder or crime'.[182]

The ECHR Memorandum acknowledges that a UWO 'may have an impact' upon Article 8 rights,[183] but insists that any interferences are justified. On the rule of law requirement, the Home Office asserts that any interference created by unexplained wealth orders would be 'in accordance with law' because the process is subject to judicial discretion and oversight. In establishing the 'pressing need' for the measure, the Home Office alludes to (but does not specify) 'strong evidence to suggest that high value property is being purchased in the UK for the purpose of concealing the proceeds of crime and corruption'.[184] It further claims that in any case, any potential interference is limited because the only information enforcement authorities can seek is details of how property was acquired, and the categories of respondents are limited to PEPs and those suspected of involvement in serious crime or those connected to such individuals. Finally, the 'legitimate aim' pursued by the measure is the 'strong public interest in ensuring that the proceeds of crime are not deposited in the UK'.[185] The immediate impact of a UWO on privacy rights reasonably

[177] Albeit art 8 cannot be relied upon to complain of a loss of reputation which is the foreseeable consequence of one's own actions (eg the commission of a crime or other misconduct entailing a measure of legal responsibility)—*Gillberg v Sweden* [GC] App no 41723/06 (ECtHR, 3 April 2012).

[178] Samuel D Warren and Louis D Brandeis, 'The Right to Privacy' (1890) 4 Harvard Law Review 193, 195, borrowing from *Cooley on Torts*.

[179] *Khadija Ismayilova v Azerbaijan* App nos 65286/13 and 57270/14 (ECtHR, 10 January 2019).

[180] NA Moreham, 'The Right to Respect for Private Life in the European Convention on Human Rights: A Re-Examination' (2008) European Human Rights Law Review 44, 47.

[181] *Dudgeon v UK* (1981) 4 EHRR 149, para 51.

[182] ECHR, art 8(2).

[183] ECHR Memorandum (n 134) para 36.

[184] ECHR Memorandum (n 134) para 37.

[185] ECHR Memorandum (n 134) para 37.

might be described as limited in nature. Although an order can require respondents to provide an account of and justify the origins of their assets, revenue, receipt of gifts, and personal and business expenditure, dissemination of this information is typically limited to a respondent's lawyers and the applicant enforcement authority. Consequently, PEPs may struggle to argue that the operation of a UWO is by itself a disproportionate infringement of privacy rights.

The more pressing privacy problem from a respondent's perspective is likely to be the extent and tenor of the publicity attending publicized unexplained wealth order cases. To date, there has been intense media scrutiny of the details surrounding UWOs. The NCA has said that it will 'always seek to report and publicise such cases wherever possible' to benefit from what the NCA believes is a deterrent effect engendered by that publicity.[186] The Civil Procedure Rules provide that judges must hold a hearing in private where they are satisfied that a case involves 'confidential information (including information relating to personal financial matters) and publicity would damage that confidentiality'.[187] Beyond that, the courts have broad general latitude to order private hearings, where they 'for any other reason [consider] this to be necessary to secure the proper administration of justice'.[188] This discretion is subject to the court taking into account any Article 10 (freedom of expression) interests that might be compromised by the decision, and the open justice principle.[189]

In *Hussain*, Murray J confirmed that the Civil Procedure Rules on privacy had been engaged when the applications for the UWOs in that case were originally made, thereby justifying the application hearing being made in private and the imposition of an anonymity order pending the final outcome of the matter.[190] He noted that 'there is no justification for a respondent's character being put forward for the type of public trial by media . . . at such an early stage of the investigation'.[191] The NCA will sometimes agree, once an application is granted, for respondent details to be anonymized for operational purposes or to avoid unduly prejudicing a party,[192] but subsequent judgments in each of the reported UWO cases have included extensive personal information on the respondents' financial and property affairs. This has established a pattern where PEPs who contest the basis on which

186 Author interview with senior NCA officials, 16 December 2020.

187 CPR 39.2(c).

188 CPR 39.2(g).

189 For a recent short treatise on the principle, see the speech delivered by Mr Justice Nicklin, Chair of the Judiciary's Transparency & Open Justice Board, entitled *Transparency & Open Justice—Opportunities and Challenges* on 9 May 2024 at the University of Newcastle Law School <www.judiciary.uk/speech-by-mr-justice-nicklin-transparency-open-justice-opportunities-and-challenges/>.

190 The anonymity order was imposed pursuant to CPR 39.4 which allows a court to protect a party's anonymity where it 'considers non-disclosure necessary to secure the proper administration of justice and in order to protect the interests of that party'.

191 *Hussain* (n 150) [84].

192 *NCA v Mrs A* [2018] EWHC 2603 (Admin).

an order is issued thereby increase the likelihood that personal information will be publicly disclosed during the appeals process.

The relatively derogatory impact of publicized UWOs against PEPs was referred to earlier in this chapter, but it is worth highlighting the issues again in a privacy context. The ECtHR has confirmed that for public officials to make statements imputing guilt to a defendant before a criminal trial would in most circumstances constitute a breach of Article 6(2) of the Convention.[193] It may be supposed that in protecting the reputation of individuals the subject of criminal processes through the presumption of innocence, the ECtHR recognizes the essentially punitive character of being the subject of enforcement authority suspicion of benefit from criminality. The reference to 'imputing' guilt recognizes that no formal adjudication of guilt is necessary to impugn a reputation through perceptions of links to criminality. Separately, the Court has found that the pre-criminal trial public disclosures by enforcement authorities of applicants' home addresses, details of their family members, and close associates (as well as their business relationships) in a press release amounted to a violation of Article 8 because it was not necessary, nor did it further a legitimate aim.[194] The Court has criticized excessive and superfluous private details being published by enforcement authorities, noting that it is possible to inform the public about the nature of investigative steps being taken by the authorities, whilst simultaneously maintaining applicants' privacy.[195] When the ECtHR examines whether Article 8 rights have been violated, it analyses the seriousness of the impugned measure's effects (including reputational effects). For a finding that Article 8 has been breached, the Court requires that the breach's effect has met an (undefined) 'threshold of severity', with applicants having to identify and explain the concrete repercussions of publicity for their private lives and the nature and extent of their suffering.[196] Given the importance of the perception of integrity to high-ranking public officials and businesspeople, it is likely that the 'threshold of severity' will be relatively easy for them to meet where their reputations are impugned through the use of a publicized UWO.[197]

The outcome of a recent Supreme Court decision means as a matter of English law, for criminal defendants, that the rules around privacy rights are even stricter. In *ZXC v Bloomberg LP*, the Supreme Court unanimously ruled against a media company in an action for the tort of misuse of private information in finding that someone who is under a criminal investigation but has not been charged will, as a general rule, be entitled to a reasonable expectation of privacy.[198] In discussing

[193] See eg *Daktaras v Lithuania* App no 42095/98 (ECHR 2000-X 489), (2002) 34 EHRR 60, paras 41–45.

[194] *Ismayilova* (n 179).

[195] *Ismayilova* (n 179) para 147.

[196] *Ismayilova* (n 179) para 110.

[197] On safeguarding the right to reputation as protected by art 8 of the ECHR generally, see Loukis Loucaides, *The European Convention on Human Rights: Collected Essays* (Brill 2007) 152–56.

[198] [2022] UKSC 5, [2022] 2 WLR 424.

public and inter-personal perceptions of individuals under police investigation and whether in the particular case the plaintiff's right to privacy should trump the media's right to freedom of expression under Article 10 of the ECHR, the Court noted:

> [T]he question is how others, including a person's inner circle, their business or professional associates and the general public, will react to the publication of information that that person is under criminal investigation. All the material [submitted in the current case] now admits to only one answer, consistent with judicial experience, namely that the person's reputation will ordinarily be adversely affected causing prejudice to personal enjoyment of the right to respect for private life such as the right to establish and develop relationships with other human beings.[199]

The Supreme Court was in no doubt that given the seriousness of the crimes alleged by Bloomberg in *ZXC* (the plaintiff was the chief executive of a foreign regional division of a particular company, and that division was under investigation by UK enforcement authorities), Article 8 was engaged. It noted the potential for 'irremediable and profound' harm to 'multiple aspects of the person's physical and social identity such as the right to personal development, and the right to establish and develop relationships' that the publication of the plaintiff's name in connection with the police investigation could engender.[200] The case has generated, and doubtless will continue to generate, significant discussion, not least because of the potential chilling effect it may create for journalists reporting factual matters and the public interest in having those matters reported.[201] A detailed discussion on the merits of the decision is not relevant for our present purposes. Its main significance here is the recognition that plaintiffs can succeed in a cause of action against media organizations (and presumably enforcement authorities) who publish their names in breach of a general reasonable expectation of privacy in circumstances where plaintiffs are indirectly or directly the subject of police investigations but have not been charged. What is not clear at this juncture is whether the ruling is a precedent for only criminal investigations, or for all investigations (including civil recovery investigations) undertaken by enforcement authorities. Civil recovery investigations ostensibly involve the suspected criminal origins of *assets* rather than the criminality of particular respondents. Even so, one might argue that substantially similar Article 8 issues are engaged: criminal and civil recovery investigations

[199] *ZXC v Bloomberg LP* (n 198) [108].

[200] *ZXC v Bloomberg LP* (n 198) [71], citing *Niemietz v Germany* (1992) 16 EHRR 97.

[201] Notably the commentary of Nicole Moreham, whose analysis was referred to by the Court of Appeal when it was hearing the matter. See NA Moreham, 'Privacy, Reputation and Alleged Wrongdoing: Why Police Investigations Should not be Regarded as Private' (2019) 22 Journal of Media Law 142.

each essentially involve a public authority investigating (at the very least, a link with) suspected criminality. Nevertheless, since *ZXC* was handed down, decisions revealing the names of respondents to civil recovery investigative orders continue to be published at relatively early stages in the investigation (in the *Grew* and *Younis* cases, for example, before any determination was made that the property the subject of the UWOs in those cases was 'recoverable property').[202]

This is all significant in the context of using civil recovery mechanisms to investigate the suspected proceeds of grand corruption. Responses to disclosure orders or UWOs sought and the orders themselves, by design, can include myriad personal details. Although not ideal from an open justice perspective, judicial responses to this problem might include either having private hearings and/or requiring that the identities of respondents be anonymized in reporting on civil recovery cases until appeal avenues have been exhausted and civil recovery orders are issued or settlements agreed. In *Hussain*, the anonymity order was lifted when it became clear as the matter progressed that the respondent would not be appealing the order.[203] This may serve as a practical model for future cases: cases that reach the end of their appeal trajectory, that are not appealed, or cases where there is clear non-compliance might be publicized. Respondents who successfully discharge UWOs should have their cases reported on an anonymized basis. Should their personal details be published while orders remain live, it is likely that they will suffer the publicly prejudicial 'smoke without fire' so often referred to throughout the *ZXC* decision.[204]

8. Targeted Anti-Corruption Measures and Discrimination

a. How Are the Measures Discriminatory?

One of the more concerning aspects of UWOs as they apply to PEPs is that respondents become answerable to them based on, amongst other considerations, their familial status and/or their employment status, and the fact that they or someone connected to them works for a state outside the EEA or the UK, or an international organization.[205] Imposing laws upon specific cohorts based on personal

[202] See *NCA v Grew (No 1)* [2023] NIKB 77, in which respondents to UWOs unsuccessfully challenged the validity of service of the orders on them outside of the jurisdiction, and *NCA v Younis* [2023] EWHC 2477 (Admin).

[203] The same eventuality ensued in *Younis* (n 202), where in the case of clear non-compliance with UWOs, the High Court had no hesitation in making public a judgment consenting to the NCA's application for final freezing orders in contemplation of recovery.

[204] In the sole unreported UWO case to date, the identity of the respondent has never been disclosed. This is possibly because of her reported links to paramilitary organizations: Margaret Davis, 'NI Woman Served with Unexplained Wealth Order' *The Belfast Telegraph* (Belfast, 1 August 2019) 11.

[205] POCA, s 362B(7).

characteristics points to a violation of the principle of non-discrimination, which is protected under Article 14 of the ECHR. This provides that the enjoyment of ECHR rights 'shall be secured without discrimination on any ground such as . . . national or social origin . . . property, birth or other status'. The prohibition on discrimination in lawmaking is based on 'normative reasons [relating] to human dignity, personal autonomy and the need for objective decision-making that is not tainted by irrational views or stereotypes'.[206] On a policy level, the norm helps to ensure that tangible and intangible social goods (including the work undertaken by law enforcement authorities) are managed and applied on rational grounds, rather than on the basis of irrelevant personal characteristics.[207] Non-discrimination is protected only as an accessory right under the ECHR, meaning it can be invoked only in connection with one of the other rights protected under the Convention.[208] This is probably why the Home Office does not expressly consider how new measures impact on non-discrimination obligations in publishing ECHR memoranda that consider the human right implications of new measures.[209]

The list of discrimination grounds under the ECHR is non-exhaustive.[210] Writing before UWOs were first proposed in the UK, Radha Ivory suggested that 'special-purpose asset recovery laws that overtly differentiate between PEPs and related parties and other people . . . are likely to involve a relevant form of differential treatment' for the purposes of Article 14 on the basis that familial relationships and the holding of governmental office are each examples of 'other statuses'.[211] An analysis of the ECtHR's case law supports this position. The Court has held that an individual holding high office is a characteristic constituting an 'other status' against which discrimination is possible for the purposes of Article 14.[212] It has also recognized the principle of 'discrimination by association' as a protected class under Article 14. By this, the Court means individuals suffering discrimination resulting from their connection to other individuals, including discrimination because of familial relationships.[213] Furthermore, UWOs against PEPs might be said to comprise a form of discrimination on the basis of 'national or social origin',[214] in this case, because the public officials involved will predominantly be public

[206] Janneke Gerards, 'The Discrimination Grounds of Article 14 of the European Convention on Human Rights' (2013) 13 Human Rights Law Review 99, 118.

[207] On the classic philosophical justifications for, and formulations of, equality, see Charilaos Nikolaidis, 'Unravelling the Knot of Equality and Privacy in the European Court of Human Rights and the US Supreme Court: From Isonomia to Isotimia' (2018) 18 Human Rights Law Review 719, 720–25.

[208] ECHR, *Guide on Article 14 of the European Convention on Human Rights and on Article 1 of Protocol No. 12 to the Convention*, Council of Europe, version updated on 31 August 2020, 6.

[209] See eg the ECHR Memorandum accompanying the Criminal Finances Act 2017, cited at n 134.

[210] art 14 protects enjoyment of Convention rights without discrimination on any ground, including 'national or social origin, association with a national minority, property, birth or other status'.

[211] Ivory (n 28) 260.

[212] *Valkov v Bulgaria* App nos 2033/04 and 8 others (ECtHR, 25 October 2011).

[213] See the ECHR's Guide on Article 14 (n 208) 12–13, citing four different cases of discrimination by reason of familial association.

[214] *Biao v Denmark* [GC] App no 38590/10 (ECtHR, 24 May 2016).

officials of non-EU and non-EEA countries. Although it might be claimed that PEP-specific provisions comprise neutrally formulated rules, in practice, because PEPs are almost always either related to, associated with, or are, non-UK or EEA officials, there is a significant likelihood that PEP-specific UWOs will disproportionately disadvantage individuals from outside of the UK or the EEA. The ECtHR has taken a particularly dim view of discrimination based on immutable personal characteristics such as nationality.[215]

b. Is the Discrimination Justified?

Where differential treatment is established, the question then arises as to whether that treatment is in some way justified. To determine this, the Strasbourg Court examines (i) whether individuals in analogous or relevantly similar situations are treated differently, and if they are, whether the difference in treatment (ii) pursues a legitimate aim (iii) in a proportionate manner.[216]

In the case of UWOs against PEPs, the first part of the test is reasonably easy to satisfy. The PEP criteria means that non-UK and non-EEA officials with prominent public functions, their families, and their connected associates are each subject to different rules from their UK and EEA counterparts.[217] Additionally, the availability of the orders means that PEPs who hold unexplained wealth face different measures to everyone else holding unexplained wealth other than those suspected of involvement in serious crime or people connected to those so involved. On the second part of the test, the legitimacy of the *aims* of the orders is not in doubt. It is objectively desirable that corrupt officials do not profit from their crimes, particularly at the expense of the citizenries in their states of origin. The government wished to ensure that the UK is not perceived as a haven for dirty money, and in introducing unexplained wealth orders, in theory at least, it furthered this aim by creating conditions that may give putative corrupt PEPs pause before seeking to launder illicit funds in the jurisdiction.

To establish the third criterion, namely, the proportionality of the measure, states must show a link between the aim pursued and the differentiation.[218] In this regard, the UK's case is less clear. Obviously, those capable of committing acts of official grand corruption and holding the proceeds of those acts in the UK form a very limited cohort populated principally by PEPs. However, grand corruption

[215] The Strasbourg Court has recognized the principle of indirect discrimination arising through laws disproportionately disadvantaging particular cohorts. See Rory O'Connell, 'Cinderella Comes to the Ball: Art 14 and the Right to Non-discrimination in the ECHR' (2009) 29 Legal Studies 211.

[216] *Molla Sali v Greece* [GC] App no 20452/14 (ECtHR, 19 December 2018) paras 133–37.

[217] The AML Regulations, by contrast, distinguish only between domestic and non-domestic PEPs, and a minimum threshold of enhanced customer due diligence under those Regulations applies to *all* PEPs, regardless of their nationality.

[218] ECHR (n 208) 18–19.

offences as a rule constitute serious crimes, so it is unclear why, in circumstances where Serious Crime UWOs are available, a PEP-specific measure was also necessary. *No* evidence has been presented by any party to show that the incidence of PEPs bringing illicit wealth into the country and laundering it through the London property market, say, is more prevalent than similar activities occasioned by non-PEP individuals (nationals and non-nationals alike) acquiring properties in the UK or using UK-based financial service providers. Suggestions that PEP-specific measures are necessary because their respondents may be domiciled in another country also do not hold water in circumstances where the NCA successfully served UWOs outside of the jurisdiction on respondents who were neither PEPs nor domiciled in the UK in *NCA v Grew and Another*.[219]

Even if a discernible link between politically exposed persons and higher levels of money laundering *could* be shown, it is still doubtful that the availability of a measure directed at *all* PEPs can be said to be proportionate. The unnecessary breadth of the definition of the term (and the consequent dilution of focus away from the highest-ranking public officials and those most likely to have access to states' coffers) was discussed in Chapter 2. Unjustified discrimination is inherently wrong as a tool of policy-making in the crime control sphere because it risks legitimizing the exercise of state power on irrational or arbitrary grounds. But infringement of the prohibition against non-discrimination is also problematic in other respects. One impact of a PEP-specific measure is to communicate to the populace at large that wealthy foreigners are somehow less trustworthy than citizens. Legitimizing such stereotypes runs the risk of embedding systemic discrimination against particular groups in policy more generally.[220]

c. Legitimacy Problems with PEP-Specific Measures

Scholars have written about differentiated procedures applying to individuals residing in society's margins in other crime and security contexts.[221] Characterizing foreign public officials and those linked to them who own property in the UK—ostensibly a relatively elite class—as 'marginalized' seems counterintuitive. When viewed alongside historic 'deviant' classes, from the mods, marijuana users, and jazz musicians of critical deviance discourse[222] to more contemporary discussions

[219] [2023] NIKB 77. The case involved the UK-owned properties in Northern Ireland of respondents who lived a couple of miles over the border in Ireland.

[220] On the nascent recognition by the ECtHR of the role of stereotyping as a structural cause of unjustified discrimination, see Alexandra Timmer, 'Toward an Anti-Stereotyping Approach for the European Court of Human Rights' (2011) 11 Human Rights Law Review 707.

[221] In particular, in the context of security and anti-terrorism laws. See David Cole, 'Enemy Aliens' [2002] Stanford Law Review 953; Cass Sunstein, 'Laws of Fear: Beyond the Precautionary Principle' (2003) 151 University of Pennsylvania Law Review 1003.

[222] As discussed by Cohen and Becker amongst other critical deviance theorists: see Chapter 4.

around suspected terrorists and young people displaying 'anti-social behaviours', PEPs seem to be located much closer to society's 'establishment' classes.[223] Nevertheless, their eligibility for UWOs demonstrates that PEPs fall into a grouping of individuals standing apart from 'fully integrated' members of society.

Measures targeted specifically at foreign politically exposed persons provoke disquiet around legitimacy for a number of reasons. First, using differentiated crime control measures in a transnational crime context exposes inconsistencies in the UK's self-perception as a champion of official integrity on a global level.[224] David Cole, writing in the context of counter-terrorism measures employed by the United States, observes that states using differentiated procedures against non-citizens 'is likely to be counterproductive at home and abroad, because it undermines our legitimacy in both spheres'.[225] He suggests that special measures targeting a particular group may serve to alienate the law-abiding members of that cohort by 'treating many of its members as suspect because of their . . . national origin'.[226] If the UK is perceived as deviating from procedural norms for non-citizens, then this erodes its moral authority when seeking to insist on similar norms being observed in other jurisdictions in respect of the treatment of individuals including its own citizens. It also undermines claims that it might have to thought leadership on an international level on legitimacy in state actions more generally.

Second, PEPs who are not themselves senior foreign public officials may become eligible respondents to UWOs, even though they have exercised no agency in becoming PEPs. The questionable legitimacy of the measure is exacerbated for this class (family members and close associates of officials holding prominent public functions) because, certainly for family members at least, they are unable to remove themselves from the category of potential respondents. In this way, they suffer stigmatization or exclusion commensurate with PEP status solely because of immutable personal characteristics,[227] without benefiting from the advantages

223 Andrew Ashworth and Lucia Zedner, 'Prevention and Criminalisation: Justification and Limits' (2012) 15 New Criminal Law Review 542.

224 HM Government, *United Kingdom Anti-Corruption Strategy 2017–2022* (December 2017). Per the Foreword by the then-Home Secretary, Amber Rudd MP: 'we have an opportunity to leverage our reputation for integrity and fair play as we establish new trading relationships. Since 2010 the UK has arguably done more than any country in the world to fight corruption'.

225 Cole (n 221) 958.

226 The use of the term 'citizen' being understood not only as a person legally being a member of a community, but as also an individual who is entitled to enjoy civil, political, and social rights within a given society, and who shares at least some measure of common cultural values with 'integrated' members of society. See Barry Vaughan, 'Punishment and Conditional Citizenship' (2000) 2 Punishment & Society 23. Vaughan distinguishes between 'full citizens' and 'partial' or 'conditional' citizens: 'people who may be moulded into full citizens but who are, at present, failing to display the requisite qualities expected of citizens' (at 26). It is into this latter category of 'not-quite' members of the community that PEPs might be said to fall.

227 See Gerards (n 206) 109–10. To be clear, the ECtHR has held that both immutable and non-immutable personal characteristics are capable of comprising grounds for discrimination under art 14.

that public officials enjoy which might mitigate the adverse impacts of possessing PEP status.

Third, and as will be expanded upon below, the PEP-focused UWO forms part of a wider trend of differentiated mechanisms targeting specified classes for crime control purposes over the past three decades which are somewhat suspect in terms of procedural safeguarding. Even though there is strong academic consensus that 'basic protections of liberty . . . are not, and should not be, deemed privileges or rights of citizenship, but human rights that stem from the fact of our common humanity, not our particular nationalities',[228] this is not reflected in crime control trends.

d. Incrementalism and Differentiation

The fact that it is not necessary to show evidence of criminality to obtain a UWO against a PEP grants an unprecedented licence to the state to 'recover' property from PEPs where respondents fail to comply with an unexplained wealth order. UWOs obtained against PEPs on the basis of sub-section 362B(3)(a) of the POCA set the bar at which the state can seize property lower even than that necessary to seize the unexplained assets of those who it is reasonably suspected have been or are involved in serious crime.[229] This low bar to the use of investigative tools by enforcement authorities forms part of an observable trend in the accretion of state power and the erosion of the rights of (i) 'non-citizens' such as PEPs, and (ii) respondents to asset recovery measures more generally.

In having UWOs target only (i) PEPs, and (ii) those suspected of connections with serious crime, the orders' availability acts as a legitimating device for the message that foreign PEPs, like serious criminals, somehow stand outside society and are thus deserving of being made subject to 'special' laws and standards. Commentators observing the gradual encroachment of security and crime control measures on civil liberties have identified the following trend. First, a law is introduced to curtail a specific perceived threat: say, terrorist activity or youths allegedly exhibiting anti-social behaviours.[230] Those to whom the law applies comprise an identifiable and limited class. The urgent or exceptional nature of the perceived threat presented by that group operates to override concerns which would arise if similar measures were directed against the populace as a whole. The state's

[228] David Cole, 'Against Citizenship as a Predicate for Basic Rights' (2007) 75 Fordham Law Review 2541, 2548; and see Lucia Zedner, 'Security, the State and the Citizen: The Changing Architecture of Crime Control' (2010) 13 New Criminal Law Review 379, 386–87.

[229] s 362B(3)(a) provides that UWOs can be issued against PEPs who hold property where there are reasonable grounds for suspecting that 'the known sources of the respondent's lawfully obtained income would have been insufficient for the purposes of enabling the respondent to obtain the property'.

[230] See Jennifer Hendry and Colin King, 'Expediency, Legitimacy, and the Rule of Law: A Systems Perspective on Civil/Criminal Procedural Hybrids' (2017) 11 Criminal Law and Philosophy 733.

new power is normalized.[231] Where it is proposed to extend that power so that its impact is no longer confined to the specified class, much of the dismay that would have greeted the measure and the attendant implications for due process rights had it been imposed against the general population from the outset will have diminished. Lucia Zedner observes that by enacting laws targeting specific cohorts of 'others' who hold little political leverage with which to protest, legislatures can evade the 'natural political resistance' that could be expected if the measures were applied to the general populace.[232] She cites as an example the use of special advocates (originally confined to cases heard at the Special Immigration Appeals Commission, their use was then extended to terrorism cases, then to parole board hearings, and then to other criminal proceedings).[233] The curtailment of the right of silence originally directed solely at suspected Irish republican paramilitary terrorists and its subsequent extension to all criminal suspects is a further example. Legislating against 'non-participants' can thus serve as a gateway to subsequently introducing similar powers against larger segments of the population. That the state has access to unprecedented and increasing power to freeze property pending an account of origin of wealth being provided should therefore not be of concern only to PEPs, but also to all participants in society, including the minister presenting UWOs to Parliament.[234] The risk in introducing the measure specifically against PEPs for now is that it will act as a legitimizing precedent allowing presumptions of recoverable property to be extended more easily and on a more widespread basis in future.

9. Proportionality and Fairness

Having highlighted specific due process and human rights concerns arising from the introduction of (i) hybrid asset recovery measures, and (ii) mechanisms targeting specific sections of the population, for completeness, it is worth critiquing UWOs against PEPs in the context of certain long-standing principles fundamental to English law. This section briefly assesses the measure in light of proportionality and fairness norms.

[231] See Peter Alldridge, *Criminal Justice and Taxation* (OUP 2017) 153.

[232] See Zedner (n 228) on this point and for a thorough discussion of the literature more generally.

[233] Zedner (n 228) 398–99. Special advocates are advocates who take instructions from and represent a defendant, and who are provided access to secret materials relevant to the defendant's case, the contents of which they are not permitted to disclose to the defendant.

[234] See Ben Wallace MP's observation when discussing why UWOs against PEPs should not be extended to UK parliamentarians, cited in Chapter 2, n 64.

a. Proportionality

The Human Rights Act 1998 imposes obligations on the courts to interpret legislation 'in a way which is compatible with the Convention rights'[235] and specifies that it is unlawful for public authorities to 'act in a way that is incompatible' with the Convention.[236] The definition of 'public authorities' includes enforcement authorities and the courts.[237] Where a public authority's actions engage a right protected by the ECHR, courts may be required to determine if the interference with the right is proportionate to the aims pursued by the particular measure employed or whether its use is excessive under the circumstances. The ECtHR recognizes that individual states are often better placed than it is itself to determine what is proportionate in their own respective national contexts. It therefore allows states a wide margin of appreciation in both determining and applying proportionality principles.[238] In the UK, proportionality has been embraced by the courts as a general standard of public law. The Supreme Court has endorsed the following test to assess whether a disproportionate violation of rights has occurred through the actions of a public authority:

> [I]t is necessary to determine (1) whether the objective of the measure is sufficiently important to justify the limitation of a protected right, (2) whether the measure is rationally connected to the objective, (3) whether a less intrusive measure could have been used without unacceptably compromising the achievement of the objective, and (4) whether, balancing the severity of the measure's effects on the rights of the persons to whom it applies against the importance of the objective, to the extent that the measure will contribute to its achievement, the former outweighs the latter.[239]

For UWOs, proportionality concerns have been addressed expressly by the presiding judges in each of the reported cases. In *Baker*, Lang J noted the importance of the principle where Convention rights were engaged.[240] In *Hussain* (a UWO case that did not involve PEPs), Murray J emphasized that in coming to his decision he had reviewed the terms of the particular orders sought to ensure that

[235] Human Rights Act 1998, s 3(1).

[236] Human Rights Act 1998, s 6(1).

[237] Human Rights Act 1998, s 6(3).

[238] See Lord Reed's dissenting opinion in *Bank Mellat v HM Treasury (No 1)* [2013] UKSC 38 [71] and Bernhard Schlink, 'Proportionality (1)' in Michel Rosenfeld and András Sajó (eds), *The Oxford Handbook of Comparative Constitutional Law* (OUP 2012) 718, 727–32, tracing varying proportionality traditions in European civil law and common law countries, perhaps further explaining the ECtHR's approach.

[239] *Bank Mellat* (n 238) [74] (Lord Reed).

[240] *Baker* (n 140) [64]. Lang J gave little by way of analysis in terms of the proportionality (or lack thereof) of UWOs because she eventually ruled on the basis that the NCA's case was founded on flawed reasoning.

they were appropriate and proportionate on the facts of the case, and had considered whether less intrusive means were available to achieve the same goals.[241]

On the first challenges to the UWOs issued in *Hajiyeva*, Supperstone J found that any violation of the defendant's right to peaceful possession of their property protected under A1 P1 of the Convention was proportionate because the requirements of the UWOs sought struck a 'fair balance', and that the interference with respondent's rights was 'no more than a modest interference with the peaceful enjoyment of property'.[242] Supperstone J emphasized that to engage A1 P1, a 'loss of value' in an applicant's interest in the property was necessary, and that 'mere inference with the enjoyment of property is not sufficient'.[243] It is reasonable to conclude that the High Court is alive to the proportionality implications of UWOs, having regard, amongst other matters, to the strength of the evidence justifying their imposition and the ensuing impact on individual rights. What is less clear is whether the High Court might be willing to issue UWOs against PEPs in the absence of reasonably strong grounds for suspecting that property is the proceeds of crime. Theoretically, it is possible for enforcement authorities to obtain a UWO against a PEP without first having to establish to the courts that either the respondent or the property the subject of the order is suspected of any having link to criminality. In those circumstances, is it proportionate to impose a quasi-criminal measure like the PEP-specific UWO against a respondent? To answer this question, it is worth considering each aspect of the proportionality test as it applies to the measure.

First, it seems clear that the stated objectives underpinning UWOs are a priori sufficiently important to justify a limitation on individual rights where there is evidence that respondents may have benefited from official corruption. The second criterion necessary to establish proportionality requires state authorities to show the legislature's objectives are 'logically furthered by the means the government has chosen to adopt'.[244] Given the objectives, one might expect that their use should be contingent on a reasonably held suspicion of a link to criminality or corruption where they are used. It is not necessary for enforcement authorities to establish any such link in seeking UWOs against PEPs. It is difficult to identify an articulable relationship between the use of UWOs and the legislative objectives without the presence of that link. Furthermore, no evidence exists to suggest that an overseas PEP is more or less likely than any other individual to hold the proceeds of crime. Moreover, the need for a PEP-specific version of the UWO, given the availability of the Serious Crime UWO, is not clear. On that basis, it is doubtful

[241] *Hussain* (n 150) [107]–[108]. Similarly, in another non-PEP UWO case, the High Court of Northern Ireland specifically cited the fact that the NCA had sought voluntary declarations and (ultimately non-enforceable) disclosure orders against the respondents in explaining their reasons for granting the UWOs sought: *NCA (No 3) Aidan Grew and Nuala Grew* [2024] NIKB 36 [107].

[242] *Hajiyeva* (n 149) [103].

[243] *Hajiyeva* (n 149) [99]–[100].

[244] *Lavigne v Ontario Public Service Employees Union* [1991] 2 SCR 211, 291 (Wilson J), cited with approval in Lord Reed's decision in *Bank Mellat* (n 238).

that the legislature's objectives in introducing the measure have been (i) met, or (ii) logically furthered, casting doubt on the measure's satisfaction of the second proportionality criterion.

The third part of the proportionality test is whether a 'less intrusive measure' is available, also known as the 'necessity' test.[245] Satisfaction of this test helps to mediate any suggestion that state authorities are overreaching or acting arbitrarily in exercising their powers. As observed by Supperstone J in *Hajiyeva*, UWOs in practice constitute 'no more than a modest interference with the peaceful enjoyment of property'.[246] If UWOs were successfully sought but the identities of the respondents were subject to reporting restrictions, at least until an investigation has been concluded, then the necessity test could be reasonably easy to satisfy. In practice, the majority of UWOs have been extensively publicized.[247] The resulting publicity as opposed to the operation of a UWO itself may form the main cause of potentially significant intrusion into the lives of respondents. Furthermore, there exist measures which are potentially less intrusive but achieve similar objectives, including for example the disclosure order, the issuance of which does not require an application to the High Court. In short then, whilst UWOs themselves are not especially intrusive, the management of UWO processes can be. It is this aspect of UWOs which may raise challenges in satisfying the necessity test.

The fourth proportionality criterion requires the courts to consider whether the severity of a measure's effects on the rights of those to whom they apply is proportionate when viewed against the objectives sought by that measure. The courts' references to 'balancing' rights against objectives have been criticized elsewhere because they (i) suggest that scenarios exist in which putatively inalienable rights can be usurped where the objectives are sufficiently compelling; (ii) suggest a cost-benefit calculation of values rather than the application of a means-end test;[248] and (iii) incorrectly assume that each (completely different) type of factor is somehow measurable against and/or is somehow capable of being offset against the other. For that reason, whilst objectively a measure requiring foreign PEPs to account for their wealth is more than proportionate when viewed against the importance of deterring the devastation wrought by crimes of overseas grand corruption, this is not really an appropriate formulation of the test. A correct conceptualization would instead consider whether, given the precedent set by the new measure and its potential adverse implications for civil liberties in society in the longer term, and given the effectiveness of the measure in practice, it was necessary to introduce the measure at all.

245 See Aharon Barak, 'Proportionality (2)' in Michel Rosenfeld and András Sajó (eds), *The Oxford Handbook of Constitutional Law* (OUP 2012) 744.

246 *Hajiyeva* (n 149) [103].

247 See eg n 21 and accompanying text above.

248 See Eric Engle, 'The History of the General Principle of Proportionality: An Overview' (2012) 10 Dartmouth Law Journal 1, 8.

b. Fairness

English common law imposes a separate and additional duty of fairness on public decision-makers empowered with discretion to adjudicate in a way capable of impacting upon individual rights. The duty has been summarized as follows:

> [W]hen a statute has conferred on any body the power to make decisions affecting individuals, the courts will not only require the procedure prescribed by the statute to be followed, but will readily imply so much and no more to be introduced by way of additional procedural safeguards as will ensure the attainment of fairness.[249]

Precisely how fairness is attained will depend on the context of the case:

> For a long time the courts have, without objection from Parliament, *supplemented procedure* laid down in legislation where they have found that to be necessary for [the purpose of fairness in all circumstances]. But before this unusual kind of power is exercised it must be clear that the statutory procedure is insufficient *to achieve justice* and that to require additional steps would not frustrate the apparent purpose of the legislation [emphasis added].[250]

This is a strong illustration of Packer's characterization of the courts as guardians of the Due Process Model paradigm. The notion of fairness overlaps with some of the ideas with which proportionality is concerned. Each permits judicial intervention by way of supplemented procedure to limit circumstances where individuals are excessively prejudicially impacted by the practical operation of a legislative measure. Each principle in essence gives the courts licence, within limits, to shield a respondent or defendant from statutorily sanctioned state overreach on a case-by-case basis 'to achieve justice'. Significantly, the fairness principle operates independently of proportionality and differs from it in important ways. It is not specifically concerned with the rights and obligations of one party (a respondent) relative to the rights of others (the state, society, etc). It instead focuses on the ideal of fairness *simpliciter*, subject to the legislature's intent. In responding to perceived failures of fairness, the doctrine can be used by the courts to require enhanced procedural protections to be attached to a particular measure rather than rejecting that measure's use entirely so that the legislative purposes can still be achieved.

The English courts have yet to undertake a detailed analysis of anti-corruption measures including UWOs against PEPs in the context of fairness. The use of

[249] *Lloyd v McMahon* [1987] 1 AC 625, 702–03 (Lord Bridge).

[250] *Wiseman v Borneman* [1971] AC 297, 308 (Lord Reid) (see also Lord Morris of Borth-y-Gest's decision in the same case) and quoted with approval by Lord Sumption in *Bank Mellat (no 1)*.

proportionality and fairness principles as interpretative tools is however a useful addendum to a discussion on the possibility of strengthening the rights of respondents through, for example, enhanced procedural protections in the context of quasi-criminal hybrid measures like UWOs. They provoke the question as to whether one solution to address concerns around the non-availability of criminal procedural safeguards to PEP-specific UWO respondents might be to extend certain of those procedural protections on the grounds of fairness and proportionality.

10. Conclusion

A key problem with UWOs against PEPs is that no harm *at all* needs to be demonstrated before an individual is implicitly condemned. Admittedly, in each of the reported cases involving UWOs against PEPs to date, enforcement authorities went beyond the strict requirements of the legislation by pointing to specific convictions for corruption offences committed overseas and established reasonable suspicions that significant sums of money had apparently been misappropriated or extorted by each of the relevant convicted public officials. This evidence likely allowed the High Court to conclude more readily at first instance in each case that granting the requested UWOs was proportionate.[251] In fact, it was open to the NCA in each case to seek Serious Crime UWOs rather than PEP UWOs. We can only assume that the former were not pursued because enforcement authorities did not want to put the courts in the position of essentially endorsing convictions against individuals by states with their own imperfect legal systems,[252] and/or because enforcement authorities wished to test judicial reaction toward the PEP-specific UWO.

In a formally criminal context, if a prosecution raised a mere allegation that an accused was guilty of something without anything to substantiate that allegation and then shifted the burden to a defendant to disprove their purported guilt, this would clearly undermine the presumption of innocence. In the context of UWOs against PEPs, the concern is that this is substantively what *can* happen. It might be assumed that, in practice, the potential for UWOs to be used against PEPs without enforcement authorities holding additional incriminating information on which to base a UWO and eventually seek civil recovery is remote. Even so, the NCA's presentation of a case against the respondents in *Baker* on the basis of reasoning which the High Court criticized as 'artificial and flawed'[253] serves as a cautionary tale of low burdens of evidence given the stakes for the respondents. Even where

[251] Albeit in *Baker* (n 140) the presumption of recoverable property was successfully overturned.

[252] In *Hajiyeva* (n 149) [67], for example, the respondent introduced an expert witness who referred to the US State Department's report (published May 2018) and concluded: 'It follows in my opinion from these and many other reports that there is no independent judiciary in [Azerbaijan], and that the chances of receiving a fair trial by reference to international standards are effectively nil.'

[253] *Baker* (n 140) [130].

an order is subsequently discharged, respondents will have already faced the ignominy of a state-made claim of (at best) benefiting from or (at worst) actively committing acts of public-sector corruption without much, if any, evidence to substantiate that claim. Where an order is undischarged, individuals face having their properties recovered, or being held answerable to the state for holding property the origins of which are not obvious, even though there is nothing inherently wrong with this as a matter of law, and even though UK and EEA PEPs (and indeed, the population at large) are not subject to analogous rules. These concerns around state intervention without a plausibility threshold of connection to criminality being met, the ensuing stigma for respondents, and the implications for the presumption of innocence and the fairness doctrine threatened by the operation of UWOs cumulatively support arguments in favour of a heightened level of procedural protection being afforded by the courts to PEP respondents. Relying on judicial discretion as a means of correcting the individual rights problems implicit in the operation of UWOs against PEPs may not be the ideal response to those problems in the longer term.

Theorists suggest that the consequences to an accused of being publicly criminally accused and condemned by the state are so serious that the tribunal determining guilt must *know* before censuring and sanctioning them that an accused is guilty, not merely believe that it is probable.[254] No justice system operating in a liberal democracy seeking to achieve communicative or expressive objectives can criminally condemn an individual for a particular act without first being more or less *certain* that the individual is culpable.[255] The obligation on prosecuting parties in criminal proceedings to establish guilt beyond reasonable doubt reflects the judiciary's concern to allocate risk of error so that wrongful convictions are minimized, whilst simultaneously dismissing 'fanciful possibilities to deflect the course of justice'.[256] It is acknowledged that in a *civil* context, this burden is unworkable because not all applicants/plaintiffs hold sufficient resources and/or powers to enable them to produce evidence to *prove* that a defendant or respondent is liable beyond reasonable doubt. Instead, the civil burden of proof operates to minimize 'the expected number of errors made by the fact-finder'.[257] The difference between the civil and criminal burdens of proof is justified, some commentators argue, by reference to the risk of greater moral harm (and accompanying censure and sanction) arising from unjust criminal convictions.[258] Mike Redmayne suggested that

254 Stewart (n 48), 411.

255 Victor Tadros, 'The Ideal of the Presumption of Innocence' (2014) 8 Criminal Law & Philosophy 449, 452.

256 *Miller v Minister of Pensions* [1947] 2 All ER 372, 373–74 (Denning LJ). For a detailed discussion on risk allocation through the criminal burden of proof, see Alex Stein, *Foundations of Evidence Law* (OUP 2005) 173–213.

257 Redmayne (n 59) 169.

258 Redmayne (n 59) 171, citing Ronald Dworkin, 'Principle, Policy, Procedure' in *A Matter of Principle* (Clarendon Press 1985).

to require plaintiffs to meet *a* burden of proof, albeit to the lesser civil standard, is to reflect 'basic principles of civility':

> We do not generally accuse people of doing us wrong unless we are able to back up the explanation with evidence, and in law this requirement is fairly easily mapped onto the rules governing the burden of proof.[259]

As discussed in Chapter 3, however, the story of asset recovery in English law over the past four decades is one of ongoing erosion and displacement of standards and burdens of proof for enforcement authorities, often by way of legislative responses to court decisions highlighting the limits of asset recovery powers. The fact that enforcement authorities are not required to back up an allegation of benefit from corruption with evidence of a link to actual corruption in applying, for example, for UWOs against PEPs represents a relatively recent example of the erosion of the presumed 'civic trust' between enforcement authorities and society in an asset recovery context. The rigid application of the criminal/non-criminal binary by the ECtHR in determining whether individuals should be entitled to procedural rights has led to the judiciary resorting to exercising discretionary powers to ensure that respondents are not unfairly prejudiced in the operation of hybrid measures. Judicial discretion and the use of ad hoc rationalizations in deciding to include or exclude evidence, or in applying or declining to apply particular measures for reasons of fairness, has been dismissed by some commentators as the 'slightly shady alter-ego of authentic rules of evidence'[260] but may serve as a pragmatic pressure valve for problems arising with UWOs. The better option may be, as Peter Alldridge suggests, to replace this binary with 'an incremental scale',[261] or to formally provide that the range of procedural rights accruing to those answerable to state-made claims of criminality should increase or decrease depending on the gravity of the accusations or the outcomes. This could prevent the procedural rights of respondents to 'civil' measures from falling through the cracks at the expense of an over-reliance on relatively unnuanced ECtHR-made legalism. In addition, on the ECHR rights analysis, it is possible to draw the following conclusions.

First, the PEP-specific UWO is prima facie a discriminatory measure. It is very difficult to ascertain a clear justification for this discrimination, particularly in circumstances where the PEP UWO purportedly targets the proceeds of grand corruption offences—serious crimes—yet the Serious Crime UWO is also available. Moreover, its introduction raises concerns around putatively legitimizing future

[259] Redmayne (n 59) 173.

[260] Paul Roberts, 'Normative Evolution in Evidentiary Exclusion: Coercion, Deception and the Right to a Fair Trial' in *Criminal Evidence and Human Rights* (n 46) 163, 164.

[261] Peter Alldridge, 'Civil Recovery in England and Wales: An Appraisal' in Colin King, Clive Walker, and Jimmy Gurulé (eds), *The Palgrave Handbook of Criminal and Terrorism Financing Law* (Palgrave Macmillan 2018) 515, 535.

incremental expansion of powers (i) against PEPs and other 'others', and (ii) in asset recovery with relatively little public or parliamentary scrutiny. Second, on A1 P1 rights, the Home Office's analysis that UWOs do not substantively impact upon property rights because any civil recovery applications will be the subject of subsequent and distinct proceedings is debatable in light of the presumption raised by non-compliance with the orders. Further, freezing assets the subject of orders for significant periods of time pending resolution of investigations is in itself a significant interference with individual property rights. There are sufficient points of distinction between the operation of the measure the subject of the *Gogitidze* decision and the design of PEP-specific UWOs to speculate that the latter could conceivably be viewed as a disproportionate infringement of Article 8 and/or A1 P1 and/or Article 14 rights by the Strasbourg Court. Third, it is broadly correct to say that the privacy and property rights implications of UWOs against PEPs are modest, particularly in circumstances where the ultimate beneficial ownership details of respondent PEPs' assets are not available on any public register. However, the reputational implications of UWOs against PEPs where they are publicized are grave, as is clear from the media coverage of the two PEP-specific UWO cases to date. Although there are strong principled and policy reasons for which enforcement authorities may wish to publicize UWO proceedings, a more proportionate approach could be to require anonymized reporting of such proceedings unless and until there is clear non-compliance or appeals have been exhausted and recovery proceedings instituted.

The upshot of the analysis set out in this chapter is that in the fervour to address the proceeds of grand corruption being laundered in the UK, the respect and recognition for individual rights forming the heart of liberal democracies were compromised. As established in the context of UWOs, there are adjustments that can be made in the operation of future anti-corruption measures to ensure that these rights are properly safeguarded. The larger question that should be asked in formulating measures in the future is whether the suggested measures, having regard to the types of individuals and impugned activities to be addressed, will likely prove effective in practice. A corollary to this question is whether any new measures or revised policy approaches would form part of a systemic and considered holistic response to the problem sought to be resolved. Some recent proposals and enactments aimed at realizing such a response are considered in the next chapter.

7
Anti-Corruption Developments and Future Reform

1. Introduction

The most credible response to the UK government's concern around the laundering of corruption proceeds in its property market would be for it to assist in developing and then enforcing a range of measures, policy, regulatory, and legal—domestically and internationally—whilst enlisting the participation of as many stakeholders as possible. Some of the criticisms of the UWO targeted specifically at PEPs made throughout this book query the measure's necessity and legitimacy.[1] Wider successful enforcement would likely bolster the output legitimacy of existing anti-corruption measures because the public would be able to observe the legislative objectives underpinning their introduction being achieved in practice. This perceived legitimacy could be further reinforced if measures like the PEP-specific UWO formed a complementary part of a well-resourced wider anti-corruption regime. This could include developing a concrete process for how funds should be returned. It could also encompass policies which inculcate in domestic Facilitators the apprehension of a credible risk of investigation and censure by enforcement or supervisory authorities where money laundering of kleptocratic proceeds is discovered.

The development of any such regime would inevitably be fraught with difficulty, partly because of the multiplicity of stakeholders (corrupt PEPs, non-corrupt PEPs, their respective associates, financial institutions, service providers, private family offices, etc) involved in laundering. This difficulty is in turn exacerbated by the plurality of those responsible for ensuring that those who breach legal and regulatory obligations are held to account. A non-exhaustive list of those parties includes domestic regulators (eg the Financial Conduct Authority (FCA), the Solicitors Regulation Authority); public registry custodians (including the Land Registry, HMRC, and Companies House); and enforcement authorities. This

[1] See the remarks of Richard Arkless MP at the second reading of the draft legislation introducing UWOs (HC Deb 25 October 2016, vol 616, col 214): 'The Bill has been instructed and drafted with high speed, admirable though that may be, but with limited consultation. Only in the last fortnight were we shown draft clauses that related to unexplained wealth orders'.

Unexplained Wealth Orders and the UK's Anti-Corruption Regime. Áine Clancy, Oxford University Press.
 DOI: 10.1093/9780198907312.003.0008

chapter considers some recent reforms and policy options under discussion in the anti-corruption literature which might contribute to a stronger, more coherent anti-corruption regime. The second section of this chapter evaluates the potential utility of settlement agreements as a pragmatic approach to recovering the proceeds of corruption. The third section turns attention to stronger enforcement against professional service providers based in the UK who facilitate—knowingly or otherwise—corrupt asset-laundering. The gatekeepers of the UK's economy include, without limitation, solicitors, trust and corporate service providers, banks and their employees, accountants, estate agents, and other professional services providers (collectively Facilitators). It is argued that more focussed regulatory and criminal law enforcement against those gatekeepers who facilitate grand corruption may improve money-laundering prevention and deterrence. The fourth section examines measures recently introduced in law to enhance asset ownership and financial transparency through reform of the UK corporate and property registries. The fifth section considers the potential efficacy of enlisting the tax regime more proactively as a value-neutral means of assessing the legitimacy of individuals' assets and income.

This chapter does not propose to present a comprehensive programme for reform of the kind needed to tackle the proceeds of corruption being laundered in the UK in a systemic way. It instead seeks to highlight that achieving the government's stated legislative objectives when introducing UWOs against PEPs is impossible through introducing a single measure of limited effectiveness. More fundamental and ambitious reform and programmes of resourcing are required. Throughout this chapter, some key themes will recur. These include problems arising from the diffusion of responsibility for dealing with the proceeds of grand corruption being laundered in the UK, as well as the regulatory, financial resourcing, and legal enforcement deficits contributing to shortfalls in enforcement action. It is argued that engaging meaningfully in anti-corruption reform and improved enforcement may bolster the perceived legitimacy and necessity of measures like the PEP-specific UWO because it may increase opportunities for their use. It also may help to refute at least partially the suggestion made throughout this volume that the introduction of such measures may be motivated primarily by political expediency considerations. As the focus of this book is on measures undertaken within the UK, discussion on potential international law interventions is not included.[2]

[2] See eg Mark Wolf and others' proposed model for an international anti-corruption court (Mark L Wolf, Richard Goldstone, and Robert I Rotberg, 'The Progressing Proposal for An International Anti-Corruption Court' (2022) American Academy of Arts and Sciences) and (gently) critical responses to it: Daley J Birkett, 'Recovering Assets at an International Anti-Corruption Court: Cautionary Tales from Rome, the Hague, and the Field' (2023) 2 Transnational Criminal Law Review 59.

2. Settlements

One pragmatic but perhaps unpopular response to the problem of corruptly acquired assets being laundered in the UK may be for more widespread employment of settlement agreements between enforcement authorities and those who are found to hold the proceeds of overseas grand corruption. Non-trial resolution processes are used across jurisdictions as responses to international corruption matters.[3] In England and Wales, section 276 of the POCA provides for judicially approved settlement agreements to recover the suspected proceeds of crime. It contemplates the High Court making consent orders staying civil recovery proceedings 'on terms agreed by the parties for the disposal of the proceedings'[4] and having discretion to add 'any further provision which the court thinks appropriate'.[5] Information on the frequency with which these orders are used and the value of assets recovered through them in practice is not available.[6] So far as this writer can determine, where settlements are made to recover assets, the agreements are not regarded as public documents and are therefore not published.

There are however some instances of enforcement authorities publishing press releases providing short overviews of settlement agreements to which they are party. In December 2019, for example, the National Crime Agency (NCA) reached a settlement worth £190m following an investigation into Malik Riaz Hussain, a Pakistani businessman with assets in England (the Hussain Settlement). Assets covered by the settlement included a £50m London property held through an offshore company and the contents of several bank accounts. The NCA released a short statement confirming the settlement and that the settlement concerned 'a civil matter, and does not represent a finding of guilt'.[7] Beyond these facts, no details (including the reasons for investigating Mr Hussain's assets) were made publicly available.[8] It is unclear whether the settlement agreement was approved by the courts (ie whether it constituted a section 276 settlement) and it is not known whether the settlement assets comprised all of Mr Hussain's assets in the UK.[9]

[3] An international study undertaken in respect of sixty-six companies on their responses to international corruption showed that over 86 per cent of countries had used non-trial resolutions (including, without limitation, deferred prosecution agreements): International Bar Association, Anti-Corruption Committee: Structured Criminal Settlements Subcommittee, *Structured Settlements for Corruption Offences: Towards Global Standards?* (International Bar Association December 2018).

[4] POCA, s 276(1).

[5] POCA, s 276(2)(b).

[6] In response to a Freedom of Information request from the author, the Home Office advised that it did not hold information on the number, or estimated value of assets recovered pursuant to, consent orders made pursuant to s 276.

[7] It subsequently removed the statement from its website. The above quote is taken from Kate Beioley, 'Pakistan Family Hands over £190m in "Dirty Money" Probe' *Financial Times* (London, 3 December 2019). The respondent may have required this public confirmation as a condition of the settlement.

[8] This is apparently standard practice: settlements made following, for example, the resolution of the Hajiyeva and Mansoor Hussain UWO matters were similarly unpublished.

[9] See eg a settlement discussed at n 21 and accompanying text below.

The proceeds of the assets in question have apparently since been returned to Pakistan.[10]

Civil recovery orders were issued against Mrs Hajiyeva's properties and Mrs Hajiyeva reached a civil recovery settlement with the NCA prior to proceeding to scheduled hearings for claims for final orders against the assets held by her. The NCA agreed with the respondent that her Knightsbridge mansion and her Ascot golf club would be sold, 70 per cent of the proceeds would be forfeited to the NCA, and she would keep the remaining millions of pounds in proceeds. No information was published on how this settlement, the culmination of the civil recovery process of the UK's first UWOs over six years after they were initially issued, was reached. Nor was any justification supplied of the rationale underpinning Mrs Hajiyeva's retention of a significant share of the proceeds of the assets the subjects of the orders. In its press release announcing the settlement, the NCA emphasized that it had 'not made any finding in relation to Mrs Hajiyeva's knowledge of how the properties were paid for'.[11] Based on the lack of publicly available information on these settlements, all that it is possible to conclude is that English enforcement authorities are open in principle to conducting civil recovery negotiations, to agreeing settlement agreements, and to keeping their terms confidential. As has been argued elsewhere in the context of non-disclosure agreements, confidentiality clauses, by keeping bad behaviour hidden, risk emboldening further misconduct and shield individuals from public opprobrium that may be deserved.[12]

The question arises as to *why* individuals who might otherwise become respondents to public legal proceedings may be willing to volunteer information on their ill-gotten gains to enforcement authorities. Law and economics writers suggest that confidentiality holds an economic value for defendants in civil negotiations because publicity could result in adverse factors including loss of reputation, litigation costs, and because public proceedings can cultivate a perception that a defendant is a 'mark' for other plaintiffs. The promise of confidentiality as a carrot in a recovery negotiation thus can expand the upper range of what a would-be defendant or respondent will sacrifice in order to settle.[13] By making available and adjusting incentives holding economic value to those allegedly benefiting from grand corruption in exchange for their cooperation with enforcement authorities, it may be possible to improve the quality of information leading to, and the amount of, assets available for recovery. Such incentives could include, where

[10] NCA, Annual Report and Accounts 2019–20, 24 <www.nationalcrimeagency.gov.uk/who-we-are/publications/467-national-crime-agency-annual-report-and-accounts-2019-20/file>.

[11] NCA, 'Luxury Properties Forfeited after Six-Year NCA Investigation' (5 August 2024) <www.nationalcrimeagency.gov.uk/news/luxury-properties-forfeited-after-six-year-nca-investigation>.

[12] See eg Catharine MacMillan, 'Contracts and Equality: The Dangers of Non-Disclosure Agreements in English Law' (2022) 18 European Review of Contract Law 127.

[13] See Richard A Posner, *Economic Analysis of Law* (6th edn, Aspen Publishers 2003) 569–71; Scott A Moss, 'Illuminating Secrecy: A New Economic Analysis of Confidential Settlements' (2007) 105 Michigan Law Review 867.

appropriate, statements from enforcement authorities expressly confirming that no criminal wrongdoing was found as part of the investigation and recovery process.[14] They might also include undertakings that, subject to full disclosure being made, enforcement authorities would cease investigating the relevant individual's involvement in a particular matter once the settlement is made, and confidentiality undertakings. The value to potential respondents of avoiding reputationally ruinous public civil recovery proceedings (particularly where those respondents are individuals like PEPs whose professional longevity is contingent on maintaining public trust) may trump the value those individuals place on retaining ownership of all of their UK-based properties.[15]

The efficacy of settlements as an alternative means of recovering the proceeds of corruption is uncertain because they are relatively untested, because there are few available data on the sums recovered through settlements, and because the appetite for individual asset holders to settle or to pursue proceedings contesting potentially public processes like UWOs will likely vary on a case-by-case basis. A version of the settlement agreement to which *companies* can become a party, the deferred prosecution agreement (DPA) has met with mixed success in the UK.[16] That said, individual asset holders' cooperation may be more feasible in non-adversarial, consensual contexts than potentially more contentious legal civil recovery processes. Consequently, enforcement authorities' investigations and verification of any statements made as part of settlement disclosure processes may be more straightforward. Cooperative individuals under investigation may also be willing to waive legal advice privilege and provide incriminating evidence on UK-based Facilitators complicit in helping them or their associates launder corruptly acquired wealth in exchange for advantageous settlement conditions or as a means of establishing good faith. In sum, more widespread use of settlement agreements may serve as a pragmatic and efficient means of recovering the UK-based proceeds of grand corruption.

Nevertheless, settlement agreement processes have some obvious disadvantages. Chief among these are the transparency and accountability implications. On the evidence of the Hussain Settlement, enforcement authorities may have the ability to finalize settlements without court approval. This raises questions as to enforcement authorities' accountability and on what authority they are acting when agreeing settlements.[17] Even where negotiations result in consent orders being agreed, section 276 of the POCA appears to contemplate judicial involvement only

[14] See eg n 9. Incidentally, there is no reason why this should not become a widespread practice in publicized civil recovery proceedings, regardless of outcome.

[15] Asset recovery actions taken by the US and France against the Vice-President of Equatorial Guinea, Teodoro Obiang, threw a spotlight on his corrupt actions and was one of the factors motivating his inclusion on the UK's sanctions list in July 2021.

[16] See Colin King and Nicholas Lord, *Negotiated Justice and Corporate Crime: The Legitimacy of Civil Recovery Orders and Deferred Prosecution Agreements* (Palgrave Pivot 2018).

[17] See n 7 and accompanying text above.

at the very last stage of the process, with the courts performing a relatively minimalist gatekeeping function in respect of substantially finalized agreements. A fundamental weakness of the process is that victim representatives have no opportunity to observe, participate in, or submit representations to the administrative meetings of which the negotiations are comprised.[18] On a cynical view, the primary motivations of enforcement authorities as directors of negotiation processes are likely to be more inherently transactional than a court's. They may, for instance, be pursuing reasonably presentable outcomes, perhaps informed by managerialist concerns, including resourcing levels.[19] Enforcement authorities also may be interested in using the negotiation process to obtain information to facilitate future domestic prosecutions as much or more than they may wish to maximize asset recovery for the assets' states of origin. Where settlement agreements are not published, this prevents widely understood first principles on dealing with the proceeds of grand corruption or with asset holders from emerging. This problem was recently highlighted by the non-publication of a settlement agreement made between the NCA and a Russian oligarch's UK-based business manager relating to the forfeiture of accounts frozen because they were suspected of transacting in breach of sanctions.[20] Whilst Westminster Magistrates' Court reportedly ratified the agreement in that case, the non-publication of either a judgment or the settlement agreement for the case deprived the public of having better insight into both sanctions enforcement and forfeiture of cash using account freezing orders; two notably under-reported areas of law. The non-publication of the rationales underpinning settlement agreements is a missed opportunity to reap communicative benefits and legal certainty around what allegedly corrupt foreign asset holders should expect if they are found to hold assets of dubious provenance in the UK. These disadvantages are a high price to pay for relative efficiency.

A further disadvantage is that 'settlement' connotes concessions being made by *both* parties to an agreement, suggesting that in addition to the benefit of confidentiality, holders of corruptly acquired assets may be permitted to retain *some* proceeds of wrongdoing in some cases. For example, in one settlement agreement reached by the NCA with the respondent to a (non-PEP) UWO and filed under seal with the High Court in October 2020, the respondent was permitted to retain four 'highly mortgaged' properties.[21] Such concessions are more problematic in the

[18] Felipe Freitas Falconi and others, *Victims of Corruption: Back for Payback* (StAR Initiative 2023) 22.

[19] Noting the limited financial resources available, for example, to the NCA's anti-corruption unit in Chapter 1. cf Mike McConville, 'Plea Bargaining: Ethics and Politics' (1998) 25 Journal of Law and Society 562.

[20] Simon Goodley, 'Billionaire Putin Ally Forfeits £750,000 in UK Sanctions Case' *The Guardian* (London, 29 July 2024).

[21] Jamie Grierson, 'Businessman to Hand over £10m Following "Unexplained Wealth Order"' *The Guardian* (London, 7 October 2020). The NCA may have decided that allowing the respondent to retain the properties would incur less expense than discharging the outstanding debt with which the properties were encumbered and handling the administrative and cost burden of discharging the

context of settlement negotiations with foreign PEPs as in the agreement reached between the NCA and Mrs Hajiyeva, because enforcement authorities hold no authority from states of origin (ie those states which are the rightful owners of that property) to cede property interests in return for cooperation or information from an allegedly corrupt PEP. Concessions can give rise to the perception that crime *does* pay, albeit the payoff is perhaps less than a corrupt PEP counterparty originally envisaged.

Finally, in practical terms, once a potential respondent is approached by enforcement authorities with an invitation to enter settlement negotiations, that respondent may take action to dissipate their assets. Alternatively, the approach may automatically trigger the operation of 'flee' clauses in trust instruments so that the legal ownership of the relevant asset is immediately transferred to a new owner, or is moved abroad (if the asset is moveable), thereby thwarting enforcement authorities seeking potential respondents.[22] It follows that enforcement authorities seeking to negotiate settlements will still need to freeze the relevant assets on an *ex parte* basis through the courts prior to any such approach.

There are no straightforward answers to these problems. The collective interest in living in a corruption-free society (or at least one free of the proceeds of corruption) competes on an ongoing basis with individual due process, privacy, equality, and property rights. The Stolen Asset Recovery Initiative (StAR) has identified the sometimes dissonant drivers between anti-corruption approaches to kleptocracy and grand corruption (prevention, criminal accountability) on the one hand, and human-rights-based impulses including the need to ensure reparations for victims on the other. It implies that a 'complete' response to corruption requires both elements to be satisfied.[23] Settlement agreements alone fail to achieve these complete responses, but where assets are returned to states of origin, they may represent at least a partial means of satisfying the claims-based rights of states of origin to reparations. Their potential efficacy and normative validity could be greatly enhanced through the development of published core principles to be observed by enforcement authorities as part of the process,[24] and a procedural architecture

mortgages or selling properties subject to security or discharging receivership duties in relation to those properties pending sale. The counterparty to the agreement was Mansoor Hussain, the respondent in *NCA v Hussain* [2020] EWHC 432 (Admin).

[22] On flee clauses generally, see John Gibbons, 'Flee Clauses: A Fresh Look in a Modern Context' (2017) 23 Trusts and Trustees 1028.

[23] Falconi and others (n 18) 6. Making an appeal for more expansive approaches towards dealing with kleptocracy and fulfilling both aspects, see John M Ackerman, 'Rethinking the International Anti-Corruption Agenda: Civil Society, Human Rights and Democracy' (2014) 29 American University International Law Review 293.

[24] The US Department of Justice, for example, publishes detailed guidance for reaching forfeiture settlements. See US Department of Justice, *Justice Manual—Title 9: Criminal; 9-113.000 Forfeiture Settlements*. <www.justice.gov/jm/jm-9-113000-forfeiture-settlements>.

that operates to allay accountability and transparency concerns to the extent possible.[25]

3. Professional Facilitators

This section first offers a short overview of the discourse around Facilitators in aiding the laundering of the proceeds of grand corruption in the UK. It then considers why regulatory action and criminal law enforcement against Facilitators who aid those perpetrating and/or benefiting from acts of grand corruption are so rare. It criticizes the policy and enforcement approaches hitherto adopted towards financial institutions and other financial gatekeepers who facilitate money laundering. Finally, it assesses two potentially controversial proposals aimed at bolstering the ease of investigating Facilitators suspected of complicity in laundering the proceeds of corruption.

a. Facilitators

Commission of a corruption offence and the subsequent laundering of its proceeds overseas are rarely acts performed alone. Whilst a corrupt principal will generally play the role of directing mind or instigator, a number of groups will be directly or indirectly instrumental in an offence. These individuals might include, without limitation, enablers in the misappropriated asset's state of origin or in the UK who omit to take action to prevent, or actively facilitate, the corrupt acts occurring and the financial institutions facilitating the deposit and/or transfer of assets. Jurisdictions whose laws permit individuals to keep details of their ultimate beneficial ownership of company shares, properties, and other valuable assets secret indirectly facilitate corruption.[26] Each of these actors assists, in different ways, in grand corruption practice.

David Garland observes that crime control in the UK from the 1970s and 1980s onwards became characterized by a culture of responsibilization, 'the attempt to extend the reach of state agencies by linking them up with the practices of the "private sector" and the "community"'.[27] Some writers have noted critically that imposing anti-money laundering compliance obligations on Facilitators constitutes

[25] For a more detailed discussion of the issues and a comparison of the American and British approaches to settlements for the proceeds of corruption, see Áine Clancy, 'A Better Deal? Negotiated Responses to the Proceeds of Grand Corruption' (2022) 33 Criminal Law Forum 149.

[26] Oliver Bullough's *Moneyland: Why Thieves & Crooks Now Rule the World and How to Take it Back* (Profile 2018) provides numerous case studies and general insight into the methods employed by corrupt officials in secreting assets out of their jurisdictions to evade investigation.

[27] David Garland, *The Culture of Control: Crime and Social Order in Contemporary Society* (OUP 2001) 126.

a responsibilization strategy whereby crime control duties traditionally conducted by state agencies are delegated in part to private actors required to engage in 'indirect crime control' activities.[28] It is difficult to discern why this is a meaningful cause of concern per se in this specific context. There are good arguments against responsibilization insofar as it relates to crimes occurring outside a regulated environment. Chief among these is the idea that the primary responsibility for taking action to prevent crimes and enforce the criminal law should lie with the criminal enforcement agencies specifically authorized, trained, and funded for those purposes. However, financial crimes, including crimes which involve the handling, or facilitating the handling, of large quantities of stolen assets transnationally through electronic financial systems, are distinguishable from other crimes. In those instances, corrupt actors engage and pay for financial institutions and other professionals' services as apparatuses of wrongdoing. Those actors rely on opaque and rapid transfers of funds and investment in assets to launder stolen wealth, and the relevant financial institutions and other Facilitators profit from providing services as part of the commission of those crimes. Liz Campbell observes that the imposition of anti-money laundering obligations on banks and other professional service providers 'might be a concession to the fact that private entities are those with adequate access and data in this context. It is hard to conceive of how the state could intervene in a comparable manner'.[29] Facilitators are, in other words, uniquely positioned to raise the alarm on potential acts of corruption.

Unlike enforcement authorities, Facilitators make their money through being privy to the granular detail of their clients' legal and financial transactions and are therefore best placed to identify transactions that are apparently inconsistent with their clients' licit income, or which are otherwise unusual. Facilitators provide opportunity and access to corrupt overseas PEPs seeking to launder and hold stolen wealth in the UK economy. Delegating monitoring obligations to Facilitators as a condition of their regulated statuses to ensure that they themselves do not become complicit in handling stolen wealth is not, in principle, an unreasonable proposition. It does necessitate, however, that the regulators holding obligations of supervision for those regulatees in turn have the resources and powers necessary to ensure a reasonably high degree of oversight and to ensure high standards of anti-money laundering compliance within their respective sectors. On the evidence of the (lack of) regulatory action and ongoing money-laundering failures within some of those sectors,[30] regulators and their charges are likely failing to disrupt the laundering of the proceeds of corruption in the UK. Doubtless, this situation is exacerbated by the tension that exists for Facilitators between having to turn

[28] Garland (n 27) 124. Referred to by, inter alia, Benson (n 34) 109; Liz Campbell, 'Dirty Cash (Money Talks): 4AMLD and the Money Laundering Regulations 2017' (2018) Criminal Law Review 102, 108.

[29] Campbell (n 28) 108–09.

[30] See eg the discussion at nn 56–59 and accompanying text below.

away business where prospective clients' activities or profiles raise red flags on the one hand, and the imperative to turn a profit on the other.[31] This tension is arguably most acutely felt in banking institutions.[32] Moreover, there exist categories of Facilitators that are not regulated, thus entirely escaping AML compliance obligations. This results in uneven anti-money laundering coverage across the financial and professional services sectors. A prominent example of unregulated Facilitators is private family offices. These are offices managing, amongst other matters, the financial affairs of high-net-worth individuals. Such offices may employ regulated professionals like lawyers and accountants but are not themselves regulated, notwithstanding their economic significance.[33]

There is limited empirical understanding of the degree to which UK-based Facilitators enable foreign corrupt PEPs to launder stolen assets. Some observers remark that there is little evidence to support suggestions that legal and financial professionals play 'critical roles' in facilitating money laundering.[34] This might indicate the under-resourcing of enforcement authorities capable of unveiling that evidence rather than proof that suggestions that Facilitators enable the laundering of the proceeds of grand corruption are overstated. There exists, however, some helpful qualitative research outlining the roles played by such Facilitators in enabling laundering,[35] and some have been found criminally liable in the UK.[36] If money laundering in the UK is as pervasive as enforcement authorities suggest, however, it begs the question of why so few Facilitator prosecutions are instituted in connection with facilitating the laundering of the proceeds of grand corruption in the UK more generally. It is acknowledged that it is difficult to investigate and prosecute the 'primary' offenders (ie kleptocrats and other foreign corrupt actors and their aides) in their countries of origin. This is especially true where the primary actors are incumbents, but it can remain the case after the relevant public officials leave office.[37] Action against Facilitators including financial institutions

[31] See the observations made elsewhere about perceptions within banks of compliance departments acting as 'business blockers, deal killers, show-stoppers, box tickers': see Nicholas Shaxson, *The Finance Curse: How Global Finance is Making Us All Poorer* (The Bodley Head 2018) 144.

[32] See n 52 and accompanying text below.

[33] David Oakley, 'How the Family Office Became One of the World's Fastest Wealth Generators' *Financial Times* (London, 12 July 2024).

[34] See Katie Benson, 'Money Laundering, Anti-Money Laundering and the Legal Profession' in Colin King, Clive Walker, and Jimmy Gurulé (eds), *The Palgrave Handbook of Criminal and Terrorism Financing Law* (Palgrave Macmillan 2018) 109, 113.

[35] eg an insightful ethnography of trust and corporate service providers, describing their methods and motivations, is provided by Brooke Harrington, *Capital Without Borders: Wealth Managers and the One Percent* (Harvard University Press 2016).

[36] See eg David Middleton and Michael Levi, 'Let Sleeping Lawyers Lie: Organized Crime, Lawyers and the Regulation of Legal Services' (2015) 55 British Journal of Criminology 647; Nicholas Lord, Liz Campbell, and Karin Van Wingerde, 'Other People's Dirty Money: Professional Intermediaries, Market Dynamics and the Finances of White-Collar, Corporate and Organized Crimes' (2019) 59 British Journal of Criminology 1217; Benson (n 34).

[37] See eg Sarah Lain and others, *Illicit Financial Flows and Corruption in Asia* (Royal United Services Institute 2017).

regulated by the FCA and other UK-based Facilitators comes within UK authorities' enforcement and regulatory jurisdictions. The official responses to date to UK-based financial institutions' behaviour in facilitating corruption have, however, been decidedly insipid. Little evidence exists to suggest that enforcement authorities or regulators have so far had much appetite to employ *criminal* justice measures where the proceeds of grand corruption are concerned. Historically, prosecutions for 'high-end' money laundering are rare.[38] As far as this writer can determine, no UK-based professional Facilitators of grand corruption have been successfully prosecuted for their roles to date, though in one civil case a High Court judge, in a subsequently overturned judgment, was scathing about the 'blind eye' former Zambian President Frederick Chiluba's London solicitor turned to the acts of grand corruption allegedly committed by his client.[39] Even relatively non-complex money laundering apparently results in few money-laundering proceedings being instituted against professional services providers.[40] This inaction may be informed at least in part by managerialist concerns on the part of enforcement authorities around prioritization and resourcing. Where there is suspected laundering of the proceeds of grand corruption, given that the primary 'predatory' offence has occurred abroad with no (immediately obvious) adverse impact on UK interests, investigating secondary money-laundering offences is less urgent a priority for enforcement authorities than dealing with domestic serious offences.[41]

It is worth summarizing *why* so little enforcement action is taken against Facilitators. The available empirical evidence makes it clear that where the proceeds of grand corruption are laundered, the processes and trust and corporate ownership structures used are complex and often multi-jurisdictional.[42] By design, the structures are opaque and tend to be constructed by highly specialized tax planners, lawyers, and trust and corporate service providers; often in conjunction with colleagues in offshore branches of the same firms. From a practical perspective, it is perhaps unrealistic to expect enforcement authorities to have in their ranks the resources and expertise necessary to disentangle every apparently suspicious structure linked to, say, both a politically exposed person and a UK-based property.

[38] See eg Chapter 3, n 42.

[39] See Smith J in *Attorney General of Zambia v Meer Care & Desai (A Firm)* [2007] EWHC 1540 (Ch).

[40] See eg Katie Benson's empirical work on solicitors prosecuted in England and Wales for facilitating money laundering working in their professional contexts. For the years 2002–2013, only twenty cases were identified, albeit Benson acknowledges that methodological constraints mean that this cannot be considered an exhaustive sample. Katie Benson, *Lawyers and the Proceeds of Crime: The Facilitation of Money Laundering and its Control.* (Routledge 2020). She notes that, in the majority of the cases identified, there was no apparent actual dishonesty, or intent or active involvement in laundering established on the part of the relevant solicitor.

[41] See the discussion in Chapter 1, n 108 and accompanying text.

[42] See the study of 150 grand corruption cases undertaken by Emile Van der Dos de Willebois and others, *The Puppet Masters: How the Corrupt Use Legal Structures to Hide Stolen Assets and What to Do About it* (World Bank 2011).

The challenge for enforcement authorities is that Facilitators, where they assist allegedly corrupt individuals, typically comprise 'legitimate occupational actors' engaging in legal, financial, and tax service provision, though these services are provided in respect of dirty money.[43] Before investing time and resources in engaging highly specialized forensic accountants on a cross-jurisdictional basis to determine whether or not a Facilitator has aided someone who may or may not be in receipt of the proceeds of corruption, enforcement authorities first need grounds on which to substantiate an allegation of suspicion. Only the most profligate spenders or careless criminals will come on to enforcement authorities' radars, conceivably leaving a large cohort of potentially corrupt actors and their Facilitators in the clear. Even then, it does not necessarily follow that PEPs under investigation for seemingly living beyond their legally acquired means, for example, are laundering the proceeds of grand corruption. Thus, the likelihood of enforcement authorities (i) becoming aware of allegations of UK-based corruptly acquired assets, and then (ii) successfully detecting the identities of, and the scope of (often confidential) services rendered by, professional Facilitators who *may* have assisted in laundering those assets, is low.

Two relatively under-examined risks faced by Facilitators in inadvertently acting for those who commit crimes of grand corruption will now be outlined. First, the means that Facilitators use to satisfy themselves that potential clients do *not* pose money-laundering risks are fraught with inaccuracy and are deeply unsatisfactory. A 'large majority' of Facilitators including financial institutions commonly outsource at least in part the task of performing customer due diligence (also known as Know Your Customer or KYC) checks to third-party private companies who for a fee will run the names of potential clients and proposed transactions through their databases. They will flag to the Facilitators whether a potential client or transaction might be of concern from an anti-money laundering perspective.[44] Traditionally, these providers maintain lists of individuals subject to sanction and people who might otherwise be worthy of caution before being onboarded as clients, either because they are PEPs or otherwise. These lists used to be compiled by researchers combing sources including public registries, media reportage, and court reports, and were 'supplement[ed] with nominations based on in-house research and methodologies'.[45] More recently, this industry has evolved so that machine learning processes can be used to scrape data sources and analyse that data to assist in fulfilling customer due diligence obligations.[46] While the use of these services is helpful to Facilitators who want to assure regulators that they are doing

[43] See Lord and others (n 36).

[44] Eleni Tsingou, 'New Governors on the Block: The Rise of Anti-Money Laundering Professionals' (2017) 69 Crime, Law and Social Change 191, 197.

[45] Tsingou (n 44) 197.

[46] See eg Laura Noonan, 'Applying AI to the War on Financial Crime' *Financial Times* (London, 21 November 2022).

everything possible to minimize laundering risk, the problem with relying on third-party services is that their evidence bases are not as sophisticated as might be assumed. Unless a potential client has been specifically named somewhere in a sanctions list or in connection with an individual, an organization, or a state publicly linked in some way to crime or corruption, they will not trigger red flags for AML compliance officers within firms. This essentially means that any corrupt 'clean-skin' who has not been linked previously through publicly available sources to sanctions or corruption may well fly under the radar of these service providers and will not be flagged as problematic to Facilitators.

A second risk is presented by Facilitators operating in advisory capacities where funds from potentially risky clients will *not* be flowing through their client accounts (ie the risk of assistance in laundering is limited to advice rather than legitimizing cash by its flow through those accounts). The danger in those circumstances is that such Facilitators may be more likely to reassure themselves that where potential clients have already passed the rigorous KYC checks of, and hold accounts with, large financial institutions, those prospective clients have essentially received the benediction of their banks for AML purposes. This can prompt advisory Facilitators to leave their guards down vis-à-vis the risks associated with those clients. This approach is one that was apparently adopted by, for example, the Home Office when engaging in their limited oversight of Golden Visa applicants, which resulted in suspected high-risk individuals moving assets into the jurisdiction.[47] One of the problems with Facilitators adopting this strategy is that financial institutions periodically are found to have significant failings in complying with their anti-money laundering obligations.[48] It follows that concluding that potential clients hold legitimate wealth just because they have been onboarded as a customer by a financial institution is far from a failsafe option.

b. Financial Institutions

The assistance of banks as Facilitators of money laundering is crucial to the commission of grand corruption activities.[49] In giving evidence to the Home Affairs Committee, the then-Executive Director of Transparency International UK,

[47] See Chapter 1, nn 39–44 and accompanying text.

[48] Danske Bank, for example, pleaded guilty to fraud on US banks and agreed to forfeit $2bn to the US Department of Justice after it was discovered that its Estonian branch facilitated the laundering of billions of dollars. See US Department of Justice, *Plea Agreement dated 12 December 2022: United States v Danske Bank AS* <www.justice.gov/opa/press-release/file/1557611/dl>. On the fines levied against banks by the FCA for their systemic anti-money laundering failures, see nn 55–59 and accompanying text above.

[49] The cash-stuffed suitcases reportedly involved in scandals linked to Sani Abacha and Ferdinand Marcos in the 1980s are less likely to be a feature of grand corruption in the age of internet banking and transfers, albeit they were a feature of the Qatargate scandal which came to light in late 2022.

Robert Barrington, noted that 'corporate culture in banks isn't necessarily in favour of turning down large clients and that is effectively what [AML] compliance officers are being asked to do'.[50] There is a tension between the commercial aims of banks (ie to increase their profits and their deposit levels) on the one hand and the banks' AML compliance obligations on the other.[51] There is often a perception in banks that given the conservative oversight approach of banking compliance departments, such financial institutions risk needless over-compliance, thereby driving away opportunities for business. As one former head of compliance for a major bank put it:

> When you have a law, those who have to interpret the law—the law firms—they want to err on the safe side. And then you have the auditors who have to audit that, they want to err on the safe side of the lawyers. And then you have your internal inspectors or audits—so you have four or five internal levels of control nowadays, who outdo themselves in being more and more compliant, because their reputation depends on not being caught out. And that becomes a kind of self-fulfilling over-compliance.[52]

It is not wholly surprising, therefore, that one of the highest fines imposed by the FCA on a bank for anti-money laundering failures to date involved a case where senior banking officers in Barclays may have *deliberately bypassed* the bank's own compliance department in approving a £1.88bn transaction involving Qatari PEPs which resulted in a £52.3m profit for the bank.[53] A £72m fine was imposed, comprising a disgorgement of the profit and a penalty of £19.77m.[54] Yet despite such a dramatic flouting of the regulations necessitating the imposition of a hefty fine, no individual was publicly found accountable by the FCA for the breach.[55]

[50] Home Affairs Committee, 3 May 2016 at 15.02 <www.parliamentlive.tv/Event/Index/fb24396c-f707-499b-b3e9-de6033acbd69>.

[51] cf Andromachi Georgosouli, 'What Makes Deterrence Credible?' in Costanza A Russo, Rosa M Lastra, and William Blair (eds), *Research Handbook on Law and Ethics in Banking and Finance* (Edward Elgar 2019) 302, 309–10.

[52] Interview with Hans-Peter Bauer, 6 February 2020. Mr Bauer who, as well as being a Wolfsberg Facilitator, was previously the head of compliance for UBS's global operations.

[53] FCA Final Notice to Barclays Bank plc dated 25 November 2015 <www.fca.org.uk/publication/final-notices/barclays-bank-nov-2015.pdf>. At para 4.25 of the Final Notice: 'Those who were identified on Barclays' systems as having [given the required AML compliance approval for the transaction] did not know that they were named on Barclays' computer system as having given this approval'. The fine covered a period where a former CEO of the FSA, Hector Sants, was briefly Barclays' chief compliance officer.

[54] Which would have been 30 per cent higher had Barclays not agreed to settle at an early stage in the FCA's investigation.

[55] For further discussion of the matter and the FCA's response to it, see Miriam Goldby, 'Breaches of AML Reporting Requirements by UK Bankers: Are Effective Enforcement Choices Being Made by Financial Regulators?' in *Research Handbook on Law and Ethics in Banking and Finance* (n 51) 317, 322–24.

The FCA's (then the Financial Standard Authority's) 2011 report *Banks' Management of High Money-Laundering Risk Situations* showed systemic failures on the parts of over half of the twenty-seven banks surveyed to apply any extra scrutiny to clients designated as 'high-risk'. Over a quarter of the institutions surveyed failed to verify clients' sources of wealth properly.[56] The scale of the banks' failings in this regard exposed some dissonance between the enthusiasm that banks displayed in developing anti-money laundering standards in conjunction with Wolfsberg, for instance, and the actuality of their practices. Following a period of minimal intervention by the FCA in proactively enforcing anti-money laundering standards compliance,[57] it has more recently imposed a number of more significant fines to banks for failure to take adequate measures against money laundering, including the fine to Barclays,[58] and fines, amongst others, of £102m, £163m, £64m, and £108m against Standard Chartered Bank, Deutsche Bank, HSBC, and Santander respectively for systemic shortcomings in their financial crime controls and AML processes.[59] Each of these institutions was a founder member of Wolfsberg.

This apparent shedding of its reticence in sanctioning banks for their lax observance of anti-money laundering obligations brings the FCA's more recent enforcement style closer to the enthusiastic and aggressive enforcement of AML requirements adopted by the Department of Justice in the United States.[60] The FCA's previous enforcement inactivity meant that there was little incentive for banks to seriously implement compliance measures which might reduce business opportunities. Its employment of more robust penalties may assist in disincentivizing the banks' hitherto demonstrably laissez-faire approaches to AML compliance. Banks employing more stringent measures in respect of politically connected ultra-high-net-worth customers may in turn present a meaningful obstacle to individuals seeking to hide the illicit proceeds of corruption in the UK, provided the PEPs against whom they are employed are actually higher-risk. The FCA has long been

[56] Available at <www.fca.org.uk/publication/corporate/fsa-aml-final-report.pdf>.

[57] Note in this regard Georgosouli's observation (n 51 at 314) that the intensity of enforcement action by the FCA is 'by and large driven by the prevailing political climate'. On that account, the FCA may have been reluctant to add to financial institutions' woes during the global financial crisis and its aftermath—but it has subsequently seemingly stepped up its credible deterrence strategy in relation to AML compliance since markets stabilized.

[58] See n 53.

[59] FCA Decision Notice to Standard Chartered Bank dated 5 February 2019 <www.fca.org.uk/publication/decision-notices/standard-chartered-bank-2019.pdf>; FCA Final Notice to Deutsche Bank AG dated 30 January 2017 <www.fca.org.uk/publication/final-notices/deutsche-bank-2017.pdf>; and FCA Final Decision Notice to HSBC plc dated 14 December 2021 <www.fca.org.uk/publication/corporate/fsa-aml-final-report.pdf>. See also FCA Final Notice to Santander UK plc dated 8 December 2022 <www.fca.org.uk/publication/final-notices/santander-uk-plc-2022.pdf>.

[60] Note eg the Department of Justice's US$1.1bn settlement with Standard Chartered in January 2019 and US$1.25bn settlement with HSBC in December 2019 in each case for, inter alia, AML failings. Both banks are members of the Wolfsberg Group. See also a US prosecutors' settlement for US$1.3bn settlement with Unicredit in April 2019.

aware of the (unwitting or otherwise) complicity of its banking regulatees in PEP corruption,[61] but its recent actions represent a more concerted focus on deterring that complicity. Nevertheless, commentators have highlighted some problems with imposing substantial fines on financial institutions as a response to AML failings. Some suggest that it is bank shareholders who primarily bear the cost of the fines. Those critics suggest that regulatory or criminal investigations should be instead aggressively pursued and instituted against the individuals (i) responsible for ensuring transactions are properly overseen and performed, or (ii) responsible for making the decisions to engage in the relevant transactions or business relationships.[62] Given the systemic compliance failings periodically uncovered in the UK's major banking institutions, imposing fines, however significant, is not yet cutting the mustard in credibly deterring dereliction of anti-money laundering duties. An increased emphasis among regulators and enforcement authorities around individual accountability is therefore overdue.

c. AML Developments

Section 330 of the POCA provides that it is an offence for individuals in the regulated sector to fail to disclose suspected money laundering.[63] Guidance issued in 2021 by the Crown Prosecution Service (CPS) in relation to section 330 offences provides that even where there is insufficient evidence to establish that money laundering was in fact planned or undertaken, a 'professional enabler' may nevertheless be prosecuted under section 330 in circumstances where they have failed to report money-laundering suspicions where there are 'reasonable grounds to suspect' an offence is planned or taking place.[64] It is not necessary to establish that money laundering has actually taken place for a prosecution to succeed. Some practitioners speculated at the time the updated guidance was issued that it would simply result in more defensive over-submission of suspicious activity reports (SARs) rather than increased conviction rates.[65] This concern has been borne out

[61] See eg JC Sharman, *The Despot's Guide to Wealth Management: On the International Campaign against Grand Corruption* (Cornell University Press 2017) 122–23, where he references a (then) FSA investigation into the finances of Sani Abacha which revealed that '£900 million controlled by Abacha, his family, and associates had passed through forty-two accounts held at twenty-three banks in the United Kingdom'.

[62] See eg Goldby (n 55).

[63] 'Regulated sector' has the meaning provided for in sch 9 of the POCA and includes, without limitation, financial institutions, legal, accountancy and/or corporate service providers, and estate agents.

[64] CPS, *Legal Guidance, Proceeds of Crime*, updated 2 April 2024 <www.cps.gov.uk/legal-guidance/money-laundering-offences>.

[65] See eg Corker Binning, *A Suspicious Change in Policy?* 9 August 2021 <https://corkerbinning.com/a-suspicious-change-in-policy/>; Shoosmiths, *Fail to Report Your Money Laundering Suspicions: The Risk of Prosecution Has Increased*, 6 July 2021 <www.shoosmiths.co.uk/insights/articles/fail-to-report-your-money-laundering-suspicions-risk-prosecution-has-increased>. Under pt 7 of the POCA, regulated firms including banks and solicitors are required to make an SAR to the NCA in circumstances where they become aware of information that causes them to know or suspect, or give reasonable

by subsequent data.[66] The guidance may suggest a frustration on the part of the CPS with the under-prosecution of Facilitators suspected of enabling laundering. In the longer term, this guidance may operate to animate enforcement authorities previously deterred by the risk of losing cases.

A second relatively recent development is that the Economic Crime Levy was introduced in 2022. It is payable by certain medium and large firms of professional service providers regulated under the AML Regulations and is expected to raise £100m per annum to fund 'new and uplifted anti-money laundering and economic crime capabilities'. Whilst this is a recent clear example of a financial responsibilization innovation,[67] the funding generated through it is helping to finance the implementation of a 'SARs Transformation Programme', introduced in the *2019–2022 Economic Crime Plan*.[68] As part of the Programme, the state's IT systems dealing with SARs were updated;[69] resourcing was increased at the UK's Financial Intelligence Unit, the NCA, to allow for improved analysis and intelligence based on data submitted; and guidance aimed at improving the quality of information submitted was published.[70]

Improving the quality of information generated by the Suspicious Activity Reporting system is to be welcomed in principle. However, significant challenges in the operation of the anti-money laundering regime in the UK and its response to the proceeds of grand corruption being laundered in the jurisdiction remain. On a broad level, these initiatives do not respond to the broader problems around responsibilization of Facilitators, including the unrealistic expectations of complex financial literacy imposed on lawyers and other non-financial experts in the operation of the AML regime.[71] Moreover, however rigorous Facilitators are in their customer due diligence, it is sometimes difficult to detect laundering risks where corrupt PEPs do not disclose that they are using nominees rather than

grounds for knowing or suspecting, that another person is engaged in money laundering (POCA, s 338). It is an offence for firms to fail to make those disclosures where suspicion is or should have been raised without reasonable excuse (POCA, ss 331 and 332). Where disclosures are made through an SAR to the NCA about a particular transaction and the NCA consents to the proposed transaction proceeding, this consent (also known as a 'Defence Against Money Laundering' or a 'DAML') serves as a defence to regulatees carrying out that transaction who might otherwise be prosecuted for money-laundering offences.

[66] A comparison between the number of SARs submitted in the financial year April 2019 to March 2020 and the number submitted for financial year April 2022 to March 2023 shows a 50 per cent increase in submissions: see NCA, *SARs Annual Statistical Report April 2022–March 2023* (March 2024) <www.nationalcrimeagency.gov.uk/who-we-are/publications/710-sars-annual-statistical-report/file>.

[67] HM Treasury, *Explanatory Note to the Economic Crime (Anti-Money Laundering) Levy Regulations 2022*, para 7.1.

[68] HM Treasury and Home Office, *Economic Crime Plan 2019–2022* (July 2019) Actions 30 and 31.

[69] On the SARs system, see n 65.

[70] HM Treasury and Home Office (n 68) 45.

[71] See generally Sarah Kebbell, *Anti-Money Laundering Compliance and the Legal Profession* (Routledge 2021). Miriam Goldby also highlights some of these, and other issues with the SAR system—see n 55.

purchasing properties in their own names. This was the case in *Hajiyeva*, where the use of nominees ensured that the relevant Facilitators' anti-money laundering systems did not detect that the ultimate beneficial owner of the assets was a PEP.[72] Some commentators query the focus on the failings of Facilitators around AML reporting, noting that banks' and professionals' failures make them 'an attractive target for folk-devilment'.[73] They suggest that too little attention has been paid to how the information submitted in SARs is processed by NCA, and what (if anything) subsequently happens where consent to transactions is withheld where Defence Against Money Laundering consents are sought pursuant to section 335 of the POCA.[74] There does not, for example, appear to exist any system that might put other Facilitators on notice that they may be approached by potentially corrupt PEPs where those PEPs have been first turned away by Facilitators who decline to act where they suspect potential laundering.[75]

Moreover, the new initiatives seem unlikely to address the more fundamental problems around defensive over-reporting and 'noise' generated by excessive and often low-quality SARs.[76] Some 859,905 SARs were submitted to the NCA in the 2022/2023 reporting period.[77] From a practical perspective, to properly investigate even a small fraction of SARs to determine whether the reported suspicions are well-founded would require vast resourcing and staffing. We can assume, given the lack of follow-up offered to SAR submitters on the specific reports that they submit, that investigation into the majority of suspect transactions is minimal or non-existent. The UK's election to adopt an 'all-crimes' approach in transposing the EU's anti-money laundering regulations means that Facilitators over-report transactions at risk of even the most trivial regulatory or minor criminal misdeeds as a means of absolving themselves from potential 'technical' liability.[78] Introducing a *de minimis* criminal sanction reporting threshold, or, alternatively, heightened and specific 'PEP laundering facilitation' and/or 'failure to prevent PEP laundering' type regulatory sanctions could be considered. Requiring Facilitators to specifically flag where suspected PEP laundering is involved when submitting SARs is a further option.

[72] See Marin Bentham, 'Top Law Firm Mishcon de Reya Used to Buy £15 Million Knightsbridge Home in "McMafia" Case' *Evening Standard* (London, 1 July 2024). Through the NCA's investigation, it emerged that Mrs Hajiyeva's mansion in Knightsbridge had been acquired using monies held in overseas accounts registered in names that had no apparent connection to either Mr Hajiyev or Mrs Hajiyeva.

[73] Michael Levi, 'Making Sense of Professional Enablers' Involvement in Laundering Organized Crime Proceeds and of their Regulation' [2021] Trends in Organised Crime 96, 98.

[74] Of which 61,978 were sought in the 2019/2020 financial year. See NCA, *UK Financial Intelligence Unit Suspicious Activity Reports Annual Report 2020*, 4.

[75] See Lord and others (n 36).

[76] See Goldby (n 55).

[77] See NCA (n 66).

[78] See Sarah Kebbell, 'Everybody's Looking at Nothing"—the Legal Profession and the Disproportionate Burden of the Proceeds of Crime Act 2002' (2017) 10 Criminal Law Review 741.

A turn from punitive action to increased regulatory enforcement where professional service providers are found to have facilitated laundering is an option to improve Facilitator deterrence. Regulatory enforcement for AML failures is light-touch in the UK. Looking at the legal profession for example, for the tax year 2022/2023, 249 money laundering-related reports were made to the Solicitors Regulation Authority (SRA), resulting in no solicitors being struck off, one being suspended, and twenty-three being fined an aggregate total of £61,600 for AML failings.[79] None of these cases apparently involved active laundering facilitation.[80] There is a notable mismatch between the gravity and number of sanctions imposed by the SRA when viewed against the scale of money laundering that enforcement authorities suggest is occurring in the UK.[81] Given the revision to the section 330 CPS guidance, regulators may be prompted to redouble their regulatory enforcement efforts to pre-empt criminal enforcement action against their regulatees.

d. Investigation

Given the apparent difficulties in establishing whether legal advisers have facilitated laundering, John Coffee has proposed two interesting and potentially contentious means of heightening enforcement against Facilitators. The first involves incentivizing whistle-blowers within firms and companies not only by ensuring that they have adequate legal protection against disgruntled employers, but by making available to them a share of the proceeds of any recovered assets.[82] Providing greater whistle-blower support and/or incentives may have the benefit not only of increasing the instances of questionable or illegal transactions supported by Facilitators being reported, but also of fostering cultures within firms and companies of acting more conservatively around such transactions given the (theoretically) higher risk of sanction and/or reputational damage.[83] Of course, cultures of whistle-blowing are also capable of fostering medium-term disadvantages, both for firm employees who potentially suffer the brunt of heightened monitoring and poorer internal relations with management,[84] and for the

[79] This is notwithstanding that the SRA review of the firm-wide AML policies of 224 firms surveyed that year showed that less than half of those firms were compliant with the AML Regulations.

[80] Solicitors Regulation Authority, *Anti-Money Laundering Annual Report 2022–23* (October 2023) <www.sra.org.uk/sra/research-publications/aml-annual-report-2022-23/>.

[81] NCA, *National Strategic Assessment of Serious and Organised Crime 2020–2021*, 54: '[it is] a realistic possibility that the scale of money laundering impacting on the UK (including through UK corporate structures or financial institutions) is in the hundreds of billions of pounds annually'.

[82] John C Coffee, *Corporate Crime and Punishment: The Crisis of Underenforcement* (Berrett-Koehler 2020) 113–21.

[83] Janine Pascoe and Michelle Welsh, 'Whistleblowing, Ethics and Corporate Culture: Theory and Practice in Australia' (2011) 40 Common Law World Review 144.

[84] Jonas Heese and Gerardo Peréz-Cavazos, 'The Effect of Retaliation Costs on Employee Whistleblowing' (2021) 71 Journal of Accounting and Economics 101385.

whistle-blowers themselves, who are sometimes (mis)characterized as misguided traitors or as untrustworthy.[85]

The idea of incentivizing whistle-blowers was previously dismissed by the FCA and the Bank of England's Prudential Regulation Authority (PRA), inter alia, on the basis that looking at the approach adopted in the United States of incentivizing whistle-blowers, there was no available empirical evidence to suggest that financial incentives would improve the quality or number of disclosures. The FCA and the PRA argued that financially incentivizing whistle-blowing could generate 'moral and other hazards' including heightened risks of poor information being provided in bad faith, malicious reporting, conflicts arising through paying whistle-blowers to testify in court, and the fact that incentives would reward whistle-blowers 'for performing what is arguably their regulatory duty'.[86] It should be acknowledged that in reaching these conclusions, these regulators may have been influenced to a degree by regulatory capture. The British Bankers' Association was a key consultee for their study, and the PRA and FCA had recently updated and improved their own internal processes for supporting whistle-blowers.[87] More generally, unlike the US context in which Coffee writes, the UK has not hitherto had the same tradition of bargaining and bounties within the criminal justice sphere,[88] nor does it have comparatively strong whistle-blower protections for employees.[89] The UK financial services industry has so far proven surprisingly watertight against leaks by its workers and advisors compared to its US and European counterparts, and its professionals are bound by strong duties and cultures of confidentiality. That said, the debate around incentivizing whistle-blowers has been resurrected of late with the head of the Serious Fraud Office recommending incentivization by noting that over 700 UK whistle-blowers have engaged with *American* law enforcement authorities in recent years. He also remarked on the huge recoveries made by the US authorities based on whistle-blower information.[90] In 2023, buoyed by the success of whistle-blowing initiatives in other areas of crime control, the US

[85] See eg Swiss Info, 'Prosecutors Target "Suisse Secrets" Bank Whistleblowers' (2 February 2023) <www.swissinfo.ch/eng/business/prosecutors-target-suisse-secrets-bank-whistleblowers/48253902>.

[86] FCA and PRA, *Financial Incentives for Whistleblowers: Note by the Financial Conduct Authority and the Prudential Regulation Authority for the Treasury Select Committee* (July 2014).

[87] IFCA and PRA (n 86) 4–6.

[88] The FCA and PRA acknowledged in their study that financial incentives from law enforcement authorities to confidential informants seemed to generate viable evidence, but such incentivization tends to occur in a very different context from whistle-blowing.

[89] Retaliation against employees by employers for whistle-blowing is not, for example, a criminal offence in England but is a federal crime in the US. See Tan Pei Meng and Ong Seng Fook, 'Comparative Analysis of Whistleblower Protection Legislations in England, USA and Malaysia' (2011) 27 African Journal of Business Management 11246. For a general overview of the UK's whistle-blowing legislation, see Folashade Adeyemo, 'Rebutting the Presumption: Are Whistleblowers Really Protected under PIDA and in the Case of the UK Banking Industry' (2020) 8 Journal of Business Law 607.

[90] Speech delivered by Nick Ephgrave, Director of the SFO to the Royal United Services Institute on 13 February 2024. RUSI has also undertaken research on the viability of whistle-blower incentives.

Treasury Department in partnership with the Department of Justice and the State Department introduced a Kleptocracy Asset Recovery Rewards Program which awards bounties of up to $5m for 'information leading to the restraint or recovery of certain assets linked to foreign corruption'.[91] The idea of incentivizing whistleblowing in the UK by strengthening anti-retaliation sanctions against employers, offering immunity from prosecution, and/or offering financial incentives is an intriguing suggestion. Based on the imprimatur of the head of the Serious Fraud Office (SFO), it is worthy of further consideration.

The second proposal, germane to lawyers' work only, is that allegedly corrupt persons (corporations, in Coffee's analysis) and their legal advisors should be pitted against each other in investigations. He suggests that where settlement negotiations are in play or where suspected corrupt actors are otherwise proving cooperative, they might be encouraged to incriminate their lawyers by waiving legal professional privilege as a condition of a deal.[92] This is a version of the rationale underpinning the introduction of deferred prosecution agreements in the corporate criminal liability sphere. These allow enforcement authorities to agree to defer prosecutions against companies accused of offences including overseas bribery, provided that those companies offer their full cooperation subject to certain conditions, including that they share information which might lead to prosecutions of individuals who instigated bribery.[93] It is clients who hold the benefit of, and the prerogative to waive, legal privilege. Such a waiver would allow enforcement or regulatory authorities access to advice which may in turn determine whether legal assistance or services were provided on an intentional or negligent basis to further corrupt aims. In many instances, a formal waiver of privilege may be unnecessary because legal advice privilege does not extend to advice of a purely commercial nature—rather it is primarily concerned with advice around an advisee's legal obligations.[94] For this strategy to be effective in practice, 'primary actors' involved in grand corruption would likely need to acknowledge to at least some extent that they and their legal advisors complicitly took steps to launder corruptly acquired assets and/or that the legal advisors were advised of a client's intention to launder and did not explain sufficiently the potential risk of criminal liability being assumed. Where a sufficiently incentivized overseas corrupt PEP,

[91] The White House, *Fact Sheet: Implementing the United States Strategy on Countering Corruption: Accomplishments and Renewed Commitment in the Year of Action* (29 March 2023) <www.whitehouse.gov/briefing-room/statements-releases/2023/03/29/fact-sheet-implementing-the-united-states-strategy-on-countering-corruption-accomplishments-and-renewed-commitment-in-the-year-of-action/#:~:text=The%20Treasury%20Department%2C%20in%20coordination,assets%20linked%20to%20foreign%20corruption>.

[92] Coffee (n 82) 122–30. He writes in the context of negotiating DPAs, but the same proposal is worth considering in the context of settlements with corrupt PEPs, examined in Section 3.

[93] In a DPA context, this strategy is seemingly ineffective in practice—prosecutions in England against executives of companies who have agreed DPAs rarely ensue and have, so far, never succeeded. See generally King and Lord (n 16).

[94] *ENRC v SFO* [2018] EWCA Civ 2006.

say, believes that a prosecution in their state of origin is unlikely, they may be comfortable about making admissions on laundering to UK enforcement authorities in making a deal relating to their UK-based property as part of a settlement negotiation. Incentives in this context might include confidentiality undertakings and/or the prospect of keeping a 'clean slate' with UK enforcement authorities.

This strategy may have the effect of focusing legal advisors' minds and forcing them to explicitly and self-defensively memorialize in their files if, when, and how they have expressly advised a potentially corrupt client of the illegality of a particular course of action. Failure to do this would suggest, at best, negligence and at worst, complicity when facilitating illegality. This may well open doors to more robust regulatory and/or criminal enforcement against legal advisors, and consequently to better deterrence. That said, Coffee's proposal also runs the risk of unintended consequences. Lawyers could turn away from providing *written* advice that could be seen as facilitating illegality, and towards orally advising their clients. Without proper written records, corroboration of facilitation beyond the primary actor's evidence may only be available through covert surveillance, including having clients wear wires to collect incriminating conversations with their lawyers. Although Coffee's proposal and this discussion of it is largely speculative, the practical upshot of his strategy might be to impose a chilling effect on the culture of mutual trust and openness on which lawyer/client relationships rely. Nevertheless, it is at least worth discussing innovations like Coffee's to animate the discourse around what *could* be done to ease investigative challenges and to deter Facilitators from enabling corruption.

4. Transparency Reforms

The policy mantra in financial crime disruption is to 'follow the money'.[95] This might explain the amount of attention paid by national authorities to putting anti-money laundering compliance structures in place within the financial sector, even if no reliable data of AML's efficacy in preventing or deterring laundering exist.[96] At the same time that there is intense policy focus on cashflow transparency, other asset regulatory systems have until recently ranged from being wholly publicly

[95] Michael Levi, 'Making Sense of Professional Enablers' Involvement in Laundering Organized Crime Proceeds and of their Regulation' [2021] Trends in Organised Crime 96, 101. The first recorded use of the expression was at the 1974 US Senate Select Committee on Presidential Campaign Activities Hearings at which Earl J Silbert was nominated to be the US attorney. See Wolfgang Mieder, Fred R Shapiro, and Charles Clay Doyle (eds), *The Dictionary of Modern Proverbs* (Yale University Press 2012) 168.

[96] Levi (n 95).

untransparent to being so porous that they were wide open to exploitation by corrupt actors. Either of these extremes is clearly undesirable in terms of situational crime prevention. This section considers recent transparency and verification developments in company, trust, and property ownership as a means of preventing corrupt activity.

As a preliminary point, it is worth questioning on a fundamental level the value of privacy in wealth management. In *Baker*, Lang J highlighted 'privacy, security, [and] tax mitigation' motivations as 'legitimate' reasons why individuals may wish to keep details of beneficial ownership through complex offshore corporate structures private.[97] Security reasons may be legitimate in circumstances where settlors or beneficial owners reasonably fear corrupt autocracies or criminals stealing their assets or practising extortion, kidnapping, etc. Security concerns aside though, it is difficult to discern compelling principled reasons why individuals should be entitled to withhold information on their financial status. Members of the general public are required, in the UK at least, to register their ownership of valuable assets like real estate and, to a lesser degree, to shares in companies on publicly searchable databases.[98] Similar transparency policies do not apply in secrecy jurisdictions, which is one reason why companies and other corporate entities registered in those countries are so popular amongst the corrupt. There are obvious commercial and personal reasons why individuals may not want details of their wealth made *publicly* available.[99] Tax mitigation might be a (sometimes) legal reason to hold assets via vehicles registered in so-called secrecy jurisdictions. However, the social value and justifiability of this and other legal reasons for claims to financial privacy are becoming increasingly unclear, particularly in the context of ongoing calls for tax justice.[100] Insisting that individual financial privacy be privileged over public or even state access to financial data seems an increasingly dated concept post-globalization. A broader public inculcation of a turn away from perceived 'rights' to financial privacy might be helpful in tackling corruption and lending legitimacy to measures like UWOs. It is submitted that it is not unreasonable per se to require individuals to provide state authorities with details of the sources and scope of personal wealth where it is required in legitimate tax or investigative contexts, especially where other jurisdictions' corporate registries facilitate the opacity of similar data where corporate vehicles are registered in *their* countries.

[97] *NCA v Baker* [2020] EWHC 822 (Admin) [97]. Lang J noted that the transfer of properties between various offshore structures was legitimately made in anticipation of a new UK law which raised a tax liability for property owned through foreign companies.

[98] For the latter, only where they are PSCs—see further Section 4(a).

[99] A comprehensive list of these reasons is provided in the ECJ's *Sovim* decision (n 140) paras 38–44.

[100] Tax justice being the idea that reform is necessary to address high-net-worth individuals and companies unfairly placing themselves in a position to be selective as to which jurisdictions (if any) they are liable to pay tax in, in a way that 'ordinary' taxpayers are not. See Peter Alldridge, *Criminal Justice and Taxation* (OUP 2017) 144–46.

a. Domestic Corporate Registries and Transparency

Corporate vehicles played a central role in obscuring the ultimate beneficial owners of illicitly acquired assets in the majority of 150 corruption cases involving senior public officials analysed by the Stolen Assets Recovery Initiative (StAR) in a 2011 study. The data provide indicators of at least some kleptocrats' *modi operandi.* StAR's study found that companies were the most widely used corporate entities in the relevant corrupt activities. The corrupt actors the subject of the study were clearly not wholly effective in concealing their crimes using companies, given the fact that they had come to StAR's attention. If anything, the study perhaps suggests that more opaque structures than single companies (eg the use of trusts or foundations organized under the laws of secrecy jurisdictions and/or corporate structures involving multiple companies across multiple jurisdictions) may be more effective to clandestinely serve the needs of the corrupt.[101] In any event, although these data suggest that companies are used as vehicles of corruption, the UK government has until recently regarded it as a business advantage that companies can be registered within twenty-four hours of first making an application via the Companies House website for a fee of fifty pounds. It is certainly cheaper and faster to register a company in England than in the main 'secrecy' jurisdictions.[102] Since 2016, in the UK, Companies House publishes personal particulars on the public register of Persons with Significant Control of companies (PSC) unless those individuals can establish that they would be at serious risk of violence or intimidation were their details to be published.[103] A PSC is, broadly, anyone who holds more than 25 per cent of the shares of, or of the voting rights in, a company as an ultimate beneficial owner. The term also encompasses individuals who have the right to exercise, or actually exercise, significant influence or control over a company or have a right directly or indirectly to remove a majority of the company's directors.[104] Those companies whose PSCs are published include all companies registered in the UK and all overseas companies owning real property in the UK.[105] The publicly accessible PSC register was introduced as part of a suite of measures 'which are intended to ensure that the United Kingdom continues to be recognized globally as a trusted and fair place to do business'.[106] Whilst well-intentioned as a plan

[101] Van der Dos de Willebois and others (n 42).

[102] Based on a survey of the companies registration process of a number of jurisdictions, namely the British Virgin Islands, the Cayman Islands, Guernsey, Jersey, Delaware, and North Dakota, the process is cheaper, less formal, and generally faster in England compared with the other jurisdictions surveyed. Each of those registries surveyed appears to have at least some minimum level of applicant verification process, either through requiring that only certified forms of identification be submitted or through requiring that companies be incorporated through company agents.

[103] Companies Act 2006, ss 790ZF and 790ZG and The Information about People with Significant Control (Amendment) Regulations 2017, SI 2017/693, regs 12–19.

[104] Companies Act 2006, s 790C and sch 1A.

[105] The latter register is the Register of Overseas Entities, maintained by Companies House and established pursuant to the Economic Crime (Transparency and Enforcement) Act 2022.

[106] Explanatory Notes to the Small Business, Enterprise and Employment Act 2015, para 3.

to improve transparency,[107] because Companies House had up until recently very few powers or resources with which to verify PSC and officer details submitted to it, those intent on obscuring their UK company ownership interests were able to simply invent false details for inclusion on company applications.[108] Traditionally, the Companies Register maintained by Companies House was viewed as 'inherently archival in nature',[109] rather than representing a trustworthy source of current information on companies. In addition to the obvious pathways to fraud that the approach opened up, this was problematic because, as research conducted by the Department for Business, Energy and Industrial Strategy in December 2019 showed, financial institutions and enforcement authorities use the PSC register to cross-check information they hold on beneficial ownership of companies.[110]

The Economic Crime and Corporate Transparency Act 2023 (ECCTA) introduced information verification requirements for PSCs and officers of new and existing companies, amongst other matters, to help 'support developing countries to stop theft of their public assets'.[111] The legislative intent in introducing the changes was to update Companies House in 'its statutory role from being a largely passive recipient of information to a much more active gatekeeper over company creation and custodian of more reliable data'.[112] Companies are now required to verify the identities of all of their officers and PSCs via the Companies House website using three personal details of each individual's identity,[113] or have those individuals register with, and register their identities via, anti-money laundering supervised authorized corporate service providers. Third-party verifiers who may be registered with the government for these purposes can include solicitors, accountants, and trust and corporate service providers.[114] At the time of writing, it is too early to establish how successful or even how rigorous the verification requirements at Companies House will prove in practice.[115] Based on the experience with measures like the UWO, anti-corruption campaigners are likely to draw on the Gramscian

[107] The UK government has said that it alone out of the G20 states has a fully public register of beneficial owners of companies. HL Deb (Sanctions and Anti-Money Laundering Bill) 20 February 2018, vol 636, col 126.

[108] See Oliver Bullough, 'Britain, Headquarters of Fraud' *The Guardian* (London, 22 April 2018).

[109] This is typical of companies registries more generally, see Van der Dos de Willebois and others (n 42) 70.

[110] Business, Energy and Industrial Strategy, *Corporate Transparency and Registry Reform* (White Paper, CP 638, 28 February 2022).

[111] Department for Business and Trade, *Progress Report on the Implementation and Operation of Parts 1 to 3 of the Economic Crime and Corporate Transparency Act 2023* (Stationery Office May 2024) para 2.1.

[112] Explanatory Notes to the Economic Crime and Corporate Transparency Act 2023, para 10.

[113] The Companies House website lists details including an applicant officer's town of birth, mother's maiden name, father's first name, telephone number, and national insurance number and/or passport number as examples of such details.

[114] Companies Act 2006, s 1110A.

[115] A cursory search on the Register of Companies on the Companies House website as of 1 August 2024 reveals a surprisingly high number of company officers who are individuals, for example, having a single initial as a surname.

notion of 'pessimism of the intellect, optimism of the will' in viewing these developments. Unlike piecemeal measures such as the unexplained wealth order, however, a systemic and mandatory process like the new verification requirements seems more plausible as a means of stymieing the laundering of grand corruption proceeds in the UK (or at least, as a means of ceasing to indirectly facilitate that laundering).

Even so, whilst significant funding has been committed to the initial phases of verification, and stakeholders including the SFO and NCA were consulted in formulating the reforms,[116] the scale of work required to re-construct a Companies Register, this time containing reliable data on companies, is formidable. As of 2024, there are 4.6m active companies registered at Companies House, with 800,000 registered during the financial year 2022/2023 alone. For those committed to holding their corruptly acquired assets through UK companies but avoiding verification processes, the requirements are, one suspects, possible for reasonably committed launderers to circumvent. There are already loopholes evident for individuals wishing to obscure their beneficial interest in UK companies. The most obvious of these is the fact that only details of PSCs with *more than 25 per cent* of a beneficial interest in the company will be registrable and publicly recorded. Foreign corrupt actors who opt, for example, to hold a UK property through a company incorporated at Companies House with four or more shareholders holding equal shares will not need to register PSC details. Alternatively, there is little to prevent individuals making false claims to negligent third-party verification service providers about the true beneficial ownership of properties or shares. If a registered third-party verifier incorrectly claims, say, that a company is owned by five PSCs with equal shareholdings, even if in reality it only has a single ultimate beneficial owner, it is vanishingly unlikely that this claim will ever be questioned unless law enforcement authorities are given good reason to doubt it. Given the apparent lassitude of regulators in creating material salient risks of sanction for their regulatees, the risk here should not be underestimated.

As with the government's other anti-corruption adjacent measures including UWOs, the intent behind introducing the reforms is laudable and at worst generates mood music suggesting an improved level of seriousness of approach in the UK's official anti-corruption philosophy.[117] However, the reforms' future success in achieving a reliable and accurate companies register in practice is contingent on sufficient resources being put in place to allow for proper verification of details and to ensure that robust enforcement measures are exercisable against those who misuse the register. Even assuming Companies House verification processes

[116] Almost £130m has been made available in funding for the implementation of this and other Companies House reforms in their first five years, including £19m committed specifically to anti-money laundering work. See Department for Business and Trade (n 111).

[117] Which of course may have its own deterrent effect.

are improved or it undertakes wider enforcement activity against parties who fail to provide accurate details when registering or updating company particulars, the number of new companies registered annually in the UK means that ensuring widespread enforcement will be very difficult.

b. Properties Owned by Trusts

Express UK trusts and express non-UK trusts holding assets in the UK are required to register with the UK's tax authority, HMRC.[118] Failure to register or to update the register with required details can attract a £5,000 fine.[119] Information required on each trust includes each trust beneficiary's full name, month and year of birth, country of residence, nationality, and the share and nature of their benefit in the trust.[120] Where a trust becomes subject to UK taxes related to their UK property (including stamp duty, capital gains tax, inheritance tax), the trustee of that trust is required to submit to HMRC within ninety days of that tax liability arising extensive information including social security numbers or passport numbers of settlors, trustees, and *all* beneficiaries named in and actively benefiting from the trust.[121]

The register is not publicly accessible but can be accessed by law enforcement authorities and those who can establish to HMRC's satisfaction that they hold a 'legitimate interest' in the identities of the beneficiaries of a trust.[122] HMRC has a wide discretion to determine what constitutes a 'legitimate interest' in this context, but in making this determination, HMRC 'must take account' of inter alia whether those seeking information are investigating suspected money laundering or terrorist financing and whether the information sought might prejudice an investigation undertaken by law enforcement authorities.[123] This approach to qualified transparency employed by HMRC is ostensibly a reasonable compromise between allowing public interest access as necessary and maintaining a level of individual privacy. It is consistent with the requirements of the most recent iterations of the

[118] A 'UK trust' is an express trust where either all of the trustees are resident in the UK, or where at least one trustee is resident in the UK and the settlor was domiciled and resident in the UK at any time when settling assets upon the trust: reg 42(2) of the AML Regulations. The registration obligation is provided for under regs 45(2) and 45ZA(3). An express trust is a legal arrangement expressly (generally in writing) created by its settlor *qua* trust (as distinct from trusts arising through circumstance like resulting or constructive trusts).

[119] This fine will only be levied if trustees fail to comply following receipt of a warning letter from HMRC: see pt 9 of the HMRC manual cited at n 121.

[120] AML Regulations, reg 45ZA(3)(a).

[121] AML Regulations, reg 45. *HMRC Internal Manual: Trust Registration Service Manual*, TRSM32050 (first published 17 May 2017 and updated as of 10 July 2024) <www.gov.uk/hmrc-internal-manuals/trust-registration-service-manual/trsm32050>.

[122] AML Regulations, reg 45(12).

[123] AML Regulations, reg 45ZB(11).

Financial Action Task Force's (FATF) Recommendations and the EU's Money Laundering Directives.[124]

Nevertheless, concerns around transparency and the accuracy of information submitted to registries of corporate vehicles in the UK and elsewhere remain. First, notwithstanding the ability of those who can establish a legitimate interest in information on trusts, there are early indications that this information is difficult to obtain. HMRC's response to a Freedom of Information query on the number of trust data requests received from those with legitimate interests and those requests to which HMRC furnished the requested information is revealing. In the first eighteen months following the ability to make trust data requests first becoming available (1 September 2022 to 3 April 2024), HMRC received a total of twenty-one requests that it deemed as demonstrating a legitimate interest in the requested information. It was able or willing to share information in relation to 'between 0 and 5' of those requests.[125] This number is exclusive of requests received from enforcement authorities, on which HMRC did not provide data. The reasons for its inability to furnish the requested information included, without limitation, because the relevant trusts 'may not have been registered on the [Trusts Register] yet, [or] cannot be identified with certainty because the details provided to HMRC were insufficient'.[126] There are a couple of takeaways from this. First, notwithstanding that this was the first opportunity for journalists and civil society groups to gain an insight into who exactly are registered as beneficiaries to trusts with interests in property in the UK since the Russian invasion of Ukraine, a surprisingly small number of requests were submitted to HMRC. Second, for those requests that were submitted, information was provided in response to very few, if any. HMRC's inability to respond to requests because of poor-quality data submitted on behalf of trusts or non-compliance with registration requirements echoes problems identified in obtaining information on and from other overseas entities holding property in the UK, discussed below.[127]

c. Properties Owned by Overseas Entities

The Economic Crime (Transparency and Enforcement) Act 2022 (ECTEA) introduced the Register of Overseas Entities, a register maintained by Companies House on which foreign legal entities including partnerships, trusts, and companies that own or intend on owning properties in the UK must register details of their 'registrable beneficiaries'. In this context, 'registrable beneficiary' is defined as

[124] Discussed further in Sub-section (d) below.
[125] Letter from HMRC Information Rights Unit to the author dated 30 April 2024 (HMRC FOI 2024/36578).
[126] HMRC (n 125).
[127] See n 136 and accompanying text below.

including an individual or legal entity who satisfies PSC criteria in respect of the legal entity or nominee holding the property.[128] Provisions are also made to capture the beneficial owners of properties that are registered in the names of entities that do not strictly have separate legal personality (eg trusts and partnerships in some jurisdictions).[129] The provisions entered into force on 1 August 2022,[130] even though what has been described as an 'oven-ready' piece of legislation had been available since 2018.[131] The Register has retrospective application: overseas entities holding UK properties which have purchased those properties since 1999 (since 2014 for Scotland) are required to provide information to Companies House on their PSCs and officers.[132] After the obligation to provide information went live in August 2022, overseas entities had six months to comply with the registration requirements after which non-compliance sanctions would be enforceable. Legal entities and their officers failing to comply with the registration requirements or annual updating and confirmation requirements can be found guilty of an offence and subject to fines including a default fine of £2,500 for each day that information is overdue and/or up to two years' imprisonment on indictment.[133] The overseas entities are precluded from acquiring or disposing of property or creating registrable security over their property for so long as registration or annual confirmations are outstanding.[134] Companies House has indicated that it will provide reminders, warning notices, and grace periods to non-compliant overseas entities and their officers.[135] One suspects that it may have no choice: obvious difficulties are likely to arise in terms of the UK authorities' enforcement jurisdiction should it seek to criminally prosecute entities registered or officers based overseas. Where fines imposed through the issue of penalty notices remain unpaid and the overseas entity and its officers fail to submit the required information and pay the fines, it is open to the Companies Registrar to enforce the debt through the courts, resulting in a charge being registered against the UK-based property held by the entity for the outstanding amount.

Academics at the University of Warwick and the London School of Economics published empirical research on the effectiveness of the obligation to register

[128] Using the same criteria to determine whether someone is the PSC of a UK company as set out in sch 1A of the Companies Act 2006, discussed above, but for overseas entities.

[129] Economic Crime (Transparency and Enforcement) Act 2022, sch 2.

[130] Pursuant to the Economic Crime (Transparency and Enforcement) Act 2022 (Commencement No 3) Regulations 2022, SI 2022/876.

[131] See Helena Wood of RUSI, *Deeds Not Words: Making the Economic Crime Plan Matter in the Real World* (6 July 2021) <https://rusi.org/explore-our-research/publications/commentary/deeds-not-words-making-economic-crime-plan-matter-real-world>.

[132] The Register of Overseas Entities (Verification and Provision of Information) Regulations 2022, SI 2022/725, reg 6.

[133] ECTEA, s 8 and sch 3 para 5.

[134] Land Registration Act 2002, sch 4A.

[135] Companies House, *Guidance: Register of Overseas Entities: Approach to Enforcement*, updated 20 May 2024.

details with the Register of Overseas Entities as of eight months following the date by which all overseas entities had to be registered. They found that, for 71 per cent of overseas entities (representing 115,000 properties), 'essential information about their beneficial owners remain[ed] missing or publicly inaccessible'.[136] Amongst the key problems identified, some 15,000 properties 'known to be held via an overseas entity' could not be linked from cross-checks at the Land Registry and the Register of Overseas Entities, and the owners of around 9,000 properties remained unregistered. Approximately 27 per cent of overseas entities (owning 69,000 properties) were part of a trust structure, with the result that the beneficial owners of those properties are not publicly accessible, albeit that information is sometimes available to government agencies.[137] A few conclusions might be drawn from these data. First, the intensity of resources required for Companies House to refer the defaulting overseas entities for prosecution and/or to institute court actions seeking liens over the relevant properties to satisfy fines is a fundamental obstacle to the legislative objective of 'increasing the transparency of beneficial ownership information relating to overseas entities that own land in the UK'.[138] This is exacerbated by the number of non-complying overseas entities involved. The scale of early non-compliance suggests that it is unlikely that the legislative objective will ever be realized in full unless there is a material and credible risk of enforcement action being taken against defaulters. Second, the prospect of enforcement is complicated by the jurisdiction of UK authorities to enforce offences against overseas entities. One solution to address this issue might be to require overseas entities, their officers, and their PSCs to provide a UK address for deemed service of warning and penalty notices as a condition of those entities holding property in the UK. Third, there is clear scope for HMRC and Companies House, to the extent that they are not doing so already, to share and cross-check information submitted to each on behalf of overseas trusts as a means of strengthening the reliability of information held on the registers maintained by each of them.

d. Much Done; More to Do

A decision of the European Court of Justice's Grand Chamber in late 2022 inflicted a severe blow against the interests of anti-corruption and transparency campaigners in the European Union.[139] In the *Sovim* matter, the Court held that

[136] Arun Advani and others, 'Catch Me If You Can: Gaps in the Register of Overseas Entities' (September 2023) CAGE Working Paper 680.
[137] Advani and others (n 136) 1–2.
[138] ECTEA, Explanatory Memorandum, para 1.
[139] See the discussion in Mathias Siems, 'Privacy vs. Shareholder Transparency: Did the ECJ Decision in *WM And Sovim SA* Impair The Global Fight Against Money Laundering?' (2023) 60 Common Market Law Review 1137, 1147–51.

members of the general public should not have access to information on the beneficial ownership of companies.[140] It determined that the rights protected under Articles 7 (respect for private and family life) and 8 (protection of personal data) of the Charter of Fundamental Rights of the European Union had been disproportionately interfered with by publicly accessible registers holding the names of company PSCs.[141] The Court identified as a problem exacerbating these interferences the fact that publicly accessible beneficial ownership information allowed members of the public to build an asset profile of particular individuals, but did not discuss why this is a problem per se. It is unclear why the Court indirectly concluded in its decision that there should be no quid pro quo from shareholders benefiting from limited liability in terms of allowing the public to know who is receiving that benefit. Moreover, whilst it acknowledged the roles of civil society groups, NGOs, and journalists as those who might have a 'legitimate interest' in access to beneficial ownership information, it paid scant attention to the role members of the general public might have as people who can notice discrepancies in public registers suggestive of corruption and tip off those organizations or individuals.[142]

As the UK is not under the jurisdiction of the European Court of Justice, the decision is not binding on it, but the concern is around the ruling's persuasive effect and the corollary risk of catalysing a transparency rollback around beneficial ownership more generally.[143] The impact of *Sovim* became evident soon after the judgment's publication, even outside the territory over which it holds jurisdiction. The Financial Action Task Force (FATF) opted not to include a consulted-upon option for its member states to 'consider facilitating public access to basic and beneficial ownership information'[144] in the most recent iteration of its updated Recommendations.[145] The Cayman Islands, British Virgin Islands, and the three Crown Dependencies all used the Court's decision to justify decisions to limit public access to details of the ultimate beneficial owners of companies registered in their jurisdictions unless accompanied by proof of a 'legitimate interest' in the information first being demonstrated.[146] The EU's sixth AML Directive removed the requirement of a 'clear rule of public access' to details of the beneficial owners of companies which was provided for in previous iterations of the Directive. It does

[140] Joined Cases C-37/20 and 601/20 *WM and Sovim SA v Luxembourg Business Registers* (ECJ, Judgment of the Grand Chamber, 22 November 2022).

[141] Charter of Fundamental Rights of the European Union [2000] OJ C364/01.

[142] *Sovim SA* (n 140) para 74.

[143] See Siems (n 139) 1150–51.

[144] FATF, *Guidance on Beneficial Ownership Recommendation 24—Public Consultation* (March 2022) para 107 <www.fatf-gafi.org/en/publications/Fatfrecommendations/R24-public-consultation-oct-2022.html>.

[145] FATF, The FATF Recommendations (FATF, 2012 version as amended November 2023) <www.fatf-gafi.org/en/publications/Fatfrecommendations/Fatf-recommendations.html>.

[146] Government of Guernsey, Government of Isle of Man, Government of Jersey, *Joint Commitment of Guernsey, the Isle of Man and Jersey: Registers of Beneficial Ownership of Companies* (13 December 2023) <www.gov.im/media/1381410/20231213-2023-commitment_final_3cd_headed-1.pdf>.

however provide detailed criteria around which groups might qualify as having a 'legitimate interest' in the data (including journalists, civil society organizations, and those who might have a financial interest in transacting with the relevant company).[147]

Where does this leave the UK and the reforms introduced by the ECCTA and the ECTEA? On a macro level, it is difficult to argue with the suggestion that requiring registration of beneficial ownership on state registers is a relatively superficial step in 'tackling the multifaceted problem of money laundering'.[148] This is supported by the evident levels of poor compliance or non-compliance exhibited by overseas entities subject to registration obligations so far, and the scale of companies' verification work with which Companies House must grapple. It is argued throughout this volume that a multi-systems approach supported by sufficient enforcement resources and expertise and a perceptible cultural shift towards zero tolerance of the proceeds of corruption is necessary. Notwithstanding the problems with the reforms introduced around companies and trusts registers, the changes wrought by the legislation are, it is submitted, a positive step towards a systematized and ambitious strengthening of information sources on who owns property in the UK. Post-*Sovim*, the UK finds itself in the novel position of having the most transparent (if not for now the most accurate) source of information on the individuals who hold the beneficial ownership of companies in Europe. There is scope for it to go still further. Arun Advani and his colleagues have suggested that the ownership interest threshold at which PSCs for overseas entities are registered at Companies House be reduced from 25 per cent to 5 per cent.[149] Given that the Trusts Register maintained by HMRC requires that the details of *all* active beneficiaries to trusts be registered, it must be assumed that Companies House adopting a similar strategy for companies and overseas entities registered with it would be administratively workable in time. Beyond that, a key risk for transparency is that the UK will seek to 'gold-plate' its adoption of measures to harmonize its anti-money laundering regime to the requirements of the latest version of the EU's AML Directive to the degree that it shuts down general public access to ultimate beneficial ownership information on companies at Companies House. More rigorous consideration of the consequences of such a step from anti-corruption and AML perspectives than was evident in the European Court of Justice's decision in *Sovim* is necessary before any such step can be contemplated legitimately, especially given the UK's perceived status as a haven for dirty money.

[147] Council Directive (EU) 2024/1640 of 31 May 2024 on the mechanisms to be put in place by Member States for the prevention of the use of the financial system for the purposes of money laundering or terrorist financing, amending Directive (EU) 2019/1937, and amending and repealing Directive (EU) 2015/849 [2024] OJ L1640/1, art 12.

[148] Paul Gilmour, 'Lifting the Veil on Beneficial Ownership: Challenges of Implementing the UK's Registers of Beneficial Owner' (2020) 23 Journal of Money Laundering Control 717.

[149] Advani and others (n 136) 3.

5. Enlisting the Tax Regime?

It is not prima facie onerous for individuals called to assist investigations, whether through UWOs or otherwise, to account for the lawful origin of their assets, as the Home Office,[150] and Supperstone J in *Hajiyeva* have each pointed out. Assuming there is a legitimate explanation for how the respondent came to acquire the property the subject of an order, the burden is largely administrative. The information sought will be often solely within the respondent's knowledge, or within the knowledge of only a few people and not a matter of public record.[151] UWO advocates might make a social contract-based argument that it is reasonable that all individuals who opt to acquire property in the UK implicitly become answerable to the UK authorities to account for their wealth in the same way, say, that UK-resident taxpayers are. In discussing rights of participation in British society, Zedner notes that 'citizenship rights of participation and protection are made conditional upon compliance with prescribed norms and upon conformity with specified requirements analogous to those of "active citizenship", set out in a welter of contractual terms, restrictions, and prohibitions'.[152] She traces this notion of legal personhood in society to Rousseau's concept of the social contract,[153] and the idea that those who fail to abide by the rules regulating society might be regarded as enemies of society. The case could be made that submission to anti-corruption measures and civil recovery investigations forms part of the consideration to be provided by those of overseas origin when opting to become property owners in the UK and consequently participants in its society (even if only from afar, if they opt not to become residents).

The measure to which the PEP-specific UWO is most akin *outside* of the proceeds of crime paradigm is the assessment to tax regime. In general, UK taxpayers are required to account annually to the tax authorities for income and gains. The state's interest in imposing the tax burden as equitably as Parliament sees fit might be regarded as a justified interference with the taxpayer's right to privacy and property rights. Where HMRC discovers that a taxpayer's taxable income or chargeable gains have been under-assessed or not assessed, it can make an assessment to tax.[154] As part of this process, HMRC officers can request the production of documents, accounts, or information to be produced by the taxpayer so that the correct amount of tax can be calculated. This form of investigation into an

[150] Home Office and HMRC, *Criminal Finances Bill: European Convention on Human Rights: Memorandum by the Home Office and HMRC* (19 October 2016) para 38.

[151] In *Hussain*, for example, the NCA sought a UWO rather than a production order from the respondent's financial service providers because the records sought were likely to be more than six years old and banks do not typically retain records beyond that period.

[152] Lucia Zedner, 'Security, the State and the Citizen: The Changing Architecture of Crime Control' (2010) 13 New Criminal Law Review 379, 389.

[153] Jean-Jacques Rousseau, *The Social Contract* (first published 1762; Penguin 1969).

[154] Taxes Management Act 1970, s 29(1).

individual's financial affairs—something to which non-tax resident individuals are not subject—is analogous to the requirements of a UWO and is relatively uncontroversial. The question then arises: how can it be credibly claimed that UWOs against PEPs are discriminatory, or involve an excessive interference with privacy, when similar measures are widely imposed against the general populace? The answer lies in all of the factors and circumstances extraneous to the interference, not the interference per se. It is the UWO process's enforcers, form, purpose, and outcome which move what could merely be an administrative or regulatory matter into the quasi-criminal realm. Table 7.1 demonstrates the 'administrative' and relatively value-neutral character of the tax assessment system as against the rather more accusatory, quasi-criminal character of UWOs.

Table 7.1 Comparison of elements of tax and UWO processes

Element	Assessment to tax	UWO
Respondents	Taxpayers	PEPs and those suspected of serious crime
Form	A notice from the Commissioners of Inland Revenue[155]	High Court order
Applicants	HMRC inspector (the NCA also has the power to seek a discovery assessment, but it is rarely used in practice)	Law enforcement authorities—to date only the NCA has applied for an order
Requirement	Production of documents, accounts, or information on income and gains	Production of explanation (together with supporting evidence) of licit sources of funds
Purpose	To ensure that a taxpayer pays the correct amount of tax	To determine whether the respondent holds 'recoverable property' for the purposes of the Proceeds of Crime Act
Consequence of failure to comply	Fines, with escalation for continued non-compliance	Property presumed to be 'recoverable property' and eligible for civil recovery

The language establishing tax assessment powers uses similarly value-neutral language when compared to the language used in the UWO legislation.[156]

[155] Note, for completeness, that HMRC is also entitled to the full range of investigation and recovery powers under pt 5 of the POCA.

[156] See s 29(3) of the Tax Management Act 1970, where the conditions under which an assessment to tax can be raised are expressed in a passive voice, imposing no implicit culpability on a respondent: 'If

Crucially, tax assessment (and indeed, the operation of the tax system generally) involves a greater degree of *ex ante* voluntary disclosure and a higher reliance on collaboration between the tax authorities and its subjects when compared to the treatment afforded to PEPs suspected of holding the proceeds of corruption. UWO cases by design involve enforcement authorities undertaking investigations, usually involving some element of financial surveillance, which originate in an assumption that the respondents under investigation have benefited from crime or corruption. The Code of Practice for enforcement authorities on the use of investigative orders issued by the Home Office encourages enforcement authorities using POCA investigation powers to consider whether there might be some merit in approaching potential respondents to investigative orders to provide information on a voluntary basis without having to resort to a court order.[157] Senior officers at the NCA have opined that while they would 'never say never' to seeking a voluntary disclosure from PEPs whose property is under investigation, it is not something they envisage happening in practice because of the perceived risk of asset dissipation.[158] It is apparent therefore that PEPs who have to interact with state authorities to give an account of their assets are exposed to a more adversarial experience than their non-PEP, tax-resident counterparts. By contrast, the (at least preliminary) tenor of communications between HMRC and its respondents on assessments to tax is that administrative clarity on the respondents' wealth is required in the interests of both parties. Furthermore, the justifications for interference with individual rights implicit in the functioning of the tax system are more readily comprehensible and logically consistent than those proffered for making UWOs available specifically against PEPs. On that basis, it is worth considering whether the property ownership framework should be revised expressly to impose information-sharing obligations on property-owners including obligations to account for the origin of property acquisition finances or face administrative sanctions of the sort imposed by HMRC, with a longer-term risk of asset seizure for non-compliance.

The relatively value-neutral approach of the tax authorities in determining the legitimacy of individuals' assets has proven effective to some degree in Australia and has been recommended as an option for other jurisdictions.[159] Exploring the use of a similar system applicable to all owners of UK properties as an option for limiting the potential for the laundering of overseas corruption might mitigate some of the rights concerns highlighted in the previous chapter.

an inspector or the Board discover that any profits which ought to have been assessed to tax have not been assessed'.

[157] Home Office, *Code of Practice issued under Section 377 of the Proceeds of Crime Act 2002: Investigations* (Stationery Office April 2024) para 20.

[158] Author interview with senior NCA officials, 16 December 2020.

[159] See JC Sharman, *Report to the Cullen Commission: Money Laundering and Foreign Corruption Proceeds in British Columbia: A Comparative International Policy Assessment* (June 2022) 26–29.

6. Conclusion

The purpose of this chapter is to highlight potential anti-corruption reforms and to assess reforms recently introduced in the UK. Where any new legal measures are adopted with the aim of countering corruption, legislators should be alive to the rights risks involved in 'special' crime control measures being assimilated into a system to the point that their use is normalized and subsequently expanded. Where public concern in response to particular problems grows to the point that it becomes politically prudent to address those concerns, it is important for the legislature to avoid hastily introducing measures, the likely effectiveness and the wider societal consequences of which have not been made subject beforehand to thoroughgoing appraisal. Ideally, there would exist an anti-corruption regime that is systemically proactive against the political, social, and economic threats posed by kleptocracies and other corrupt actors. Where reactive measures must be introduced, they should be carefully designed, costed, stress-tested, and legally scrutinized before being presented to Parliament. An ineffective system designed as a counterweight to the excesses of foreign corrupt regimes that indirectly results in harsher laws being imposed against the domestic citizenry (as is the risk with the future expansion of UWOs) is clearly counterproductive.

Whilst none of the discrete topics discussed in this chapter is likely to inspire a great deal of excitement in the media or amongst the public, in many cases they represent pragmatic and/or systemic reforms likely to quietly aid the valuable work of disincentivizing the laundering of the proceeds of grand corruption in the UK. The key point sought to be made more broadly is that for anti-corruption approaches in the UK to be effective, they must be multi-faceted and innovative. The discussion of recent and potential developments in the anti-corruption space in this chapter will, it is hoped, foster further discourse around the characteristics of effective anti-money laundering reform in the future.

Conclusion

1. Introduction

This book has evaluated the UK's anti-corruption regime, to the extent that it could be described as having a coherent and effective system of the sort. The potential for those benefiting from grand corruption to invest dirty money in the UK damages both states of origin and the UK itself. Grand corruption directs resources in victim states away from basic services like health, sanitation, and education and towards private residences in Belgravia and Mayfair—deepest Londongrad. It distorts the economies of countries in the Global South, with graft committed by leaders begetting further graft on a wider basis, and cultures of kleptocracy engraining themselves in the fiscal practices of victim states. In hosting illicit wealth, the UK undermines claims it has to moral leadership as a bastion of the rule of law, and by its omission to counteract this effectively, establishes itself as a friend and an enabler of the officially corrupt. Consequently, it is imperative that the UK not only is seen to be tackling the proceeds of grand corruption flooding through the jurisdiction, but also actively puts the state's enforcement authorities, financial gatekeepers, and others in the best possible position to deter those assets from entering the country in the first place. Where they are already here, UK authorities must track those assets down, seize them, and return them to the citizenries of their states of origin.

This book is the first that undertakes a holistic assessment of how the UK's anti-grand corruption system operates in practice. It takes a wide view of civil recovery tools, criminal sanctions, transparency reforms and alternative routes to deterrence and asset recovery, and examines how each fits into the national anti-corruption landscape more generally. It then zooms in on the granular detail of how each is used and how effective they are in practice. On a policy level, this monograph has framed the discussion through discussing the UK's response to public concern around grand corruption through its examination of the PEP-specific UWO. It has critiqued the measure's design, its operation, and its wider impact within the context of its status as a recent addition to a longer-term litany of legislative responses to outcry on the perceived prevalence of dirty money within the jurisdiction. It has applied critical deviance theory and considered the work of contemporary crime theorists in assessing the socio-legal narratives surrounding

Unexplained Wealth Orders and the UK's Anti-Corruption Regime. Áine Clancy, Oxford University Press.
 DOI: 10.1093/9780198907312.003.0009

the development of the 'PEP' concept in international anti-money laundering law and the UWO's introduction under the POCA. Applying a broader perspective still, the book has identified some key drivers of the jurisdiction's attractiveness as a harbour state for the proceeds of overseas graft. It has considered the efficacy of further existing and potential options to fighting the proceeds of foreign official corruption being laundered in the UK. It has highlighted the individual rights implications of targeting foreign political elites in particular and of the operation of the anti-kleptocracy system more generally. The book presents a picture of the anti-corruption regime in the UK that is something of a curate's egg. The UK has in the past proven effective at facilitating the recovery of the proceeds of overseas kleptocracy, and enforcement authorities benefit from a legislative architecture that, theoretically at least, places a wide array of tools at their disposal in pursuing dirty money. Its government does well in signalling opprobrium towards kleptocracy by periodically unveiling new innovations aimed at dissuading corrupt elites from investing in the UK. Crucially, however, that messaging is undermined by the lack of resourcing and by adopting piecemeal attempts at reform as a substitute for undertaking the harder systemic reform work of constructing well-considered and well-financed anti-corruption apparatuses capable of addressing all relevant sectors. The upshot is that despite the best efforts of civil society groups, enforcement authorities, and others to implement new measures, it is ultimately possible to view much of this anti-kleptocracy messaging as no more than relatively trite window-dressing, devoid of political value.

This concluding chapter draws together some findings from the analysis conducted throughout this volume. First, it lays out conclusions on the legitimacy, proportionality, and necessity (or lack thereof, as the case may be) of the PEP-specific UWO and discerns why it has proven so ineffective as an anti-corruption tool in practice notwithstanding its initial promise. The findings of this discussion and the wider analysis of the UK's anti-corruption regime throughout this volume then inform a series of high-level proposals for policy-makers to consider in devising effective and proportionate approaches to dealing with overseas corruption and its proceeds in future.

2. UWOs: Legitimacy, Proportionality, Necessity

The immediate consequences from an individual rights perspective for respondents subject to UWOs are largely excusable in the context of investigations into the proceeds of grand corruption. However, the measure's inclusion in the Criminal Finances Bill in 2016 largely constituted a literally and (as it subsequently transpired) figuratively cheap, optically beneficial opportunity for the government to assure the public that it was 'doing something' about the proceeds of overseas official corruption being laundered in the UK. The rationales behind PEP-specific measures and the aptness of the 'PEP' concept as currently defined have been inadequately scrutinized by lawmakers. In its PEP-specific form, the unexplained wealth order has been applied in a way that has survived judicial scrutiny only once in practice. Consequently, the advantages of having a PEP-specific version of the order are increasingly unclear. While its existence may be justifiable insofar as it has on one occasion operated to deprive someone of the benefit of alleged grand corruption, this book argues that in the grander scheme of anti-corruption activity, the introduction of UWOs against PEPs was neither wholly necessary nor wholly legitimate.

a. The Measure's Legitimacy

In the introduction to this book, legitimacy was defined by reference to input legitimacy and output legitimacy. In assessing input legitimacy, the validity of the processes by which UWOs against PEPs were developed and enacted was assessed. Chapter 2 examined the origin of the focus on PEPs in international anti-corruption and anti-money laundering contexts, while Chapter 4 reviewed the socio-political and legal narratives preceding the introduction of UWOs against PEPs. Given the significance of the anti-money laundering rules to the UK's financial sector and the centrality of PEPs within anti-money laundering and anti-corruption systems, four aspects of the evolution of the 'PEP' concept are particularly striking.

First, whilst PEP-specific rules apparently first appeared in Swiss domestic banking regulation, they came to international prominence through rules developed by bankers rather than by policy-makers or legislators. It was in the banking industry's interest to be seen to be 'doing something' to address corruption by refocusing attention away from its own culpability in enabling that corruption and towards a specified cohort. The promulgation of the PEP concept was therefore made at a remove from what we would regard as normal society-centric policy development. Its genesis lacked the consultation, expertise, and public debate and scrutiny typically accompanying the creation of significant legal rules or ideas. Second, the development of PEP-specific laws seems to have occurred in a remarkably crude and piecemeal manner. Very little has been presented by way of empirical justification by the Financial Action Task Force (an organization with questionable legitimacy in its own right) in advocating for PEP-specific rules. Moreover, *no* public debate ensued either in the UK or in the EU on the PEP concept before it was adopted wholesale into their respective AML laws. Third, the definition of the 'politically exposed person' in its current incarnation bears relatively little resemblance to the concept as originally contemplated. The contours of the 'politically exposed person' as initially conceived have now been diluted to such an extent that focus is, according to those who first developed the concept, much obscured from the state leaders and senior government members whom it was created to target. Fourth, over twenty years since PEPs became a feature of the anti-money laundering landscape, there *remains* no reliable empirical evidence substantiating the suggestion that PEP-specific rules are effective as a means of deterring money laundering and/or corruption more generally.

With regard to the development of UWOs designed specifically to apply to corrupt overseas PEPs, Chapter 4 considered whether the orders might reasonably be said to constitute the kind of poorly constructed measure that is characteristic of hurried legislative responses to moral panics. The deviance identified in the historic cases of panic discussed may have justified some form of official reaction in each case. However, the creation of categories of folk-devils on which to focus opprobrium allowed policy-makers to avoid the harder work of adopting more considered and expansive approaches to the situational contexts in which that deviance was fostered. The same criticism can be levelled at PEP-specific UWOs. On a close analysis, the socio-legal narratives surrounding the measure's introduction featured all the criteria necessary to reach the conclusion that a panic-induced, politically expedient, and ultimately somewhat ill-considered statutory power was introduced. Its clearest benefit from the government of the day's perspective is that it allowed it to enact a measure to show that it was addressing the issue of corruption proceeds being used to acquire property in the UK, whilst not actually having to spend financial capital on the problem, and not inconveniencing the UK's financial system in any way.

It is worth remembering in this context that the PEP-based UWO was tacked on as a late addition to the Criminal Finances Bill in which it was introduced.[1] Had the government been intent on achieving its stated legislative objective of making investigations easier and deterring corrupt PEPs from laundering the proceeds of corruption in the UK, one or both of the following consequences would have ensued:

- First, mindful of the resources of the deep-pocketed kleptocrats the measure purportedly targets, the government would have thrown significant financial and political support behind the enforcement authorities empowered to apply for UWOs.
- Second, the government would have undertaken a thoroughgoing reassessment of all of the reasons why 'dirty money' from allegedly corrupt PEPs is infiltrating the UK's property markets and financial systems and would have established its harmful impact on society. It would then have duly undertaken exacting law and policy reform to address the UK's cross-sectoral porousness to the proceeds of overseas official corruption. This would have

[1] See Chapter 7, n 1.

involved, without limitation, considering the roles played by regulated sectors, flaws in the design and operation of the AML system, the transparency and verification problems in the UK's corporate regime, the government's own under-resourcing of overstretched law enforcement authorities, and the relationships the government was cultivating with states holding morally ambiguous views on administrative propriety.

At the time, neither of these courses of action, each of which would have suggested an intention on the government's part to *do* something about proceeds of corruption, eventuated. Such proposed acts might be dismissed as unrealistic or overly ambitious. However, it is notable that other jurisdictions have, for example, taken a far more proactive stance on resourcing their law enforcement authorities sufficiently to allow them to take robust action in actively pursuing the proceeds of crime and corruption,[2] and the UK itself subsequently enacted laws to reform corporate transparency. With regard to the input legitimacy of the measure, therefore, there are a number of good reasons to hold reservations both on the institutions and on the processes behind the development of the PEP concept, as well as on the factors motivating the UK government's decision to hastily include PEP-specific measures in the array of civil recovery tools available as part of the proceeds of crime regime.

Output legitimacy was examined by reference to key preconditions for legitimacy in anti-corruption contexts. These are the inclusiveness or non-discrimination of the measure, the impact on individual rights through the state's use of it, and the measure's effectiveness in practice. Assessments of the PEP-specific UWO's legitimacy in these contexts overlap with the conclusions drawn on the order's justifiability and its necessity, which are now respectively discussed.

b. UWOs against PEPs: Justifiability

Measuring justifiability in this context involves determining the objectives of a piece of legislation and, assuming that the measure is effective in practice, assessing whether its potential impact on individual and societal rights can be said to be justified in light of those objectives. First, to the extent that UWOs impact on privacy and property rights, that impact has proven relatively minimal in practice. In my analysis, I drew comparisons between the interference with those rights by UWOs and the operation of the tax system. Even though civil recovery investigations implicitly hold a more criminal tenor than tax investigations, requiring an individual

[2] See eg Chapter 7, n 17 and accompanying text. In the United States, then-President Biden declared anti-corruption efforts a core US national security interest focus at the start of his term. The US's anti-corruption efforts have so far fared more poorly under the second Trump regime—see n 27 below.

to account to the state for their assets, given that it is information far more easily accessible to the individual than the state, is not an especially onerous obligation. It is only if and when enforcement authorities subsequently opt to apply for civil recovery orders (strictly speaking, a process subsequent to and separate from UWO applications) that most significant interferences with property and privacy rights may come into play.

Second, on the procedural rights of respondents, it is argued in Chapter 6 that owing to the measure's quasi-criminal character, respondents to UWOs should be entitled to more heightened levels of procedural protection than those typically afforded to parties in civil proceedings. It notes however that the High Court in fact already observes heightened standards by rigorously requiring proportionality and fairness principles to be met by enforcement authorities in addition to satisfying the Statutory Tests. The procedural rights of respondents are perhaps thus already subject to a higher level of protection than, say, other types of civil respondents to state litigation. It would be nevertheless preferable to ensure that this becomes a clear and judiciable ongoing expectation on the part of respondents by enshrining it in legislation rather than relying on judicial discretion. Separately, suggestions that UWOs involve a reverse burden of proof being imposed on respondents are perhaps overstated. Again, it is submitted that it is not a particularly onerous imposition on respondents in practice given the relative ease of access to the pertinent information on respondents' parts.

In summary, given the humanitarian and human rights consequences of grand corruption for the populaces of its victim states, the individual rights impact on respondents to the UK's anti-corruption machinery is relatively modest and therefore justifiable. Four caveats apply to this conclusion. First, although applications for tools like the UWO and the AFO are typically made in private, challenges to PEP-specific UWOs have so far been made in public and are capable of attracting significant and aspersive publicity. The benefit of open justice to society as against the impact on individual rights wrought by the publication of potentially reputationally ruinous personal information is a perennial subject of academic and legal discourse. A significant development in this sphere is the Supreme Court's decision in *Bloomberg LP v ZXC*[3] to the effect that a person under *criminal* investigation is, in general, entitled to a reasonable expectation of privacy in relation to that investigation prior to being charged. It does not appear that respondents to *civil* orders made as part of, for example, civil recovery investigations are entitled to the same expectation, even though similar considerations of social and public stigma that informed the Supreme Court's decision in *Bloomberg* apply. In the interests of consistency with the principles endorsed in the Supreme Court's judgment, courts should perhaps consider keeping the identity of a civil recovery investigation's respondent subject to reporting restrictions until that respondent has exhausted

3 [2022] UKSC 5.

appeals trajectories (albeit, given the public interest in understanding how civil recovery works, those restrictions ought not apply to the general details of the matter).

Second, the potential duration of asset holders' inability to deal in their properties for so long as they remain frozen while a UWO matter remains unresolved, and the ensuing and potentially unfair impact on property rights, behoves enforcement authorities to use their best efforts to expedite their handling of the process and avoid unnecessary delays insofar as is reasonably possible.

Third, making available a PEP-specific category of UWO, particularly in circumstances where the Serious Crime UWO is available, risks further entrenching a perception (already widely held, based on the media surveys included in Chapter 4) to the effect that foreign PEPs as a cohort have a propensity towards corruption. There is no evidence available to demonstrate that these individuals are more or less likely to deal in illicit wealth than members of the population more generally. The availability of PEP-specific UWOs therefore joins the phalanx of crime control measures that are targeted at a specific section of the population, and that are capable of unjustly stigmatizing that collective as folk-devils. In each of the PEP-based UWO investigations to date, there appeared to be prima facie justifications for enforcement authorities to rely on the Serious Crime UWO rather than the PEP UWO. It is preferable for enforcement authorities to rely solely on the Serious Crime UWO, given that it requires an evidential nexus between serious criminality and the relevant assets to be established by enforcement authorities.

Fourth, and related to the foregoing, this book highlights the legislative tendency in crime control matters towards incremental expansion of state powers against the whole population after those powers first become normalized when used against a specific group. Drawing on the incremental expansion precedents identified in the context of asset recovery powers set out in Chapter 3, this book urges attentiveness and wariness towards any future proposals that UWOs be expanded for use against the population more generally.

c. The Measure's Necessity

The question of the PEP-specific UWO's output legitimacy (ie its impact in practice) overlaps with the question of its necessity. Insofar as a case can be made that the measure is effective in achieving its stated statutory objectives, this may support an argument that its introduction was imperative. UWOs against PEPs have not proven effective in meeting the statutory aims specified by Parliament upon their introduction. Some commentators have gone so far as to characterize the measure (fairly) as a 'dud'.[4] Chapter 3 outlines some general problems with

[4] Oliver Bullough, *Butler to the World* (Profile Books 2022) 203.

the measure's design and explains why it has failed to meet the goals enumerated by Parliament. There is no evidence available to suggest that the measure has deterred the holding of corruptly acquired assets in the UK, though admittedly it is impossible to quantify the value of the proceeds of grand corruption being held in the jurisdiction at any given point. Nevertheless, some four years *after* the UWO first became available for use, media coverage and parliamentary discussion of the Russian invasion of Ukraine served to highlight *again* the perceived prevalence of corrupt PEPs and dirty money in the UK, suggesting that the expressive component of the measure—the UK's purported rejection of foreign 'dirty money'—had proven ineffective in practice. As to the aim of repatriating assets to states of origin, as at the date of writing there exists no evidence that any proceeds realized from the only successful enforcement authority application for UWOs against a PEP—the *Hajiyeva* matter—have been returned to Azerbaijan. Finally, as the PEP-specific version of the measure has been successfully used only once to date, and in circumstances where reliance on the Serious Crime UWO or a request to enforce a confiscation order from the Azerbaijani authorities may well have proven equally effective as a means of recovering Mrs Hajiyeva's assets, arguments that UWOs of a kind designed to be used specifically against corrupt foreign elites with political links can ease enforcement authorities' investigative burdens are unconvincing. The measure has proven ineffective in achieving the objectives underpinning its introduction.

As to whether the introduction of PEP-specific UWOs was *necessary*, Chapter 5 examined alternative and pre-existing available means of investigating and retrieving the proceeds of grand corruption. Whilst transnational and domestic *criminal law* routes to asset recovery through post-conviction confiscation processes perhaps constitute the most expressively satisfying and complete forms of justice from victims' perspectives, the nature of complex transnational financial crimes means that investigation and prosecution of those crimes is unfortunately seldom feasible in practice. Similarly, states of origin pursuing assets using civil processes through the UK's courts to recover their stolen assets are likely to encounter numerous practical and legal difficulties. For civil investigation powers where the relevant assets are located in the UK, enforcement authorities benefit from an impressive armoury of measures, not least disclosure orders, account freezing and forfeiture orders, and customer information orders. It is tempting to conclude that such orders are under-enforced, perhaps because of straitened enforcement authority resources. That said, there are no civil investigation tools that perform *identically* to the UWO: that is, a power to have a respondent explain the source of their wealth (or explain how their wealth was *not* illicitly acquired) or else face having a presumption of recoverability raised against their property. The measure has the potential to transcend some of the evidential challenges faced by enforcement authorities in seeking to criminally prosecute grand corruption offences. As it has been used so little in practice, it is difficult to gain a clear picture as to whether this novel power represents a significant boon to enforcement authorities. However, the fact that it has been established that UWOs can be served outside the jurisdiction, and, once validly served, can be enforceable is potentially useful intelligence for enforcement authorities working in a proceeds of grand corruption recovery context.[5]

In summary, therefore, the PEP-specific UWOs against PEPs might be viewed as justifiable and, perhaps, necessary. Unfortunately, however, they have proven ineffective and come laden with the baggage of deficient legitimacy.

3. Anti-Corruption Policy: Future Approaches

UWOs are invoked frequently in Parliament as 'proof' that the UK is taking action against the fruits of official corruption being hoarded in the London property market.[6] In early 2022, following Russia's invasion of Ukraine, the British government once again claimed that it was 'doing something' in response to an outcry about the proceeds of corruption, this time in the form of dirty money allegedly being laundered by Russian kleptocrats in London. On that occasion, it made amendments to the UWO rules in a way designed to 'strengthen and reinforce the UWO regime to ensure the powers can be used to maximum effect'.[7] The relevant legislation was passed by Parliament in a remarkably short space of time.[8] Like the original UWO legislation, the new laws were (i) introduced swiftly following media and public outcry on the proceeds of foreign corruption; (ii) purportedly designed to ease the burdens of enforcement authorities in seeking civil recovery; and (iii) intended to convey a message (accurately or otherwise) to the public that the government was proactively tackling the proceeds of corruption being laundered in the UK. No further UWO applications against PEPs have been reported since the UWO laws were amended in 2022.[9] There is evidence to suggest that other facets of the UK's anti-corruption machinery are similarly under-enforced or ineffective.[10]

Since UWOs against PEPs were first introduced, and as alluded to throughout this volume, very little reported enforcement action has been taken to address those laundering the proceeds of grand corruption in the UK. Substantially more sanctions have been imposed, Magnitsky laws were expanded, the Economic Crime (Transparency and Enforcement) Act 2022 expedited the introduction

[5] *National Crime Agency v Grew (No 1)* [2023] NIKB 77.
[6] See n 28 in the Introduction to this volume.
[7] Economic Crime (Transparency and Enforcement) Bill—Explanatory Notes (HL Bill 126) para 15.
[8] This time, eight days from its first reading in Parliament.
[9] As of 1 January 2025.
[10] Robert Barrington KC, 'The Governance of Corruption in the UK' in Fen Osler Hampson and Robert I Rotberg, *Grand Corruption: Curbing Kleptocracy Globally* (Routledge 2025) 172.

of the Register of Overseas Entities, and the Economic Crime and Corporate Transparency Act 2023 sought to provide for improved corporate verification processes. Still, little asset recovery from PEPs is evident. A pattern may be emerging in the UK whereby an incumbent government announces an intention to adopt, or even adopts, new laws in response to concerns of the public around the proceeds of grand corruption being laundered in the UK property market but then fails to provide the financial and/or political support to authorities necessary to enforce those laws.

Some lessons have emerged in this book's discussion of anti-corruption measures through the prism of the UK's experience with the proceeds of kleptocracy and grand corruption. Other academics have already identified the pressing need for a root-and-branch reappraisal of the UK's philosophy and policy towards deterring the proceeds of grand corruption from being laundered within the jurisdiction.[11] Heathershaw and others frame grand corruption (and the UK's seeming acquiescence to it) post-globalization as a fundamental threat to the Rules-Based International Order. They urge a range of direct domestic policy changes to be adopted as a matter of urgency. These include the government of the UK expressly acknowledging the threat of grand corruption to the rule of law and global security, an incorporation of the concept of kleptocracy in statute, and the state prioritization of transparency for all public institutions.[12] A radical official overhaul of the kind contemplated by these commentators on a policy level would complement the more granular-level suggestions made throughout this volume. It would aid in creating an environment in the UK that is at worst uncomfortable and at best impossible as a place for kleptocrats and other beneficiaries of grand corruption to invest and enjoy their illicitly acquired assets. Elsewhere, Robert Barrington has persuasively argued that there is a leadership vacuum (and, consequently, vanishingly little political accountability) within the UK's anti-corruption apparatus. He has cited robust leadership models that might usefully be considered for anti-corruption coordination from other realms of governmental activity.[13] These recommendations are wholeheartedly endorsed here.

Beyond these suggestions, some headline points to be made on the potential reform options flagged in this book are now summarized with a view to informing policy approaches in the future.

[11] See, in particular, written evidence submitted to Parliament by John Heathershaw and others, *Towards a Strategy for Countering Kleptocracy: Five Steps to Address the UK's Kleptocracy Problem* (11 March 2022) and the works written by the same authors cited therein.

[12] Heathershaw and others (n 11).

[13] See Barrington (n 10). In addition to UWOs, he points to the foreign bribery regime and the UK's falling standing on Transparency International's Corruption Perceptions Index as indicators that the UK's anti-corruption regime is not fit for purpose in its current form.

a. Data in Policy Development

There is a dearth of data available nationally and internationally on known cases of grand corruption. Consequently, researchers and policy-makers are unable to effectively map commonly recurring (i) states of origin, conduit states, and destination states contributing to acts of grand corruption on a transnational basis; and (ii) techniques used by transgressors to facilitate those crimes. Some useful empirical work has been produced by researchers seeking to establish stronger evidence bases for anti-corruption policy using information harvested from various data leaks in tracing the global routes on which dirty money tends to travel.[14] There is scope for even more detailed data to be produced transnationally and shared by enforcement authorities on a cross-jurisdictional basis, including information on how successful recoveries were made, how prosecutions were finalized, and/or the methods adopted by corrupt parties in misusing financial systems. The accuracy of this kind of work would be contingent on the input of enforcement authorities in states of origin and destination states making contributions through resources like the Stolen Assets Recovery Initiative database. The findings of any such work would, of course, be subject always to the caveat that any new policy measures introduced to address kleptocratic misconduct will be effective only for the asset-holding paradigm which exists at a particular point in time. Those truly intent on laundering the proceeds of corruption outside their countries of origin will always find innovative and proactive ways of circumventing anti-corruption obstacles by exploiting legal privacy rules and complex ownership structures. Nevertheless, increased understanding around known instances of how, where, and by whom assets are laundered would allow for more sophisticated risk-based policy approaches to be adopted by policy creators, enforcement authorities, and potential Facilitators.

b. Expertise and Resourcing

Adequate resourcing is fundamental to the success of any currently proposed and new measures aimed at hampering grand corruption and the laundering of its proceeds. Possibly the most potent indicator of political will to tackle a particular problem is the allocation of resources allowing for aggressive enforcement. The *Baker* case laid bare the financial challenges faced by the UK's enforcement authorities and their limited anti-corruption budgets when viewed against the legal

[14] A notable recent example is Dan Haberly, Tom Shipley, and Robert Barrington, *Corruption, Shell Companies, and Financial Secrecy: Providing an Evidence Base for Anti-Corruption Policy* (Centre for the Study of Corruption, University of Sussex 2023).

and financial war chests available to allegedly corrupt PEPs[15] One curious aspect of the introduction of unexplained wealth orders was the seeming failure to foresee and make provision for some obvious characteristics of allegedly corrupt PEPs, namely, their deep pockets and their apparent willingness to take extraordinary measures to obtain and retain their allegedly stolen assets. It is easy to make these criticisms in hindsight, but the failure of the PEP-specific UWO to gain traction in practice strongly suggests that some basic stress-testing and modelling of outcomes was not undertaken upon that measure's inception. The *Impact Assessment* setting out the projected costs and frequency of use of UWOs suggested an estimated upper limit cost of £10,000 to the state for each case, with an anticipated twenty cases per annum.[16] Given that even an uncontested UWO requires enforcement authorities to meet the Statutory Tests, instruct lawyers, and make a High Court application or applications for interim freezing orders and unexplained wealth orders, this estimate now seems risible. Charges of rampant under-resourcing for oversight and implementation might also be reasonably levelled at other facets of the UK's anti-corruption infrastructure, most notably its anti-money laundering regime.

When adopting measures that have proven effective in other jurisdictions, it is important to examine the policy and socio-legal contexts in which those models succeeded. It is not sufficient merely to pick the most attractive and easiest-to-implement aspects of a relevant model, disregard its more expensive and less straightforward aspects, and expect it to reap benefits outside of the context in which it proved effective. A law firm tasked by the US Department of Justice with evaluating the relative successes (or lack thereof) of UWO-style mechanisms when they were introduced in Ireland and Australia drew comparisons between the 'active and judicious enforcement' and the high level of state resourcing of the powers in Ireland, where the orders have been broadly regarded as a success, as against the perceived failure of UWOs in the Australian jurisdictions analysed.[17] Unless proper attention is paid to 'the fundamental capacity and capability issues within the UK's operational response to economic crime',[18] no improvement in prevention, deterrence, or recovery abilities in terms of the proceeds of overseas

[15] See Bullough (n 4) 200–05 and see also the attribution of the relative success of UWO-style mechanisms in Ireland to robust state investment and political support (Booz Allen Hamilton, *Comparative Evaluation of Unexplained Wealth Orders* (October 2012) 148–49).

[16] *Criminal Finances Act—Unexplained Wealth Orders Impact Assessment No: HO0282* (20 June 2017) 8.

[17] Booz Allen Hamilton (n 15) 148–49. Note that one reason for the success of UWO-type measures in Ireland is the notably low standards of evidence sufficient to allow for respondents to be put to proof on the origin of their assets. See Colin King, 'The Difficulties of Belief Evidence and Anonymity in Practice: Challenges for Asset Recovery' in Colin King, Clive Walker, and Jimmy Gurulé (eds) *The Palgrave Handbook of Criminal and Terrorism Financing Law* (Palgrave Macmillan 2018) 565.

[18] Royal United Services Institute, *Getting the Economic Crime Plan Done: Why Economic Crime Matters for Johnson's 'Global Britain'* (RUSI 13 January 2020).

grand corruption are likely. Other commentators have emphasized the need for a material and salient risk of enforcement where financial crimes are involved.[19]

When observers talk about 'political will' to meaningfully address behaviours, they are often using this as a euphemism for committing sufficient economic and administrative/bureaucratic resourcing to address problems. Based on admittedly limited and imperfect data, there unsurprisingly appears to exist a correlation between providing adequate resourcing through funding and requisite expertise on the one hand and successful enforcement and recovery of the proceeds of corruption on the other.[20] Absent meaningful resourcing accompanied by clear political will, the introduction of novel anti-corruption measures is a largely hollow exercise.[21] The longer-term success of the corporate transparency and verification measures introduced under the Economic Crime and Corporate Transparency Act 2023 and the Economic Crime (Transparency and Enforcement) Act 2022, for example, will only be achieved if there is sufficient funding of both to ensure systems-wide rigour in accepting only verified, accurate information, and to allow for a credible enforcement regime to disincentivize non-compliance.

c. Systemic Transparency in Tackling Laundering

There exist some promising (though very early) signs to suggest that demanding higher levels of transparency from property-owning corporate vehicles on the identities of their ultimate beneficial owners may impact on the behaviours of those purchasing properties from overseas. Preliminary data suggest that since the introduction of the Register of Overseas Entities, the number of companies based in tax havens making new purchases in the UK property market has fallen.[22] It is unclear what the specific drivers for this trend are, but to the extent that some would-be corrupt holders of real estate have been dissuaded by an intensified detection risk as a result of the new transparency requirements, this may represent a diminution in the value of dirty money flowing through the British economy.

[19] See Jennifer Arlen, 'The Potential Promise and Perils of Introducing Deferred Prosecution Arrangements Outside the US' in Tina Søreide and Abiola Makinwa (eds), *Negotiated Settlements in Bribery Cases: A Principled Approach* (Edward Elgar 2020) 156, 168.

[20] See the Booz Allen Hamilton discussion of Ireland in the report cited at n 15, and Liz Campbell and Áine Clancy, 'The Principled and Practical Limits to Unexplained Wealth Orders' (2024) 52(1) University of Western Australia Law Review 29.

[21] See Cass R Sunstein, 'On the Expressive Function of Law' (1996) 141 University of Pennsylvania Law Review 2021.

[22] Matthew Collin, Florian M Hollenbach, and David Szakony, 'The End of Londongrad? The Impact of Beneficial Ownership Transparency on Offshore Investment in UK Property' (2023) The United Nations University World Institute for Development Economics Research Working Paper No 2023/11.

d. Risk-based Policy Design

The operation of unexplained wealth orders has proven revealing in terms of the pressure points and spending preferences of, and the defensive strategies adopted by, allegedly corrupt PEPs. Policy-framers should assume that wealthy PEPs will aggressively oppose any investigative action taken against them by enforcement authorities, using expensive counsel and exhausting appeal trajectories in the process. We know from cases like *Javadov*[23] and *Hajiyeva*[24] that politically connected respondents challenging investigative orders will seek to maintain their privacy for as long as possible, including by making judicial review applications or further submissions to the courts. The relative success of enforcement authorities in being awarded uncontested account forfeiture orders and account freezing orders, which are rarely reported upon or publicized, compared to other types of civil recovery proceedings is instructive in this regard. Such cases should also be mined for potentially useful intelligence on, inter alia, the UK-based lawyers, financial institutions, estate agents, and other Facilitators involved in relevant transactions, as well as the strategies employed by corrupt elites to circumvent those Facilitators' compliance systems. This knowledge may be useful in devising future anti-corruption strategy and innovation.

Separately, the Financial Conduct Authority's work on scoping and refining the potential risk factors associated with foreign PEPs is a welcome step in systematically grasping the context in which financial institutions' customers transact, the content of those transactions, and the risks associated with the sources of funds for those transactions. To the extent that, as part of its consultation on PEPs, the FCA publishes recommendations for systemic compliance system reform, it is likely that those recommendations will meet resistance from its regulatees because compliance reforms carry cost implications for those institutions. One hopes that the FCA (and, later, other Facilitators' supervisory bodies which undertake similar work) will operate outside the sphere of regulatory capture in advocating for risk-based reforms.

e. Sectors Vulnerable to Laundering

Cases like Mrs Hajiyeva's highlight the need for closer monitoring of the trade and ownership of high-value assets as potential money-laundering risks more generally. The National Crime Agency eventually abandoned its claim against millions of pounds worth of her jewellery, something that was 'understood to have been prompted by a desire to free its investigators and resources to focus on other

23 *R (Javadov) v Westminster Magistrates' Court* [2021] EWHC 2393.
24 *National Crime Agency v Mrs A* [2018] EWHC 2534 (Admin) [6].

targets'.[25] It was not established that Mrs Hajiyeva's jewellery collection represented the proceeds of corruption. Nevertheless, the case serves as a worthwhile reminder to revisit the supervision of, and vulnerability to, money laundering of sectors like the fine art, jewellery, and collectible wine markets. Separately, numerous yachts and aircraft of various oligarchs have been frozen worldwide as part of the sanctions regimes of various countries and territories (including the UK's). As discussed in Chapter 1, it is extraordinarily difficult for individuals who do not have a direct interest in those aircraft or vessels to access the details of the ultimate beneficial owners of such highly mobile and liquid tangible assets where they are held on registries in the UK. These registries are ripe for transparency reforms.

f. Political Opportunity and Buy-in

Chapter 1 discussed how, until recently at least, the UK has nurtured a political economy that, given the pressures on the UK's government post-Brexit to maximize foreign direct investment, seemed almost to acquiesce to the flow of corruptly acquired assets into the jurisdiction. The recent systemic changes introduced to the corporate transparency regime is reason for tentative optimism that the UK will prove a less comfortable landing site for stolen wealth in future.[26] There is scope for soft global political capital to be gained here. Throughout the Biden administration, the United States telegraphed its moral leadership as a global anti-kleptocracy champion. Given that the Trump administration has failed to do likewise, cancelling overseas aid funding and issuing an executive order to pause enforcement of offences under the Foreign Corrupt Practices Act,[27] it is open to the UK to inherit this position, using influence and expertise developed through the Foreign, Commonwealth and Development Office to encourage anti-corruption best practices in other jurisdictions. As Heathershaw and others have recommended elsewhere, as part of this endeavour, the UK should be open to actively pursuing joint counter-kleptocracy enterprises with overseas partners.[28]

Should the UK take up the mantle of global anti-corruption leadership, it will be necessary for it to acknowledge explicitly the reality of globalization and encourage states to move away from traditional Westphalian ideals of sovereignty in criminal

[25] Martin Bentham, '"McMafia" Banker's Wife Given Back Seized Jewellery Worth Millions' *The Standard* (London, 9 September 2024).

[26] The retreat from public corporate transparency in the European Union and in the UK's Crown Dependencies and Overseas Territories is discussed at Chapter 7, n 139ff and accompanying text. For the US, see Casey Michel, 'Hidden Figures: Anonymous Shell Companies, Secret Trusts, Money-Laundering Enablers—How the United States Stashes the World's Shady Cash' (2024) 49 Mother Jones 23.

[27] Casey Michel, 'Trump is taking a sledgehammer to the anti-corruption cause' *Financial Times* (London, 13 February 2025).

[28] See Heathershaw and others (n 11) para 12. The UK has successfully engaged in such partnerships in the past. See eg Chapter 5, n 65.

law enforcement in the longer term. Internationalist and transnationalist responses must be developed if transnational crimes are to be effectively challenged and enforced.[29] Policy-makers must appreciate this when seeking more emphatic means of addressing official corruption and transnational crime. In the shorter term, the UK has an opportunity to display political leadership by lobbying for and encouraging stronger implementation of, for example, UNCAC and OECD Anti-Bribery Convention obligations in other state (and, in the case of the latter, by taking action to address its own failures in implementing the OECD Working Group's recommendations in full).[30] Supporting the active enforcement of the offences created under those instruments, and prioritizing more robust enforcement of its own international law obligations thereunder would allow the UK to show moral leadership by example in a meaningful way.

g. Panic-Proofing Future Measures

One of the triggers for panic-based legislation can be an information deficit in media and public circles around how existing laws function or how new laws are proposed to operate. This is something that was recently highlighted by the apparent assumptions made by some parts of the media and certain politicians that where the assets of Russian oligarchs were frozen pursuant to sanctions made against them, those assets would automatically be seized. The Foreign, Commonwealth and Development Office, think-tanks like the Royal United Services Institute, and NGOs like Transparency International UK do valuable work in educating the public on graft and anti-corruption options and initiatives. It may, in some circumstances, be necessary for them to expand their remits to ensure that media editors and politicians are accurately briefed when publicly engaging in anti-corruption rhetoric. This will in turn allow for better quality public discourse when further measures to tackle grand corruption are under discussion and will further assist in avoiding the pitfalls encountered as a result of introducing panic-induced and ultimately relatively ineffective measures like the PEP-specific UWO.

4. Concluding Remarks

The experience of UWOs against PEPs as recounted in this book might be regarded as a cautionary tale on how the UK government should approach the problem of

[29] Peter Alldridge, 'Money Laundering and Globalization' (2008) 35 Journal of Law and Society 437.

[30] See OECD Working Group on Bribery, *Implementing the OECD Anti-Bribery Convention: Phase 4 Follow Up Report on the UK, Updated 2021*, 8: 'the Working Group regrets that no steps have been taken to address long-standing recommendations to ensure the independence of foreign bribery investigations and prosecutions, or to enhance detection through AML-reporting mechanisms'.

the laundering of overseas corruption more broadly. Whilst there may be political capital to be gained internationally by advocating for more aggressive anti-graft approaches globally, unless the resources necessary to enforce anti-corruption measures domestically are expended, it seems reasonable to regard those actions as primarily gestural rather than practical. The gravest and most immediate impact of overseas grand corruption will be experienced far from the UK. For the UK's enforcement authorities and its government alike, especially where resources are limited, prioritizing action in respect of domestic crimes with more readily visible victims makes sense politically. It is therefore not difficult to understand why UK has a tendency to enthusiastically pass new anti-corruption laws, yet then immediately ceases to take further action to ensure that they are adequately supported. As other commentators have noted, however, this approach is excessively short-sighted, given that a failure to suppress kleptocracy and grand corruption in turn supports the rise of shadow states and criminal networks, whose deleterious reaches extend far beyond the borders of their states of origin.[31] By making a case for a renewed and methodical approach to anti-corruption policy design, this volume seeks to champion the broader significance and potential efficacy of anti-corruption activism on the part of governments. This is difficult work and necessitates high levels of political will. The over-simplification or overclaiming that we have seen on the part of policy-makers is no substitute for this will. In making an appeal for greater prioritization of this area of law, an appeal is made that any new measures should be justified, proportionate, and legitimate in nature to ensure that respect for the rule of law is valorized as far as possible.

[31] See eg Henri Decœur, *Confronting the Shadow State: An International Law Perspective on State Organized Crime* (OUP 2018).

Index

For the benefit of digital users, indexed terms that span two pages (e.g., 52–53) may, on occasion, appear on only one of those pages.

Tables and figures are indicated by an italic *t* or *f*.